Mass communications

The rise of mass communications has fundamentally reshaped the modern world. In this new, comparative introduction, Rowland Lorimer surveys not only the different types of media and their attendant technologies, but the theories used to understand the subject.

Unlike other studies, Lorimer's provides students with a truly international perspective, drawing on examples from the UK, USA, Canada, Australia, Japan and various European countries.

The book begins with an examination of the historical and contemporary roles of communication in society, followed by an analysis of the mass media in modern society. Four fundamentals of mass media – law and policy, ownership, professionalism and technology – are explored in detail. This is followed by key sections on audience response and media content. A comprehensive glossary completes the book.

Written with the assistance of Paddy Scannell, this book will enable students at every level to understand the geopolitics of mass communication and the likely impact of modern media systems on national cultures in the future.

Rowland Lorimer is Professor in the Communications Department and Director of Canadian Centre for Studies in Publishing, Simon Fraser University, Vancouver.

Mass communications

A comparative introduction

Rowland Lorimer
with Paddy Scannell

Manchester University Press
Manchester and New York

Distributed exclusively in the USA and Canada by St. Martin's Press

Published by Manchester University Press
Oxford Road, Manchester M13 9NR, UK
and Room 400, 175 Fifth Avenue, New York, NY 10010, USA

Distributed exclusively in the USA and Canada
by St. Martin's Press, Inc., 175 Fifth Avenue, New York, NY 10010, USA

British Library Cataloguing-in-Publication Data
A catalogue record for this book is available from the British Library

Library of Congress Cataloging-in-Publication Data
Lorimer, Rowland, 1944–
    Mass communications : a comparative introduction / Rowland Lorimer
with Paddy Scannell.
       p.   cm.
    Includes bibliographical references (p.   ) and index.
    ISBN 0–7190–3946–0 (hardback).—ISBN 0–7190–3947–9 (paperback)
    1. Communication—Social aspects.   2. Mass media—Social aspects.
I. Scannell, Paddy.   II. Title.
HM258.L674   1994
302.2—dc20   94–19057

    ISBN 0 7190 3946 0 *hardback*
    ISBN 0 7190 3947 9 *paperback*

Photoset in Linotron Sabon
by Northern Phototypesetting Co. Ltd, Bolton

Printed in Great Britain
by Redwood Books, Trowbridge

Contents

Figures and tables

Figures

Tables

Preface and acknowledgements

This book represents an attempt to bring a comprehensive and critical perspective to the study of mass communication in North America and Europe. Its critical position follows Cassirer's formulation of the responsibility of intellectuals – to bring forward a critical intelligence, ethics and art as opposed to an uncritical and supportive, descriptivist, or even administrative stance (Real, 1986). It also takes account of the four areas of emphasis identified by Becker (1985) as within the purview of critical theory: rhetorical or literary explications of a media text; cultural studies relating media specifics to cultural patterns; evaluative comparisons of media industries and practices against potential social, political and economic change; and, political economy examinations of the institutional infrastructure of media and information in capitalist society. The resulting stance does not greatly differ from the analytical stance taken by regulatory agencies and policy developers who must consider the interests of all the major players in the system and the public good. It also finds complements in research reported in many journals, especially *Media Culture and Society*, and in widely-used exploration of mass communication in Latin America (Moragas Spa, 1981) and Canada (Lorimer and McNulty, 1984, 1991).

Mass communications has been long in the making and has involved the efforts of a great many people. I would especially like to thank in rough order of their first involvement: Jean McNulty, Michael Harrison, Nancy Duxbury, Eleanor O'Donnell, Anita Roy, Richard Collins, The Association for Canadian Studies through funds made available by the Canadian Studies Directorate of Heritage Canada (financial support), Susan Richards, Basil McDermott and Clare Hetherington, Les Étiennes, Gilles Charveriat and Hélène Zweguintzou, Sylvie Coundray, Alan Hancock, David Mitchell, Ed Slopek, Edna Einsiedel, Paddy Scannell, Ian Klassen, David Ze and Julia Henderson. Each was critical to the completion of this book in the form you see it. Some made contributions and provided support well beyond the call of duty.

As the cover makes clear, I owe a very great deal to Paddy Scannell, who would probably have never become involved were it not for Suzanne Williams. Without Paddy's colleaguely guidance and direct contributions the value of this book would be diminished substantially and considerably. In addition to help throughout, he is, in effect, the co-author of Chapters 7 and 8.

I wish to dedicate this book to my family.

References

Becker, S. L. (1985), 'Critical studies: a multidimensional movement', *Feedback*, 27, pp. 24–7.

Lorimer, Rowland and Jean McNulty (1984), *Mass Communication in Canada*, McClelland and Stewart, 2nd edn. 1991, Toronto.

Moragas Spa, M. (1981), *Teorias de la Communicacion*, Gustavo Gill, Barcelona.

Real, Michael (1986), 'Demythologizing media: recent writings in critical and institutional theory' in *Critical Studies in Mass Communication*, pp. 459–86.

Abbreviations

ABC	American Broadcasting Corporation
AFP	Agence France Presse
AM	amplitude modulation
AP	Associated Press
ATT	American Telephone and Telegraph
BBC	British Broadcasting Corporation
CANA	Caribbean News Association
CAT	computer-assisted teaching
CBC	Canadian Broadcasting Corporation
CBS	Columbia Broadcasting System
CD	compact disc
CIS	Confederation of Independent States
CNC	Centre National du Cinema
CNN	Cable News Network
CRTC	Canadian Radio-television and Telecommunications Commission
DAT	Digital Audio Tape
DBS	Direct Broadcast Satellite
DPA	Deutsche Presse Agentur
EFE	Spanish news service
FCC	Federal Communications Commission
GATT	General Agreement on Tariffs and Trade
GHz	gigahertz
GNP	gross national product
HBO	Home Box Office
INTELSAT	satellite consortium (see Glossary)
ISDN	Integrated Services Digital Network
ITAR	Information Telegraph Agency of Russia
ITC	Independent Television Commission (UK)
ITU	International Telecommunications Union
KHZ	kilohertz

MHZ	megahertz
NAFTA	North American Free Trade Agreement
NBC	National Broadcasting Corporation
NFB	National Film Board of Canada
NHK	Japanese public broadcast company
PANA	Pan-African News Agency
RCI	Radio-television Italia
SCS	Satellite-to-Cable systems
TASS	Telegraph Agency of the Soviet Union
TVRO	TeleVision Receive-Only
UPI	United Press International
USSR	Union of Soviet Socialist Republics
VHF	very high frequency
WARCs	World Administration Radio Conferences

Chapter 1

Communication and society

This book is a study of mass communication on a comparative basis. That is to say, it is a study of the impact of modern technologies of communication on many different countries and, at the same time, the developing inter-connections between countries as modern media have come to circle the globe.

Harold Innis and Marshall McLuhan were the first modern scholars to study the connection between the means of communication available to a people, and the ways in which their means of communication contribute to shaping the character and scope of their society, its economic life, politics and culture. Where speech is the only means of communication the group is small, and face-to-face interactions define and organise the scope of social life.

Innis (1950) noted the importance of written technologies for the estab-lishment and maintenance of empires – the building up of power blocs spread over large spans of time and space, for example the Roman Empire. Co-ordinating, administering and policing such a vast imperium required written systems of communication to keep records, to circulate decisions, laws and so forth, in short to maintain links between all the scattered parts. It also needed an educated elite to perform such tasks. Literacy has always been close to economic and political power. Innis concentrated on the relationship between the media of communication and the character of societies in the ancient world. He noted the 'bias' built into different media – some emphasis-ing time, others emphasising space – with different implications and conse-quences for social life. Messages written on paper or papyrus are lightweight and portable, and transmit information rapidly across space. Messages carved on stones (for instance on mausoleums, or triumphal arches) are permanent and unmoveable monuments to time which preserve information through many generations.

Thus, in a very general and fundamental way, the temporal and spatial characteristics of the available means of communication in any society impose boundaries upon the scope and scale of its activities. Within those boundaries they contribute to shaping the character of social institutions and social interactions.

McLuhan, a scholar of English literature, took up Innis's ideas and extended them to the modern period. McLuhan started with the impact of printing – 'typographical man' – and the ways in which the printed book was a powerful means of spreading ideas and knowledge in early modern Europe (1962). He went on to contrast what he called print cultures with the newer electronic cultures of modern media, especially radio and television (1964). He was the first real analyst of the impact of new media of communication (radio, TV, photography, film) on what we think of as modern societies, although certain British modernists, for example Wyndham Lewis, preceded him and had a parallel concern (Tiessen, 1993). He expressed his ideas in a distinctive, aphoristic way, referring to them as 'probes', and they had a great impact in the 1960s in North America and Europe. Perhaps his most important and lasting perception – particularly for the perspective of this book – was that the impact of modern media could no longer be thought of as particular to this or that society. What was new about electronic media was their global impact: they created, for the very first time in history, the possibility of instant communication between any two points on the globe – 'the global village' in McLuhan's famous image.

Electronic media have powerful transforming effects on the character of social time and space. In effect they help to establish the world-historical character of modern life (Giddens 1990): it is increasingly difficult not to know about what is happening elsewhere in the world today. Global television is indeed a real phenomenon when hundreds of millions of people, scattered all over the world, have simultaneous access to an event such as the Olympic Games (Dayan and Katz, 1992). Television today is intimately linked to the character of international politics, business and war. Through television, cultural narratives, images, songs and jokes circulate round the world. When a programme like *Dallas* is watched in over a hundred different countries around the world (see, for instance, Silj (1988) for its impact on European audiences, Liebes and Katz (1986) for its impact in Israel) it is clear that electronic media contribute to the formation of a global culture, underpinned by global capitalism, and with serious implications for local (national) societies and cultures. A key aspect of the 'gap' between North and South, the so-called developed and developing regions of the world, is a communications divide – the unequal flow of information and entertainment between the first and third worlds (see ch. 9).

The ideas of McLuhan and Innis form the backdrop for this comparative approach to mass communication as a global system. Their ideas have been much debated and criticised, but it was they, more than anyone else, who stressed the importance of a) studying the forms of communication available in any culture for their impact on the character of that society and particularly for their effect on the social organisation of time and space, and b) for extending this approach to the analysis of global comunication today.

One of the dangers of the McLuhan–Innis approach is what Raymond Williams calls technological determinism (Williams, 1974): with a central emphasis on media form, other elements of the communication process, such as media content or how media products are made by producing institutions, are sidelined. Partly because of McLuhan's emphasis on technology, the new wave of Marxist media theorists of the 70s saw his ideas as reactionary. McLuhan was dismissed as the guru of Madison Avenue, an apologist for advertising. But in the 80s, and in the context of postmodernism, the recognition of globalisation as a key cultural and economic phenomenon of the late twentieth century has brought about a renewed interest in McLuhan's pioneering work on the social character of media of communication. In the US, Meyrowitz (1985) has been influential, with his argument that electronic media (above all TV) weaken the once strong link between physical place and social space. Whereas previously place and space were inseparable – the latter being an extension of, or embedded in, the former – communications technologies such as the telephone, for instance, allow two people in very distant physical places to share the same social, communicative space. Similarly television gives people access to events anywhere in the world without being there, while at the same time creating new social contexts of interaction for viewers.

At its simplest, and drawing heavily on McLuhan and Erving Goffman's dramaturgical perspective (see, e.g., 1959), Meyrowitz's argument that electronic media, by invading social spaces hitherto kept apart, tend to undermine traditional settings of social interaction that maintained distinct and separate social identities. For example, he thinks the boundaries between children and adults and men and women have been blurred by the impact of broadcasting, with consequences for the character of social relationships. In India the social organisation of domestic space in the household tended to keep men, women and children apart from each other for much of the time, thereby maintaining their distinct and separate traditional social roles and identities. The arrival of TV sets in the households of rural India has considerably disturbed traditional relations between the sexes and between young and old by bringing them into each other's presence in the context of watching (Malik, 1989). In the UK Giddens (1984, 1990) has stressed the relevance of McLuhan's ideas about the social organisation of time and space as fundamental to any analysis of the concrete forms of social life and interaction.

We embark on our study with a general overview based on McLuhan and Innis. In later chapters we will introduce other points of view and other elements to which neither paid particular attention. We will strive to avoid the limitations of this perspective. We will consider, among other factors, such elements as the influence of law and policy, professionalism and professional ideals, the nature of communications institutions, proprietorship, international conventions and trading patterns, and audiences. Appropriate to an overview, both Innis (1950) and McLuhan (1962), and the Toronto School which followed in their wake, for example, Ong (1982) and Goody (1977), placed their emphasis on media writ large. McLuhan's phrase 'the medium is the message' refers to how a society organises itself around its dominant medium of communication. In developing this perspective Innis, followed by McLuhan and then others, distinguished between three different types of society based on the predominance of certain types of media: oral, literate and electronic societies.

Oral society

Innis claimed that the means of communication set basic parameters to the functioning of any society. More specifically, he analysed how oral and literate societies functioned completely differently because of their predominant means of communication. For example, as a literate people we are governed by what is written in law and by the principles and statements of our written constitutions. In oral societies people were governed by the knowledge vested in the community and specifically preserved by certain speakers. These speakers or minstrels developed and maintained their knowledge by means of epic poems and what Innis called epic technique (Innis, 1951). Epic technique involved creating poems in rhythmic six-beat lines – hexameters – with certain rigidities and elasticities. The rigidities allowed for memorisation, while the elasticities permitted adaptation to local conditions and vernacular speech. Forms, words, stock expressions and phrases acted as aids while the local language and situation provided the basis for ornamental gloss. The development of such techniques meant that epic poetry was in the hands of persons with excellent memories and poetic and linguistic abilities. The techniques for memorising and reciting epics were often passed on within families of professional storytellers and minstrels. According to Innis, such families probably built up a system of memory aids that were privately owned and carefully guarded.

   In ancient Greece mastery of words or recitation came to mean intellectual sovereignty. The epics permitted constant adaptation, as required by the oral tradition, and also allowed for the emergence of completely new content to describe conditions of social change. What was socially relevant was remembered, what was not was forgotten. Changing perspectives permitted the incorporation of sacred myths from earlier civilisations. These myths could be transformed and humanised as they were turned into the content of an epic poem. The Greeks could thereby foster the development of an inclusive ideology as they expanded their empire, and this ideology could serve colonising efforts extremely well.

The dynamics of the oral tradition in a more modern context (rural Yugoslavia from 1937 to 1959) are described by Lord (1964) in *The Singer of Tales*. One of his many telling observations is that, for the oral bard, the recording of the words of a song is a totally foreign experience. Nor, when the recording is finally accomplished, has the bard any use for it. It exists in a dead form, a particular performance at a particular time in a particular setting, utterly useless. It does not represent the correct or best version, which is approximated by subsequent performances. Nor does it capture, as 'live recordings' do for us, the spirit of the moment. The point is that the oral poet lives in an entirely different world and operates with entirely different cognitive processes than do we. The pianist Glenn Gould's 'literate' perspective (Payzant, 1984) is the antithesis of this: he believed a perfect performance (especially of a composer such as Bach) could be created in the recording studio through splicing bits from many different performances. The concert stage merely interfered with musical perfection.

The oral tradition and its ability to preserve the past, to transform that past as necessary, to base law in custom and to explain all events within a natural cosmology, point to the stability of oral societies and their tendency to preserve, extend and adapt culture. Rather than being concerned with the continued existence of formal structures and institutions, oral societies are most successful at extending the dynamics of interaction. As Innis phrased it, they were **time biased**, that is tending to extend themselves over the centuries. Change in such societies tends to induce an adaptation that preserves ways of acting, but in new circumstances. The ancient Greeks, for example, perpetuated a stable, continuous, but adapting culture.

Modern oral societies

The influence of oral processes has by no means passed. In many African societies there have been opportunities to examine the effects of oral versus literate processes. In the 1900s when British colonial administrators attempted to record histories of certain tribes to facilitate the administration of British justice, the origin myths of certain groups were carefully recorded. One myth – recorded among the Gonja of northern Ghana – told of the founding of the country by a particular figure who then divided the country amongst his sons, who became tribal chiefs of the various subsections of the country. This myth describes rather well a federation of related tribes. What amazed researchers who returned to interview the Gonja in 1956–57 (Goody, 1975, p. 35), was the transformation of the origin myths. When asked to recount these myths in the face of the further subdivision of the country, tribal narrators told the same story but the number of sons had increased. When questioned about earlier recorded versions of their myths, these oral people professed lack of understanding of the 'inconsistencies in the evidence'. When asked which number of sons was correct, in effect they answered 'both'.

The point here is not that members of oral societies are foolish, forgetful, naive, or even inconsistent, but that the ways in which oral societies preserve knowledge and cultural integrity are fundamentally different from those of literate society. Where literate cultures emphasise the 'letter of the law', as it were, oral cultures emphasise its meaning. According to the logic of an oral society, if there now exists a federated country of so many parts, given the nature of the mythical form, it must have developed from a founder followed by so many sons. The myth serves and justifies present-day reality. The same is true of the myths of literate cultures, but the relation between the present day and the past often involves a much more labyrinthine series of connections. In literate cultures, in face of massive numbers of volumes of recorded history of figures and events, history need not be synchronic, that is to say, it need not be synthesised into a few ideas that encompass a vast passage of time. History in literate societies can be both synchronic and diachronic – ideas that span time and narratives that are faithful to chronology can exist simultaneously. The result, in literate society, is that as each generation reads its history they may interpret the same many and varied events in the light of the ideas of the day: history is continually re-written.

It is not only tribal societies that exhibit oral processes. Every community has its gods, its heroes and anti-heroes, borrowed and adapted, religiously adhered to by insiders, reviled by its enemies. Music seems to play an especially strong catalytic role in helping such societies bond. Indeed, the response of societies to new musical forms is worth noting. It is a tribute to the powerful role of new musical forms and to their autonomy from central societal institutions that popular music is continually subjected to censorship. Eastern European countries under Communist rule exercised such censorship, particularly in relation to jazz. In Western countries the absolute bans of the Eastern bloc are replaced with strictures on the medium through which the work can be communicated. For example, rock-music stations and television broadcast channels do not play certain songs and videos, although these may be available through record and video stores.

Literate society

Greece, for Innis, represented an oral society, whereas Rome represented a literate society. It was not that Greece was unaffected by writing. On the contrary, a number of authors, notably Havelock (1976), claim that the basis of the enormous contribution Greek civilisation made to modern civilisation is to be found in writing, in their invention of the phonetic alphabet. Innis also cites contemporary statements from the time of the emergence of writing that indicate a realisation of the significance of the change from oral to written forms. For example, in Plato's *Phaedrus* Socrates reports a conversation between the Egyptian god Thoth, the inventor of letters, and the god Amon. Amon says:

> This discovery of yours will create forgetfulness in the learners' souls, because they will not use their memories; they will trust to the external written charac-ters and not remember of themselves. The specific you have discovered is an aid not to memory, but to reminiscence, and you give your disciples not truth but only the semblance of truth; they will be bearers of many things and will have learned nothing; they will appear to be omniscient and will generally know nothing; they will be tiresome company, having the show of wisdom without the reality.

Socrates continues:

> I cannot help feeling, Phaedrus, that writing is unfortunately like painting; for the creations of the painter have the attitude of life, and yet if you ask them a question, they preserve a solemn silence, and the same may be said of speeches. You would imagine that they had intelligence, but if you want to know anything and put a question to one of them, the speaker always gives one unvarying answer.   (Plato, *Phaedrus*, 1973, p. 84)

Such statements are reminiscent of some discussions of television and its numbing effect on the mind. And so they should be, for the transformation from an oral to a literate society is as major a change as from a literate to an electronic society. They also point out the degree to which knowledge and wisdom were negotiated in oral discourse, rather than derived from a logical analysis of proposed concepts.

Rome and the Roman Empire represent literate society because the operating concepts and processes of Rome were derived from the written rather than the spoken word: possession of a piece of land or object became subject to an abstract notion of legal property, which had never before been conceived of. In other legal proceedings, the influence of writing could be seen in the fact that trained lawyers were responsible for defining the exact nature of a dispute within written laws (a literate function), and only then was the case handed to laymen (as a jury, for instance) to determine a settlement among the claimants (an oral community function, to gauge the significance of the crime to the community). But the Roman ability to invent an institution to supplant practices founded on the oral process was most marked in the development of contract law. A contract changes an oral pact into a legal obligation. It is a precise written record of an agreed obligation between persons or other legal entities.

Such inventions allowed for both an orderly and a vast expansion of the Roman Empire which, as Innis phrased it, gave it **a space bias**, that is a tendency to extend itself over a larger and larger territory (Innis, 1950, 1951). Crucial to the exercise of the administrative power of the Roman Empire was the conception of forming abstract laws to apply in all situations, and recording these laws by writing them down on a portable medium such as parchment so they could be consulted in numerous locations. These develop-ments reflected an attempt to replace spoken poetic language with clear, ordered, unambiguous, logical written prose.

In their writings, Cicero (106–43 BC) and other Stoic philosophers invented the ideas of the world state, natural law and justice and universal citizenship in an ethical sense. All these were characteristics of a literate society, as were libraries, which were scattered throughout the empire. Without writing, without the ability to pursue the static representation of ideas, where, by a mere eye movement, two ideas could be juxtaposed and compared, without the ability to see many individual instances and abstract the general case, such ideas could never have existed.

Most other writings about literate societies focus on modern societies. While they discuss the nature of the influence of writing they do so within a context of an evolved technology and developed social, political and legal institutions (see, for example, McLuhan, 1962; Goody, 1977; Olson, 1980). The basic claim of these authors is that writing has provided the means for the development of logical, linear and sequential thinking. Literate thought is logical because it must be presented in such a way that anyone can understand the meaning of a written passage without benefit of knowing the context within which the passage was written and without the possibility of further reference to the author. It can stand by itself as a statement that is consistent both internally and with reference to other common knowledge. Literate thought is linear and sequential because only one idea can be presented at a time, followed by another and then another. This contrasts with what can be done on television, where a picture can be providing context while a spoken text, i.e. a written script, can provide other aspects of meaning. It also contrasts with what is available to a speaker, who with facial or bodily gesture can communicate certain aspects of a message while communicating other aspects in words. In addition, in most situations the speaker also has the benefit of monitoring his or her audience during the communication, a direct form of feedback not available with print or with electronic communication.

Electronic society

It is only in the past half-decade or so that scholars have given serious consideration to the transformations in our society that result from a growing reliance on electronic communications. Perhaps because scholars depend so heavily on what we associate with writing, that is, the ability to write clearly and think logically and conceptually, we have not been able to imagine how electronic information processes are going to change that process dramatically.

A shortcoming of McLuhan's work, understandable for his time, is that his examples are from entertainment media such as television rather than information-processing media such as computers. In concentrating on broadcast television and radio he enters a domain foreign to most scholars, a domain from which they get little information of value to their scholarship. They are thus inclined to see McLuhan's media as a system serving needs other than their own, professional needs and therefore have been reluctant to consider the dynamics of electronic information-processing thoughtfully.

However, as information processing by electronic means becomes more prevalent, that is, as computers become more pervasive in everything from cars to cameras, it is easier to see the importance of McLuhan's ideas. As scholars begin to take advantage of computers and communication technology in their own writing, information gathering, information monitoring and personal and professional communications, they begin to understand new patterns of information production and consumption, which in turn lead to new biases in the creation and dissemination of knowledge.

McLuhan himself made much of the notion of a global village. By that he did not mean that we would soon become members of one big happy family, but that we would have the information-gathering capacity to be intimately, perhaps too intimately, aware of the goings-on of all people in every kind of situation around the world. Global news organisations mean that it is not difficult for us to find out about nearly every country and its current situation. Nightly we find out about many countries in which 'newsworthy' events have recently happened, yet most of us know that our nightly news services rarely avail themselves of news available from parts of the world that for one reason or another are not considered to be of primary interest. What is going on now in the Falklands? In Grenada? In Turkey with the Iraqi Kurds? These are all areas that commanded world attention for a while. In Australia in the early 1980s, an hour-long news programme on that country's Special Broadcasting Service was designed to disseminate news from areas not covered by other stations, and especially from countries that had supplied many recent immigrants to Australia. The service provided a different image of the world and a quite different image of the news-gathering and presentation process than that presented on British, European, American, or Canadian television. Ted Turner's Cable News Network (CNN) has that capability but it is difficult to know if it will be realised. As Chapter 5 argues, so tied are the US media to the interests of the state that unless there are foreign policy implications for the US, events and areas of the world will not be covered. What this means, of course, is that if CNN fails to respond to this opportunity, there is a market niche opening for such a world information service or consortium of services.

Our linkage with the whole world is always incomplete but steadily more inclusive as the global electronic village transforms our environment, extending our realm of knowledge and transforming our attitude to our own local environment. Various studies indicate that people who rely on television for information have a vision of the world that over-estimates the violence and disorder in the world, a view apparently derived from news and other programming that concentrates on violence (see Gerbner, 1978). At times people seem to ignore their own quiet surroundings for the more dynamic impact of the world as presented on television.

Television demands the enactment of a small drama with visual interest for the creation of a news story. Information is not collected and later transformed into a form presentable through television; rather, the event is most often staged and then 'clips' of it are used for television. The television crew must get everyone to act in a way that will make good television; people must be stage-managed so the material can be sifted through to produce what is perceived to be 'good' television. Or the newsmakers can stage the event themselves. The presentation of news on television is not so much a transformation by analysis as a selection. Those who can create good television are those who become newsworthy. Newsworthiness itself shifts focus away from logically interesting to visually interesting items, not a new plank in a political platform but the presence of a prime minister or president in an esoteric or visually interesting location.

Numerous other examples of substantial changes to the structure and use of information echo the elements McLuhan identified as intrinsically different between literate and electronic communication. Every major stock exchange has computerised its stock trading. Such electrification has reduced confirmation on stock orders from two or three minutes to seconds. This emphasis on speed does nothing to enhance the proper value of stock reflective of performance and potential. It emphasises quick stock-market play as opposed to long-term stable investments. In another area, Martin Eslin (1980) has argued that, with the advent of television, the predominant form of argumentation or presentation of facts has come to be dramatisation. Theatricality has replaced reasoned analysis.

Vivid examples of information presentation that reflect both literate and electronic information processes can be found in the world of advertising. Products that we are meant to purchase because they are of value to our health often reflect literate values. Advertisements that make reference to surveys of either results-of-use or consumer preference mimic logical argumentation to convince us to choose their product. The term 'mimic' is used here because there is no attempt in such advertisements to ensure exact understanding of actuality; instead, their creators make claims that, though logically constructed, tell only part of the story. The audience is led to believe it is receiving the whole story.

Products that we are meant to purchase for our own enjoyment or for the enhancement of our self-image tend to reflect the image-oriented values of electronic society. Lifestyle ads, such as those used to sell beer, foreground an image of the beer drinker and his/her sensibilities. A marketing vice-president for Labatt (a leading Canadian brewer) has explained that the difference in taste of any one mainstream brand is so elusive that the customer has to keep consuming to remember that difference (Grady, 1983). The point is that *the image of the consumer is what is being sold and consumed.*

A North American ad series that is an excellent combination of implied literate reasoning and image-based electronic values is one created for Campbell's soup. A ball of yarn coloured and shaped like a Campbell's soup can is stuck through with knitting needles and accompanied by the caption 'Better than a sweater'; it has the immediate draw of a powerful image, accompanied by the subtlety of the logical reasoning behind why one would consume soup in cold weather. The complete ad series plays on this theme.

Extending McLuhan and Innis

The legacy of Innis and McLuhan has been affected by their opaque intellectual and writing styles. Much time has been spent, especially by Canadian scholars, attempting to prove that their insights were genuine and salient to the field. As we noted earlier, in the UK in the 70s, McLuhan was dismissed as an apologist of the advertising industry. However, such authors as Eric Havelock (1963, 1976), Jack Goody (1975, 1977), David Olson (1980), Walter Ong (1982), Elizabeth Eisenstein (1983) and Anthony Giddens (1990) have taken these insights at their most general level and developed more systematic analyses of particular phenomena.

In the following section, in order to provide a more thorough understanding of both his overall theoretical framework and the nature of contemporary society, we will extend McLuhan's analyses, especially of electronic society. (Meyrowitz (1985) has carried out the same sort of analysis but in a much different manner.) To assist in this endeavour we have constructed Table 1. In this table, column 1 describes the communicational forms we discussed above with a slight expansion. That expansion is a division of electronic communication into three parts – oral, audio-visual and textual-numeric. Column 2 describes the communicational context and dominant technology of the form; column 3 outlines the analytical framework that complements most directly the communicational form; and column 4 describes the social philosophy/belief system that derives from each analytical framework. As Table 1 illustrates, we are positing that each communicational form is part of a different context or technology, and encourages a quite distinctive manner of thinking, out of which is derived a distinctive social belief system.

TABLE 1   *The social structure of communication*

Communicational form	Communicational context/dominant technology	Analytical framework	Social philosophy/belief system
Oral	• face-to-face • multifaceted e.g., voice modulation, gesture	• interpretation of intent • consistency of actions with character	• focused on personalised environmental constants • pluralistic
Literate	• indirectly social • individual interacts with text • text can stand alone	• logical • linear • conceptual • structuralist • scientific method	• hierarchical • development of conceptual constants • single concept supremacy • scientific
Electronic oral	• mediated by radio and telephone	• memory-based • impressionist • intent and character oriented	• capture of the *Zeitgeist*
Electronic audio-visual	• television • iconic • dramatic • socially produced	• impressionist • multi-interpretative • post-modernist	• pluralistic • celebratory of variety, particularity, novelty
Electronic textural-numeric	• computers/ telecommunications • text- and machine-oriented	• trends analysis • inferential statistics • specialised knowledge and hence viewpoints	• extensivity possibly leading to elitism • potential for widespread systems, i.e. freenets

Oral and literate communication: an overview

Oral communication takes place through face-to-face interaction where both speaker and listener can hear and see each other. Each can look for, listen to and use all kinds of inflection to create and interpret meaning. As E. T. Hall (1980) has explained so vividly, we do so within lived cultural patterns. Oral communication is fundamentally social. As investigations have shown in a variety of areas, including anthropology (Goody, 1977), communications (Innis, 1950, 1951; McLuhan, 1962, 1964; Ong, 1982), history (Eisenstein, 1983) and classics (Havelock, 1976), it is associated with an analytical framework focused on interpreting the intent of actors, whether those actors are human beings or a pantheon of gods. Oral communication leads to belief systems in which environmental constants such as the sun, moon, stars, signs of the zodiac, earth, air, seas, rivers, trees, rocks, animals and so forth are made into persons or metaphors of persons. The world is filled with personal interactions between, for example, the sky and water. They (sky and water) lie together at the horizon and bear children (clouds), who pass over our heads shedding tears of joy as nourishment for our crops. Each member of society – by virtue of time and date of birth or family membership or sex – is a member of one or more groups, such as aquarians, moon worshippers, the bear clan. Thus certain rules apply to members of one group that do not apply to another, rather like the game rock-scissors-paper, where paper covers a rock but is vulnerable to scissors. The pluralism inherent in this system also provides a variety of interpretative structures that vie for allegiance and are not necessarily consistent one with another.

Literate communication, on the other hand, is only indirectly social. Both writer and reader engage differently with a written text, one creating, the other interpreting. The text must have internal consistency and comprehensiveness. It must be capable of standing apart from its author as a meaningful statement in and by itself. Literate analysis is linear – moving from point to point. It is not contextualised, as is oral communication, by body language and tone of voice. Literate communication leads to the development of general and specific explanatory concepts that form into a system or general theory. These explanatory concepts have a hierarchical relation one to another and, over the course of time, form an explanatory framework – in specific instances, a scientific theory. For example, the behaviour of objects relative to other objects was defined by a number of specific laws until Newton suggested the notion of gravity to explain such behaviour. Later, Einstein proposed his general theory of relativity and Newton's notions were recast as specific instances within Einstein's more encompassing framework. In each case, old concepts were eclipsed by new ones.

The hierarchical nature of the conceptual frameworks developed in literate society focuses the development of ideas on producing and testing conceptual constants, leading towards the supremacy of single general concepts that seem to explain all related phenomena, as in relativity theory. Consistent with this tendency, literate societies are less amenable than are oral societies to a plurality of explanatory frameworks that gain or lose apparent validity, and hence allegiance of followers, as world events unfold.

Electronic oral communication

Electronic society can best be understood by dividing it into three parts.

Electronic oral communication, exemplified by radio and the telephone, is socially mediated by technology and focused on the human voice and the rhetorical structure of the message. Like oral communication it relies on the memory of the listener; however, in terms of creation it differs from oral communication in that it is often created first in written form and then delivered orally as in newscasts. When not created first in written form, it is often edited after the fact to create the intended impression. Parallel with oral communication itself, the oral content of both television and radio have a quite different logic from written discourse (Scannell, 1991).

Electronic oral communication is affected by how the speaker con-textualises his/her message by a) voice modulation, b) the manner in which ideas are expressed, such as choice of words and whether the ideas are expressed within a narrative form, and c) the overall interrelationship of ideas in the message as a whole, for example the sequencing of ideas or placing opposing ideas in the mouths of different actors. To some degree electronic oral communication is dramatic performance.

The analytical framework complementary to electronic oral communica-tion is memory-based and impressionistic of both the message and the messenger. As the words go by, some phrases stick in your mind, not just their meaning but the phrases, the exact words. And the exact words are framed more broadly in two ways. One is in the vaguely remembered whole, but more vivid than that whole discourse is an imputed personality of the speaker – the kind of person who would speak that way on that subject. Like the analytical framework associated with oral communication itself, under-standing is based on perceived and projected interpretations consistent with the inferred character of the speaker.

The derivative social philosophy from electronic oral communication is oriented to the ability of certain speakers to capture in words, in ringing tones, the largely unarticulated attitudes and understandings – sometimes called the *Zeitgeist* – of the audience. The phrase 'does it ring true' is often operative. In different words: does the information put forward appear to be consistent with what I already know and is it reasonable that the person giving it to me would know? This perspective can lead to reliance on the 'believability' of certain speakers, such as talk-show hosts or investigative reporters, independent of whether their content stands up to detailed scrutiny. Smooth-talking politicians, especially those who wear the mantle of power well, can use this media 'bias' to their advantage. As many members of the public have said of a politician they have listened to on the radio, 'she sounds sincere' or 'you can tell she knows just from the sound of her voice'.

Electronic audio-visual communication

Electronic audio-visual communication is most obviously exemplified by television. Like electronic oral communication, it is also only indirectly social and mediated by technology. It re-creates or re-presents the social through its pictures and spoken words. Based on its orientation to visual images, it can be said to be an iconic or image-oriented medium (see Bruner, 1978). It shares with electronic oral communication the characteristic of being a dramatic medium. Together these properties allow it to attempt to re-create the sound and sight of persons completely focused on significant events.

The production of audio-visual images is a social process that, in the final analysis, is usually directed by a single individual, but that involves a large and diverse team of specialists. Each member contributes to a complement of images by lighting, framing, dialogue, ambience, or editing style, which combine to create the intended impression (see ch. 8). In a sense, electronic audio-visual communication is the re-creation of face-to-face communication in a fully visualised context conceived by the literate mind.

It would appear that because an infinite number of images and impressions can be created by even slight variations in the produced piece of communication – a camera frames a person inappropriately for the intended message – the complementary analytical framework most appropriate to this form of communication requires flexibility and room for difference of opinion. Such a framework, or rather, frameworks are post-structuralism, postmodernism and dramaturgical analysis each of which we will explain in later chapters. They all allow for substantial variations but point to the organising attributes of the produced message. Note that this analytical framework shares plurality with oral and electronic oral communication.

The social philosophy arising from the need to understand an image-based world is pluralism, an acceptance of variety, particularity and novelty that celebrates the human condition. In practice, this pluralism appears to be constrained by one or other prevailing school of thought or expression, probably a vestigial bias deriving from our literate backgrounds. The emergence of moral relativism, as well as layered personal identities, is also consistent with this form of communication. A focus on presentation of both self and ideas, as well as an ability to command the forces of communication, overrides content and consistency as the foundations of effective communication. Currently, for example, there is no great moral outcry from the public when politicians are elected on one platform and, once elected, completely reverse themselves.

Electronic textual-numeric communication

Electronic textual-numeric communication, exemplified by the processing of information by computers and telecommunication, is the least social communicative form of the five discussed here. At its most social, it may involve an individual creating input and another, or the same, individual doing some final interpretations of output. However, computers may suffice for all aspects – inputting, reception and analysis. The information typical to this form of communication is monitored (e.g. the number of items sold at a particular cash register) or sampled (e.g. a market or political poll). The communicators involved – both information creators and audience – have the capacity to analyse and benefit from vast quantities of detailed information. It is commonly large institutions, which have been able to expand due to the ability of computers to process large quantities of data, that have acquired that capacity and learned what information is critical to carry out ever-increasing large-scale operations. Examples are banks, insurance companies, central governments, stock analysts, global advertising agencies, even large urban public libraries. Digitisation of information gives electronic textual-numeric communication the ascendancy, for it is not only megadoses of numbers and words that can be tamed by supercomputers but also sounds and images, indeed anything that can be formally defined as information.

The complementary analytic framework most suited to this form of communication is descriptive and inferential mathematical analysis and statistics. These techniques are a means of summarising patterns in data. Married to extensive information-processing capacity, such techniques can reveal the secrets of brainwave or weather patterns, correlate life expectancy with location, lifestyle, diet, gender or any other recordable variable.

The countertrend in electronic textual-numeric communication is widespread electronic empowerment through public access to information databases. Such public access facilities are generally called **freenets** and they are being set up in a variety of major cities in the developed world. Essentially, freenets are computer networks which provide free access to computer-based discussion groups in which contributors come from all over the developed – and sometimes the developing – world. The limitation of freenets is that at best they provide access to a certain range of information products and to a limited number of telephone lines for discussions by means of typed-in entries. They are weaker in their provision for the systematic collection, processing and analysis of data to create, disseminate and discuss meaningful information.

The derivative social philosophy from the primary form of electronic textual-numeric communication (i.e. not the countertrend) focuses on the amount of data and the transformation that is necessary to bring phenomena into a digital regime, and on the organisation appropriate to and necessary for its analysis. In short, analytical expertise directed by planners and strategists must be combined with copious information-processing capacity, to be interpreted by other experts knowledgeable of both trends and trend analysis. Large-scale data collection and analysis becomes a pre-condition to valued knowledge and interpretation not necessarily because such a scale is superior but because it is possible. For instance, an infrared satellite picture of a farmer's field can tell him which parts are ready for harvest. But then again, so can his eyes if he cares to walk out to the field and take a sample of the grain. The difficulty in the latter case is that he cannot sample as widely, and if he has a vast acreage the job is best done by satellite.

All things being equal, the more extensive the information at the command of the analyst, the more accurate the analysis can be. These organisational foundations of electronic textual-numeric communication have the potential to lead to elitism, even if they do not do it directly, essentially because social issues can be formulated in terms that can be addressed by digitalised data. Those who have the technical and analytical capacity to work with extensive data become claimants to the wisdom of the day. This orientation could easily lead to a sort of institutional feudalism within large corporations reminiscent of governing courts, seigneurs, war lords, or, in more contemporary forms, global conglomerates, oligarchies, monopolies and Japanese-style business (involving both lifetime employment and state/business co-ordination). Whether the freenets will be effective counter measures to elitism remains to be seen. At this point the possibility of entrenching information utilities into the basic services of society and guaranteeing access to all seems a pipe-dream, let alone providing the majority of the population with the skills necessary to use such services.

Other viewpoints

The shortcoming of the McLuhan/Innis framework is that it tends toward a technological determinism. It is not that either author was an avowed technological determinist. McLuhan, for instance, once noted: 'we shape our tools; thereafter our tools shape us'. Thus it might be claimed that McLuhan starts in society and with human agency, but the 'we' in McLuhan's statement (i.e. human agency) was not consciously theorised as a starting point for an explanatory framework for communications.

Other viewpoints which address the media certainly exist. They are mainly rooted in material realities. They range from pure Marxism through Louis Althusser, Antonio Gramsci and Raymond Williams, to current cultural theorists, feminists and the work of Anthony Giddens, with added broadening by those more oriented to the audience, such as Ien Ang and David Morley. The work of many of these authors will be introduced in later chapters, particularly chapters 7 and 8. For now and for illustrative purposes, consider the perspective of Raymond Williams. Williams (1974) makes the case that social forms of communication, of which communications technologies are a part, arise from the organisation of society and reflect that organisation. These perspectives are important to understand and will be discussed in more depth in later chapters.

It is also important to understand that starting points are a function of literate form. The linearity and conceptuality that is intrinsic to written communication, especially the essay form, demands a central, unitary concept around which an explanation is organised. That centrality and unity have less to do with the phenomenon being studied than they do with the form of explanation being used. Thus, it is our view that while tools are developed in societies, for example block printing in China, for them to become an influential technology demands a social structure which provides a potential reward for those who may have access to the technology. If there is no opportunity for the reward of technology-based entrepreneurship, then the potential of a particular technology will not be fully realised.

Summary and conclusion

This chapter began with an introduction to the McLuhan-Innis framework and a discussion of its relevance to a comparative examination of mass communications. The overview provided by this framework was outlined and its potential danger of leading towards a reductive technological determinism was pointed out. We then examined the characteristics of societies organised around various media forms. We began with a summary of what McLuhan and Innis regarded as the fundamental characteristics of oral, literate and electronic societies. Noting that each of these three types of processes are present in contemporary society we took a second look at the social structure of communication in oral, literate and electronic societies. To give electronic society a full discussion we distinguished between oral, image-based and textual-numeric electronic communication.

We argued that each communicational form arises in either a dominant communication context or technology, that each form and context give rise to a complementary dominant analytical framework and that all three – form, context and framework – create a derivative social philosophy or belief system.

In so far as all these communicational forms are present and active in contemporary society we have not tried to reduce the dynamics of contemporary society into a single concept. Rather, we have laid the groundwork for a media-based interpretation of phenomena in society. Because the mass media are various – TV, movies, books, radio, sound recordings, magazines, electronic networks and so forth – it is unlikely that one medium will completely eclipse the others, but it is entirely possible that particular media forms could become married to particular sectors of society or human activity. It is reasonable to expect that out of such liaisons, shared points of view located in various sectors of society could be built. From these differently-located shared perspectives could emerge claims to – if not actual – political and social power. Understanding the media dynamics on which each perspective is based thus offers insight into social process.

The chapter closed with a nod to other overviews of communication and society and briefly noted the nature of the difference between them and the model put forward here.

References

Bruner, Jerome (1978), *Human Growth and Development*, Clarendon, Oxford.

Dayan, D., and E. Katz (1992), *Media Events. The Live Broadcasting of History*, Harvard University Press, Cambridge, MA.

de Kerckhove, Derrick (1984), 'McLuhan versus Orwell in 1984', *The Globe and Mail*.

Eisenstein, Elizabeth (1983), *The Printing Revolution in Early Modern Europe*, Cambridge University Press, Cambridge.

Eslin, Martin (1980), 'The exploding stage', *Ideas*, CBC Radio, October, University of Toronto.

Gerbner, George (1978), *Trends in Network Television Drama and Viewer Conceptions of Social Reality*, Annenberg School of Communications, University of Philadelphia, PA.

Giddens, Anthony (1984), *The Constitution of Society*, Polity Press, Cambridge.

Giddens, Anthony (1990), *The Consequences of Modernity*, Polity Press, Cambridge.

Goffmann, Erving (1959), *The Presentation of Self in Everyday Life*, Doubleday, Garden City, New York.

Goody, J. R. (1975), *Literacy in Traditional Societies*, Cambridge University Press, Cambridge.

Goody, J. R. (1977), *The Domestication of the Savage Mind*, Cambridge University Press, Cambridge.

Grady, Wayne (1983), 'The Budweiser gamble', *Saturday Night*, February, pp. 28–30.

Hall, Edward T. (1980), *The Silent Language*, Greenwood Press, Westport, Conn.

Havelock, Eric (1963, 1976), *Origins of Western Literacy*, Ontario Institute for Studies in Education, Toronto.

Innis, Harold (1950), *Empire and Communications*, University of Toronto Press, Toronto.

Innis, Harold (1951), *The Bias of Communication*, University of Toronto Press, Toronto.

Liebes, Tamar, and Elihu Katz (1986), 'Decoding Dallas: notes from a cross-cultural study', in G. Gumpert and R. Cathcart (eds), *Inter/Media*, Oxford University Press, New York.

Lord, A. B. (1964), *The Singer of Tales*, Harvard University Press, Cambridge.

Malik, S. (1989), 'Television and rural India', *Media Culture and Society*, 11 (4), pp. 459–84.

McLuhan, Marshall (1962), *The Gutenberg Galaxy: The Making of Typographic Man*, University of Toronto Press, Toronto.

McLuhan, Marshall (1964), *Understanding Media: The Extensions of Man*, McGraw-Hill, New York.

Meyrowitz, Joshua (1985), *No Sense of Place*, Oxford University Press, New York.

Olson, David R. (ed.) (1980), *The Social Foundations of Language and Thought*, Norton, New York.

Ong, Walter (1982), *Orality and Literacy: The Technologizing of the Word*, Methuen, London.

Payzant, G. (1984), *Glenn Gould, Music and Mind*, Key Porter, Toronto.

Plato (1973), *Phaedrus*, Penguin, Toronto.

Scannell, Paddy (ed.) (1991), *Broadcast Talk*, Sage, London.

Silj, A. (ed.) (1988), *East of Dallas. The European Challenge to American Television*, British Film Institute, London.

Tiessen, Paul (1993), 'From literary modernism to the Tantramar Marshes: anticipating McLuhan in British and Canadian media theory and practice', *Canadian Journal of Communication*, 18 (4), pp. 451–68.

Williams, Raymond (1974), *Television: Technology and Cultural Form*, Fontana, London.

Chapter 2

Mass communication and modern society

The notions of oral, literate and electronic media provide a panoramic and somewhat historical view of the role of communication in society. Superimposed on these fundamental communicational forms are the specific media of modern society. In being composed of oral, literate and electronic elements the modern mass media have an impact on society that derives not only from the organisational biases inherent in such communicational forms but also from a complexity of variables that define their nature – the laws under which they operate, the technology they use, their organisational form, the professions they employ, their perceived aims and goals, and their orientation to their audiences. The purpose of this second chapter is to outline these variables and define the basics of their influence on the media and society.

In *Key Concepts in Communication* O'Sullivan and his co-authors (1983) provide a short empirical orientation to mass communication, which is: 'usually understood as newspapers, magazines, cinema, television, radio and advertising; sometimes including book publishing (especially popular fiction) and music (the pop industry)' (p. 130). They go on to note that mass communication should probably be thought of as a proper noun, a term that denotes something but is not descriptive of it. The reason? The word mass encourages us to think of the audience as a vast undifferentiated agglomeration of individuals lacking social bonds and alienated from society by unskilled, meaningless work, subject to the vagaries of markets and the willingness of capitalists to pay a living wage. The word communication tends to mask the social and industrial organisational nature of the media and promotes a tendency to think of the communication that takes place through the media as analogous to interpersonal communication. Having introduced these caveats (as well as the fact that they know of no successful definition), the authors aim for a more formal definition: 'Mass communication is the practice and product of providing leisure entertainment and information to an unknown audience by means of corporately financed, industrially produced, state regulated, high technology, privately consumed commodities in the modern print, screen, audio and broadcast media' (p. 131). In spite of its relatively recent formulation, the conception of mass communication put forward by O'Sullivan *et al.* is already becoming dated and problematic. Most importantly, it only partially distinguishes between the mass media and mass communication. Such a differentiation is important because it can provide a basis for a deeper understanding of the interaction between communication and society.

A historical example

Curran (1982) makes the useful point that every medium of communication to large numbers of people, although perhaps mass *communication*, should not be considered part of the mass *media*:

> a variety of signifying forms apart from face-to-face interaction – buildings, pictures, statues, coins, banners, stained glass, songs, medallions, rituals of all kinds – were deployed in pre-industrial societies to express sometimes highly complex ideas. At times, these signifying forms reached vast audiences. For instance, the proportion of the adult population in Europe regularly attending mass during the middle ages was almost certainly higher than the proportion of adults in contemporary Europe regularly reading a newspaper. Since the rituals of religious worship were laid down in liturgies, the papal curia exercised a much more centralised control over the symbolic content mediated through public worship in the central middle ages than even the controllers of the highly centralised and monopolistic press of contemporary Europe.   (p. 202)

When we speak of the mass media, then, we are speaking of the modern electronic and print-based mass media. Mass communication is a broader matter, and to gain a full understanding we should also regard the communication functions performed by the church, architecture, education systems, paintings, sculpture, coins, rituals and the like as mass communication. Indeed, including these forms in our study may enhance our understanding of the mass media as mass communication.

A contemporary example

Another example may contribute to that understanding and elucidate the differences between the mass media and mass communication. The example is adapted, with the author's permission, from an essay by Umberto Eco called 'The multiplication of the media' (1986, pp. 148–50).

   1 A firm produces polo shirts with an alligator on them and it advertises them.
   2 A generation begins to wear these polo shirts.
   3 Each consumer of the polo shirt advertises, via the alligator on his or her

chest, this brand of polo shirt (just as every owner of a Toyota is an advertiser, unpaid and paying, of the Toyota line and the model he/she drives).

4 A TV broadcast (programme), to be faithful to reality, shows some young people wearing the alligator polo shirt.

5 The young (and the old) see the TV broadcast and buy more alligator polo shirts because they have 'the young look'.

Which is the mass medium? The advertisement? The broadcast? The shirt?

Who is sending the message? The manufacturer? The wearer? The TV director? The analyst of this phenomenon?

Who is the producer of ideology? Again, the manufacturer? The wearer (including the celebrity who may wear it in public for a fee)? The TV director who portrays the generation?

Where does the plan come from? This is not to imply that there is no plan but rather that it does not emanate from one central source.

Eco concludes: 'Once upon a time there were the mass media, and they were wicked, of course, and there was a guilty party. Then there were the virtuous voices that accused the criminals. And Art (ah, what luck!) offered alternatives, for those who were not prisoners of the mass media. Well, it's all over. We have to start again from the beginning, asking one another what's going on' (1986, pp. 148–50).

Since Eco's passage was written, there has been an advance in the way many people think about the media, brought about in part by questioning along the lines Eco has indicated. For example, consider the Rolling Stones. The Rolling Stones, in being famous, are one element of mass media content that is widely known. In being widely known they have had to form themselves into a company and have thus transformed themselves into industrially organised media properties. As a significant content element – in other words a well known pop group – the Rolling Stones have ready access to the mass media, that is, television, radio, magazines, newspapers, books. They share that ready access with company logos, alligator shirts, sports heros, the Olympics, political leaders and the World Bank. Their presence on the world stage, made possible by the mass media – records, movies and the like – transforms them into media vehicles themselves; what we might call second order mass media. They gain the ability to be vehicles for messages (and/or products) that are extensions or transformations of the identities that brought them onto the world stage in the first place. Thus they can promote other products through their achieved presence in the lives of audience members. Hence we have the Rolling Stones line of clothes, not a very successful line, but a line nonetheless.

With the existence of an ever-increasing number of media, secondary media vehicles and a proliferation of technological forms and capacities, we appear to be moving away from the mass media as they were originally understood, that is, as media who carried a small set of information and entertainment products to most of society. We have created an extensive mass media system no longer simply aimed at the general aggregate audience but which has a sufficient capacity to distribute a variety of specialised information and entertainment packages directed at fragmented or segmented audiences, small groups whose shared characteristic is their media selection, small communities of interest but not of geography.

Telecommunications

A second area properly labelled mass communication is modern telecommunications. Formally defined, telecommunications include 'any transmission, emission or reception of signs, signals, writing, images or sounds or intelligence of any nature by wire, radio, visual or other electromagnetic system' (Canada (1970), c. 233, s. 1). Strictly speaking this includes broadcasting, but because broadcasting itself is such a large area of concern, telecommunications normally refers to what is included in this definition when broadcasting is removed.

Traditionally, the term 'telecommunications' has included the telephone and telegraph industries; with the advent of communications satellites and computers, the term has expanded to cover satellite transmissions and data links. In recent years, thanks to inventive communications engineers, a vast array of services has emerged that integrates the capacities of computers, satellites, glass fibres and light-based as well as electromagnetic-based transmissions. We now have in the consumer and business markets alone e-mail, electronic bulletin boards, videophones, databases, videotex, faxes, cellular radio (phones), pocket range phones, packet radio and vastly expanded satellite capacity, to say nothing of the traditional services such as telex and cable television.

These are properly regarded as mass communication because they are designed to be, and are on their way to being, universally available. As the International Telecommunications Union notes, the goal of their organisation is to have a telephone within access of every individual in the world. As individuals' access to personal computers and data and voice lines increases along with affordable transmission capacity and electronically accessible information (databases), these services are indeed becoming part of our system of mass communication. As such services ensconce themselves in our day-to-day lives, they are changing the nature of our communities, weakening our links with the physical space and community that immediately surround us and strenthening our connections to world-wide events, phenomena and communities.

A revised definition of mass communication

Given this expansion, and to build on the definition of mass communication proffered by O'Sullivan *et al.*, we need to incorporate a wider range of phenomena than the mass media and specifically draw attention to the capacities for affordable storage, transmission and widespread retrieval of a vast array of information which are intrinsic to mass communication. To revise their definition, mass communication is the practice and product of providing information and leisure entertainment to

> large, often unknown, and increasingly fragmenting audiences. When under-taken by means of modern technologies, this process involves institutionally financed and organised, [state regulated, high-technology] organizations that provide commodities and associated free services in print, on the screen, elec-tronically, and by electromagnetic broadcast. When undertaken by more tradi-tional means, mass communication includes any means of providing informa-tion, images, and/or leisure entertainment to large numbers of people from all social strata and demographic groups but who are homogeneous in their behaviour of choosing to attend to an information source.
>
> (adapted from O'Sullivan *et al.* (1983), p. 131)

The mass media

The mass media are a subset of mass communication. While we might tease out mass media elements from our definition of mass communication and discuss those elements, this job has essentially been done by McQuail (1983). The following section builds on his definition and explanation. The mass media:

1 are *a distinct set of activities* (creating media content);
2 *involve particular technological configurations* (television, radio, videotex, newspapers, books);
3 are associated with *formally constituted institutions* or media outlets (systems, stations, publications and so on);
4 operate according to *certain laws, rules and understandings* (professional codes and practices, audience and societal expectations and habits);
5 are produced by *persons occupying certain roles* (owners, regulators, producers, distributors, advertisers, audience members);
6 convey *information, entertainment, images and symbols* to a *mass audience*.

1. A distinct set of activities

The mass media can be considered to be a distinct set of activities in their communicative function as well as in their form. The common-sense image of the nature of communication is that of a conductor, such as a pipeline for water or an electrical wire for electricity. Some piece of information that exists at point 'A' or time 'A' or in the mind of person 'A' is transposed, largely unaffected by its mode of transmission, to point 'B', time 'B', and/or into the mind of person 'B'. In contrast to this viewpoint, a predominant emphasis in socially oriented (as opposed to technically oriented) communication theory is on the transposing function, which is really seen as a transforming function. This latter viewpoint stresses the role of the media as active symbol- or meaning-producing agents which assist us in defining key and subordinate characteristics of reality. They are thereby distinguished from other non-communicative activities.

To use the words of two different kinds of theorists to describe this transforming function, the media 'construct' (see Berger and Luckmann, 1966) or 'signify' reality. Berger and Luckmann use the word 'construct' in the same way as you might think of builders using bricks and mortar to construct a house. Using the elements at hand – in the case of the media, people, events, objects, and so on – they create a meaningful whole. Semioticians use the word 'signify' in a rather special sense. As Chapter 8 explains in more detail, semioticians work with signifiers, that is, words; signifieds, that is, objects or events to which the words refer; and signs, the totality of meanings we associate with the signifiers and signifieds. Thus to signify wrestling as theatre is to call attention to the various elements in a wrestling match as elements of a theatrical presentation. Done well, such signification can provide new insights into familiar phenomena.

Modern communication theory also posits that this function is not a secondary or derivative activity. As Bennett argues, the ideas that long held sway insisted that:

> the media can reflect only what is there . . . the world of signs is granted only a shadowy, twilight existence; it 'hovers' above 'reality' as an ethereal appendage to it, deriving such substance as it has merely from what is reflected in it.
>
> More recent developments in the theory of language have pulled in a direction directly contrary to this, stressing not only the independent materiality of the signifier – the fleshiness of the sign – but also the activity and effectivity of signification as a process which actively constructs cognitive worlds rather than simply passively reflecting a pre-existing reality. . . . Sign orders world.
>
> (1982, p. 187)

In summary, the mass media are a distinct set of activities because they have a primary and non-derivative signifying or reality-constructing function. While reality construction can be said to be non-derivative, the totality of the building blocks of meaning-making derive from the social milieu, from the ideas and images that have currency within any particular society. It is the meaning we apply that gives meaning to reality. The mass media are major contributors to our perceptions, both on the basis of the information they carry and the interpretation they place on that information. But our perceptions are also organised by the prevailing dynamics of our communities, our acquired ideas and even our personalities – in short, the totality of ongoing functioning of our consciousness.

Other characteristics of the mass media draw in our definitional net more closely.

2. Particular technological configurations

Considerations of the role of technology in the modern mass media are not exhausted simply by identifying them as modern as opposed to ancient. In examining the context in which these modern technologies have developed, together with their particular properties, we gain a sense of the role of technology itself in the functioning of the various mass media.

As noted in Chapter 1, Raymond Williams (1974) points out that technologies do not arise from the brain of a genius working in isolation from any social context; they arise from and are incorporated into society on the basis of the structure and functioning of society. For example, television did not arise as an inevitable offshoot of the search for scientific knowledge but rather from the interests and conceptions of technical investigators and industrial entrepreneurs, who, on the basis of their cultural background and their technical expertise, were able to imagine an electronic medium of sound and visual communication suitable to the home.

Television is but one example of a modern mass medium. As we know, there are many more and each decade brings several brand-new ones. One company, Sony, has been particularly active in bringing forward new technological configurations. Two of their great successes (they have had failures) were the Walkman and the compact disc (CD). In the case of the Walkman, the Japanese company Sony took existing cassette playback technology, improved a battery-operated version of it, miniaturised it and made it resistant to shakes and joggling, thereby creating a vast market for the pocket-sized cassette recorder. In the case of the compact disc, Sony took a new technology (videodiscs) invented by a competitor, the Dutch company Philips, which was hailed for the amount of information it could carry and for the fidelity and flexibility of retrieval of that information. Sony reduced the disc to a manageable size, capable of holding slightly more information than that contained on a long-playing (LP) record. In the cases of both the Walkman and the CD, success was built on an analysis of the social use to which the technology could be put. As with television, in both these cases particular technological configurations were chosen and marketed.

3. Formally constituted institutions

The implications of technological configurations of the media cannot be discussed for long before a consideration of their associated industrial structures must be included. The mass media are industrial structures for the production and processing of content. Media institutions may be private corporations owned by a few shareholders, publicly-owned corporations, or state enterprises.

Private-sector institutions

Private media may be defined as corporations owning media enterprises for profit. Their primary purpose, obviously, is to gain the maximum revenue at minimum cost. This principle of action guides the entire scope of their operations; however, it is a principle that must be and is applied in a sophisticated manner. Media institutions must build audiences. They do so by spending money to provide content of interest to their target audiences. Revenue comes from the sale of content to audiences (newspapers), the sale of audiences to advertisers (newspapers and TV), or both. Furthermore, sales of content to other media outlets who must similarly build audiences (network TV to affiliated stations) can bring revenue.

On the expense side of the ledger, the major cost in operating a broadcasting station, newspaper, book-publishing house, or film studio is creating or purchasing content. In addition to creative and journalistic writers, the cost of materials, studios and so forth must all be included. Thus the cost of producing an episode of a TV serial can run over £500,000. On the other hand, game shows can be made and imported programmes purchased, especially old reruns, for about £5,000. For newspapers, news wire copy is inexpensive, syndicated material a little more. On the other hand, employing a columnist for a year, including expenses, can easily run to £100,000. While this last figure represents a major outlay for an individual paper, for a newspaper conglomerate it is much more affordable.

For all media outlets, costs and profits must be weighed against perceived responsibility to the community, but this is especially so for broadcasters who, as a condition for obtaining a broadcasting licence must detail how their programming will contribute to the community. They must also take into account audience sensitivity; for instance, for specific types of programmes such as news and public affairs programmes, local and national production is preferred by most audiences. This preference is less strong in most countries for dramatic productions and sitcoms.

In some cases privately-owned media emphasise their social contribution over the bottom line. Newspaper examples of this are *The Times*, *Le Monde*, *The New York Times*, *Le Devoir* (of Montreal), and at certain points in their histories, *The Globe and Mail* (of Toronto) and the *Jerusalem Post*. In their glory days, each of these papers was able to trade on its prestige as the paper of the elite to support its service to the community. More recently, such papers have evolved into 'flagship' papers of conglomerates, who maintain them as prestige outlets and for the generation of content that can then be used throughout a chain or conglomerate. They might also be seen as loss-leaders in the conglomerate's attempt to interest the consuming public.

Public-sector institutions

The other major type of formally constituted media institution is the public-sector institution. These are institutions owned and/or regulated – but not controlled – by the state, that is to say, the directors of the institution are not employees of a government minister and responsible for carrying out his or her orders.

In Western nations, public media corporations are usually operated at 'arm's length' from control of the government (although the length of the arm varies greatly). In some countries, such as Britain, they are responsible to a ministry – the Home Office – but they are not guided day-by-day by the ministry. In other countries, such as Canada, they are responsible to an arm's-length regulatory board, the Canadian Radio-television and Telecommunications Commission (CRTC).

In contrast to Western public media corporations were the state-owned and/or subsidised enterprises of the former socialist countries. Such enterprises were closely linked to the state by directives and by subsidies. In Soviet Russia *Pravda* was owned by the Communist Party itself, while *Trud* (Labour) was run by the labour unions (the president of which was a member of the ruling Politburo, a rough equivalent to the Cabinet). Both newspapers operated like government departments, interpreting information in the interests of the state – a pattern that is also emerging in developing countries.

Like private-sector businesses, public-sector corporations must also balance revenue and costs. The advantage that public-sector institutions have is that they receive revenue from government, generated either by special levies, such as licence fees, or through general government revenue. Sometimes such revenue is in addition to advertising; at other times it replaces advertising revenue. However, this revenue is not an unconditional gift. The funds are to assist the corporations in fulfilling special public service responsibilities usually defined by a broadcasting act. These special responsibilities often include reference to minority languages, children and senior citizens, local production, certain types of information and so forth.

Public and private-sector institutions

Whether the media are owned publicly or privately is obviously a major factor affecting the relationship between the media and the state. Where private ownership is dominant, considerations of profit-making and advertiser interests tend to prevail over considerations of public service. (It is, of course, possible for private ownership of a mass media system to be organised on a non-profit basis, but this is relatively rare.) Where public ownership prevails completely and accepts no advertising, potential advertisers complain of an inability to get information to consumers, while consumers sometimes complain of the lack of escapist programming that allows them to forget the issues and concerns of the day.

4. Certain laws, rules and understandings

As we have argued, the technological and institutional form of mass media systems are significant factors in their performance. However, they are far from the only factors involved. Almost all media systems operate within specific national societies and, as such, are subject to formal legal constraints as well as less formal patterns of expectations.

On the formal side, in the case of broadcasting, the relatively limited number of radio frequencies that have been available to each nation-state have obliged national governments to exercise some control, in the form of licensing requirements, over the frequencies used within their borders. In the case of publishing (newspapers or magazines) most developed countries exercise little overt control. No licences are required and media content is not restricted, except by broad laws directed at libel, sedition and pornography. In some countries censorship, especially over political content, plays a significant role. Various indirect government controls, such as taxation, subsidies, business policies and distribution subsidies, can be and are employed to influence the media in developed countries.

The formal laws or statutes of a country have a major impact on the mass media. They will be discussed more fully in Chapter 3 and are only introduced briefly here. Speaking generally, for broadcasting, countries usually have regulatory agencies that operate within – or at arm's length from – government departments. These agencies have administrative responsibility for the country's broadcasting act. For the print media, regulation is far less common. However, subsidised distribution, paper subsidies, ownership and competition laws and other means can be used to create and maintain an industry of a certain character.

Another key statute is a country's copyright act, which creates intellectual property. It transforms the material reality of a person's intellectual efforts, for example a script or a movie, into a piece of property that can be owned by someone. Moreover, it attaches certain rights and privileges to that ownership. Copyright stimulates creators to create by providing a means for them to achieve payment for their efforts and prohibiting the use of their creation without their permission and/or in exchange for payment. Copyright does not protect ideas; it protects the expression of ideas.

Each statute that affects the operation of the media must be translated into concrete reality. To do so, *rules* are created that are consistent with the principles of the legislation; for example, quotas of certain types of programmes may be set. Copyright law regulations provide the framework for publishers to contract with authors for the right to publish and distribute their books. They also allows movie-makers to buy the movie rights for a book. And it may allow authors to form collectives to contract with institutions for photocopying rights.

The laws and rules that govern the behaviour of the mass media have developed from certain understandings that society has of the potential value of the media. At the most general level, in Western societies, the media are encouraged to provide 'continuity, order, integration, motivation, guidance and adaptation' (McQuail, 1983, p. 64). To reach this multifaceted goal, the media must reflect the values and goals of society. However, in any liberal democracy these values and goals are a matter of continuing debate. The presence of this debate gives the media substantial latitude within which to make their social contribution. It also raises the question of how one determines whether the media are contributing appropriately. Certain media spokespersons claim that if people are watching television, given that they have the freedom not to watch, then the television station is obviously making an appropriate contribution to their enjoyment of their leisure time. At the other end of the spectrum, others will claim that the media should set much more ambitious goals for themselves, to provide, for example, enlightening rather than escapist entertainment. This debate, which will receive further attention in subsequent chapters, is a debate over the public interest.

5. Occupying certain roles

The number of people involved in the mass media and the number of roles people play are vast. The most obvious players are the journalists. But there are also owners, editors, technicians, actors, administrators, secretaries, designers, advertisers, members of regulatory bodies, politicians who control the purse-strings, lawyers, public interest group members and audience members. The influence of the major players is dealt with throughout this book. Here we will make a few general remarks, primarily on outside influences.

Business influences
The influence of businesses on the mass media is exercised both through advertising and through the demands generated by the corporate form of the media outlet. Decisions by businesses on where to advertise and how much to spend collectively affect the fortunes of individual media enterprises. To attract advertisers media managers, at the very least, try not to offend (or

potentially offend) advertisers by ensuring that their content does not clash with the advertisers' messages. Lately, especially in movies, there has been a tendency for the media to foreground commercial products in return for payment, for example, a main character in a movie makes a point of asking for a Guinness rather than a beer. This is called 'product placement' (see Wasko, Phillips and Purdie (1993), who also provide a list of product placements in five films). Sometimes advertisers are explicit in demanding that certain content is not placed near their ads and increasingly the media are obliging. In North America, the 'editorial' content of property sections of newspapers is increasingly being handed over to advertising departments. Similarly, according to industry sources, in Canada, often over 75 per cent of local television news is generated by publicity departments of various firms or advertising agencies attempting to gain attention for some person or product.

Government influences

The influence of government, exerted from outside the mass media, has several dimensions. At the bureaucratic level, the government is a major source of information for the mass media; in many instances it is the only source for specific types of information. The flow of information from government to the mass media benefits both parties. The government needs access to media outlets to inform the general public of its programmes and expenditures. The mass media need the information supplied as a readily usable source of media content for new current affairs and public affairs materials. However, this cosy exchange of favours creates a mutual dependence. The main drawback of this dependence is that the public interest may slip from its privileged spot as the driving force of media operations in favour of a mutual trading of favours between government and the media. For example, because of time constraints and limited resources, media workers tend to rely heavily on news releases and hand-outs prepared by the government. By failing to look behind these announcements, the media outlets run the risk of acting as the propaganda arm of the government.

The government's influence on the mass media also exists at a highly political level. Politicians are newsworthy, and daily coverage of political events is an essential part of mass media content. Rivalries between individuals and parties are extensively portrayed in the mass media and balanced coverage between the government party and opposition parties has to be handled carefully by media practitioners.

Related to both the bureaucratic and political levels of government is the phenomenon of government advertising. Advertisements can provide information on government programmes, can be straightforward political campaigning, or can exist in the grey area of general promotion of the federal or provincial government. Total advertising revenue from government sources form a substantial part of the revenue for mass media; national governments often outspend any one commercial advertiser. In the 1980s the Conservative government in the UK spent millions of pounds in advertising as they privatised national utilities (gas, electricity, water, etc.).

Governments also have an influence on the mass media through the power to regulate and control. Both at the federal and provincial levels, government has the authority to approve legislation, to impose taxes and in various other ways to affect the means by which mass media organisations conduct their operations. Private corporations have a strong tendency to resist or seek to reduce government control over their operations by raising the banner of 'freedom of the press'.

Legal influences

A third influence on the mass media is that of the legal system, in particular the decisions of the courts. One obligation of the courts is to interpret existing statutes in instances where specific mass media practitioners or owners are thought to have operated outside the law. A much more widespread influence on content, however, has to do with various sections of the criminal and civil codes that cover such offences as sedition, promulgating obscenity, propagating hate literature and issuing false messages. Court decisions on cases of these kinds tend to influence all mass media practitioners – particularly journalists – and are used as indicators to guide future actions taken in the selection of media content.

Audience influences

The fourth influence on the mass media is the audience. Denis McQuail has suggested that the audience can influence media content in six different ways:

1 As *critics and fans*, audience members can comment (often approvingly) on the nature of specific content pieces or content producers.

2 Through *institutionalised accountability* audience members can seek to influence mass media organisations. This is often easier to do with public corporations than private corporations. Politicians who have an influence on the allocation of funds to public broadcasters often feel that it is their duty to comment on its public performance. For the printed media, press councils – made up of owners' representatives, journalists and the public – can act on behalf of readers who complain about specific content in newspapers.

3 Through the *market*, audience members can choose between media outlets and, through such choices, determined by ratings data, exert some influence on the mass media. However, any individual audience member acting alone cannot exert much influence by this means.

4 Through *direct feedback* to mass media outlets, audiences can make their views known and hope to influence future actions. 'Letters to the editor' are the standard form of feedback for the press, while broadcasting stations rely on phone calls.

5 Through the use of *audience images* formed in the minds of content

producers the audience can influence media content. The difficulty here is
that the audience has little control over the formation of those images.

6 Through *audience research* mass media practitioners can gain a more precise
idea of audience interests and responses to specific media content. However,
here again, the audience has little influence on the design of the research. This
is in the hands of advertisers and producers intent on selling products.

(adapted from McQuail, 1983, pp. 168–70)

The influence of owners and media professionals

To this point we have been looking at outside influences on the operation of
mass media organisations. Of course, the internal structures of these organisations and the people who work in them also exert considerable influence on
the mass media systems.

Above the managerial levels are the ultimate owners of the media corporations (or the owners' representatives). In the case of public corporations, the
owners are the taxpaying public, but through Parliament and other governmental bodies responsibility for the operation of the corporation lies with a
governing board of some type, usually a board of directors. In the case of
private corporations, the owners are shareholders or individual entrepreneurs (usually the former). Shares may be widely held among many
investors or closely held by the members of a particular family. Owners may
be actively involved in management of the media corporation or may rely
largely or even entirely on senior managers. Internally, media corporations
can be viewed as social systems with their own structures and history.

Besides these general role categories, many specific roles are played out.
The programme directors, producers, executive producers, programme assis-
tants, editors, technical people and sales managers all have at least a dual
allegiance to their profession and to the company for which they work. How
they play out these roles, and the social system that emerges within the
corporation, can influence greatly the resulting output of the station,
network, or paper. Of particular interest is the way creative people are
attracted to organisations that must use, but inevitably restrict, their
creativity. Gallagher (in Gurevitch *et al.*, 1982) provides an insightful
account of how these individuals and their organisations negotiate in such a
way that there is control and predictability over programmes and at the same
time room for creativity.

6. Information and entertainment, images and symbols

In the following discussion the words *information* and *entertainment* are to
be taken in a narrow sense. On television, for instance, we are given information (news and current affairs) and entertainment (sitcoms, drama) programming. In newspapers, the same two words cover, on the one side, news,

opinions found in editorials and columns, advertisements and even the comic strips, and on the other, travel, leisure, gossip columns and the comic strips.

To say that the mass media convey *images* and *symbols* is to look at content from a different angle. Whether through words or pictures, in print or electronically, the mass media present us with images of the world. There are two classes of images, both of which we discuss in Chapter 8. The first is denotative, that is to say, those which are explicit, objective, there for anyone to see. They are stated rather than implied. A descriptive analysis of a photograph identifying the various elements or a rational argument presents us with denotative images. The second class of images is the connotative associations that are implied and/or that we infer from the context that surrounds the denotative images. They may have a visual base and derive from the composition of a still photograph or from the timing and juxtaposition of a series of video shots, or even from the layout of a printed page. Alternatively, and poetry is a very strong example, they may derive from any characteristic of a written text, for example the flow of words, the images presented, the imaginative reality which the poet sets up.

Symbols can include everything from the letters of the alphabet to something as complex as an icon. An icon is usually a visual image of a sacred person, such as Christ or the Virgin Mary, but the word has been used increasingly in a secular context to mean an image that stands for much more than itself. As we noted in Chapter 1, iconic means image-based. The meaning we intend for the word 'symbol' is a general one, a term that stands for a larger reality. That larger reality derives in part from the symbol itself, for example the peace dove, but perhaps even more from the interpretive tendencies of the audience. Thus, at every level of our existence from the biological through to the psychological – the social, the cultural, the political and so forth – the meaning of a symbol is an interaction between the composition of the image and the interpretive predispositions of the audience. A death mask has a biological base; a flag has a socio-cultural as well as an aesthetic base; an appeal to democratic rights has a political base. A synonym for symbolic meaning is connotative value.

The images the media present are rich in their symbolic meaning or connotative value whether or not the media intend them to be. To some degree, the success of all media products, from movies through books to television stations and newspapers, depends on the presentation of images that are layered with symbolic meaning. From one perspective it could be said that the sum of the meaning of the images and symbols presented to us by the media represents the ideological currents of society, at least those ideological currents that find their way into mass media form. Given that, the media play a fundamental role in articulating and consolidating ideological control in society.

7. The mass audience

The word 'mass' implies large numbers. In some sense it might be best for us to leave the meaning of the word at that. However, like information, entertainment, images and symbols, the word has many different meanings. At a basic level there is a value connotation implied by the word 'mass'. A negative connotation is related to the mob; a positive, to the wisdom of the aggregate.

In an early article, Blumer (1939) contrasted a number of different kinds of collectivities to arrive at a meaning for 'mass'. Simplifying and adapting Blumer's ideas somewhat, we can say that in a small group all members know each other and are aware of their common membership. The crowd is limited to a single physical space, is temporary in its existence and composition and if it acts, it does so non-rationally. The public is customarily large and widely dispersed. It is often represented by largely self-appointed 'informed' people who speak publicly and in rational discourse to validate their statements and appointment. McQuail summarises Blumer on 'mass':

> The term 'mass' captures several features of the new audience for cinema and radio which were missing or not linked together by any of these three existing concepts. It was often very large – larger than most groups, crowds or publics. It was very widely dispersed and its members were usually unknown to each other or to whoever brought the audience into existence. It lacked self-awareness and self-identity and was incapable of acting together in an organised way to secure objectives. It was marked by a shifting composition within changing boundaries. It did not act for itself, but was rather 'acted upon'. It was heterogeneous, in consisting of large numbers from all social strata and demographic groups, but homogeneous in its behaviour of choosing a particular object of interest and in the perception of those who would like to 'manipulate' it.   (1983, p. 36)

In short, a mass audience is not to be thought of as a seething mass of unthinking automatons vulnerable to the intentional or unintentional manipulations of media practitioners. Rather, it is a convenient shorthand term for the great numbers of people who constitute the 'mass entertainment' audience. However, rather than being homogeneous, vulnerable and passive, the mass audience is better conceived as a great number of individuals who, from their various backgrounds bring a variety of readings to media content derived from such categories of human activity and interaction as the psychological, social, economic, political, cultural, spiritual, as well as others based on age, nationality, ethnicity, region, and gender.

Beyond a mass audience

With the proliferation of the media the audience is fragmenting to such a degree that the notion of a mass audience, in the sense of a significant percentage of the population watching common programming, such as the evening news on the BBC, is increasingly problematic. Especially with the expansion of single-content channels – news (CNN), music (MTV), old movies (Home Box Office) – the audience is fragmenting or segmenting. Rather than being informed and therefore socialised by a few channels of radio and television, audience members are being socialised into a part of society – a market niche in the view of media producers and advertisers – that is represented by their own media selectivity. With the globalisation of services – such as CNN, MTV and HBO, the ability of national societies to coalesce around a central set of concerns, symbols and even political boundaries, may weaken (see Collins (1990) for a discussion of this phenomenon and for a different interpretation of its implications).

Summary

This chapter began with a conceptualisation of mass communication and the mass media. We set out formal definitions of both and explicated the basic elements of those definitions.

We then set down a seven-part definition of the modern mass media and explored its implications. The mass media were defined as a distinct set of activities, involving particular technological configurations, associated with formally constituted institutions, acting according to certain laws, rules and understandings, carried out by persons occupying certain roles, which together convey information, entertainment, images and symbols to a mass audience.

With this brief overview of the major elements of the mass media we have tried to accomplish two things. The first is to demonstrate how media of communication are intrinsically interwoven into the societies of which they are a part. To be specific, without a legal and regulatory framework, proprietorship, professions, institutions, technology, and leisure time, the modern mass media would not exist. Similarly, if the media did not build on established modes of communication – words, images, narrative, drama, analysis, personalities – they would fail for lack of understanding or engagement.

Our second aim has been to set the stage for an in-depth examination of the five major structuring features of the modern mass media: 1) law and policy 2) ownership 3) the producer professions 4) technology and 5) audiences. We will turn to these features in the following chapters. We will then examine the production of media content in Chapter 8, followed by an examination of the dynamics of the world media system we have created – who benefits, who suffers. We will conclude in the final chapter with an overview of the media in a cultural framework.

References

Bennett, Tony (1982), 'Media, "reality" and signification' in M. Gurevitch *et al.* (eds.), *Culture, Society and the Media*, Methuen, London.

Berger, Peter, and Thomas Luckmann (1966), *Social Construction of Reality: A Treatise on the Sociology of Knowledge*, Doubleday, New York.

Blumer, H. (1939), 'The mass, the public, and public opinion', in A. M. Lee (ed.), *New Outlines in the Principles of Sociology*, Barnes and Noble, New York.

Canada (1970), *Radio Act*, Revised Statutes of Canada, Ottawa, c. 233, s. 1.

Collins, Richard (1990), *Culture, Communication and National Identity: The Case of Canadian Television*, University of Toronto Press, Toronto.

Curran, James (1982), 'Communications, power, and social order' in M. Gurevitch *et al.* (eds.), *Culture, Society and the Media*, Methuen, London.

Eco, Umberto (1986), 'The multiplication of the media' in Eco, *Travels in Hyperreality*, Harcourt Brace Jovanovich, New York.

Gallagher, Margaret (1982), 'Negotiation of control in media organizations and occupations' in M. Gurevitch *et al.*, (eds.), *Culture, Society and the Media*, Methuen, London.

Gurevitch, M. *et al.*, (eds.) (1982), *Culture, Society and the Media*, Methuen, London.

McQuail, Denis (1983), *Mass Communication Theory: An Introduction*, Sage Publications, Beverly Hills.

O'Sullivan, T., J. Hartley, D. Saunders, and J. Fiske (1983), *Key Concepts in Communication*, Methuen, Toronto.

Wasko, Janet, Mark Phillips and Chris Purdie (1993), 'Hollywood meets Madison Avenue: the commercialization of US films', *Media, Culture and Society*, 15 (2), pp. 271–93.

Williams, Raymond (1974), *Television: Technology and Cultural Form*, Schocken Books, New York.

Chapter 3

Mass communications law and policy

The mass media are fully integrated with and indispensable to modern society. The media gather, analyse and disseminate current information. Individual citizens, social organisations and businesses rely on the mass media to tell them what is going on in their community, the nation and the world at large. Governments rely on the media not only to inform the people of their nation and the world, but also to be informed about what various sectors of society believe about, and want from, the state. Thus the mass media are a vital link in an information system that encompasses all levels of society and its governance.

But just because the mass media are a vital link between government and people, contributing to both the political life and the general character of society, it does not follow that they are neutral conveyors of information. The mass media are social institutions that function within particular political and legal constraints, employing a distinctive mixture of trained personnel, following specific information-gathering procedures, to create material for either visual, auditory or conceptually-oriented media. They have a particular view of their role in society and work under particular financial constraints. They are also, in many cases, owned by proprietors and operated by managers who have a distinct view of the world, which they promote in their organisation. In short, they are distinctive participants in the political, economic, social and cultural power dynamics of society.

It also does not follow from the role of the mass media as a vital link, that the two-way flow of information between the people and the government that is necessary for the smooth and just functioning of society works perfectly and flows equally in both directions. Just as information does not necessarily flow freely between the people and government, so it also does not flow freely between various classes and such social sectors as business, labour, church and the intelligentsia. On the whole, the media function in a manner that reflects the conjoined interests of the power elites in society, that is, those groups who are in a position to allocate resources in society (see C. Wright Mills, 1959).

Despite these constraints, the media play a crucial role in all modern societies. Moreover, the more open a society is to all voices, the more vital is the role of the mass media in keeping it open and accessible to the many and varied interests of individuals and groups at all times.

The place of the media in society

Western press traditions speak of the media as the fourth estate. The first three estates within the state as a whole are the church, the landowners and the bourgeoisie; in the UK, the Lords (Spiritual and Temporal) in the upper house and the commoners in the lower house of Parliament. *The interest of the fourth estate is purported to be the active pursuit of information in the name of the public good* (see Boyce, 1978 for a critical history of the term). The media maintain their credibility and their claim to the status of the fourth estate by their performance. Stated somewhat differently, the media contribute information and analysis within a wide context in which a variety of individuals and groups compete to interpret the real meaning of events (Curran, 1990). At times this contribution is made with the interest of the public in mind, at other times it is more self-interested.

Historically the media have carried out their operations in four different sites or locations within society:

1 within the state
2 as part of social or political movements or parties
3 through private enterprise
4 by means of public enterprise at arm's length from the state itself.

Each of these locations tilts the interests and the orientation of the media in a particular direction. Each introduces a bias focused on the interests of those who control the site in question; Curran (1991) has provided a recent reappraisal of the interaction between the mass media and democracy. Partly in reaction to the particular site of the media in society, and also reflective of the pre-eminent form of democratic idealism of particular societies and times, there are differing perspectives on how the media and journalists ought to function (see, for instance, Habermas, 1984; Siebert, Peterson and Schramm, 1956). These perspectives encompass the following:

1 furthering the interests of the owning/controlling entity, whether it be the state, social or political movements, or the business class. This perspective is the explanatory framework most applicable to the state-controlled or party-owned press, the commercial press, the radical press and special interest publications;
2 pursuing free speech unencumbered by other considerations. This is

usually called a libertarian perspective for its exclusive emphasis on individual liberty and free speech;

3 informing by freely and widely seeking and considering information and
opinion on behalf of and in response to audiences. This is commonly called
the social responsibility perspective.

The legal and policy foundations of mass communication

The media also operate within certain legal and policy constraints. While
every country has a host of laws and policies that are relevant to media
functioning, nine types of laws are directly relevant. They are:

1 the freedom to communicate, covering both ownership of media enterprises and the gathering, receiving and imparting of information;
2 acts regulating broadcasting, telecommunications, and in some countries,
press entities; these statutes govern the operations of broadcasters in
exchange for using a limited resource, i.e. the radio spectrum;
3 industrial support policies directed by governments specifically at cultural
industries;
4 freedom of, or access to, information legislation, designed to make govern-
ment-gathered information available for public scrutiny;
5 laws limiting free speech such as libel law, intended to protect the good
reputation of individuals. These differ considerably from country to
country;
6 copyright laws, designed to protect intellectual property. Increasingly
these are being applied to the creation of television news and documentary
programmes;
7 laws governing public disclosure, which usually apply to 'public' companies who have sought investment by members of the public through
selling company shares on a stock exchange;
8 laws governing the dissemination and use of technology;
9 contract and company law.

These laws and policies both facilitate and constrain the structure and
functioning of both national mass media systems and international mass
communication. We will direct our attention to international law and policy
and to a selection of national mass media systems in developed countries. We
will begin our discussion with broadcasting, then turn to telecommunications, and end with the cultural industries, that is video and film, book and
periodical publishing, and sound recording. Table 2 summarises the major
issues discussed in this chapter.

International legal foundations of broadcasting

The international legal foundations of broadcasting – and of all communica-

TABLE 2   *The focus of communications law and policy*

	Broadcasting and cable	Telecommunications	Cultural industries
International level	*General principles and ideals* • freedom to seek, receive and impart information • duties and responsibilities of journalists • sometimes culture (e.g. Council of Europe, see p. 110) • intellectual property • trade in services • information sovereignty	*General principles* • frequency allocation • satellite footprint control • geostationary orbit space allocation • technical standards • co-ordination and integration of national systems • dataflow	*General principles and ideals* • status of artist • preservation of art • cultural development • copyright
National level	• domestic content • nature of audience served • language • ownership • regulation by state • fairness and balance • advertising and sponsorship • culture • policy process • libel and constraint law	• access • ownership • rate balancing • regulation • industrial development	• status of artist • cultural and community development • domestic participation in production • market bias • technology and culture • audience access to domestic content • copyright laws and rights, e.g. reprography and lending • development of artistic expression • education

tion – are to be found in international covenants that deal with the *freedom to communicate*, to which any nation that chooses is a signatory. Article 19 of the *Universal Declaration of Human Rights* (1948) sets out provisions concerning freedom to communicate, endorsed by the *International Covenant on Political and Civil Rights*, enacted in 1966:

1: Everyone shall have the right to hold opinions without interference.

2: Everyone shall have the right to freedom of expression; this right shall include freedom to seek, receive and impart information and ideas of all kinds, regardless of frontiers, either orally, in writing or in print, in the form of art, or through any other media of his choice.

3: The exercise of the right provided for in para 2 of this article carries with it special duties and responsibilities. It may therefore be subject to certain restrictions, but these shall only be such as are provided by law and are necessary for the respect of the rights or reputation of others or for the protection of national security or of public order or of public health or morals.

Article 20 of the *International Covenant on Political and Civil Rights* also states:

Any propaganda for war shall be prohibited by law.

2: Any advocacy of national, racial, or religious hatred that constitutes incitement to discrimination, hostility or violence shall be prohibited by law.

Other international conventions reiterate or expand these provisions. The *American Convention on Human Rights* (signed in 1969 and enacted in 1978) applies to the Western hemisphere and largely reiterates the 1948 *Universal Declaration of Human Rights*. The *European Convention on Human Rights* recasts Article 19 of the Universal Declaration slightly in its Article 10:

1: Everyone has the right to freedom of expression. This right shall include freedom to hold opinions and to receive and impart information and ideas without interference by public authority and regardless of frontiers. This Article shall not prevent States from requiring the licensing of broadcasting, television or cinema enterprises.

2: The exercise of this freedom, since it carried with duties and responsibilities, may be subject to such formalities, conditions, restrictions or penalties as are prescribed by law and are necessary in a democratic society in the interests of national security, territorial integrity or public safety, for the prevention of disorder and crime, for the protection of the reputation or rights of others, for preventing the disclosure of information received in confidence or for maintaining the authority and impartiality of the judiciary.

A second convention, the *European Convention on Transfrontier Television* (1989), is also applicable in this field; detailed rules have been set out for this through EEC directive (89/552/EEC). They cover several fields, including the right to reply in broadcasting, advertising and restrictions to advertising, sponsoring, co-operation and co-production in Europe and promotion of European audiovisual production.

In an international context, the counterbalancing concept to unrestricted freedom to communicate is information sovereignty. Information sovereignty is the ability of a nation or community to control the dissemination of information across and within its boundaries to preserve its cultural integrity and distinctiveness, while maintaining respect for basic human rights freedoms to seek, receive and impart information. Two examples of actions aimed at maintaining information sovereignty would be the setting of quotas on how many foreign films may be shown in a country, or passing legislation to ensure the creation and maintenance of national databases in key areas. The relation of the concept of 'information sovereignty' to 'freedom to communicate' at the level of nations or communities can also be thought of as parallel to the relation between a social responsibility and a libertarian view of the media. The notion of information sovereignty has been championed in the MacBride Report (1980), a Unesco publication with the formal title *Many Voices: One World: Report of the International Commission on Communication Problems.* As Chapter 9 details, the MacBride Report was written in an attempt to redress the imbalance in information flows between the developed and the developing world.

In addition to the international covenants to which nations voluntarily commit themselves, nations create their own statutes and agreements. Within the national context, the legal foundations of broadcasting are to be found in the written constitutions of countries (except the UK, which does not have a written constitution), and in articles that refer to freedom of expression, freedom of speech, prohibition of prior censorship, sometimes the freedom of audiovisual communication, the freedom to operate a business and so forth. Parallel to the international sphere, most nations have developed restrictions in broadcasting related to public morality and order, national security and youth protection.

Some national broadcasting laws and policies

Specific regulations governing the administration of broadcasting are generally to be found within a nation's broadcasting Act itself or associated statutes, such as competition Acts. Some of the key provisions of national broadcasting Acts in Europe and North America follow. The countries included in this survey are Austria, Canada, Denmark, France, Germany, Italy, the Netherlands, Sweden, Switzerland, the United Kingdom and the United States.

All European and the Canadian broadcasting Acts make provision for at least one public broadcasting organisation. In the United States, public broadcasting was added to the system as an afterthought in 1967 in the form of the Public Broadcasting System (PBS). All, with the addition of the US, but with the exception of Austria, provide for the possibility of private sector commercial broadcasting.

All countries place restrictions on foreign ownership of broadcasting stations. Some, such as France and Canada, admit up to 20 per cent foreign participation. The others, usually by direct prohibition, forbid foreign ownership completely. To help govern relations between owners and journalists, about half the countries have specific provisions designed to promote editorial independence, that is, to separate journalists from owners so that owners cannot unabashedly promote their own interests and perspectives.

All countries have provisions for a regulatory authority to supervise the structure and character of their broadcasting systems. Most often, in Europe, this authority is vested in the executive of government, cabinet or its equivalent. In Britain, the 1990 Broadcasting Act created an Independent Television Commission (ITC) as the regulator of non-BBC television broadcasters and cable television services and the Radio Authority to regulate commercial radio. In the US, the regulator is the Federal Communications Commission (FCC) and in Canada, it is the Canadian Radio-television and Telecommunications Commission (CRTC). In some cases the responsibilities of these bodies extend into programming, at other times separate regulatory bodies have been set up. In still other cases control over programming is in the hands of the broadcaster.

In addition, all countries have provided for overseas transmissions by short wave. In Britain, the BBC World Service is funded by the government directly and thus is separate from the other radio and television services, which are funded by the licence fee. In Canada, Radio Canada International (RCI) was separated recently from the CBC. In the US, the Voice of America is funded by the United States Information Service. In France and Germany, the law provides for a separate public organisation to undertake this task.

With respect to concentration of ownership, only France has restrictions on the extent of the control any one person may have of any broadcasting enterprise. In terms of cross-ownership within broadcasting, that is, ownership of more than one station, France appears to be the most restrictive. On the other hand, Germany emphasises both regional control and regional content. In a dramatic sequence of events, after years of public monopoly, Italy provided the opportunity for the emergence of perhaps the most powerful broadcasting-based media player, Silvio Berlusconi. (Ch. 4 provides a more detailed account of Berlusconi's rise as a media mogul.) In Canada, concentration is decided on a case-by-case basis without benefit of firm laws, except that cable company owners cannot hold interests in broadcasting.

In the US the following situation applies. Historically, the FCC limited the number of stations of any one owner to seven television stations, seven AM radio stations (stations that operate by means of amplitude modulation in a band between 530 and 1610 kHz (kilohertz), seven FM radio stations (stations that broadcast by means of frequency modulation in a band between 88 and 108 MHz (megahertz). (These two categories of radio stations are roughly equivalent to Medium Wave and VHF in the UK.) Recently, the number of stations in each category was changed to twelve. Although this restriction limited the number of stations that the three major networks – CBS, NBC and ABC (the Columbia Broadcasting System, the National Broadcasting Corporation, and the American Broadcasting Corporation) – could own, a system of affiliates developed so that the networks were able to become national. Affiliates are stations owned by independent operators who sign a contract with one of the three networks to air their programmes. They devote about 65 per cent of their time to network programmes.

Cross-media holdings between the press and broadcasting are also subject to specific laws in many countries. In the UK, for instance, newspaper proprietors are forbidden from owning more than a 20 per cent interest in a broadcast licence. In Italy and France, the rules are more complex and contain regional and national provisions but hold to about the same level for major newspaper proprietors. In Canada, cross-media ownership is decided on a case-by-case basis and in terms of local market monopolies, as well as the extent of national market share. The motivation behind constraining cross-media ownership appears to be to prevent restriction of news coverage and interpretation. Thus, newspapers are targeted rather than magazine-owning companies. But a second concern – control over advertising – also exists. Generally, an effort is made to ensure that advertisers are not forced to deal with only one company.

Programming activities are discussed in national broadcasting Acts in terms such as impartiality, accuracy, objectivity, integrity, fairness, plurality, completeness, thoroughness and balance. In addition, most countries incorporate specific public responsibilities into a broadcaster's licence. The UK and Italy call for a sufficient minimum amount of time to be devoted to high quality news programmes. Those countries that are not silent on the matter call for independent and fair news services, or for meeting the responsibility of keeping the audience informed.

Most countries pay specific attention to political parties, elections and the access to the airwaves that public authorities may need. Generally, the principle embodied by such regulations affirms keeping the audience informed while encouraging impartiality on the part of the broadcaster. The exception is Italy, where news services of the various channels are aligned with dominant political parties. In Germany, there is a traditional system of *Proporz* or proportional representation, whereby producers, editors and even journalists are appointed to broadcasting stations in proportion to the electoral strength of their respective political parties (Homet, 1979).

In examining the provisions of various countries it appears that the principle of impartial communication of information is the basis for the restrictions that are placed on religious broadcasts and ownership. Provisions for educational authorities to use the airwaves are more facilitative. In educational broadcasting, specific attention is paid to the needs and vulnerabilities of children and, indeed, to the community at large. With regard to the general level and tone of programming, many countries have specific prohibitions against violence, pornography, blasphemy, incitement to hatred and endangering national security. Other countries rely on self-policing by the industry to maintain general community standards. Linguistic minorities also receive some attention, usually in officially multilingual countries; Canada and Switzerland are notable for their provision. Channel 3 in Scotland must provide some programmes in Gaelic. Channel 4 in the UK is committed to providing programmes that reflect the interests of ethnic and minority groups.

Canada, France, Italy, the Netherlands and the UK each have quotas relating to the originating country of programmes, the producing entity (e.g., in-house, an independent producer), the original language of the production (France) and whether the material was originally a feature film. In an overall sense, the challenge for Europeans is, to create a European audio-visual culture in the face of strong linguistic allegiances. Working against this effort are 1) treaties such as GATT that encourage free trade; 2) readily available programmes from outside Europe in some European languages; 3) US domination of the market.

Advertising is an area that, perhaps more than any other, is governed by industry norms as well as laws and principles. All countries except the US have restrictions on the amount of advertising a station can broadcast. Some have regulations regarding the spending of advertising revenue. Most insist that advertising must be blocked off and identified as such. The Netherlands has full programmes of commercials, while the UK, like some other countries, has a code of principles to which broadcasters must adhere in making or broadcasting advertising. Generally speaking, subliminal content cannot be broadcast. In an increasing number of countries, including the US, advertisements for alcohol, tobacco and some legal drugs, as well as for religion, is prohibited or restricted. While sponsorship of programmes is possible in most countries, in some there are strictures that either prohibit the sponsor from directly benefiting, or insist that the sponsor be clearly identified.

With regard to financing, public sector organisations are generally forbidden to make a profit, while private sector corporations may. Licence fees are charged for reception of radio and television in all countries except Canada and the US. These fees are either distributed to public sector broadcasters or distributed more widely, based on cultural or public service criteria.

The role of journalists depends primarily on press and media traditions and general principles to which the broadcaster must adhere. A few countries provide for the participation of journalists – and the audience – in the decision-making process of public broadcasting organisations. Five countries – Denmark, France, Germany, Italy and Sweden – provide for the right of reply. In others, such as the UK, the provision is considerably weaker and the procedure for obtaining a correction more protracted. In broadcasting, for instance, a complaint must proceed through the Broadcasting Complaints Commission, the BBC, the ITC or the Radio Authority. In the press it must be addressed to the Press Complaints Commission, a voluntary industry body with no legal powers but which in March 1990 adopted a code of practice to which members of the industry publicly committed themselves.

Cable

Cable operations, as extensions of broadcasting, tend to be governed in a way that extends the basic principles of broadcasting as they are manifest in any particular country. In many countries, a specific licence is given to cable operators to allow them to operate. Some countries call for ownership only by citizens of the country in question. The reasoning here is that cable, as part of the country's communications, is so important to the country's well-being that this means of communication cannot be placed in the hands of foreigners, who from time to time may have conflicts of interest with those of the country in question. The US, Italy and the UK are the clear exceptions. They have not extended broadcast ownership restrictions to the cable industry. Most, although not the UK and Italy, also set content controls. In the US, public access must be guaranteed, and local government control over licensing of cable systems ensures that pressures for national, regional and local content, as well as ownership, are strong. In most countries, cable has been used for signal enhancement and for importing programmes, most recently via the reception and distribution of satellite signals, to urban neighbourhoods.

Satellite communications

Satellite communications come under both national and international jurisdiction and encompass both broadcasting and telecommunications. At present, few countries have joined the UK in putting legislation in place requiring those who initiate signal transmission to gain permission from a government body, specifically the ITC (Independent Television Commission), for satellite broadcast. This is partly because, until recently, the main use to which domestic and international communications satellites have been put has been to transmit broadcast signals to cable systems. With increasing direct broadcast by satellite (DBS) activity, there will be increased regulatory action in this area. For now regulation is vested primarily at the international level.

There are three branches of international law that directly impinge on satellite communications:

- international telecommunications law
- space law
- law bearing on the international circulation of goods and services.

International telecommunications law

Telecommunications have been defined as follows: 'Telecommunication means any transmission, emission or reception of signs, signals, writing, images or sounds or intelligence of any nature by wire, radio, visual or other electromagnetic system' (Radiocommunication Act, *Revised Statutes of Canada*, 1985, c. R-2, s. 2). In strictly technical terms, then, broadcasting is a type of telecommunication. However, in policy terms, broadcasting is treated separately in all countries. In less technical terms, the telecommunications sector refers mainly to the telephone and data communications industry and the services it provides. Basically, telecommunications services can be categorised into five types: voice telephony, public message (telegram), switched teleprinter and other text services (Telex and TWX), data communications and programme transmission (audio and video signals, especially for broadcasting).

Of primary importance to telecommunications is the International Telecommunications Convention, a convention that dates back to 1865 and is the basis for the International Telecommunications Union (ITU), which has over 160 members. This convention, which is under continuous revision by its nation members, has the mandate to regulate a finite but inexhaustible resource, the radio frequency spectrum, for its best and most efficient use. The radio frequency spectrum is a subset of the electromagnetic spectrum lower than 3,000 gigahertz (GHz). The ITU allocates and registers frequency assignments and co-ordinates efforts to eliminate harmful interference between broadcasting in different countries through World (or regional) Administrative Radio Conferences (WARCs). The ITU is concerned with all means of telecommunications, wired or wireless, closed (from point to point) or open (from one point to the general public). This boundary between closed and open systems is the boundary that divides broadcasting from telecommunications.

Satellite communications are a subset of all telecommunications. Telecommunications satellites sit in geostationary orbit, about 36,000 kilometres above the earth's equator, orbiting the earth at exactly the speed necessary to remain in a constant position with respect to the earth. They provide the means for fixed satellite services, which are intended to be closed systems used to transport signals from one point to another on earth. They also provide the means for direct broadcasting satellite (DBS) services to the general public. An intermediate form of service, not strictly broadcasting, is that provided by such companies as the Cable News Network (CNN) or Rupert Murdoch's Sky channels. The signals these companies send up are weaker than DBS signals, are often scrambled and are intended to be received primarily by cable systems, which increase their power and distribute them to individual homes, hence satellite-to-cable services or systems (SCS). The reason such signals are scrambled is to allow owners to sell their signals to individual subscribers.

Since 1971, the ITU has begun to allocate space in geostationary orbit and frequencies available for satellite signal transmissions – whether they be for data, television or other purposes – in each of three regions. Region 1 includes Europe, the Commonwealth of Independent States (the CIS, including the Ukraine, Georgia, etc.) and Africa; Region 2 includes North and South America; and Region 3, Asia, Australia and New Zealand. Within each region, frequencies are assigned to countries yet, inevitably, there is overspill, that is, signals beamed back to earth from the satellite cover a wider area than a single country. Through managing locations on the frequency band and different polarisations, interference between signals in neighbouring countries can be minimised. However, neither of these two mechanisms addresses the availability of signals. This is addressed by designing a footprint that approximates the shape intended to be covered. A footprint can only approximate the boundaries of a country, and a weaker signal surrounds the full strength signal, as shown in Figure 1.

International space law

International space law impinges on the operations of satellite communications. The United Nations' Outer Space Treaty of 1967 is the basis of space law. Four of the main principles of that treaty are as follows:

- outer space is not delimited from air space (where nations exert sovereignty) but 36,000 kilometers is taken to be outer space,
- outer space is not subject to national appropriation,
- activities in outer space shall maintain peace and security and promote international cooperation and understanding,
- the state which registers a space object is considered to be the owner and has responsibility for that object.

(United Nations, 1967)

In response to the Outer Space Treaty and arising from a concern that technologically advanced nations might appropriate all positions in the geostationary orbit, a meeting of equatorial states took place in Bogota, Columbia in 1976. A declaration was passed claiming sovereignty on behalf

Figure 1   Footprints of the ASTRA (1A and 1B) Direct Broadcast Satellites. The ASTRA satellite system, owned by Société Européenne des Satellites, is composed of four satellites capable of transmitting 32 television channels across Europe. There are four sets of footprints for each satellite, as each satellite has two polarisations each with two modes.
Note: The numbers in the figure indicate the minimum diameter (cm) of a dish antenna needed for good home reception.
Reproduced by permission.

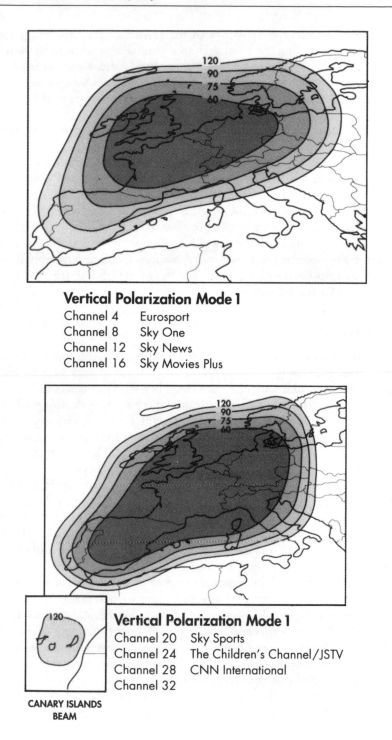

Vertical Polarization Mode 1

Channel 4   Eurosport
Channel 8   Sky One
Channel 12   Sky News
Channel 16   Sky Movies Plus

Vertical Polarization Mode 1

Channel 20   Sky Sports
Channel 24   The Children's Channel/JSTV
Channel 28   CNN International
Channel 32

**CANARY ISLANDS
BEAM**

of equatorial nations over portions of the geostationary orbit lying above those nations, or, failing that, that such space be used for addressing the needs of developing countries. On the other side of the issue is the United States, which has been trying to promote the idea that all geostationary space should be allocated, at least temporarily, to those nations that have the ability to use it.

The cultural contribution that mass communications can make is universally recognised. Moreover, the electronic media have been put to explicit educational use in every nation of the world. At the international level no specific provision has been made to ensure that international communications serve cultural and educational ends. Two non-binding agreements have been discussed but they have not progressed very far. One is the 1972 Unesco Declaration of Guiding Principles on the Use of Satellite Broadcasting for the Free Flow of Information, the Spread of Education and Greater Cultural Exchange. The other is the 1982 United Nations General Assembly Resolution on Principles Governing the Use by States of Artificial Earth Satellites for International Direct Television Broadcasting.

Intellectual property law

A third area of international law and policy affects international mass communications. It deals with the handling of cultural objects such as books, records, cassettes, film and so forth – in other words, objects that contain intellectual property. The main international convention dealing with intellectual property is the Berne Convention, to which all major nations are now signatories. Basically the Berne Convention allows the author to own, for a period of time, the expression of his or her intellectual labours and to assign ownership to others (such as publishers). Intellectual property law recognises two fundamental elements of intellectual work: property rights and moral rights. Property rights are those economic rights that may be exploited by the author through selling or assigning his or her rights to copy the work in question and are foundational in Anglo-Saxon copyright law. Moral or personal rights derive from the work as an expression of the author's personality and are foundational to Continental copyright law. In French the term is *droit d'auteur*. Moral rights are most strongly expressed as perpetual, inalienable and imprescriptible. The provision of perpetual rights forbids anyone at any time from claiming ownership of, distorting, or mutilating any piece of intellectual property which the claimant did not create. The inalienability of personal rights means that they cannot be sold or otherwise transferred to another person, although they may be waived. The notion of imprescriptibility forbids the taking away of such rights by any state or other authority. Of some significance is the fact that the stronger the protection of moral rights the more difficult can be the trading of intellectual property.

Also, the recognition of authorship, especially in films where there are multiple authors, is a key factor in exploiting maximum value from intellectual property.

The Berne Convention undergoes almost continuous revision in that it calls for 'national treatment' of foreign copyright holders. So when a country changes its laws, Berne changes. In addition, periodically a meeting of the convention is held to discuss evolving issues. Such meetings may culminate in an agreement among some or all signatories at a particular time and place. This is what happened in Florence, Italy in 1952, which gave us the Florence Agreement (the Agreement of the Importance of Educational, Scientific and Cultural Materials). Twenty-four years later, in 1976, the General Conference of Unesco adopted a protocol to the Florence Agreement which contains three special undertakings for states:

- not to apply customs duties or other charges on the importation of books and educational, scientific or cultural material,
- to grant necessary licences and/or foreign exchange for certain kinds of articles, for example, books for public libraries, official government publications and articles for the blind,
- to facilitate importation of educational, scientific or cultural material imported for showing at public exhibitions.

(Couprie and Olsson, 1987, p. 3)

Overview of broadcasting

While the material presented thus far has reviewed various characteristics of the broadcasting systems of a variety of countries, we will now review some specific distinguishing features of the broadcasting systems in Europe and North America. The Netherlands is known for the control exercised over broadcasting by a range of community groups. Italy is known for its recent re-regulation allowing the emergence of Berlusconi. Germany pays particular attention to regionality by vesting control for broadcasting in the *Länder*, while both Sweden and Denmark appear to keep individual broadcast operations local enough not to attract foreign ownership. France exerts extensive state control, particularly in ownership and content. The UK's production and export of high-quality drama and sitcoms has diminished in profile in the 1980s and 90s and the 1991 allowance of competitive bidding for licence renewals promises to be interesting for its long-term consequences. Canada has long been known for permitting copious quantities of foreign – mainly US – programming, while in direct contrast, the US is known both for the difficulty of penetrating its markets and for its programme exports. Japan is also making some initial moves to assemble one or more giant global communications conglomerates.

In general, the whole of Europe is experiencing an expansion of services and hence not only productions from their EC partners but also imports from the US. Some commentators have called this 'Canadianisation' because the balance of national and international content is expected to approximate what has existed in Canada since the advent of cable. The other major trend has been a decreasing dominance of national public sector broadcasting companies and increasing participation by the private sector in broadcasting systems.

All countries see their broadcasting systems as fulfilling a cultural role. To a greater or lesser extent, individual aspects of that culture – such as Canada's bilingualism and multiculturalism – are specifically addressed in individual clauses of a nation's broadcasting Act. The usual exception made to this statement is the US, but to exempt the US is probably to misunderstand the nature of American culture and society.

The unique case of the United States of America

The US sees its culture and interests expressed in the pursuit of unfettered individual initiative. It also promotes the conception of human activities in economic or market metaphors, and has created a broadcasting system that approximates those principles. The confusion seems to arise out of the US insistence that unfettered individual initiative and low prices are universal desiderata that all nations should pursue. Moreover, the US often maintains that the specific mechanisms which other nations use to nurture their cultural distinctiveness are illegitimate because they contradict free market laws and interfere with the ability of the US to export – note the name – its 'entertainment' products. Of course, these perceptions and preferences for guiding principles – for broadcasting, communication, trade and, indeed, the organisation of social activity – are nothing more than cultural orientations that, in one form or another, have been fairly common throughout history in dominant imperial powers.

The particular cultural orientation of the US broadcasting system is founded on US laws. Most fundamental are the relevant clauses of the US Constitution, which because it was written at a particular time in history has thereby frozen the conception of social institutions around the freedom and emancipation of the individual. The US broadcasting system is founded simply and solely on the notion of free speech and, specifically, the First Amendment to the American constitution: 'Congress shall make no law respecting an establishment of religion, or prohibiting the free exercise thereof; or abridging the freedom of speech, or of the press; or the right of the people peaceably to assemble, and to petition the Government for a redress of grievances'. In Section 326 of the US Communications Act of 1934, the relationship of the broadcasting system to that amendment is stated explicitly:

> Nothing in this Act shall be understood or construed to give the Commission
> [that is the FCC] the power of censorship over the radio communications or
> signals transmitted by any radio station, and no regulation or condition shall be
> promulgated or fixed by the Commission which shall interfere with the right of
> free speech by means of radio communication.

This attachment of broadcasting so closely to the constitutional rights of the
individual US citizen is a significant constraint on the system. Effectively, it
rules out planning a system with cultural goals, for to attempt to have any
goals beyond free speech is to act in a way that must inevitably affect, if not
infringe, the free speech rights of individuals. And most interesting is the fact
that in face of its unique status, rather than explore the value of the myriad
other methods of using broadcasting for positive cultural ends, the United
States has attempted to persuade other nations to accept its way of doing
things (see Blanchard, 1986). As is apparent, it has not succeeded.

Some specific comparisons

A major difference between Europe and North America in the control over
broadcasting is the openness of the policy-making process. In both Canada
and the US the policy process could be said to be more open than in Europe. In
Canada, for instance, for over twenty years it has been the practice of the
federal government – and more recently of some provincial governments – to
encourage public discussion and comment about current issues requiring
policy action both in broadcasting and telecommunications. Under the procedures of the CRTC, policy questions, broadcasting licence renewals, conditions of service and rate structures for federally-regulated telecommunications companies and broadcasting companies are all considered at public
hearings in cities across the country. In addition, the federal Minister of
Communications may encourage public discussion and reaction on various
proposed policies.

On a number of occasions in Canada since the mid-1960s, task forces,
commissions of inquiry and special committees have been set up to examine
particular problems, and the reports of these bodies have been made available
to the general public. Indeed, since 1928 it has been the practice of the federal
government to employ the inquiry processes of royal commissions and parliamentary committees on many occasions to examine aspects of the broadcasting system and to obtain public comments. This public involvement, as well
as the more usual consultations with industry associations and between
government agencies and departments, provides the federal government with
a considerable range of information on which to draw in developing policy.

However, if the policy process is more open in North America, access by members of the public to influence broadcasting is much easier and more extensive, at least in some European countries. The Netherlands is probably the best example, with its broadcasting associations. These associations effectively choose which programmes will be broadcast on the channel they control. Sweden follows close behind, with the involvement of citizens in the control of what is broadcast. The placement of ownership of broadcasting stations in local communities assists this process in Denmark, and concern for regionality in Germany works in the same direction.

Citizen participation in creating and transmitting television programmes in North America is effectively limited to providing studio access and transmission time on community access channels, on cable systems, to those who request it. No consideration has been given to public participation in determining what is broadcast. As a result, community-based programmes covering political, social and cultural activities may commonly be found only on cable in both the US and Canada. In the US, especially on cable systems, the strident voices of individuals exercising their freedom of speech rights over any consideration of the interests of community is also not uncommon. In Quebec, cable operators have turned of the community channel over to community organisations, which has proven to be a valuable stimulation to locally based and oriented programming.

The conclusion we must reach, then, is not that individual citizens and groups are more involved in North America and less involved in Europe. Rather, where policy appears to be the prerogative of government in Europe, it is open to participation in North America. And whereas the organisation of participation by individuals and groups in production is taken somewhat seriously in some European countries, and is not limited merely to studio time to produce programmes for little-watched channels, this is less the case in North America.

If broadcasting is taken to include cable and satellite communications the situation looks slightly different. When cable television was first introduced in Canada in the 1960s, it was seen as a Trojan horse, a vehicle that would usher in a host of US television programmes that would constrain the ability of Canadians to communicate with each other over the din of American entertainment. Cable did just that. Audience share for Canadian stations decreased and the CRTC was forced to create a mechanism called simultaneous programme substitution to keep the private stations from losing bags of money. This mechanism allows the Canadian broadcast company to schedule the programmes it has purchased from the US networks at the same time as they are being shown on the Canadian cable system by a US broadcaster. Further, the Canadian broadcast version, complete with its advertisements, is allowed to pre-empt the US signal. In other words, the Canadian version of the show, which differs only in the content of the advertisements, is shown on both its channel and the channel of the US station. Thus the advertisers on the

Canadian station gain access to the audience of both stations and the Canadian broadcast company collects advertising revenues based on that expanded audience.

Cable systems have ceased to be viewed as a Trojan horse, not because they have ceased to bring in American signals but because a bigger and better Trojan horse has been built, in the form of overspill from communications satellites. In face of easy reception of US direct broadcast satellites (DBS) the Canadian government has supported the maintenance and development of cable, partly to discourage Canadians from purchasing satellite dishes. Why? Because Canadian cable operators can be regulated by the state to ensure that the mix of signals provided includes Canadian signals. The reception of Canadian signals by Canadians serves the dual purpose of maintaining Canadian culture and maintaining advertising revenues for Canadian programme producers.

Both cable systems and communications satellites are expensive undertakings that, by virtue of their technology, can take advantage of economies of scale. Broadcasting thus has an increased vulnerability to pressures for concentration of ownership. As a result, in many countries very large players are emerging, such as Ted Rogers of Rogers Cablesystems, Ted Turner of CNN, Rupert Murdoch of Sky, Fox, and News Corp. and so on, who make money through global – as opposed to local, regional or national – distribution. While different situations prevail in North America and Europe, currently economics appears to be the legitimised prevailing arbiter of the design of national and international communications systems. There is also, understandably, a political stress on European as opposed to national markets, and the technology favours large-scale activities. In this context, the social and cultural concerns for the development and enhancement of national cultures that led to the establishment of European broadcasting systems may be submerged.

The press in comparison with the electronic media

The printed press and electronic media have slightly different histories in both Europe and North America. This is partly because the press is an older institution and partly because nations have found it necessary to allocate a scarce resource, the radio spectrum, by means of licences.

There is virtually no interference – positive or negative – in establishing and publishing newspapers in most countries in Western Europe, the exception being France, where the state uses a variety of mechanisms to ensure a lively commentary on matters of national and regional importance. Where registration of news organs is required, it is a formality. Distribution is slightly different: France, Germany, the Netherlands and Sweden provide tax and postal concessions and Britain exempts papers from value added tax (VAT). Whereas in broadcasting there is the requirement of balance, there is a tacit assumption that press journalists will both have an opinion and express it. On the whole, the press is expected to operate according to the journalistic ethics of the day and to regulate itself to ensure fairness. The UK Press Complaints Commission is the body used for arbitrating issues where that fairness comes into question. Among other countries, in Germany a right of reply exists and in Sweden a press ombudsman assists in maintaining fair treatment. Continual concern, but little action, over the emergence and operation of newspaper and media oligopolies has been expressed fairly continuously since World War II.

The role of the press is generally more critical and investigative than that of the electronic media. However, the exact role it plays in each country varies. Its role seems to depend on such factors as social relations between politicians and journalists, on press traditions, on the openness of information, on the association between political parties and journalists, professional accreditation, and on the perceived relations between the policies of the government and the will and interests of the average citizen. We will return to these factors in Chapter 5.

Non-broadcasting telecommunications law and policy: the common carriers

Telecommunication companies, that is telephone, telex, and data carriers, are generally referred to as 'common carriers'. The basic characteristic of a common carrier is its obligation to carry whatever messages (i.e. content) any customer wants to send and to charge equitable rates for that carriage service. A carrier may not tamper with the message, nor is it involved in creating any of the messages carried for customers (although this requirement may be modified through changing technological opportunities). The creation of the 'content' is what makes broadcasters different from common carriers; broadcasters are involved in content creation and are legally responsible for all the content they transmit, even if some programming is purchased from other sources.

Traditionally there has been one, publicly-owned, nation-wide telecommunications system, for example, British Telecom, France Telecom, ATT (American Telephone and Telegraph), Telecom Australia, connected to one international system – for the West it is INTELSAT – that provides links overseas. With increasing emphasis throughout the 80s on privatisation and technological development, considerable pressure exists, emanating from the private sector, to allow it to provide telecommunications services. Customarily, but not entirely, these companies are interested in providing value-added services in high traffic areas. Value-added services enhance basic telephone services or data transmission, voice mail is one example. Certain countries have begun to respond to these demands by granting licences to private telecommunications companies. In the UK the best example is Mercury; in the US it is Sprint. And as is already apparent these alternative companies are joining together in their own world-wide networks.

Regulation of telecommunications

Since their beginning in the 1840s, the telegraph and telephone industries have most often been regulated monopolies. Regulation of telephone and telegraph rates and service was deemed necessary for protection of the public interest because of the companies' operation as natural monopolies, that is, in the longer term, it was believed that only one company could provide efficient service in any one area. (It is a moot point whether such monopolies could ever have been described as 'natural' since they were authorised by statute and regulation.) In any case, due to the proliferating technologies of communications transmission, it is no longer taken for granted that one large company such as British Telecom should have exclusive rights to provide any telecommunications service in a specific territory.

Telecommunications issues

For telecommunications, the fundamental issue is always that of fair access. This revolves around the principle that individuals (households or businesses) are entitled to receive adequate service at equitable and non-discriminatory rates. While no one seriously expects that a person living in an isolated area will receive exactly the same range and price of services as someone living in a large urban area, the usual principle is that there must be no deliberate deprivation of service and the rates charged must be shown to be just and reasonable.

Related to this principle is another, that all customers in similar circumstances must be treated equally and the charges for services must be publicly known. This requires all telecommunications carriers to post their rates and to specify clearly who pays what for which level of service. Specific issues that arise in telecommunications are related to disputes about the equity of established rates, whether one type of customer service is being cross-subsidised at the expense of another (e.g. households by businesses, rural residents by urban residents and so on) and whether the costs of service are being properly calculated by the carrier.

We have already referred to the third major issue in telecommunications – *competition*. The most contentious issue here is rate balancing. Once competition is allowed for elements of the system, for example long-distance calls, the telecommunications system as an integrated whole begins to break up. Why is this a problem? Essentially the problem arises because the cost of providing long-distance services has decreased so much over the years that, in the past decade, the traditional carriers have used high charges for long-distance calls (which are mainly made by businesses) to subsidise the operation of local urban services (which are used to a greater extent by members of the public). Once competition is introduced this source of cross-subsidisation is removed from the traditional carriers, and in order to compete they must raise the cost of local telephone calls. This is exactly what has happened in the US and the UK (see Hanafin, 1991).

The US has gone furthest in introducing competition. Long distance rates have been reduced considerably, in fact so much so that Canadian businesses find it lucrative to use US carriers to cross Canada and to communicate with other nations. Canadian businesses have recently increased their lobbying for telecommunications competition on the assumption that such competition would lower long-distance rates. They argue that with costs more than double those of the US they need a level playing-field in telecommunications costs to compete. Figures 2 and 3 illustrate what savings competition can bring. Figure 2 shows the differentials in rates between national carriers and competitive services within Germany. Figure 3 shows the differential rates within Europe. Note that the bars represent the price of a call in one direction minus the price in the other direction. In short, whereas there is a very small differential between calls to and from Britain and Portugal, there is a substantial difference, over 2 **ecus** for a three-minute call, between calls to and from Germany and Spain. In other words, while Britain and Portugal charge approximately the same tariffs, Spain charges considerably more than does Germany for long-distance calls. Obviously there is room for rationalisation. But it is an open question whether the type of competition that takes place in the US is the best solution. US telephone users must listen to a brief advertisement for every system they use; the phones of up to three companies can be found in various locations in one hotel; at times users cannot phone certain locations, usually outside the US, from the phone they are using; and each company's card only works in its own phones. The American system is a mess and the provision of a simple, straightforward telephone service has deteriorated badly.

As if this was not enough, a substantial competitive struggle between the cable and phone industries is emerging with regard to a whole host of digitalised communication services. Both cable and the telcos (telephone companies) are capable of delivering a range of digitalised services to every home. The telcos have the advantage of addressability, that is they can direct and bill on a per unit basis to every home. The cable companies have a greater carrying capacity and thus are better able to cope with information-rich

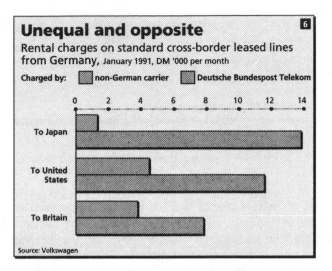

6
Unequal and opposite
Rental charges on standard cross-border leased lines from Germany, January 1991, DM '000 per month
Charged by: non-German carrier Deutsche Bundespost Telekom
0 2 4 6 8 10 12 14
To Japan
To United States
To Britain
Source: Volkswagen

Figure 2 Telecommunications charges for lines out of Germany
Source: The Economist, 5 October 1991, p. 27. © 1991 The Economist Newspaper Group, Inc. Reproduced by permission. Further reproduction prohibited.

7
Don't call me, I'll call you
Differences in the prices of EC phone calls, 1990
Price of a three-minute call in one direction minus the price in the other direction
0 ecus 0.5 1.0 1.5 2.0
Spain to Germany
Italy to Denmark
Spain to Holland
Italy to Britain
Spain to France
Greece to Germany
Belgium to Portugal
France to Holland
Germany to Denmark
Britain to Portugal
Source: Touche Ross Management Consultants
First country is the more expensive of the pair

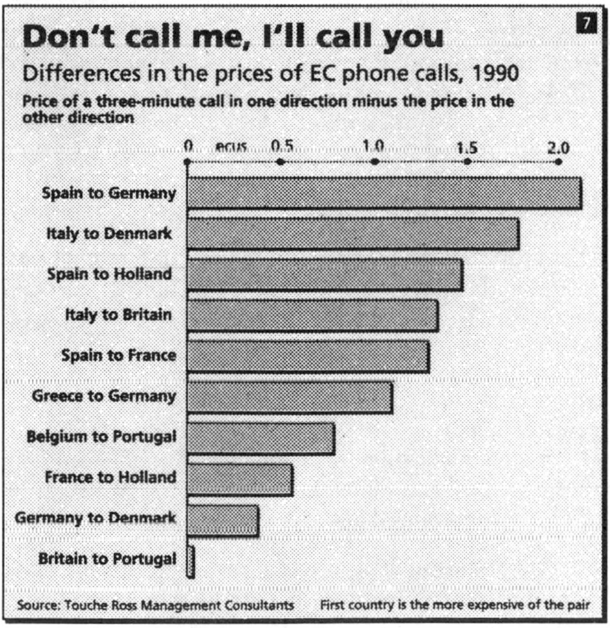

Figure 3 Price differentials in EC phone calls
Source: The Economist, 5 October 1991, p. 28. © 1991 The Economist Newspaper Group, Inc. Reproduced by permission. Further reproduction prohibited.

services such as television pictures. As yet, no country appears to have taken the matter in hand well enough to ensure that the average citizen will not lose out.

Cultural industries

The term 'cultural industry' was first used by Horkheimer and Adorno (1972) in the *Dialectic of Enlightenment*, although the idea can be found in an earlier essay by Walter Benjamin (1969, originally published in 1936). Both Benjamin and Horkheimer and Adorno used the term to speak of the emerging production of music, theatre, and general entertainment which appeared to be replacing locally produced, participatory cultural expression. Since that usage the term has been neutralised and has generally been converted to the plural – 'cultural industries'. Currently, it covers activities that involve the creation and distribution of cultural goods and services employing industrial or commercial practices.

Given the current definition, cultural industries can be seen as encompassing broadcasting or restricted to such activities as book and periodical publishing, video and film, and sound recording. Other rarer uses of the term add to the above three areas newspapers, photography, art reproductions, new audio-visual and multimedia products and services and advertising. Our discussion will be confined to film and video, and book and periodical publishing.

International cultural industries policy

The most relevant international provision that applies to cultural industries is Unesco's Recommendation Concerning the Status of the Artist (Unesco, 1982). The recommendation calls on countries to take responsibility for the following:

1 proper remuneration and control of the artist over his/her work especially in light of new technology,
2 ensuring that communication dissemination technologies contribute to artistic encouragement and stimulation, and
3 creating working conditions that foster artistic creativity.

Beyond this recommendation little exists at the international level, a dramatic contrast to national scenes. Beginning with the industrial revolution, but particularly following the development of film, sound recording and television, and since the end of World War II, there has been a significant expansion of the state's role in cultural activities. The challenge in cultural industries policy is to ensure an adequate level of distribution of cultural products reflective of the values of the producing and consuming society in face of

1 technologies of mass distribution such as broadcasting and telecommunications, and
2 the resultant availability of expensively produced but cheaply delivered generic entertainment products.

This challenge is not confined to small countries, developing countries, countries with weak economies and countries that share a language with other, more powerful nations: it is a universal challenge. In Japan, for instance, the Cultural Agency's attention is oriented to the Japanese language, fine arts, copyright, religion and conservation of cultural assets. The fostering of indigenous cultural production and consumption is infused throughout all government ministries. Minowa (1982) notes that the Japanese government intervenes in cultural industries and broadcasting in the following ways:

1 direct management (sometimes in the form of semi-governmental management),
2 licensing,
3 regulation of activities,
4 subsidisation,
5 granting of privileges in taxation and assessment of public-service rates,
6 public spending to buy the products of cultural industries,
7 arrangement of legal environment (including legalisation of resale price maintenance and institution of the copyright law), and
8 research and counselling.   (1982, pp. 141–2)

In France, with the election of François Mitterrand in 1981, came the allotment of FF8 billion to the then culture minister, Jack Lang, for cultural support, including the development of a new television channel. The United States has its National Endowment for the Arts, which subsidises art, artists and cultural organisations, while Britain has, among other public sector agencies and programmes, the British Council to promote British culture overseas. Not surprisingly, former socialist countries such as Czechoslovakia and Hungary have fairly sophisticated means of stimulating such activities while others, such as Cuba, have a well-articulated ideology. The Scandinavian countries, along with Spain, Portugal, the Netherlands, Italy, Austria, Australia, India, Brazil and Canada, have active governmental support programmes for their cultural industries. There is widespread acceptance of the need for stimulative and maintenance measures by states for their own cultural industries. The accepted rationale for such measures is to be found not in the economics of the industries but in their cultural value (see, for example, Nielsen, 1986, p. 45).

National film and video policy

The basic dilemmas specifically applicable to film and video production are: the amount of money that must be advanced for a single production; the delay in earning back investment; restrictive distribution channels; the age profile of the audience; the necessity of organising production, marketing and distribution; ever-increasing competition with 'old product' distributed via broadcast, satellite and cable, and the necessity of extensive marketing and promotion. These factors produce certain risk-minimising strategies that maximise immediate market potential rather than artistic creativity, for example the star system.

In the USA, a low budget film costs about US$1 million to produce, and the average Hollywood product, about $24 million. Up to $50 million can be spent marketing a blockbuster. When such sums are at stake, financiers are reluctant to hand money over to untried but talented artists. Thus arises the need for producers, that is, members of the business community who have the experience and know-how to assemble and manage the human and material resources any film or video production requires. The producer must also find a path to distribution. Not only must hard-nosed business people be persuaded to sign a distribution contract, but, in addition, those who are persuaded must be in a position to place the film in an appropriate market so that it will reach an audience likely to be appreciative. These factors have led to centralisation in the film industry and a Hollywood, US-based oligopoly, which has been challenged by small entrepreneurs only in the past two or three years.

Increasingly, and echoing one of the concerns of the Unesco Recommendations on the Status of the Artist, countries are enacting regulations requiring broadcasters to acquire a certain percentage of their material from independent producers. This may free up film and video distribution somewhat but a counter-trend, the purchase and display of old movies and TV series by broadcasters and especially satellite broadcasters, will be competing for audiences. Additionally, broadcasters will be looking for 'reliable product', that is, film or video productions that can fit into a broadcaster's view of what audiences want at particular times of the day, to advance the interests of particular advertisers.

While broadcasters, audiences and advertisers combine to constrain made-for-TV film and video, films made for theatrical release must cope with a fairly narrow age profile among the movie-going public – predominantly teenagers and young adults – as well as the desire of movie investors to make millions. A review of the ten top films in the UK in September 1993 illustrates the point.

Film title	*Gross receipts in UK, week ending 22 September*
1 The Firm	£1,720,698
2 Jurassic Park	871,654
3 In the Line of Fire	824,654
4 Sliver	486,436
5 Much Ado About Nothing	559,808
6 Made in America	287,534
7 Hot Shots! Part Deux	236,197
8 The Crush	154,676
9 Dennis the Menace	114,370
10 What's Love Got To Do With It	103,481

(Source: *Variety*, 4 Oct. 1993)

The question to ask is what age such films are designed for? The answer is mostly children, adolescents and young people. Given this target market, is it likely that a full range of artistic expression will find its way onto film?

Wide-ranging means are used by various countries to keep open the artistic possibilities and cultural relevance of film and video. Because the United States is by far the dominant producer of film and video entertainment product for global distribution and consumption, we will begin with consideration of its film development mechanisms.

A multinational survey of film production

The major difference between the United States and most other countries, *vis-à-vis* film and video, is that the US has such a dominant share, it might be termed a monopoly producer of international feature film product in and for the developed world. This position was achieved over the years by means of a vibrant and thriving industry built in part on an American love of technology, a need to socialise its immigrant population and the fervent belief that the American political system represented the most advanced form of democracy and therefore should be exported to other countries. In short, the social, political, technological and industrial will were in place.

As the film industry established itself, largely in the reliably sunny climate of southern California, it built mechanisms – in the early years the large studios – for the reinvestment of profits and for the attraction and development of acting, technical and managerial talent to ensure a continuous release of lavish productions. It conceived of movie formulae which were both products and advertisements for themselves. An industry press further promoted American productions. Beginning modestly with examinations of American realities, for example, the renowned film pioneer D. W. Griffiths' film *Birth of a Nation* (1915), the film industry later turned to English and European classical stories, the morality tales that are infused in Western civilisation, and Roman and biblical sources for film extravaganzas such as *Ben Hur*, *The Robe* and *Spartacus*.

The obvious success of the industry, together with the wealth and notoriety of movie stars and movie moguls, attracted many more people wishing to participate in the industry than it could ever assimilate. In playing into the myth that any person can rise from humble roots to a position of wealth, social recognition and power, and a secondary myth that one can have a lavish lifestyle without hard work, the industry came to have its pick of domestic and international talent. The purist attitudes of many a successful stage actor were eventually softened by the lure of megabucks.

The industry and the country also developed an educational infrastructure that ensured a continual flow of acting, technical and managerial talent into the industry. At first these talents were developed largely by apprenticeship or, in the case of acting, by the many amateur and professional opportunities that existed on the stage. However, in due course, beginning in California and spreading throughout the country, film schools encompassing all aspects of film production, distribution, consumption and criticism were created to meet an ever-increasing need for knowledgeable entrants into an industry over-supplied with willing workers.

The result has been the establishment of a dynamic, self-sustaining and extremely profitable industry that generates enough opportunity and cash for there to be a continual evolution of both the product and the industry structure. The industry can count amongst its achievements substantial domestic employment, derivative industries, a high level of export sales, the articulation of American values for domestic consumption, and advancing US ideology abroad. As a result of these accomplishments, the industry has sufficient clout with the US government that the head of the American Motion Picture Association is apparently able to command the support of the President, the Secretary of State, the Secretary of Commerce and the United States Trade Representative on the matter of possible restriction of export opportunities of US movie and video products (*Canadian Communication Reports*, 31 December 1989, pp. 2, 3).

In no other country is the film industry so dynamic, therefore in the name of cultural articulation and development many other states intervene in the market-place to support national film industries. The main mechanism that France uses is the *Centre National du Cinéma* (CNC) Advances Against Receipts programme. Until mid-1991 any French director could submit a script and hope for a grant which would be returned to the agency (CNC) for reinvestment should the film make money. The chance of success was about 10 per cent; an average grant was US$350,000. Besides the low success rate and relatively low amount of the grant, a second difficulty emerged in the allocation of grants. Whereas first-time directors were reviewed by their own panel, second-time directors were lumped in with established names and their success rate dropped to almost zero. Since mid-1991 the agency has had to pay greater attention to the relative experience of directors.

Of course, $350,000 does not make a film. With grant in hand, the director must find a producer, the person who puts the business deal together and manages the project and its finances. In France, there is a two-year deadline on getting the project underway. A ten-year delay for a film to reach the screen is not unheard of, as with, for example, the comedy, *Delicatessen*.

In the UK market, pressure is severe and public culturally-oriented support sparse. There are a variety of private funding sources, all market oriented, but only a few are in a position to be major investors. Unlike other countries, including Canada and Australia, in the wake of Thatcherism the UK provides no tax breaks for investment in film or broadcast programmes. Also, Britain has no equivalent to the US majors, such as Paramount, MGM, and Columbia (now a subsidiary of Sony). Its largest film company, Rank, limits itself to the pre-purchase of the rights to foreign distribution.

The private producers who assist directors in obtaining financing are also limited in numbers and in funds. According to *Variety* (May 1991, p. C25), only three British companies, backed by consortia of lenders, have standing funds for investment in film. Five other private producers operate but must raise money project by project.

The limited public-sector assistance that is available is provided by British Screen Finance and the British Film Institute's National Film Development Fund. The former supports mainly low budget films, the latter, script and project development. Both share an annual budget of £4.5 million, less than Telefilm Canada's annual budget by a factor of eighteen, and in Canada film-makers can also approach the provinces with federal money in hand. Only one major private-sector script and project development funder, Allied Film-makers, is in operation. Limited commercial development funds are available through one public-sector source, Persona, financed by BBC Wales and SC4, and two private-sector sources.

The television channels are frequently involved in financing films – in 1990, in 22 of the 38 feature films shot in Britain – mainly in the purchase of television rights at the pre-production stage. So are sales agents, companies that may acquire international distribution rights prior to production. They may be prepared to put up minimum amounts of money as a guarantee that they will purchase such rights.

Hollywood studios also play a significant financial role in financing British film production, but usually only with large and ambitious projects. In these cases the producers usually have a standing relationship with the studios or are at least known to them. The few banks that specialise in media and entertainment can also be approached for financial support, as can innovative financial deal-makers and helpers. For example, two insurance companies now will guarantee return on investment. While such insurers charge high premiums, the guarantees are worth their cost if the producer is desperate for further funds from banks.

In Canada, the central role of the National Film Board in (primarily documentary) film-making has been eclipsed by a myriad of factors. Financial support for the NFB has been cut, while support for a private-sector independent film industry has grown under both Liberal and Conservative governments. Funding began in earnest in 1967 with the founding of the Canadian Film Development Corporation (CFDC). It expanded significantly in 1974 with the Capital Cost Allowance (CCA) allowing investors to deduct 100 per cent of their investment as a tax credit, and was rationalised and further expanded through the 1980s with the transformation of the CFDC into the powerful and reasonably well-endowed Telefilm Canada. In response, and in parallel with Australia's state film development corporations, seven provincial film development corporations have been founded to assist in attracting that support to their provinces. Finally, the joint federal/Quebec Cité du Cinema film facility with its production equipment and studio space provides useful infrastructure.

Most of the policies focus on much-needed production and development support, but another major problem is the lack of screen time for Canadian productions on Canadian cinema screens. About 2 per cent of screen time in Canada goes to Canadian films. The reason for this lack of market access is the historic structural relationship between the major American studios and the Canadian exhibitor chains (which own the vast majority of first-run, urban cinemas). There are now only two major chains of Canadian movie theatres, Famous Players and Cineplex Odeon. They have established contractual arrangements with the seven Hollywood majors (Paramount, United Artists, Columbia Pictures, MGM, Universal Pictures, Twentieth-Century Fox and Warner Bros.), which both produce and distribute film products. From a business point of view, these agreements are beneficial to the financial security of all the parties involved. The problem is that the independent Canadian producers and distributors are largely excluded. Because control over cinemas is vested in the provinces, the federal government is powerless to invoke quotas on screen time. Only Quebec has attempted to insist on some participation of domestic distributors. In doing so they incurred the wrath of at least one Hollywood major, Paramount, which took retaliatory action by refusing to allow distribution of its English-language films to video rental shops in the province.

National publishing policy

In the context of cultural industries, the word 'publishing' generally refers to book and magazine publishing but not newspapers. Publishing is an area of cultural production with a long history. The manner in which countries deal with publishing differs as a result of the age of the country, its language and its publishing history.

Generally speaking, European countries, each with their own language, established publishing industries prior to the twentieth century. The strength of these industries roughly followed the strength of the cultures and economies of the respective nations. The establishment of colonies, along with copyright law, assisted in developing and maintaining these industries. Thus, for example, British book publishing companies set up branch operations in their colonies in India, Africa and North America, while Spain and Holland did the same with their colonies. In most cases the coloniser companies obtained and maintained control over the lucrative publishing for the institutions they introduced in education and law. In doing so, not only did they maintain ideological influence but they also garnered whatever profits were to be made.

Being colonisers and thus in control of the legal system of the colony, they were able to use copyright to ensure markets for home producers and prevent the development of indigenous publishing. Thus imperial (British) copyright law of 1841 gave no protection to anything published in Canada. As a result, British publishers were free to reprint Canadian work without recompense to the author or the original publisher.

The United States broke through this control in the years following the American Revolution (1776) by piracy, mainly of popular English novels by authors such as Charles Dickens. True, for a while the situation worked to the disadvantage of American writers, who were less likely to be published because they had to be paid royalties, whereas the British got none. But it also allowed the development of indigenous firms which could then turn their attention to American publishing. It was only with the emergence of American writers like Mark Twain, whose interests were very much at stake, that a copyright law was forced through Congress in 1909.

In contrast, the colonial status of other 'new world' nations prevented such piracy. Canada, for example, lived under the dual disadvantage of imperial copyright law and the spill-over of cheap American reprints. Only when the Canadians started pirating American works was there any US concern expressed regarding international respect for the law. The double jeopardy that Canada was placed in undermined both indigenous publishing and distribution operations based in Canada. The use of piracy to establish an industry continues today in Asia, not only in book publishing but also in sound recording and videotapes.

In modern times, public support for book publishing is available in many countries, in parallel with support for film and video, but different mechanisms are used to deliver that support and information on government support policies is much harder to obtain. Support for creative writing is widespread in the form of education, awards, residences, festivals, publishing grants, readings and commissions through a variety of public-sector bodies, either local, regional or national. In certain countries non-fiction or documentary writing is also supported. In fewer countries, direct support for publishing firms is available. Such support programmes were strong in the former socialist countries, and continue to be in smaller European countries and in Canada.

Canada can be considered as a case in point. In the late 1960s, Canadian governments decided to support an indigenous book-publishing industry. They began with a bail-out of two firms and then designed continuing support programmes. The rationale for providing support was based on three factors. The first was the value of an indigenous industry oriented to publishing work that dealt with national, regional and local issues. The second was to provide a vehicle for Canadian creative writers to reach an audience. The third was that English-speaking Canada is an easy and open market for US and UK publications which could be sold at prices based on large domestic print runs, and therefore low per-unit costs, that were impossible for Canadian publishers to achieve.

While the industry called for structural intervention, for instance by requiring that imported books be distributed by Canadian-owned companies, the government provided two types of programmes. One was to cover deficits for the publication of culturally important books. The second was to stimulate industrial development so that at some point Canadian-owned firms might become financially stable and gain a larger market share, especially of traditionally profitable publishing sectors such as educational publishing.

The actual programmes, especially the industrial development programmes, were original and innovative. By 1992, the federal government was inoculating the industry with $140 million over five years, in addition to postal subsidy compensation – purportedly a 160 per cent increase in annual funds over the previous five-year plan. They had also put in place a cultural development bank from which publishers would be eligible to secure loans. Export assistance was available. In addition, nearly every province had some form of substantial support – either grants or both grants and loans.

The point has been reached where a number of Canadian-owned publishers of fiction, poetry and Canadian-oriented non-fiction are receiving as much from grants as they are from sales. Such a statistic makes it sound as if the government has somehow been persuaded to support a moribund industry. On the contrary, these publishers regularly command about half the places on the non-fiction national and regional best-seller lists. Almost without exception, a new release of a well-known Canadian author climbs immediately into the first three places. A few Canadian authors are now known world-wide, such as Alice Munro, Margaret Atwood, Antonine Maillet, Robertson Davies, Brian Moore and Margaret Laurence. What the grant-equals-sales statistic means is that Canada's market is too small to support profitable book publishing when it must be conducted within the constraints of an open market in which American, British and French books can be sold at run-on prices. The pity of the matter is that in spite of this government assistance, in English-speaking Canada Canadian-owned companies have no more appreciable market share than they had twenty years ago.

The major difference in French-speaking Canada is that the Quebec government has been willing to take complementary actions in related fields, especially in education. A combination of initiatives has produced some real inroads for Quebec publishers. Quebec's extensive concern with culture is reflective of the attitude of the French government: the state is accepted as a leading actor in both cultural and educational matters. Being French-speaking, yet North American, Quebec finds itself out-of-tune with educational books from France and out-of-language with American texts. Having responsibility for education and fighting with the federal government for complete responsibility for culture, Quebec found itself in a good position to encourage the development of a healthy – but not self-sustaining – industry, steadily gaining market share.

Programmes with the extent of Canada's are not to be found in Europe or the US. In these countries well-established firms, active across both less and more profitable markets, cross-subsidise the publication of new authors. In both France and Britain minor subventions are available for restricted categories of writing, whereas in the US private foundations provide support for authors and for social and political causes (and hence publishing). The CIA has been active in supporting book publishers in the past, both within and outside the US, and presumably such activity continues. The enormous post-secondary US educational system, especially in comparison to Europe, also provides opportunities for institutional support of publishing and authors. The purchase of movie rights in the US is a significant market. And being the most powerful nation on earth never hurts in attempting to sell books on a variety of American subjects. In contrast, traditional colonial markets provide support for European publishing. For example, whereas Britain exports approximately 35 per cent of its book output, the US exports about 10 per cent.

In short, either through institutions, industry activity or direct support, developed nations find ways to ensure the continuous replenishment of creative writers whose voices and ideas will become those of the nation. However, international tensions sometimes arise when the rules of ensuring such cultural renewal cannot be agreed upon. Having outgrown piracy, the US is the most active nation in attempting to suppress it, with the UK close behind. Because both are well positioned in the present world market, both favour cultural industries such as publishing operating within the rules of a

free market. Smaller countries, and especially developing countries, risk
cultural inundation if they abide by such rules.

Summary and conclusion

This chapter began by setting out a socio-political context for a discussion of
the law and policy involved in the national and international mass media and
mass communication. We identified common sites from which media operate
in different societies and the inherent biases associated with each position,
and thus how the media were constrained in addressing socio-political
concerns.

We then turned to the legal foundations of the media. Starting with the
international context we followed with a discussion of broadcasting laws and
policies in a selection of European and North American countries. Within
broadcasting we considered cable and satellite communications and noted
how these technological innovations are changing the face of the broadcast-
ing-derived mass media. In a separate section we discussed telecommunications in the form of telephone and data communications, and noted the
globalising tendencies inherent in development in this area.

The final section of the chapter dealt with cultural industries, specifically
video and film and publishing. By reviewing the support systems available in a
few selected countries we gave an indication of the means necessary, over
many different countries, to secure works reflective of some degree of artistic
creativity, with some relevance to the producing culture, that has some access
to audiences.

References

Benjamin, Walter (1969), 'The work of art in an age of mechanical reproduction' in
    Hannah Arendt (ed.), *Illuminations: Essays and Reflections*, Schocken Books, New
    York.
Blanchard, Margaret A. (1986), *Exporting the First Amendment: The Press Govern-
    ment Crusade of 1945–1952*, Longman, New York.
Boyce, George (1978), 'The fourth estate: a reappraisal of a concept' in G. Boyce *et al.*
    (eds.), *Newspaper History from the 17th Century to the Present Day*, Sage/
    Constable, London.
Canada, Dept. of Communication (1989), *Canadian Communication Reports*, Dept.
    of Communication, 31 December, Ottawa, pp. 2, 3.
Canada, Task Force on Programme Review (Nielson Task Force) (1986), *Culture
    and Communications*, Minister of Supply and Services, Ottawa.
Canadian Radio Television Commission (1974), *Canadian Ownership in Broadcast-
    ing: A Report on the Foreign Divestiture Process*, Information Canada, Ottawa.
Commission of European Communities (1984), *Television Without Frontiers*, Green

Paper on the establishment of the common market for broadcasting, especially by satellite and cable, Office for Official Publications of the European Communities, Luxembourg, COM(84) 300 final.

Communications Canada (1988), *Canadian Voices, Canadian Choices: A New Broadcasting Policy for Canada*, Supply and Services, Ottawa.

Couprie, Eliane, and Henry Olsson (1987), *Freedom to Communicate under the Law: Case Studies in Nine Countries*, Media Monograph no. 9, Manchester University, The European Institute for the Media, Manchester.

Curran, James (1990), 'The new revisionism in mass communication research: a reappraisal', *European Journal of Communication*, 5 (2–3) (June), pp. 135–64.

Curran, James (1991), 'Mass media and democracy: a reappraisal' in James Curran and Michael Gurevitch (eds.), *Mass Media and Society*, Edward Arnold, London, pp. 82–117.

Gawlik, Ladislav (1982), 'Creative and performing artists and the media in Czechoslovakia' in Unesco, *Cultural Industries: A Challenge for the Future*, Unesco, Paris, pp. 112–19.

Habermas, Jürgen (1984), *The Theory of Communicative Action*, trans. Thomas McCarty, Beacon Press, Boston.

Hanafin, J. (1991), 'Forum file: index on telephone deregulation', *Canadian Forum*, October (citing the American Federation of Consumers), p. 48.

Head, Sydney W., and Christopher H. Sterling (1990), *Broadcasting in America: A Survey of Electronic Media*, Houghton Mifflin, Dallas.

Homet, Roland S. (1979), *Politics, Cultures and Communication*, Praeger, New York

Horkheimer, M., and T. W. Adorno (1972), *Dialectic of Enlightenment*, Herder and Herder, New York.

Kleinstuber, Hans J., Denis McQuail, and Karen Siune (eds.) (1986), *Electronic Media and Politics in Western Europe: Euromedia Research Group Handbook of National Systems*, Campus Verlag, Frankfurt, New York.

Kofler, Brigit (Unesco Communications Division) (1991), *Database on Broadcasting Laws in Western Europe and North America*, Unesco, Paris.

Mills, C. Wright (1959), *The Sociological Imagination*, Oxford University Press, New York.

Minowa, Shigeo (1982), 'A purely liberal strategy: public and private intervention in cultural industries in Japan' in Unesco, *Cultural Industries: A Challenge for the Future*, Unesco, Paris, pp. 141–2.

Neilsen, Erik (1986), *Economic Growth: Culture and Communications: A Study Team Report to the Task Force on Program Review*, Supply and Services, Ottawa.

Organization of American States (1969), *American Convention on Human Rights*, Washington, DC.

Osgyani, Csaba (1991), 'New Hungarian film foundation launched', *Variety*, May 6, p. 328.

Globe and Mail (1989), 'Paramount withholds videos from Quebec', April 14, p. C1.

Siebert, F. S., T. Peterson, and W. Schramm (1956, 1971), *Four Theories of the Press*, University of Illinois Press, Urbana.

Siune, Karen, Claude Sorbets, and Asle Rolland (1986), 'A framework for comparative analysis of European policy-making' in Denis McQuail and Karen Siune (eds.), *New Media Politics: Comparative Perspectives in Western Europe*, Sage Publications, London.

Smith, Anthony (1991), *The Age of Behemoths: The Globalization of Mass Media Firms*, Priority Press, New York.

Unesco (1980), *Many Voices: One World: Report of the International Commission on Communication Problems* (MacBride Commission), Unipub, Paris.

Unesco (1980), *Status of the Artist*, UN Standard Setting Instruments, General Conference, 21st Session, Belgrade.

Unesco (1982), *Cultural Industries: A Challenge for the Future* (Unesco Recommendation Concerning the Status of the Artist), Unesco, Paris.

United Nations (1966), *International Covenant on Political and Civil Rights*, United Nations, Paris.

United Nations (1967), *Treaty on Principles Governing the Activities of States in the Exploration and Use of Outer Space*, United Nations, Paris.

United Nations (1976), *Declaration of Equatorial States Concerning the Geostationary Orbit and National Sovereignty*, United Nations, Paris.

Variety (1993), 4 October.

Chapter 4

The structure and role of ownership

The laws and policies that govern communications and, especially, ownership of communications enterprises, are generally distant from most people's minds. Yet communications and media institutions are intimately connected to their societies. British sitcoms and drama reflect British values, as do Indian, Brazilian or Australian movies. The commercial values of American society are reflected in its television system and in the types and production values of movies it releases. The philosophical turn of mind of the French cannot be avoided in their writing, art and electronic media products. The aesthetic values of Japan are likewise visible in creative works, especially when they are made for domestic consumption. In short, in the same way that both moral rights and property rights are recognised as part of the potential intellectual property of individuals, so cultures are intimately connected to the content and form of their communication systems.

In general, capitalism makes no allowance for such relations between cultures and their institutions. The little allowance that does exist is confined to intellectual property law and is covered by the notion of moral rights which accrue to individuals. Moral rights are generally weak and they are weakest in those countries most active in the trade of intellectual property. Also, in general, trends point towards further weakening of moral rights.

No *economic* system makes allowance for such relations between cultures and their institutions. As we have seen, especially with the collapse of Eastern Europe and the USSR, state communism as a culturally-sensitive economic system is apparently far worse than capitalism. In communist regimes, economic power is vested in the hands of a political elite isolated by position, reference group and ideology, and committed to the reproduction of political dogma to the exclusion of cultural expression. In capitalist countries, market dynamics can devastate a country's cultural output, as the market and lack of government policy has done to the British film industry.

On the international scene, because of different economic growth rates between countries, which may concentrate wealth in one for a number of decades, if no legal protection is in place, a country can find its media

Source: Royal Commission on Newspapers (Canada). Reproduced by permission, November 1993.

industries in the hands of foreign owners, as is happening in the US thanks to Japanese investment. Columbia Pictures is now owned by Sony and Matsushita owns MCA. If the industry survives, it is often managed by nationals, at least up to the second highest level of management, but under the weight of competition in the market, management must plot with owners to keep the firm competitive. This means that, if not before, then once the firm is foreign-owned, its activities must almost inevitably be seen in global and economic rather than national and cultural terms.

It is also true that capitalism maximises inexpensive distribution of slickly produced goods to as large a number of consumers as possible. However, there is also an inherent drift towards concentration of ownership, resulting in the emergence of extremely large firms and hence oligopolies, that is to say small groups of large firms that control the vast majority of the market. Within oligopolies, competition to satisfy the customer is carried on in a relatively limited way and products become more and more similar. To illustrate the point, bearing in mind that all of the top ten movies are created with the dominant audience in mind (see Chapter 3), one might analyse each and identify the common elements – cars, explosions, a love story, winners and losers, special effects, young lithe bodies and so forth. Is this the limit of consumer preference? Does such a system maximise opportunity for the articulation of variety, of the wonderful multiplicity of human cultures and societies that we know exist in the world? The short answer is no.

With the emergence of global firms and global distribution systems, resulting in the development of what might be called global tastes, the French café may be replaced with the fast food franchise, the neighbourhood pub with the beer hall, the furniture shop with the discount warehouse and culturally distinctive programmes with generic mass-media entertainment. Why? Because the neighbourly and distinctive, that is, the cultural, are more costly and generally less profitable than the mass generic. And just as firms exist under economic pressures so the average disposable income of individuals is shrinking. In other words, the ability of most people to pay a premium for goods and services is decreasing rather than increasing. This is not to say that global firms will be the only ones operating, but it will be surprising if they are not dominant.

However, the naked rule of the market can be, and is, easily tempered. In communications and especially in broadcasting and cultural industries, it is tempered by cultural mandates. These mandates are to be found within the broadcasting acts of nations and in government support programmes for culture and the arts. These cultural mandates translate into state intervention in the marketplace, or political economics, that is, the injection of cultural and political goals and frameworks within which economic activity can be carried out.

The purpose of this chapter is to examine the economics of communication and culture, specifically ownership structures and trends, and the nature of their current and future influence.

Historical background: function and ownership

The roots of media institutions are found in social, cultural, political and, most importantly, business opportunities. Gutenberg's press was an invention that responded to growing literacy, and to an opportunity to make the Bible and other tracts available to a wider audience. The establishment of the newspaper press, in the sense of an institution rather than a machine, was originally a response to a need to record and circulate official government information. However, once printing escaped the palace walls, printers soon saw other business opportunities.

In the case of the British press numbers of laws and taxes were used from the sixteenth century to control newspaper and other printed output, such as pamphlets, so that the content would reflect the interests of the ruling elite. Only in 1855 were the knowledge taxes abolished, and the paper taxes in 1861. This pattern of control was, of course, repeated with adaptation throughout Britain's colonies. However, with the continuing transformation of society throughout the nineteenth century from an agricultural to an industrial base, including, amongst other things, the creation of wage-earners living and working in close proximity in urban centres, and without round-the-clock work responsibilities; an expanding bourgeoisie; increasing literacy; and technological developments in printing and paper manufacture – all elements of what, in general, we call the Industrial Revolution, this control began to weaken. Printer/publishers were increasingly able to turn to commercial ventures, social and political groups, and consumer demand for work. Government printing contracts declined in terms of the overall amount of printing work that was available, and thus became a less important or negligible source of revenue. As the connections between printer/publishers and the government (and the gentry) weakened, the printer/publishers were far less inclined to curry government favour by controlling the ideas expressed in their publications. Printing/publishing became one of many trades within an increasingly large and economically and politically influential bourgeoisie, with whom they identified. Without much ado they became the messengers – and in some cases the voice – of the emerging classes, much as they had been messengers of the established elites. Printing equipment was increasingly able to handle larger print runs and more content. Together these developments led to intense and insistent pressure for the freedom of printers to pursue their economic interest.

Free press, free market

The battle to establish the economic interests of private press owners was not only fought on economic grounds. In the nineteenth century, the press put itself forward as an estate representative of a distinct set of interests, in the sense that it represented the distinct set of interests of one group of the body politic. That group was the general public, the people, or, as it might have been termed then, the 'common man', the other estates being the church, business, or landowners. The inherent contradiction between public service and private ownership was suppressed. The press won recognition as an estate in part because democratic ideals notwithstanding, the economic manifestations of these ideals were coincident with the economic interests of all owners of property. The interests and privileges requested by the press were in accordance with – and no more than – the generally accepted business theory and practice of the day. That theory, which still holds sway in capitalist countries, posits that individuals' pursuit of their economic self-interest will maximise the economic interests of the whole. The mechanism that leads to this happy confluence of interests is Adam Smith's theory of the 'invisible hand', named after the Scottish political economist who proposed it. The invisible hand guides individuals to pursue a societal need through each responding to a self-interested, economic opportunity.

The press asked for nothing more than any other business. But in dealing with information, which even during the Industrial Revolution was recognised as somehow different from other commodities, the press found it prudent to fight (and win) in public on idealistic, non-economic grounds, that is to say, the pursuit of free speech.

The public role in broadcasting

Broadcasting built on the foundations that had been laid by the press. However, there was a major difference between the two media: the public participation in ownership of broadcasting. Public (that is, government) involvement in broadcasting was a response to at least five factors. First was the legacy of free press ideals, the degree to which the press had been able to provide a vehicle for the voices and aspirations of the people. Second was the scarcity of the radio spectrum. Although inexhaustible (it cannot be used up), it is finite – it has space for only a certain number of stations. Third was the technology-created chance to design a whole new system of communication with a knowledge of the contributions and shortcomings of the press. Fourth was the established traditions of the British and other civil services, specifically working for the public good under the principles of political impartiality and neutrality. Fifth were the capitalistic instincts of Guglielmo Marconi. As the first person to transmit intelligence electronically from one point to another without the use of connecting wires, Marconi was in a good position to exploit his position. His methods for doing so – through patents, leasing rather than selling his equipment, and controlling who operated his equipment – allowed Marconi to create for himself a virtual international monopoly of the airwaves. The nations of the world were able to break his monopoly by declaring the airwaves to be a public resource. They were then able – and were to some extent forced – to regulate the airwaves.

Once in the business of regulation, governments needed to identify a guiding principle. That principle was that the airwaves should be regulated for the general public good. This notion of the public good seems to be both an extension of the notion of the press as the fourth estate and a twentieth-century articulation of an eighteenth-century notion of the democratic ideal.

In the eighteenth century, the democratic ideal was expressed as the emancipation of the individual from the constraints of elites in society through the granting of such rights as free speech. The media derivative was a free press acting as a fourth estate. The twentieth-century notion of the democratic ideal was expressed as the emancipation of social action from the excessive influence of both state and market through enlightened legislation, the power of landowners and the church having faded. The broadcast media derivative was a neutral and impartial public-sector organisation operating at arm's length from both the government and business guided by culturally-mandated legislation and a socially-representative board of directors.

The early years of broadcasting brought forth public broadcasting institutions. But private businesses, especially in the United States, applied continuous pressure to be allowed to exploit the airwaves for their interests. They argued, like the press had before them, that market theory (Adam Smith's invisible hand) would ensure that the general public good was best served by the profit-seeking behaviour of individual businesses. In the US they won the day. In Europe, until recently, private business was precluded from owning broadcasting undertakings or, as happened in Canada, was allowed to do so alongside public institutions. The contemporary trend in all countries is toward increased private-sector involvement.

Public-sector media ownership

A number of different forms of ownership have evolved in media institutions. On the public side are organisations, associations and corporations differently reflective of the plurality of their societies. On the private or commercial side are enterprises which are stand-alone entities (although this is rare), or are enterprises variously connected to other corporations. We will first examine public ownership and then take up private or commercial ownership.

Public enterprise has a long and distinguished tradition in every Western country. Its most common use has been in instances when a national social need was clearly identifiable yet a market was not organised or seemed incapable of adequately serving the needs of the country. In communications the setting up of national broadcasting services such as the BBC is the classic example. State education, postal and health services are others.

Public ownership of the broadcast media has followed in this tradition. Its general purpose was to bring information and entertainment, images and symbols reflective of the diversity of the country and of the world to the greatest number of citizens as possible. The social value was that the audience might generally benefit from such exposure and, in certain countries, that compatriots might see themselves as members of a single nation.

The ethic of public enterprise

The central ethic of the public corporation, as we have noted, is connected to the democratic ideal. More specifically it is to provide a public service to both the users of the service provided and to the population as a whole. Under such an ethic, charges are sometimes levied for services rendered, and at other times costs are paid for through general government revenues. In still other instances, revenue raised by general taxes is combined with user fees. On the consumer's side, user fees are often determined in part by what others must pay and in part by how much the service actually costs. For example, while rural users often pay more for telephone services they do not pay the full amount of the additional costs to bring in the service. In this way an attempt is made to provide universal and equitable access.

A public service ethic also means that the object of public corporations is not to demonstrate the existence of a market or pursue profit while trying to serve the public purpose. In most countries profit-making by publicly-owned corporations is forbidden and in some others certain or all public media corporations are prevented from accepting advertising. These restrictions exist to ensure that the public corporation is not compromised in its ability to serve the public purpose by its need to seek revenue. It also guards against all-out competition between the public and private sectors for advertising income.

Public service means that economics is only one factor to be considered in an overall equation. The other major element of the equation is determining the public interest, not in a unitary or authoritarian fashion but in a way that reflects the many and varied interests and viewpoints that are part of any society. (See McQuail (1991) for a recent attempt at outlining the public interest in the context of media performance.) This public-interest ethic or approach means that while the central concern of private or commercial media outlets is to attract audiences and sponsors, the publicly-owned outlet must weigh its public service mandate – such as appealing to all ages and people in all locations, or training top-level journalists – against economic reality. The public corporation can consider, on the merit of the case itself, whether it will carry children's programmes without advertising, develop socially-oriented programmes for the poor, or underwrite programmes for the aged. Having made the decision, it must then find the means to carry that decision through.

Forms of public ownership

Historically speaking, the characteristic West European model of broadcasting ownership is a national public monopoly. Its organisation and finances may be controlled by the state but it is fairly independent from government in its programme policies. The original BBC model was adopted by France, Italy and the Scandinavian countries, and was also the dominant element in many other West European countries as well as in Australia and New Zealand, Africa and the Indian sub-continent. In Belgium and Switzerland, like Canada, each linguistic group has its own BBC-type broadcasting service. In West Germany, where the states or *Länder* are responsible for broadcasting, a number of regional monopolies come together to form the national networks (Rolland and Østbye, 1986).

The UK and Greece have moved to a duopoly – one public monopoly and one private monopoly – with the UK now moving well beyond that with increased private-sector participation and authorisation of satellite channels. Finland's national broadcaster (YLE) sells time to a private company. The latter finances its programmes by selling commercials. In Italy, the national broadcasting monopoly, Radio televisione Italiana (RAI), a joint-stock company controlled by the government, has been broken by means of a burgeoning increase in local stations, subsequently formed into a national network composed of many local stations, although technically not carrying the same programmes at the same time and therefore not a network. In Norway, although a legal monopoly exists for the national broadcasting company NRK, many local commercial stations have been approved by the government. In Sweden, while the possibility for several broadcasting companies exists in legislation, a formal agreement protected by civil law has been signed between the state broadcasting company and the government, giving it a monopoly.

Generally speaking, the nature of the organisation and operation of the national broadcasting company reflects the fundamental characteristics and concerns of the country. Thus in the Netherlands, the traditional pillars of society – religious groups and political parties – are represented in separate, independent broadcasting organisations co-ordinated by the Dutch Broadcasting Foundation, NOS. The *étatisme* or state involvement of the French government in cultural fields is represented in its highly centralised structure of broadcasting, which exists alongside a concern for regionalism. The British broadcasting system reflects Civil Service ideals of impartiality and neutrality. Similarly, multilinguality is reflected in Belgium, Switzerland and Norway by means of programmes in more than one language. German regionalism, re-emphasised by the Allies in the post-war years, has led to a regionally-based system and a great debate over whether plurality from within (the differing beliefs and approaches of journalists) allows greater freedom of speech than plurality from without (a multiplicity of owners), especially in the context of a commercially-dominated system with its constant search for the largest audience.

The dynamics of cultural identity also play a major role in the design of broadcasting systems. Regional cultural identity is important to Norway as well as Germany and France. National cultural identity is predominant as a concern in Italy, the Netherlands, France, Finland and Denmark. The French have seen themselves as bastions against Anglo-Saxon or English-language imperialism. Italy has expressed its concerns in terms of 'cultural colonisation'. Each of these countries has established quotas governing national and imported content. Denmark and Finland have favoured importation from a variety of countries over quotas to keep foreign content from overwhelming national culture. Diversity has been a main concern in Germany, the Netherlands, Norway, Finland, Sweden and Italy. However, where access by organised minority groups is somewhat restricted in Germany it is definitely facilitated in Italy, Finland, Norway and Denmark (Bakke, 1986).

The play of various pressure groups is also reflected in national broadcasting systems. Religious groups make their influence felt in the Netherlands, Norway and Sweden; ethnic groups in Italy and Spain; cultural-ideological groups in the Netherlands and Norway; linguistic groups in Belgium, Finland, Norway and Sweden; geographical groups in France, Norway and Germany; and private companies and trade unions in Finland.

In North America, the broadcasting systems of the US and Canada can be seen in the same context. Canada's system, with its mixture of public and private elements, is an attempt to deal with bilinguality, multiculturalism, the size of the country and its low population density, regionality, its proximity to and hence vulnerability to overspill of programmes from the US, its concern for a national identity and its roots in Europe. The US system, predominantly commercial in character, with a small but important education-oriented Public Broadcasting Service (PBS), reflects the dominance of commercial and free speech values in that society.

Among the variety of these ownership forms, the public-interest ethic has been dominant. However, in recent years these state monopolies have been and are being challenged by aggressive American and Luxembourgian free-speech-based private sector or commercial entrepreneurship, the use of cable and satellite technology and a predominance of programming for target markets of young people with disposable income and people looking for entertainment rather than enlightenment. Luxembourg is involved in this competition because companies are able to set up in Luxembourg under a very permissive regulatory regime and then broadcast to the whole of Europe.

Private-sector media ownership: the private enterprise ethic

The general ethic of the private or commercial media outlet is long-term profit-making. The corporation is responsible to its shareholders to do just that. Privately-owned commercial companies, that is, those not publicly listed on a stock exchange or privately-controlled companies, have more freedom. The only other circumstance in which a commercial company does not have to prioritise profit-making is under regulatory insistence. Otherwise, a company not aggressively pursuing profit makes itself vulnerable to take-over. For regulatory insistence on serving the public interest to work, it must coexist with the need of such companies to make a profit, otherwise such companies will simply not abide by the regulations. For example, cable companies can be encouraged to keep their equipment upgraded by allowing them to recover half the cost of equipment upgrading through subscription fees. This means the public effectively pays half the cost for any installation of fibre-optic cable by a private corporation. While such an installation may marginally increase picture quality and channel capacity, it also, incidentally, makes the company more competitive with telephone companies in carrying long-distance signals and increases its net worth. Because cable companies are monopolies, the consumer has no choice but to ride with the ambitions of both government and industry in technological development.

Policy directed at the production and display of high-quality national content programming has had varying success from country to country. This is essentially because only in certain countries have governments and industry been able to identify mechanisms that simultaneously encourage high-quality national content and either increase or maintain profits. Until the late 80s Canada could be cited as an example of a country in which the private sector could not be persuaded by any form of policy to pursue the development and sale of high-quality, nationally oriented programmes. In contrast, the UK has been successful, and, arguably, Australia has been somewhere in between. The status of the UK as a centre of English-speaking peoples, the articulation of the notion of the public interest, and the concomitant role of export markets has contributed greatly to the ability of the UK private sector to produce such high-quality programming.

In spite of its limited abilities to pursue cultural goals, the private sector is making continuous gains in its participation in media industries, especially in broadcasting. Its success appears to be attributable to three factors. One is a general correction that is going on in developed economies. In the post-war years developed countries followed one element of Keynesian economics, that is, state spending to encourage economic growth. However, even when periods of boom were underway, Western states did not stop spending, perhaps in anticipation of greater booms. The result was that many nations saddled themselves with potentially crippling debt, and with what some regard as over-generous welfare programmes. A general trend in Western countries from the early 80s has been to look for areas of state expenditure that can be cut. Publicly-owned media has been one area where public spending has been cut and an expansion of services has been realised through increased private participation.

The second reason that the private sector has been able to make substantial inroads into broadcasting and other electronic media is that the broadcasting industry has come of age. Public (and existing private) corporations have demonstrated through their functioning which audiences can be served by what means to make what level of profit. Programme types, employee levels, working relationships and so forth have all been established. The knowledge infrastructure now exists and can be transferred to new firms through the hiring of qualified personnel.

Thirdly, new technologies – specifically communications satellites – have been developed that challenge the ability and legitimacy of states to control electronic communication. When a signal from outer space can deliver pro-grammes to all homes in a country, in the context of international covenants affirming the freedom to receive information, what should the state's position be? In the face of insistent requests from the private sector to be allowed to engage in profit-making activity that can serve a market, if not a public good, it is difficult for states to claim that cultural goals directly contradict such activities. This is especially the case in the presence of technology able to facilitate such activities. If audiences watch, limited in enlightenment though many commercial programmes may be, cultural content is being transmitted. There are also basic human rights that come into play, specifically the right of an individual to receive information.

Forms of private ownership

The single enterprise

The single enterprise is a business form in which control rests with a group of shareholders, or perhaps a single owner, who do not represent other related companies. Examples of this form of ownership were plentiful in the early days of newspapers and broadcasting, and such firms are still a major feature of the book and magazine industries. However, they are fading in some countries much faster than others due to laws that fail to protect their continued existence in the face of larger enterprises that are always looking to add more properties to their stable.

Horizontal integration: the chain

The second major type of firm is the linked company or chain. A chain is a group of similar companies, for example, a group of cable companies, radio stations or newspapers would constitute a chain. Chains can also be described as horizontally integrated: the links do not buy or sell to or from one another but are a number of enterprises, usually in different locations, doing the same business. Such companies achieve efficiencies or economies of scale by sharing resources, such as columnists, programmes, advertising departments and so forth.

Vertical integration

Another form of linkage is through vertical integration, in which companies under the same owner supply and consume each other's products. Thus when telephone companies purchase from equipment companies owned (or controlled) by the same group of investors, or when a major newspaper owns a newsprint supplier, such companies could be said to be vertically integrated.

Cross-media ownership

A further type of linkage more closely associated with horizontal than vertical integration is cross-ownership or cross-media ownership. Cross-ownership of media companies refers to companies that own more than one type of media company, for example, more than one of a television station, a radio station, a newspaper, a magazine publisher, a book publisher, a cable company, or a telephone company, in one specific market. Cross-media ownership is the form most often legislated against in broadcasting legislation. This effectively prevents firms from controlling access to information through a number of different channels.

The conglomerate

The last type of linked ownership is the conglomerate, which combines a variety of linkages, usually inclusive of horizontally and vertically integrated companies and sometimes cross-ownership of companies that operate in different markets. Two types of conglomerates can be distinguished, the media conglomerate and a more general or non-media conglomerate. The media conglomerate does the majority of its business in the media; the general or non-media conglomerate has its foundations in non-media firms. For example, the Thomson corporation is first a media conglomerate but also has holdings in other fields such as travel and retailing (see Table 3).

Trends in ownership form

A strong trend in ownership of media companies is the buying up of small companies by larger companies. This is leading, quickly rather than slowly, to increased corporate concentration in the media and, as a result, to

TABLE 3   *The holdings of some major media corporations*

Company	Principal activities	Employees	Finance
The News Corp. CEO Rupert Murdoch	Newspaper, magazine and book printing and publishing in Australia US, UK, Asia, China Radio, television and film operations and production (e.g. Fox and BSkyB) Information, research, data securities, couriers, data communications	approx. 30,700	Net profit 1990 A$343,305,000 Total assets A$25,000,000,000
The Thomson Corporation CEO Ken Thomson	Newspaper printing and publishing Specialised information services and professional publishing Financial services Leisure and commercial travel	approx. 45,800	Net income US$292,000,000 Total assets 1991 US$8,166,000,000
Bertelsmann AG	Over 75 book and record clubs, publisher and direct mail marketers, trade & professional markets, periodicals, encyclopedias, maps and atlases in Germany, UK, Canada, US, Switzerland, Spain, Netherlands, Italy, Belgium, New Zealand, France and Australia Music, film, television Printing and manufacturing: over 20 companies, mostly in Germany and in Europe Music and video: over 16 companies in North America, Europe, Japan Electronic Media: 23 companies, mostly in Germany Gruner and Jahr	approx. 45,100	Net income DM 510,000,000 Total assets 1990 DM 7,209,000,000
Time Warner Inc.	Publishing magazines and books Music production, distribution and copyrights Entertainment production and distribution: film and television, video cassettes, pay TV, cable and cable programming	approx. 44,000	Net income 1992 US$86,000,000 Total assets US$27,366,000,000

Source: Moody's International Manual (1993), Moody's Investment Services, New York.

oligopolistic practices. When ownership within an industry shifts increasingly to the hands of the few rather than the many, the emergent business structure is said to have an increasing degree of corporate or ownership concentration. Corporate concentration in any single industry, such as the media, arises through horizontal integration, that is, a combination of chain ownership and cross-ownership. The resulting situation is that a small number of conglomerates assume a national or international presence as information and entertainment providers. It also means that in some locations, all media are owned by one of the few corporations and it is the rare (and often outlying) location where at least one medium is not owned by one of the prevailing few companies. Most markets are affected in some way or other by these dominant few. Industry in general is said to be concentrated when horizontal integration is combined with vertical integration. The media industries are thus dominated by relatively few large corporations.

The means by which corporations can be linked are both symptoms and causes of further concentration. Linkages may exist among holding companies and subsidiaries, through stock options, insider holdings, convertible shares and interlocking directorships, as well as control over nominee accounts and blocks of shares. The four companies listed in Table 3 are all good examples of interlinked conglomerates. Bertelsmann's empire in the United States alone in 1991 comprised Bantam Doubleday Dell Publishing (publishing hardcover, mass market and trade paperback books of general fiction and non-fiction for adults and young readers), which included Doubleday & Company Inc., Doubleday Book Shops, Inc., The Trumpet Club (a juvenile book club), Laidlaw Brothers (school textbooks and other educational materials), Dell Publishing, and Doubleday Books and Music Club; Bertelsmann Printing & Manufacturing Corp., which included firms involved in paperback reprinting and binding, directory publishing, book printing and binding, and book cover decorating; Bertelsmann Music Group, which included Arista Records Inc. (a record manufacturer), BMG/Music (which internationally manufactures and markets records and tapes, and manages a record and tape club) and RCA Records US (with operations similar to BMG/Music in the US).

Why does corporate concentration arise? The accompanying cartoon presents one version of events. It is usually assumed that corporate expansion is stimulated by the expectation of greater efficiency. The first type of efficiency is derived from a greater number of companies doing the same thing under one overall owner (i.e. horizontal integration). The knowledge and organisation necessary to the operation already exist and can be repeatedly applied from firm to firm.

The second type of efficiency derives from cutting suppliers and those whom one supplies out of the market by becoming supplier and end-product producer oneself. If an owner can buy from another company he already

Source: The Financial Post, 4 July 1988. Reproduced by permission of the artist, Ed Franklin.

owns and sell to a third he owns as well, then nobody but the one owner makes a profit. In addition, because the one owner knows the needs of one business and the output of another, the former is assured of continuous supply while the latter is assured of a known and reliable market. There is no need for a vast sales department, or for the continuous processing of competitive bids from suppliers. Vertical integration is thus another level of efficiency, and profits can be divided amongst companies for the greatest tax advantage come tax collection time.

Efficiency may be the main reason for growing concentration, but a number of other reasons are no less significant.

1 *High profit levels.* Information, communications and entertainment are all growth industries that are benefiting from new products, new technologies and new means of distribution. Communication products, for example old movies, television series and books, have a long shelf life; run-on production costs, such as movie prints, are low, and new markets are continually emerging as standards of living creep upwards in the developing world and free flow of information is maintained. The common base profit level for cable companies in Canada is 24 per cent. Newspapers that are monopolies in their own geographic area regularly turn profits higher than that. The emergence of global media companies, the vast majority of which began after World War II, is also evidence of high profits.

2 *Growth for its own sake and borrowing power.* Established large corporations are in a good position to expand. On the basis of increasing volume of business and high profit levels, companies have access to loans of working capital that may exceed present operating needs. Once they have stabilised the operations of their acquisitions and marginally reduced their debt through revenue, they are welcomed back to the acquisition trail by financial institutions. The cartoon on page 89, complete with the smiling faces of the board members, nicely captures the happy position of such companies.

   With regard to borrowing power itself, a small company may not be able to borrow enough money to upgrade its physical plant in order to remain competitive or launch a new product. But frequently a larger company will buy out the smaller company, even paying a premium to the owner, and then will be successful in borrowing the needed funds. The necessity of borrowing for technological upgrading, expanding product lines, or expanding into foreign markets can all lead to corporate concentration.

3 *Buy-outs versus start-ups.* It is often easier and, for a number of reasons, cheaper for a company to buy an existing company than to build one up from the ground. Sometimes, just when an individual entrepreneur has brought an enterprise to the verge of real financial success, a conglomerate with the needed financial resources to provide the final expansion or marketing will buy out the entrepreneur and subsequently reap the profits.

4 *Replacement of the rich.* People die, and shareholders are people. When shareholders die, their shares often come onto the market. When these holdings are large, often only large corporations can quickly organise the resources to take up the shares. Ownership thus becomes further concentrated.

5 *Small national clubs.* In some media, restrictions against foreign ownership lead to increased concentration of ownership. In broadcasting companies in most countries, foreign ownership is either restricted or limited to no more than 20 per cent. In the print media, tax legislation has been used to prevent foreign owners from acquiring control. Grant eligibility in areas such as book and magazine publishing can also discourage foreign ownership. The result is that new foreign owners are effectively prevented from entering the market-place. Each of these provisions, along with trends towards concentration of ownership, leads to the possibility of a relatively small national elite holding the bulk of media properties.

6 *Decreasing risk in a changing industry.* Large companies may also wish to buy into emerging industries because they represent potential competitors or outlets for products they are already producing. For

example, cinema chains and newspapers were early investors in cable television and broadcasting. In both cases these technologies represented new competition. The activities of Japanese companies, specifically Sony, in buying up software (CBS Records and Columbia Pictures) and, predictably, distribution companies, to add to their hardware manufacturing and retail holdings is not buying up the competition but rather vertically integrating on a scale rarely seen before the 1990s. Itoh, Toshiba and Matsushita have made similar acquisitions. The new twist in this level of integration is that such companies now – or will shortly – control enough that they can demand that consumers acquire certain hardware formats in order to have access to certain entertainment and information, much as the Nintendo company does on a smaller scale with its machines and games. Similar examples, although not quite on the scale of these Japanese companies, abound. Large companies regularly buy up small media producers, run them for a while as separate entities and then fold them into larger competing operations. This is happening as much in book publishing companies as in the electronic media.

7 *Media ownership as status and as an ideological vehicle.* Roy Thomson acquired *The Times* and the *Sunday Times* for reasons of status and for much the same reason his son, Ken, was able to sell them to Rupert Murdoch. Two Canadian newspaper magnates, Roy Thomson and Max Aitken, gained peerages becoming Lord Thomson of Fleet and Lord Beaverbrook. Other British-born press lords – Rothermere, Hartwell and Stevens, owner of the *Daily Mail*, former owner of *The Daily Telegraph* and Chairman of Express Newspapers respectively – have faired equally well in acquiring or inheriting status from press ownership. *The Daily Telegraph*'s new owner, Conrad Black, combines a pursuit of status with the promotion of ideology. To further his ideological aims, Black contemplated purchasing the perennially money-losing Canadian magazine *Saturday Night* as long ago as 1973. At that time he was consulting with American conservative ideologue William F. Buckley, Jr. on the possibility of turning it into a right-wing magazine of political commentary to, in his words, 'convert an existing Canadian magazine into a conveyance for views at some variance with the tired porridge of ideological normalcy in vogue here as well as the U.S.A.' (Newman, 1982, p. 183). Black has described the media as 'an industry like the others, though more profitable than most, and *more strategic than any*' (emphasis added) (*Financial Post*, 19 May 1988, p. 14).

8 *Shaking out the industry.* Many new industries begin with copious quantities of small marginal businesses. For example, many independent operators leapt into the video rental business in the mid-80s. Once consumer behaviour had become predictable, the large operators, with greater access to capital, stepped in and grabbed the lion's share of the

market. Many of the independent operators who survived became franchise holders in chains.

9 *Media regulation*. Regulation contributes to increased concentration in media industries in a variety of ways. Setting profit levels high allows room for corporate growth and the purchase of the weaker by the stronger to the net financial gain of both, but with little or no gain to the consumer. Lack of control of funds-transfers between non-regulated and regulated companies owned by the same entity allows profits to be transferred in and out of the regulated company to the best advantage of the owner. The lack of control over the selling price of a company may lead to a buyer paying, let's say, twice as much as the company is really worth. The buyer can then go to the regulator with a request for rate increases to allow for a reasonable rate of return on investment, for example, 20 per cent. The buyer requests 20 per cent of the price paid, not the net worth of the company as evaluated by, for instance, an independent tribunal. Thus the buyer can pass the unwise debt he has incurred, and the need for profit, on to the consumer. The consumer may end up paying twice as much for services as he/she might under a system of competition. Granting such requests can also lead to concentration because it allows companies to pay unwarranted prices with impunity. The buying and selling of broadcast licences, allowed in some countries but not in others, also can contribute to increased corporate concentration.

On the opposite side of the coin, regulation and other government action can be used to restrict or slow ownership concentration. Ownership can be restricted to regional operations, as happens in the electronic media in Germany. Operating subsidies can be provided to non-dominant media outlets, as happens in Norway and Sweden with newspapers. Advertising revenue can be diverted from one medium to another, as happens in the Netherlands with television revenue being diverted to newspapers. A variety of distribution and production subsidies can be used for print or electronic publications as happens in France. In short, a variety of mechanisms to restrict ownership concentration can be put in place.

10 *Competition policy*. It is difficult to show that the public interest is harmed unless a monopoly exists across all media in one location. There are enough factors other than their monopoly positions that influence the behaviour of media outlets to be able to show that a monopoly does not necessarily lead to decreased journalistic quality. And journalistic quality is a very difficult concept to define in a court of law. Rarely has precipitous action been taken on media concentration in any country in spite of numerous commissions and inquiries. In part this is because while per cent share of market is often higher than economists generally deem to be

desirable, in terms of absolute size in the wider world of business, media companies do not stand out as giants among pygmies.

Implications of commercial ownership

The commercial or private-sector corporation exists in a different world from that of the public corporation. Private corporations exist to make a profit. They perform a service in order to remain in business so that they can generate wealth for their owners. There are two major perceived social benefits of private enterprise. The first is that, by virtue of Adam Smith's invisible hand, needed, desired and affordable services are stimulated into being by economic opportunity. Second, because in some cases communication services are advertiser-supported, they are 'free' to the consumer, for example television and radio programmes in North America, where there are no licence fees.

The prospect of a single independent media corporation operating a newspaper or a television or radio station, or publishing magazines or books, is not at all an unusual or unpleasant one. In all likelihood, the scale of operations is such that the owner lives in the community, is anxious for the development of the community and attempts to provide a service to the community while seeking to make a profit. As with any independent operator of a business, their social outlook is likely to reflect their economic interests. One would not expect to find stories denigrating the owner or the owner's close associates in the company's productions, even if they were managed by employees. One would learn to allow for these biases, which could be tolerated as long as they remained within the pale. Given the present state of the media – newspapers, magazines, radio, television, movies, sound recordings and books – one might never feel constrained by either the information or the entertainment provided by one media outlet. About the only unknown, given the present state of media industries and ignoring the spectre of a possible takeover for the moment, is the degree to which the owner might feel it necessary to purchase professional advice, for example on material and formats, from outside. That is, if the firm was a heavy user of the various consultancy firms that now exist to advise on nearly every aspect of the design of information services, the community character of the firm might be submerged in, for instance, its desire to employ the latest tricks for maximising audiences.

The multi-enterprise media corporation

Once we leave the environment of the independent media corporation and enter the world of companies related in ownership to other media and non-media companies, the whole scene, save the pursuit of profit, changes. Taboo subjects are extended to all the business affairs of the owning entity. The media company will ease the business atmosphere for the non-media company as much as it can without being charged with undue bias. Vertical relations also come into play in a simple media/non-media association. For example, advertising can be sold within the company at a price that minimises taxes for the company as a whole. The newspaper holdings of the Thomson Corporation and the advertising of the various retail and travel companies Thomson also owns are a good case in point. The former owner of Columbia Pictures, Coca-Cola, continuously plugged its products in movie after movie put out by Columbia (Miller, 1990).

Conglomerate relations

When the simple association of media and non-media companies is extended into a reasonably sized conglomerate, the potential extension of self-censorship and insider financial relations extends to at least the same extent. What employee journalists find themselves able to talk about, what potential favouritism exists in advertising rates and placement, what potential abuse there is for tailoring soft news items to the travel and business interests of the conglomerate – all become major items of concern, not only for employees but also for the public and, in the case of broadcasting, for the regulator.

It might appear from this discussion that a conglomerate-owned news-paper is nothing but a propaganda tool for its sister companies. 'Nothing but' is too strong, but there is little doubt that media corporations advance the broad interests of all of their owners' activities. On numerous occasions owners use the considerable platform of their media companies to promote their own interests and ideas. Rupert Murdoch and Conrad Black are contemporary examples, as was Robert Maxwell. Others are shyer and have journalists write their thoughts or put forward their ideas in unsigned editorials or under pseudonyms. Three good sources for gaining an understanding of the role of press and media owners are biographies, journalists' memoirs, and company histories.

Conglomerate journalism

In an environment increasingly dominated by media-related and non-media-related conglomerates, there is good reason to discourage in-depth investigative reporting. Media conglomerates have joined other global corporations, and as a group these are portrayed by their owners and managers as the harbingers of all things bright and beautiful. Investigative reporting into the unseemly behaviour or power trading of members of the global club or even into the business community as a whole is inconvenient at best and undermining at worst. In the environment of the conglomerates, journalists are encouraged to create a complementary visual and ideological environment for advertised commercial products. While such writing falls short of being an advertorial (sometimes also called an informercial), it is certainly far from seeking after truth in the name of the public. Even journalists charged specifically with attending to the interests of the public are vulnerable to the softening of news values, in some quarters called the McNews syndrome, especially in monopoly markets. The word 'McNews' derives from the fast-food chain McDonalds, where quick and formula-prepared bland fare is offered to the customer.

Journalists and other content producers working within a media conglomerate are well rewarded for their efforts. It may be a long way down to the average journalist from the seven-figure salaries of the news anchors on the US networks, but once such a person has established him or herself in the market, the process of bargaining for a salary takes on the flavour of any other entertainment media personality's negotiations.

A conglomerate, whether of media companies or otherwise, allows for so-called economies of scale. A conglomerate such as the Mirror Group, for example, can employ a columnist and use him or her throughout the conglomerate for a fraction of the cost and arguably produce better-quality content. Managerial techniques successful in one location can also be adopted throughout the conglomerate, as can promotional strategies, special features and the like. Once one radio station in a group finds a successful formula all the costs of the research and development can be amortised through the company as a whole, and other stations in the conglomerate can adopt it with only fine tuning. Similarly, the bargaining position of a television network is much stronger than a single independent station. Such factors minimise costs. Finally, managers as well as managerial techniques can be transferred from paper to paper or station to station. With a conglomerate there are opportunities for advancement within the company, a situation that encourages company loyalty rather than journalistic integrity.

Service to the consumer

Media companies would argue that any economies of scale that can be achieved mean a higher level of service to the consumer. No single paper, for example, could afford to hire the number of columnists which any member of a conglomerate offers readers. On the surface, these economies and qualitative improvements are not to be denied, but McCormack (1983) has argued that the pursuit of such economies distances newspapers from their traditional readership.

In another area, book retailing, independent bookstores provide a wide range of books from the classics to the contemporary for their clients. The chains tend to stock fast-selling items that are given limited shelf-life, depending on their computer-monitored sales. The cultural values of the two types of stores are vastly different. In Britain, even given the up-market orientation of Dillons and the general market orientation of W. H. Smith, it is not possible to maintain a vibrant national literary community through the marketing practices of the chains. In North America the chains are clearly mass-market vehicles quite insensitive to the maintenance of a literary culture.

Monopoly control

The central issue of corporate concentration is monopoly control. The two types of monopoly are 'natural' monopoly and effective monopoly. Economists and policy-makers define a 'natural' monopoly, if one can ever be said to exist, as the result of limited technology. They apply the word 'natural' to indicate that competition cannot exist in the long run except by duplication of facilities. A licensing and regulatory structure is put in place to substitute for competition. The monopoly ensures that by avoiding duplication the greatest number of households can be serviced for the lowest cost. Telephone and hydroelectric companies are often natural or regulated monopolies.

An effective monopoly, rather than being granted to a company by government, is gained by a company buying up or establishing companies that have total control over the market in which they operate, that is, all significant competitors have vanished. In media, the combination of radio, television and newspapers can provide a company with an effective media monopoly in a certain locale. In other, more common, instances, one company may have a newspaper or television monopoly but not a media monopoly. Monopolies are being weakened by the communications satellite. Communications satellites are now being used to distribute both newspapers and television nationally and internationally.

In markets with monopolies, now the common situation for newspapers, the monopoly owner completely controls what news is covered, how it is covered, the ratio of advertising to news and the slant taken on the news, that is, analytic and informative or sensational. The threats to such a monopoly are the possible alienation of its audience and the remote possibility of some other company taking a run at its market. The monopolist is also constrained to some degree by the other media in the same market, provided that it does not own those media outlets.

The role of 'other media' is considerable and is increasing. With regard to newspapers, the presence of weeklies, magazines, and national and international papers constrains the worst monopoly practices. In broadcasting, the multiplicity of radio and television stations available by cable, broadcast and satellite also restricts monopoly practices to a degree.

Alienation is a very real threat to the monopolist, for the readership or audience is what the company sells to advertisers. It would be a mistake, however, to assume that media outlets are continually seeking ways to enhance the informative value of their product and thus please their audiences. More often they attempt to capture the audience with anything that works and is not too costly to produce, such as game shows. The advertorial is also a case in point. An advertorial is a piece of writing undertaken by an employee of, let's say, the Port Authority of Liverpool, which describes (in glowing terms) the services of the port. While informative it also puts everything in the best light, appearing to be a piece of journalism while it is really a soft form of advertising. It fills the 'news space' in that it is not advertising in the normal sense. Because it is not advertising, it costs the advertiser nothing for placement. And because it is not written by a journalist, the generation of the content costs the paper nothing. Everyone gains, except journalists and readers.

Polling is also beginning to take its toll. Through the years media outlets have often acted as social antennae, bringing emerging issues to the attention of the community, whereas sagging audience figures are now often addressed with polls of the tastes and attitudes of the audience. Using such polls tends to turn the media into reactive rather than proactive entities, hence contributing more to a stagnation in community values than to their growth.

The threat of an emergent competitor is minimal, because the conglomerate-linked company has the financial resources to withstand any kind of circulation or ratings war. However, the establishment of community newspapers, which are often give-away vehicles for advertising and are sometimes down-market tabloids, has provided a platform, minimal though it might be, for potential competition for established middle-of-the-road newspapers. The drawback with the emergence of such competition is that its commitment to journalism and information is far less than the traditional newspaper.

The larger social issue of corporate concentration

If the corporate barons become too powerful, the people may lose control of their economic destiny. Corporate chief executives are not responsible to the public except in a very indirect fashion. If they form too powerful a class for any government to control, then no one can force them to live up to their public responsibilities. Such a concentration of control may lead to social and cultural instability (Hatter, 1985).

A highly concentrated media industry also leads to a narrowing of perspective. This is not because journalists become narrow-minded but because news is generated by fewer sources at the international, national, regional and local levels. Economic recession leads to faster concentration, while expanding economies may generate information renewal in the form of all kinds of small companies producing the Western equivalent to *samizdat*, or an underground or alternative press.

If there is any certainty in the behaviour of governments with regard to media concentration it would appear to be as follows. When governments feel threatened or helpless in getting the information they want to the public they begin to take steps to control further expansion. Thus the public interest is replaced by the interests of the government. This is not the healthiest state of affairs but perhaps one step short of allowing business a free hand to control completely the dissemination of ideas in society. In other words, it would appear that a political will exists to resist monopoly power at the level where the power of private capital threatens political power.

Private media ownership, Cases I and II: the brilliant careers of Axel Springer and Leo Kirch

In Europe in the years immediately following World War II, the Allies, each in their own sector, attempted to set up a broadcasting system that would prevent a single party and a single person from ever dominating the media so absolutely as did Hitler and the National Socialists. In Germany, the BBC's public service model won the day against the French (state-oriented) and the American (commercially-oriented) systems. Plurality was further assured within the broadcasting system by the constitutional allocation of broadcasting powers to the states within Germany, the *Länder*. The Allies did the same in Japan, but with the Americans the dominant force, Japan ended up with a media system dominated by American commercial values and with a subordinate sector in the public-educational sphere modelled on the BBC, NHK (Nippon Hoso Kyokai).

The Allies attempted to introduce plurality into the newspaper business as well. Here the presence of American-style, free-wheeling, libertarian reportage and commentary opened up German journalism considerably. In terms of ownership, the control the Allies had over the granting of licences in the late 1940s ensured that no large player emerged during that time. But as the controls were lifted, Axel Springer, the Rupert Murdoch of post-war Germany, burst onto the scene, building his papers by formula and extending his ownings through acquisitions.

Axel Springer's (1912–85) first publication was the *Altoner Nachrichten*, a modest periodical established by his printer-father. During the Nazi regime the publication was closed down and the print works bought out. In the post-war era, in the British-controlled zone of Germany, Springer was able to obtain three licences for different publications, no mean feat in a time of severe paper shortages. His first two publications were oriented to broadcasting, one a monthly critical review and the other, listings. Shortly after acquiring them, he took the critical journal down-market by focusing on the simple and the sensational, turning it into a bi-monthly called *Kristall*. About this time he launched his first daily newspaper, the *Hamburger Abendblatt*, and in 1953 purchased *Die Welt* from the British (Humphreys, 1990).

The success of the Springer papers was based on a more accessible journalism than had been customary in the German press. Traditionally, the German press was intellectual, heavy with reasoning, highly moralistic, culturally literate and philosophical. Springer papers were based on a calculated sentimentality, which portrayed ordinary people as good-hearted but sometimes misled. Above all, according to Springer himself, he helped the German people avoid reflection on their Nazi past (Brüseke and Grosse-Ötringhaus, 1981). The Springer formula was led by lurid headlines, a limited vocabulary and preoccupation with scandal. It was

> an anodyne mixture of entertainment, serialized novels, puzzles, horoscopes, local sections, the heavy use of clichés and generally 'big-city romanticism'. All events seemed to be reduced to anecdote, the human interest story now reigned supreme. Much of the content now focussed on human catastrophes and sensationalism. (Humphreys, 1990, p. 94)

It disarmed the press of its critical and objective function and demobilised the political press, paving the road to an affluent society and the German economic miracle with images.

Springer's political passion was to speak for the ordinary people or 'Volk'. He was closely connected to Konrad Adenauer, Chancellor of West Germany from 1949 to 1963, a paternalistic, highly conservative, semi-authoritarian man who himself attempted to gain control over a television network while Chancellor. Springer was militantly nationalist and anti-communist to the extent that he mounted a neon sign on top of his building in West Berlin that flashed 'Free Berlin Lives' continuously over the Wall at East Germans. His other political target was the German student left. *Bild-Zeitung*, one of Springer's newspapers, pictured the student leader Rudi Dutschke as a dangerous quasi-terrorist. A failed assassin of Dutschke in 1968 cited details of Springer newspaper commentaries that had inspired his attempt on the student leader's life. A well-known German investigative journalist, Günter Wallraff, infiltrated the *Bild-Zeitung* and concluded that the precarious employment conditions of many of its journalists played a powerful role in exerting 'editorial discipline' (Wallraff, 1977, p. 979). He also described the process of editorial filtering that distorted the reporters' original statements and found evidence of fabrication.

Springer was among a group of four publishers who formed a private commercial television satellite consortium (PKS) and gained control of a more largely held satellite communications operation called SAT 1. He also entered a partnership with the more socially liberal Bertelsmann group in a pay-TV company, Teleclub, operating in Hanover. By the 1990s the Axel Springer Group held approximately 28 per cent of the market for German daily newspapers. As Humphreys notes:

> the right-wing Axel Springer Verlag has long occupied a dominant and unchallenged position among the West German newspaper publishers. It enjoys near complete regional monopolies in Hamburg and West Berlin (86.4% and 71.4% respectively), and produces West Germany's most successful tabloid, the *Bild-Zeitung*, which has a circulation of over five million. [This is a highly sensational tabloid with an underlying philosophy that is militantly anti-socialist and illiberal in the extreme with a readership of approximately 10 million.] Moreover, the *Bild-Zeitung* alone dominates the West German market for 'Boulevardzeitungen' [street sales]. The Axel Springer Verlag also produces both of West Germany's national Sunday newspapers, the *Bild am Sonntag* and the *Welt am Sonntag*. In addition, the Axel Springer Verlag produces one of the country's best-known and most widely distributed 'national' ('*überregionale*') quality dailies, *Die Welt*, and its largest evening newspaper, the *Hamburger Abendblatt*. Other well known Springer papers are the Berlin *BZ* and *Berliner Morgenpost*. With holdings in many other papers and publishing houses, Axel Springer established one of the largest press empires in Western Europe, employing over 12,000 people and with an annual turnover in 1987 of around DM 2.7 billion.
>
> (1990, p. 85)

In addition to these vast holdings, the Springer group operates its own domestic and overseas news service, the *Springer Auslandsdienst* (SAD). It is in second place in the German market behind Heinrich Bauer Verlag (32 per cent share) for popular illustrated magazines, with a 13 per cent market share.

A prodigal son

Since Axel Springer died in 1985, with no obvious single heir, the film entrepreneur Leo Kirch appears to have been gaining control of the Springer holdings. At the time of Springer's death, three Burda brothers (of the Burda Group, another large West German print/media company) owned 24.9 per cent of the Springer shares. Springer's heirs inherited 26.1 per cent. Through a public sale of shares just before Springer's death, Leo Kirch acquired first 10 per cent then 20 per cent and, through intermediaries, apparently more than 26 per cent of Springer's holdings. Springer's heirs blocked a take-over by Kirch, but in 1988 Kirch countered by gaining control of PKS (Programmgesellschaft für Kabel und Satellilenrundfunk, originally a joint public-private-sector venture), which in turn was the largest single shareholder in SAT 1.

Prior to his run at Springer, Kirch's company Beta/Taurus was a major supplier of film, drawing on a vast archive, to the SAT 1, other private sector television operations, the public sector television channels, movie theatres and his own and his son's television companies. He is reported to have access to over 50,000 hours of film usable as television programmes, including 15,000 hours of feature films and numerous series. The value of these resources is estimated at DM 1 billion.

Case III: Silvio Berlusconi

In 1976 the Italian Constitutional Court declared the television monopoly held by the government-owned Radio televisione Italiana (RAI) illegal. This declaration legitimised many local stations and encouraged many more to begin broadcasting. Into this deluge marched Silvio Berlusconi, a real-estate and construction magnate. By 1980, through his company, Fininvest, he had acquired ownership of three national television networks, Canale-5, Italia-1 and Rete-4. (By 1990, the audience reach of these three networks was approximately equal to that of the national public broadcaster, RAI, which also controls three channels.) He then created four specialty channels, Italia-7, Junior TV, Capodistria and Sport. By 1984, he had acquired control of three more networks owned by three large publishing houses, Rizzoli, Ruscone and Montadori. For a short time in 1984 Berlusconi had to shut down his operations when the Italian courts declared national private tele-vision ownership illegal. However, within the week, Premier Craxi reversed the law. By 1987, the annual gross revenues of Berlusconi's holdings were US$8 billion.

Berlusconi's productions amount to 180 hours of television programmes per year and 70 theatrical or feature-length films, which play in his chain of theatres along with those he imports from the US. He is the country's largest importer of US films and owns Italy's largest advertising agency. Berlusconi may become vulnerable to anti-trust legislation, although his political con-tacts have previously served him in good stead. And two other challengers are in the wings, a partnership of Brazil's TV Globo with Fiat, and the much smaller Odeon TV. In addition, 300 rival television stations remain outside any network.

Berlusconi has made forays into other European countries, which may stand him in good stead as the European Community moves closer to one market. However, he has only been able to achieve minority shareholder positions and thus has also been considering the acquisition of Montadori, a major Italian publisher. In West Germany, Berlusconi owns 45 per cent of Kabel Media, a cable company that reaches 2.5 million homes, and 45 per cent of a major new channel, TELE 5. Apparently he has an agreement that will bring him access to Germany's transponder space on the Luxembourg-based Astra satellite. In France, he and Robert Hersant each own 25 per cent of La Cinq, a company that has failed to live up to the expectations of the French audience as a genuine alternative and failed to turn substantial profits for either of the two main shareholders. In Spain he owns 25 per cent of Gestevision-Telecino. In both France and Spain he unsuccessfully attempted to gain control of both companies from his 25 per cent holding base (Smith, 1991). Berlusconi also has holdings in Belgium, the Netherlands and Portugal.

Conclusion

The ownership of media corporations is a significant element in understanding the nature and operation of the media in modern society. Ownership involves the assembling and allocation of resources and thus a general ordering of priorities. It also reflects the faith that society places in those who are trusted with ownership. Ownership form, be it public, private, large or small, gives priority to certain goals and encourages certain types of allocations while discouraging others. Just as laws and policies provide a structure within which the media are integrated with society, so in the patterns of media ownership we can see one aspect of that integration.

The drift from public to private-sector ownership in combination with increasing size and conglomeratisation reflects the expansion of the market into a greater variety of activities, the increasing integration of national markets into larger groupings, and a set of laws and policies which encourages (to the point of carelessness, as Robert Maxwell amply demonstrated) the emergence of transnational players who are prepared to assemble resources and operate on a global scale. The long-term consequences of the dominance of this type of ownership form is unknown. However, through the expansion of technological capacity, it is already producing countertrends in some countries in the form of community-based and educationally-oriented regional owner/operators.

Summary

Capitalism or private ownership deals with relations between people and property in a manner that has a limited capacity to encompass the full potential of communication media in society. Yet private enterprise has come to own and control much of this cultural domain in Western society. While the press is almost entirely privately owned by commercial corporations, broadcasting has a mixture of public and private ownership. Satellites and cable, like the press, show a predominance of private ownership.

Public ownership rests on an ethic of serving the public interest. The goals and operations of public enterprise are legislated to bring information, entertainment, ideas and images that are salient to the political, cultural, societal and individual identities of audiences of a particular locale, region or country.

The goal of private owners is to make profits by selling audiences to advertisers. There are a variety of forms of private ownership and many are represented in media companies. However, the dominant business form in the mass media is the multi-enterprise conglomerate; the dominant industry structure is oligopoly. The predominance of this industry form has major implications for the generation and dissemination of content, as cultural objectives are suppressed.

In spite of an already high level of ownership concentration, forces leading to increased concentration are clearly identifiable. They include growth for its own sake, acquired borrowing power, the greater ease of buying a company over starting one from scratch, providing capital to financially strapped entrepreneurs, taking over large share blocks from the estates of the rich, diversification, and a nurturing legal, tax and regulatory framework. Little is being done in any country to combat continuing trends towards increased concentration, while entrepreneurs such as Berlusconi, Springer and Kirch amass great fortunes and considerable control over the ideas circulating in society.

References

Bakke, Marik (1986), 'Culture at stake' in Denis McQuail and Karen Siune (eds.), *New Media Politics, Comparative Perspectives in Western Europe*, Sage, London.

Brown, Allan (1986), *Commercial Media in Australia: Economics, Ownership, Technology, and Regulation*, University of Queensland Press, Brisbane.

Brüseke, F. and H.-M Grosse-Ötringhaus (1981), *Blätter von Unten: Alternativzeitungen in der Bundesrepublik Deutschland*, Verlag 2000 GmbH, Offenbach, p. 11 (cited in Humphreys).

Hatter, D. (1985), 'Corporate concentration: charmed circle still firmly in control', *Financial Post 500*, pp. 58–61.

Humphreys, Peter J. (1990), *Media and Media Policy in West Germany: The Press and Broadcasting since 1945*, Berg, New York.

McCormack, T. (1983), 'The political culture and the press in Canada', *Canadian Journal of Political Science*, 16(3), pp. 451–72.

McQuail, Denis (1991), 'Mass media in the public interest: towards a framework of norms for media performance' in James Curran and Michael Gurevitch (eds.), *Mass Media and Society*, Edward Arnold, London, pp. 68–81.

Miller, Mark Crispin (1990), 'Hollywood: the ad', *The Atlantic Monthly*, 265, pp. 41–68.

Newman, Peter C. (1982), *The Establishment Man*, McClelland and Stewart, Toronto.

Rolland, Asle and Helge Østbye (1986), 'Breaking the broadcasting monopoly' in Denis McQuail and Karen Siune (eds.), *New Media Politics: Comparative Perspectives in Western Europe*, Sage, London.

Smith, Anthony (1991), *The Age of Behemoths: The Globalization of Mass Media Firms*, Priority Press, New York.

Wallraff, G. (1977), *Der Aufmacher, Der Mann, der bei Bild Hans Esser war*, Verlag Kiepenhauer und Witsch, Cologne.

Wallraff, G. (1979), *Zevgen der Anklage: Dic 'Bild'-Beschreibung wird forgesetzt*, Verlag Kiepenhauer und Witsch, Cologne.

Chapter 5

The functions of journalists

As the people who actually produce information and entertainment, journalists and other media content producers are central to the whole media enterprise. In this chapter we examine the role of the professional journalists in some detail. We also take note, in less detail, of other media content producers. Interestingly, although so central to the medium, journalists commonly make up a mere 10 per cent of newspaper employees. Throughout this chapter, we will talk about print and electronic journalism, and unless stated otherwise, comments apply to both.

A professional profile

Journalists do not fully represent, in terms of their backgrounds, the various classes and groups of society; in general they are drawn from the middle class and, until recently, from the most numerous racial group in society. In developed countries they have the following characteristics:

- a higher level of education than the average person in society,
- more and more have professional training,
- the majority are young, in their 30s,
- there is a diminishing preponderance of men,
- print journalists are usually better educated than those in the electronic media, especially commercial radio,
- incomes are generally somewhat higher than the national average,
- many tend to leave the profession in their 40s and 50s for better paying jobs,
- the more highly educated, the more critical journalists are of their profession and their employers.

(Desbarats, 1990, pp. 88–93)

Some further context is revealing. Journalists tend to advance relatively quickly out of their basic role as reporters to become editors and columnists or, just as often, to leave journalism to work on the other side of the fence, for government or private enterprise as information officers. Presidents and prime ministers regularly lure journalists away from news outlets by doubling their salaries. Such jobs make good use of their skills. They involve designing and orchestrating information to be fed to the media. Knowing from their journalistic background what makes reporters pay attention, they design press releases, photo opportunities and leaks so that certain information is bound to be emphasised in the news. Journalists also find themselves able to move back and forth between government, private corporations and the media with relative ease. Such ease of movement illustrates the degree to which such institutions share the same basic viewpoint. It also illustrates a basic liberal pluralism to which many journalists adhere with relative comfort.

The ideals of journalism

The journalistic profession, like the teaching, legal and medical professions, has a set of guiding ideals to which its members make primary reference. Generally speaking, contemporary journalism finds the basis of those ideals in the position and role of journalism and the media in society. The journalistic ideal is centred on a quest for information and based on a commitment to treat 'events and persons with fairness and impartiality, but also [to consider] the welfare of the community and of humanity in general in a spirit devoid of cynicism' (*Royal Commission on Newspapers*, Canada, 1981, p. 24). Journalists see, and most declarations of human rights enshrine, this ideal of freedom of the press as an extension of the basic right given to all individuals, freedom of speech.

The assertion of professional ideals has assisted journalism in establishing its right to seek information and to maintain a measure of independence from the constraints within which journalists must work, specifically, a legal framework that, historically, has been oppressive, the government of the day, employers, particular working environments, the pressure of interest groups within society and technology. From a longer term view, these professional ideals have also played a role in establishing laws and practices for journalism.

Journalists do not take the ideals of their profession lightly, nor do they consider those ideals and their profession as peripheral to the workings of Western democratic society. Most journalists believe that press freedoms are the very reason we have responsible democracy, rather than vice versa.

The majority of journalists are idealistic. They tend to see themselves as inveterate seekers after truth, devoted to the facts and to either the public or the reader. However, their ideal reader or viewer tends to resemble an idealised rational citizen rather than the average citizen. Journalists are usually aware of the need to assume responsibility for the consequences of their actions. The output of this mainstream of journalists, whose working practices we will be exploring throughout this chapter, forms the basis of our knowledge of our own and other societies.

Two sub-groups of journalists on either side of the above-described norm can be identified. One group identifies largely with media owners and business interests. Members of this group are prepared to interpret the public's preferences as measured by consumption patterns, that is, what they read or watch. These preferences conveniently translate directly into subscription and audience figures, advertising lineage and profits. Whatever raises these figures, they argue, is what the public wants. This group is more willing to sensationalise, emphasise the bizarre, invade the normal bounds of privacy or work right at the limit of the law in order to get a good story. They tend to feed the seemingly insatiable public appetite for details of the lives of others who are rich, famous, powerful and/or who may have experienced tragedy. They are also willing to fulfill the public's desire for intrigue and high drama, in stories often expressed in the most lurid terms and pictures.

The other sub-group identifies with a larger set of social or public interests. They often see their job as being to look beneath the surface at the power dynamics of society and how these are played out in both the events of the day and the manner in which these events are presented to society. This group may be long on interpretation, selecting information and sometimes theorising, and short on following the dynamics of a story as it unfolds. Such journalists see their role as exposing the dominant ideas and interpretations of society, or sectors within society, which favour the dominant, powerful, or privileged, whether they are on the left or the right of the political spectrum.

The boundaries of the mainstream and the groups on either end of the political and ideological spectrum vary from nation to nation, especially on a dimension of analytical/descriptive writing. The average French journalist is more analytical than the average American journalist, who it taught to focus on description of events and to give free rein to opinion rather than analysis as a result of the emphasis on libertarianism in the US. Within a single country such as Britain, a *Daily Mirror* reporter is likely to be less analytical than a *Times* reporter, largely because of the interests and position in society of their respective readerships.

Differences in journalists' orientations can often be readily observed in approaches to new patterns of social behaviour. Take terrorism as an example: when a new form of terrorism emerges, those oriented to audience preferences tend to wade in and exploit it for all they can. The mainstream report events and also report on the effects of their and others' reporting. The ideologically committed tend to use such events as a springboard for restating their case that society is fundamentally misguided, misgoverned or unjust. As time passes, the state and the profession work out a mutually acceptable *modus operandi* and form an accepted set of interpretive structures with built-in variations. Usually this involves keeping the media informed and, at the same time, appealing to them not to unnecessarily endanger people's lives. Schlesinger (1982) discussed this strategy in connection with the 1980 seizure of the Iranian embassy in London. It was successful in that instance, and has been successful whenever journalists have been willing to cooperate. Indeed, it would appear that the close relations between the state and the media have given governments courage to demand that the media surrender their independence in times of what the state sees·as external threat, but which others may see as when it has seemed convenient for the state. The role of the media in the Gulf War, the Falklands War in 1982, and the US invasion of Grenada in 1983 are all good cases in point.

The manipulation of the media by the 'spin doctors' of the military and of government in the Gulf War was masterful. (Spin doctors are persons, usually former journalists, who are responsible for presenting information in a light most favourable to their clients. They work best when alternative information is difficult to acquire.) Firstly, the number of journalists each country was allowed to send was based on the size of their fighting force. Other nations had to rely on a media pool. Journalists of each nation were attached to their own troops and restricted in their movements by troop movements. Journalists were not allowed to travel anywhere without 'minders' and certain areas were forbidden. (Minders are members of the military who supervise journalists and ensure they obey the set restrictions under which they are allowed to work.) Death and destruction sustained by either side was generally kept from the media. In general, any transgressions by one journalist resulted in increased restrictions for all. This resulted in scapegoating and immense peer pressure not to overstep or even test limits. All of these techniques, by the way, are reminiscent of the manner in which prisoners of war are treated, an interesting way to treat the media of one's own society which illustrates the tension between the media and other interests in society. Masses of disinformation, for example irrelevant technical facts, were fed to the media to emphasise the image of the war as a triumph of technology. A picture of an apparently dumb 'smart bomb' was never broadcast. While Patriot missiles 'took out' Scuds, little was heard of the debris that then dropped to earth. Healing metaphors, such as 'surgical strikes', were continually used by official spokespersons. In the end, the North American and European public were deceived (see Winter, 1992 and Mowlana, Gerbner, and Schiller, 1992), and the picture painted of the war was systematically distorted.

Governments and police forces are not beyond tricking the media as well. In Canada, in the spring and summer of 1990, during what has been called the 'Oka Crisis', a group of Mohawks erected a barricade across a road preventing access to the town of Oka. The Mohawks were protesting the permission granted by the white municipality for the building of a golf course on land they regarded as theirs. During the day, Canada's army, well known as peace-keepers, behaved in a firm but reasonable fashion; they were contained and calm. By night, once the majority of reporters had left, the army engaged in a variety of harassing activities designed to demoralise the protesters and throw their plans into disarray (Borovoy, 1990). Journalists who chose to remain behind the Mohawk barricades so that they could experience the full force of the army treatment were portrayed as having compromised their objectivity. The army took steps to immobilise their cellular phones, cut off food and generally make reporting so difficult that their employers had to ask for a court injunction to stop the army from interfering with the media in doing their job.

Law and policy and the practice of journalism

The foundation of journalistic practice lies in the law and policy that affect the operation of the media. Discussions of that law and policy are usually found in literature dealing with media ethics. That literature is not confined to discussions of how journalists should conduct themselves in difficult situations; rather, it discusses the principles that govern the behaviour of journalists, owners and governments, and what consumers – the average reader or viewer, the knowledgeable or critical reader or viewer, and advertisers – can expect from the media.

As outlined in Chapter 3, journalists work within international law and policy and national law and policy, both of which derive from notions of free speech. At the international level, Section 19 of the *Universal Declaration of Human Rights* is operative and reflects other international covenants as well as national laws. To state it again:

> para 1: Everyone shall have the right to hold opinions without interference
> para 2: Everyone shall have the right to freedom of expression; this right shall include freedom to seek, receive and impart information and ideas of all kinds, regardless of frontiers, either orally, in writing or in print, in the form of art, or through any other media of his/her choice.
> para 3: The exercise of the right provided for in para 2 of this article carries with special duties and responsibilities. It may therefore be subject to certain restrictions, but these shall only be such as are provided by law and are necessary for the respect of the rights or reputation of others or for the protection of national security or of public order or of public health or morals.

Article 12 of the Declaration also applies to press functioning, dealing with infringement of privacy, and attacks on honour and reputation. With regard to such infringements it states 'everyone has the right of protection of the law

against such interference and attack'. These two rights, while not contradictory, exist in tension with each other. Their interplay is affected substantially by national laws, codes and practice and, in Europe, EC statutes.

At national and EC levels there is considerable variation in relevant
statutes. Every developed nation has a statement of freedom of speech rights.
Many also have codes of press and media conduct, as well as bodies to oversee
the application of these codes. The codes derive from freedom of speech, the
right to privacy and reputation, and libel laws.

The commonalities between developed nations are well expressed by the
Declaration of Rights and Obligations of Journalists operating in the
European Community. This declaration was approved at a meeting of representatives of journalists' unions from six EC countries held in Munich in
1971. The preamble asserts a number of general principles. The first is that
'the right to information, and to freedom of expression and criticism is a
fundamental right of humankind'. Obviously, this is derived from the *Universal Declaration of Human Rights*. Given this right, it notes that 'the rights
and duties of a journalist originate from this right of the public to be informed
on events and opinions'. In other words, it is in the service of public rights that
journalists gain their freedom to operate. Further, no special rights are
asserted for the benefit of journalists.

In the third paragraph of the preamble, the document asserts that 'the
journalist's responsibility towards the public takes precedence over any other
responsibility, particularly towards employers and public authorities'. Again
the service to the public is underlined and given primacy over both media
owners and the government and bureaucracy of the day. The fourth paragraph recognises that the search for and dissemination of information could
justify undesirable activity. Thus it says 'the mission of information necessarily includes restrictions which journalists spontaneously impose on themselves. This is the object of the declaration of duties formulated below'.

The final paragraph deals with working conditions and morale. It states: 'A
journalist, however, can respect these duties while exercising his profession
only if conditions of independence and professional dignity effectively exist.
This is the object of the following declaration of rights.'

Declaration of duties

The essential obligations of a journalist engaged in gathering, editing and
commenting on news are:

1 To respect truth whatever be the consequence to him/herself, because of the
   right of the public to know the truth;
2 To defend freedom of information, comment and criticism;
3 To report only the facts of which s/he knows the origin; not to suppress
   essential information nor alter texts and documents;

4 Not to use unfair methods to obtain news, photographs or documents;

5 To respect the privacy of others;

6 To rectify any published information which is found to be inaccurate;

7 To observe professional secrecy and not to divulge the source of the information obtained in confidence;

8 To regard as grave professional offences the following: plagiarism, calumny, slander, libel and unfounded accusations, the acceptance of bribes in any form in consideration of either publication or suppression of news;

9 Never to confuse the profession of a journalist with that of an advertisement salesperson or a propagandist and to refuse any direct or indirect orders from advertisers;

10 To resist every pressure and to accept editorial orders only from the responsible persons of the editorial staff.

(cited in Clement Jones, 1980, pp. 76–7)

Every journalist worthy of the name deems it his/her duty to observe faithfully the principles stated above. Within the general law of each country, the journalist recognises, in professional matters, the jurisdiction of his/her colleagues only; s/he excludes every kind of interference by governments or others.

Declaration of rights

1 Journalists claim free access to all information sources, and the right to inquire freely into all events affecting public life. Therefore, secrets of public or private affairs (connected to public life) may be kept from journalists only in exceptional cases and for clearly expressed motives;

2 The journalist has the right to refuse subordination to anything contrary to the general policy of the information organ of which s/he is a contributing member such as it is laid down by writing and incorporated in his/her contract of employment or clearly implied by this general policy;

3 A journalist cannot be compelled to perform a professional act or express an opinion contrary to his/her convictions or his/her conscience;

4 The editorial staff must be informed on all important decisions which may influence the life of the enterprise. At minimum, it should be consulted before a definitive decision is taken on all matters related to the composition of the editorial staff, e.g. recruitment, dismissals, restructuring and promotions;

5 Taking into account his/her functions and responsibilities, the journalist is entitled not only to the advantages resulting from collective agreements but also to an individual contract of employment, ensuring the material and moral security of his/her work as well as a wage system corresponding to his/her social condition and g ranteeing his/her economic independence.

(cited in Clement Jones, 1980, p. 77).

This 1971 document is significant for two reasons. First, it represents the basic principles on which journalists across Europe were able to come to common agreement. Secondly, it identifies all but two of the major areas of constraint within which journalists must work. Those areas are:

1 international and national law and information policy;
2 the orientation, actions and preferences of the government of the day;
3 the policies, practices and attitudes of owners;
4 the philosophies, practices and attitudes of their colleagues, including their editorial bosses; and,
5 pressures from societies and sub-groups within society.

There are two constraining elements which are not specifically mentioned. The first is technology; the second is freedom of, or access to, information. This latter aspect, which enhances the ability of journalists to provide accurate information and analysis is much more developed in North America, especially in the US. While society has a general interest in providing journalists or anyone else with the freedom to pursue information and understanding, few specific institutions in society share that interest. It is not in the short-term interests of the government of the day nor in the interests of private institutions. Thus nations have been involved for some time in creating Freedom of or Access to Information Acts. The basic principle of these acts is that, in the name of democracy, most government information should be available to the people. Exceptions should be rare and should be justified, for example, by reference to national security, the protection of the privacy of individuals, or the confidentiality of advice of public servants to cabinet ministers.

The reason for the double-barrelled name reflects two different governing traditions. 'Access to information' is appropriate to countries, such as Britain and its former colonies, where information collected and created by the government (the Crown) is seen to be the property of the Crown unless the Crown is prepared to release it. In the US, the same information is seen to be the property of the people because 'the people' are paramount in the Constitution. Thus 'freedom of information' is a more appropriate label.

A survey of national law and policy

In the following section we will illustrate the flavour of the principles laid down in the European document as they are applied in various developed countries (not all in Europe). We will examine France, Germany, Italy, Scandinavia, the UK and the US, and make brief mention of Australia, the Netherlands and Japan.

France

Concern with the functioning of the press and journalism in France dates back to the *Code de la Presse* of 1881. An important and more recent definition of the role of the media and journalists was set out in the *Déclaration des devoirs des journalistes* in 1954. It summarised the duties of journalists in seven points: honouring the truth, defending the liberty of information, publishing information only from known sources, not using dishonourable methods to gain information, facilitating the right of correction, preserving personal character and resisting government control.

This 1954 document was supplemented by the 1971 EC document reproduced above and a 1973 charter agreed to by four different French journalists' groups called *The Right to be Informed*. This charter is exemplary in its thoroughness and deserves detailed attention. The philosophy of the charter emphasises two points. The first is that the nation, in the form of the government of the day, has a responsibility to ensure that the public is informed. In France, this has been taken to mean that the nation has a duty to assist businesses which help the public exercise this right. In providing that assistance, a distinction has been drawn between publishing houses whose principle objective is profit and those that perform a public service. Three criteria have been laid out to distinguish public service-oriented publishing. First is that 'effective responsibility for handling editorial matter and for appointing the managing director and the head of the editorial service shall rest with the journalists'. Secondly, 'at least half of the column area shall be devoted to political, economic, social and cultural news'. Thirdly, 'a substantial part of the newspaper's income shall come from sales'. These three criteria provide a wide basis for a broad programme of government subsidies.

The second point of emphasis is contained in the charter's preamble, which outlines what journalists perceive to be a major shortcoming in the functioning of the media. They feel that it is the responsibility of the totality of the media to keep everyone informed about political, social, economic and cultural life. In practice, they feel that news gathering and dissemination is subject to pressures from money and power through the concentration of ownership in institutions of expression and distribution, commercial imperatives and government control. They claim that the right to be informed presupposes 'the freedom to gather, receive, transmit, publish, and distribute ideas and information in accordance with . . . principles' which are outlined in the charter. These principles are:

1　Freedom of access to news sources.
2　The duty of government to communicate freely all the news under their jurisdiction and to exercise neither direct nor indirect censorship.
3　Recognition in law of the journalist's right not to divulge confidential sources.

4 Access to mass media facilities for organizations representing various currents of opinion; broadening the right to reply.

5 The freedom to distribute without let or hindrance newspapers and periodicals published in France or abroad in any language whatsoever. This entails abrogation of laws which now restrict this freedom.

6 Protection against monopolies and concentrations. Private business and financial groups should not be allowed to set up a national, regional or local monopoly in radio, television and newspapers. The independence of the press and mass communications media in respect of the state should be written into the law.

7 Government and community assistance should facilitate the right to be informed.

8 Publications specializing in views and comment should be provided with special assistance; but this aid must not be such as to ever permit it to become a means of exercising political pressure.

9 The collective national charter should also include a definition of journalists' rights and obligations in accordance with the resolution in Munich on 25 November 1971 by the European journalists' unions setting out the moral principles of the profession and its guarantees of independence.

10 The national education system should promote the critical study of the news media; student newspapers should be accorded official recognition and be entitled to assistance provided for other newspapers.

11 The unhampered distribution of publications purveying news and views will be guaranteed in educational establishments, barracks, and prisons.

12 Measures pertaining to related sectors such as newsprint and distribution services will be worked out by all the parties concerned.

(cited in Clement Jones, 1980, pp. 20–1)

A further flavour of the operation of journalism in France comes from an article written by a US commentator, C. R. Eisendrath, which was published in 1982 by Praeger, a publisher that has received CIA support. Eisendrath points out that Article XI of the 1789 *Declaration of Rights of Man and Citizen*, gives every French person the right, in principle, to be 'free to speak or publish . . . except as prohibited by law'. But as Eisendrath notes, extensive laws exist which are prohibitions against that freedom. The most significant are those that protect the state, its institutions and its elected and appointed officials from criticism. One of the characteristics of this law is that the more powerful the person and the more central the institution is to the functioning of the state the more highly protected it is in law (Auby and Ducos-Ader, 1976). Thus in law the President is virtually immune to criticism. However, in practice President Charles de Gaulle went to court 350 times to restrain the media from continuing to criticise him on various matters. This suggests that the immunity is restricted to disallow full exploration of particular matters (as in Watergate, as the author notes). This protection extends all the way to municipal employees, to foreign governments and their diplomats.

Other institutions receive special protection. They include *les grands écoles*, chambers of commerce, academic councils, the Legion of Honour, the courts and the armed services. The former President Valéry Giscard d'Estaing, when in office, used the notion of 'discredit to the judicial system' to stop *Le Monde* discussing his acceptance of jewels from the ruler of a former French colony. Anything concerning the military that may damage its effectiveness or morale is vulnerable to suit. Anything that might attack the credit of the nation, whether undermining confidence in its currency or the value of its public funds, is also vulnerable. It is also the case that the French state may initiate action on behalf of protected people and institutions.

French libel law also deserves some attention. As in most European countries, libel is dealt with by both the criminal and civil codes and extends to all who participate in or are responsible for the creation and distribution of information and opinion to the public. Again, consistent with many countries, the usual presumption of innocence is reversed in libel cases. Under libel law, the accused must support and justify his/her statements. The distinctive characteristics of French libel law are several. In France, libel can express true facts: that they are stated and damaging is enough to be libellous. Libel is also rather extensive. Three categories of defamation exist. *Diffamation* involves verifiable evidence. *Injure* encompasses epithets and insults with no particular factual content. *Offense* and *outrage* are more general transgressions such as pornography or interference with the course of justice. These three categories provide for a wide range of restriction of expression. There are also time limits and other categories of restrictions that can be applied to certain statements. Facts that are more than ten years old that damage a person's reputation can be a basis for a libel suit. Also, crimes specifically pardoned or amnestied are sealed off from further discussion. The working reality of this latter law is that national leaders routinely give amnesty to ordinary crimes and frequently those involved in particularly troublesome historical periods such as World War II.

France also has strong right of reply legislation. Any embodiment of public authority accused in the press of misperformance has the right to demand a free insertion up to twice the length of the original piece. Any person defamed has the ability to force a compensating insertion, whether or not the piece written about them was correct. Further, they may be able to make a case for insertions in publications other than the one which contained the offensive piece.

France has other distinctive characteristics beyond its unique libel law. There is a system of yearly grants to newspaper publishers that requires approval each year by legislators. These grants can amount to 12 per cent of financial turnover to publications with no more than one-third ads. The grants are justified as an aid to keeping the public informed. In this and other ways the state injects itself positively into commercial, and, in this case, media affairs. Such a style of state action is often called *Colbertism*. Other examples of Colbertism include

- not taxing 80 per cent of reinvested profits to improve productive capacity;
- providing subsidies for postal distribution and for information gathering;
- reducing professional taxes for journalists by 30 per cent;
- exempting news publications from value-added taxes;
- making fully registered journalists eligible for certain optional and mandatory bonuses and premium pay for night and hazardous work;
- providing life insurance, summer and winter vacations, job security and the right to resign if a paper's political orientation affronts a journalist's honour, reputation, or general integrity; and
- subsidising the foreign distribution of French newspapers and underwriting Agence France Presse (AFP).

Such practices may appear to call into question the foundations of free media operation in France. However, such practices are not uncommon in other countries. It is probably also the case that the French media are no more closely bound to the state than are, say, the American or British media, although their media laws and policies differ significantly. In the wider context of all developed countries, all three nations have a rather close relation between the state, the government of the day and the media. There is little question that American news is guided by American foreign policy. It informs the public so that they can make sense of that foreign policy.

With regard to France, it is probably safe to say that the nature of the interaction between the media and the state illustrates the importance France attaches to its media of news and commentary. It also, characteristically, injects the state into news operations not only in the ways outlined above but, as the preceding chapter points out, though direct ownership.

Germany

The traditions of German journalism point to turgid political and philosophical tracts requiring a high level of knowledge and linguistic decoding abilities. Prior to World War II, to write on a topic was not so much to report events but to enter a rule-bound discourse with well-established champions and adversaries. To be taken seriously was to gain the approval of established figures, essentially an authoritarian enterprise. These traditions represented a considerable barrier to the participation of the ordinary citizen in the full range of affairs and debate in society. Room was also created for the conceptually accessible writings in support of National Socialism (Humphreys, 1990). While little heed was paid to these publications prior to Hitler gaining power, once in power the circulation of National Socialist publications soared (Humphreys, 1990). Nurtured by an established acceptance of authority, they were allowed to feed upon their own rhetoric and gain in extremism.

In the aftermath of World War II, at least two major influences made themselves felt on the German media. First was the rule of the Allies, each in its own sector. The main purpose of the Allies was to avoid national control of the media in any future German state, hence emphasis was placed on regional control. Another major influence was the shoot-from-the-hip journalistic style of American journalism, beholden to no authority, not even its own government, and oblivious to the unspoken rules of German, or even European, cultural history. Both influences, along with others such as the British orientation to public service, opened up the German media and journalism to greater participation, a greater range of opinion and diminished polemics.

Perhaps the major issue in journalism in Germany today is still the protection of the journalist against pressure from his/her employer. In one study conducted inside the Springer operation, paternalism is combined with uncertain employment conditions and encouragement of a journalistic style which erases the past and sugar-coats a capitalist future (Humphreys, 1990). On the other hand, German journalists have been at the forefront of reform, playing a key role in the development of the 1973 EC code of duties and rights and exposing owner influence. In Germany, journalists cannot be required to write against their consciences. The constitutionally-mandated responsibility of the *Länder* for media affairs and culture has been jealously guarded, especially in broadcasting, against attempts at incursions by the central government. Concentration of ownership in media industries is a continual focus of public discussion and has largely been avoided in broadcasting. Unfortunately, as Chapter 4 points out, considerable concentration has been achieved in the print media. The ideological orientation of the press has been defanged by a plurality of owners, the practice of hiring journalists in proportion to the strength of political parties, and journalistic protection. Finally, Germany has led the way in consulting with journalists on the hiring of senior editors, an initiative that reflects co-operative employer/employee relations in the country.

In the post-war years and after the lifting of Allied control of the media, codes of conduct were formulated, beginning with the magazine *Stern*. Many other 'house' agreements followed and they had many points in common. House agreements usually include participation in decision making on matters affecting the staff's work, changes in ownership, the pay and working conditions of journalists, editorship and the position of the reader. These house agreements led to the establishment of a German Press Council, whose overall aims are:

protecting freedom of the press, and assuring unrestricted access to sources of

news; ascertaining and removing grievances in the press, observing the structural development of the German press and warding off the formation of
monopolies and groupings endangering freedom; and representing the German
press before the government, parliament and the public, especially in the case of
draft laws affecting the existence and functions of the press.

(Clement Jones, 1980, p. 22)

This national voluntary German Press Council, especially with its provisions
for representation and co-operation, reflects the tripartite state/business/
labour co-operative management of German society. The development of
press laws are discussed and agreed upon by the press before they are taken
forward to legislation. German journalists also practice strong professional
discipline, seemingly to avoid government control. Clement Jones (1980)
draws particular attention to the responsibility journalists have for accuracy,
noting that the press code calls for unconfirmed reports, rumours and sup-
positions to be identified as such and illustrative pictures identified as not
documentary in nature.

Right of reply is weaker than in France in that it only applies to matters of
fact. However, it is stronger in that it requires the news organisation to itself
initiate an 'adequate retraction'. What is adequate can involve expression of
regret or not, timing, placement and the involvement of relevant persons
outside the news organ. Concern for privacy is respected, yet less so than in
France, in that if a person's private conduct affects the public interest then
there is some obligation to report on the matter. There is also strong wording
on discrimination: 'nobody can be discriminated against as a result of race,
creed or nationality' (Clement Jones, p. 23).

Italy

The general perception of the Italian press and media is that they are sensa-
tionalistic and intrusive. This perception was captured well in a headline for a
story in *The Economist* about a series of Benetton ads featuring a man dying
of Aids, a newborn baby with umbilical cord attached, a black woman
breast-feeding a white baby, and a nun and a priest kissing. The headline was
'More controversy, please, we're Italian'.

Italy's press tradition has lacked a pure devotion to informative news
values and editorial independence from business interests. Radio televisione
Italiana (RAI), a joint-stock company controlled by the government, was also
one of the first European broadcasters to experiment with commercials to
supplement licence fees. These commercials were presented in clusters in a
prime-time period marked off for the purpose. This commercialism probably
contributed to the slow emergence of the decision that the RAI's television
monopoly was unconstitutional. In terms of direct state control, the government plays a formal role in the licensing of journalists and party-based

reporting is well established in both television and newspapers.

Clement Jones (1980) has argued that the sensationalist quality of Italian press and journalistic functioning can be explained by the fact that newspapers have often been owned by industrial magnates, who have used their media properties 'as a means of exerting pressure on the government, on politicians, or other economic groups' (p. 27). He implies that the lack of influence of codes of journalistic ethics derived from their lack of explicitness and the subordination of press journalism to industrial activity. The lack of ethical sensibility would seem to have been exported to the world at large through the adoption of the Italian word, *papparazzi*, for photographers who pry into the private lives of movie stars, nobility and other 'newsmakers'. This subordination of the press to other activities vests with the printers' unions the greatest concern for the preservation of the press (as opposed to owners or journalists). Television journalism may hold more promise in Italy; however, the alignment of television news programmes with the major political parties and the influence of advertisers may recreate the obvious subordination of media to other interests.

Overall, the structure and function of the Italian media appears to reflect the general tenor of the functioning of all social institutions in Italian society. As such, it may be that the tentative reliance Italians place on their media is appropriate to their functioning. Certainly, from the outside, it appears that media, government and even the law function within wide boundaries in Italy. Notwithstanding this apparent lack of order, the economy fairly consistently shows signs of stability and strength, and the GNP now exceeds that of Britain.

Whatever the actual state of the media and the level of trust Italians put in them, there has been continuous lively debate over the functioning of the press in Italy. In 1958 the National Federation of the Italian Press, having put out an apparently ineffectual ten-point declaration of principles in the previous year, attempted to persuade journalists and their employers to exercise 'scrupulousness and self-control' to diminish sensationalist reporting. The issues addressed in the 1957 code are as much an identification of what is wrong with the Italian press as they are basic statements of principles. For instance, it speaks of 'the public's right to be fully and objectively informed regardless of ulterior interests' and that 'the facts be interpreted without bias and faithfully reported' because, apparently, ulterior motives and bias often play a role (Clement Jones, 1980, pp. 26–8).

Italy has a mechanism called the Press Court, which is conducted entirely by the legal profession and thus has some attendant prestige. However, its powers are merely that it can make a moral judgement about the behaviour of a press organ, and there the matter stops.

Scandinavia

It would be a mistake, and indeed in the case of the UK a misrepresentation, to discuss press systems without some discussion of the Nordic countries. The main reason for this is that the Nordic countries have led the way in putting forward codes of conduct and establishing a self-monitoring and -corrective press system. In Sweden in 1916 the Newspaper Publishers Association, the Union of Journalists and the Publicists' Club established a Court of Honour to investigate complaints against the press. During the 1960s Sweden set up a Media Council to receive complaints, and also established a press ombudsman to initiate complaints against the press, to act as advocate and to mediate between the Council and the public.

The codes of conduct of all the Scandinavian countries are notable for their tolerance and dispassion. In Sweden misdemeanours of civil servants caused by negligence are not to be reported unless they are very grave or there is a principle involved; the names of people accused of crimes and those sentenced to less than two years' imprisonment are not to be published or hinted at by giving other information; detailed descriptions of crimes are to be avoided; the personal backgrounds of those convicted and offences irrelevant to the case are not to be published in headlines, posters and so forth; race or nationality are not to be emphasised unless they are relevant. Such rules complement the strong emphasis on the rehabilitation of criminals rather than their punishment.

The Code of the Union of Swedish Journalists states that 'the media should exercise their functions of watching society with vigor and intrepidity. This should be done within the limits determined by the common interest, which must not be confounded with a curiosity harmful to the sanctity of privacy'. In the 1960s, discussion took place within the media of the role of advertising and editorialisation. The Newspaper Publishers' Association (note not the journalists) moved to stop the infringement of advertisers into editorial space because '. . . it is a betrayal of the reader, carries a risk of corrupting the journalist, and of damaging the credibility of the press. [It also] . . . deprives the instigators of their motivation to pay their way through advertising' (Clement Jones, 1980, p. 31).

The United Kingdom

The first code of conduct for journalists in Great Britain was announced in 1936. Its aims were to separate fact from opinion and to protect journalists from their employers. In 1946, amidst much criticism of the press, a Royal Commission was set up that recommended the Nordic Media Council as a model for self-regulation. In 1953, led by the journalists, with foot-dragging by the owners and editors, a Press Council was set up. In 1961, a second

Royal Commission was set up and, following it, lay members and a lay Chair were added to the Press Council. To date, a Press Council code of conduct does not exist. On the other hand, both the National Union of Journalists and the Institute of Journalists have their codes which exist on top of case law, the body of decisions that have been made in the courts which customarily carries the common law forward in Britain.

Journalists are the prime movers in determining appropriate conduct for the profession. The National Union of Journalists took the lead in drawing up guide-lines for the reporting of race and race relations. Lack of leadership from editors and owners led to a diminution of press quality during the 1960s and 1970s. The printers' unions asserted themselves in moving towards closed union shops and restrictive labour agreements. Quality has recovered somewhat through journalists asserting their concerns on editorial content and the input of new owners. In the 1980s, a series of colonial and immigrant owners, specifically Robert Maxwell, Rupert Murdoch and then Conrad Black, broke the unions, with Murdoch and Black moving their premises from Fleet Street to the Docklands and modernising their plants. They were able to cut their printing staffs by a half to two-thirds and reap great financial rewards. For instance, Black paid £30 million for *The Daily Telegraph* in 1986 and by 1992 was turning a pre-tax profit of £40.5 million.

In 1977, a third Royal Commission into the Press was set up, as was a Commission of Inquiry into Broadcasting. Among other suggestions, the Royal Commission recommended that a government charter on the press and journalists' responsibilities and freedoms be drawn up, that the Press Council be strengthened and the percentage of lay members increased, that contentious opinion based on inaccurate information be grounds for censure and that journalists be protected from writing against their conscience and in their relations with their employers. Not much happened until severe pressure from Members of Parliament and the establishment of a Departmental Committee (the Calcutt Committee) forced the industry to adopt a Code of Practice in March 1990. The Code of Practice encompasses the following areas:

1 Accuracy
2 Opportunity to reply
3 Comment, conjecture and fact
4 Privacy
5 Listening devices
6 Hospitals
7 Misrepresentation
8 Harassment
9 Payment for articles
10 Intrusion into grief or shock

11 Innocent relatives and friends
12 Interviewing or photographing children
13 Children in sex cases
14 Victims of crimes
15 Discrimination
16 Financial journalism
17 Confidential sources
18 The public interest.

In June 1990 the Calcutt Committee reported having been given terms of reference which included 'to consider what measures (whether legislative or otherwise) are needed to give further protection to individual privacy from the activities of the press and improve recourse against the press for the individual citizen' (Press Complaints Commission, 1993).

In the electronic media, both general operations and journalistic functioning were examined during Margaret Thatcher's premiership. The Committee on the Future of Broadcasting stressed that broadcasting should continue to be a public service, independent of the government in its day-to-day operations, that a Broadcasting Complaints Commission (BCC) should be continued and that the media have a responsibility to combat racism. The Complaints Commission was set up by statute in 1981. Its current function and authority derive from the Broadcasting Act of 1990. Complaints may be made by those involved in the programme or by those with a direct interest in a particular programme, and which they see to be unfair, unjust, or invading their privacy. Both the Commission and the complainant have recourse to the courts. Complaints about the depiction of sex or violence, bad language or bad taste, background music, programme scheduling, and a programme which is in the course of production or which has not yet been broadcast must be made to the relevant authority, the BBC, the ITC (Independent Television Commission), the Radio Authority, or the Broadcasting Standards Council. The BCC deals with slightly over 100 complaints per year. The majority are from individuals acting in a professional capacity, although companies and other individuals are well represented. The most complained about programme type is documentaries and leisure programming (one category) (BCC, 1993).

The United States

As noted, the First Amendment of the United States states: 'Congress shall make no law respecting an establishment of religion, or prohibiting the free exercise thereof; *or abridging the freedom of speech, or of the press*; or the right of the people peaceably to assemble, and to petition the Government for a redress of grievances' (emphasis added). This amendment has generated an industry of commentary in itself. It also appears to have generated a plethora of codes of conduct for virtually every media group, including journalists, editors, newspaper owners, radio and television workers, script-writers, advertising people and motion picture people. While evidence of a laudable concern, the number and specificity of codes make it difficult for the public to penetrate media organisations and pin down exactly what group should receive a complaint and which is most likely to act.

In 1923, the American Society of Newspaper Editors set out the canons of journalism in seven sections: responsibility, freedom of the press, independence, the triad of sincerity, truthfulness and accuracy, impartiality, fair play and decency. It elaborates as follows: the *responsibility* of a newspaper is 'to attract and hold readers restricted by nothing but considerations of public welfare. The use a newspaper makes of the share of public attention it gains serves to determine its sense of responsibility, which it shares with every member of its staff' (cited in Clement Jones, 1980, p. 74). The 1923 canons note that *freedom of the press* is a vital right restricted only by explicit law. The press should be independent from the promotion of private and partisan interests. *Good faith, accuracy and truthfulness* are the foundations of good journalism. *Impartiality* demands that fact and opinion be clearly separate. *Fair play* suggests that unofficial charges should not be published, nor private rights invaded 'without sure warrant of public right as distinguished from public curiosity', and that the newspaper has a duty to correct promptly and completely. *Decency* dictates that base conduct in detailing crime and vice is deliberate pandering to vicious instincts and should yield public disapproval.

The *Code of Professional Journalists* adopted by the American Society of Newspaper Editors in 1973 has a number of distinguishing features. In overview, it notes that 'the agencies of mass communication are carriers of public discussion and information, acting on their constitutional mandate and freedom to learn and report the facts' (cited in Clement Jones, 1980, p. 75). The 1973 code emphasises public enlightenment, its relation to justice and the Constitutional role of the media to seek the truth. Under six headings it sets out standards of practice as follows: under *responsibility* it underlines the public's right to know and the relationship between the general welfare, news and enlightened opinion. It sees *freedom of the press* as an inalienable right carrying with it freedom and responsibility. Under *ethics*, it states that journalists must be freed from any obligation other than the public's right to know. Gifts and potentially compromising activities should be avoided, substantiation should be sought, the seeking of news that serves the public interest should be paramount and sources should be protected. Within the category of *accuracy and objectivity*, emphasis is placed on truth-seeking, justifiability of headlines, the separation of news and opinion, avoidance of partisanship that departs from truth, the labelling of advocacy as such and the responsibility to present informed opinion. The section on *fair play* mentions the dignity, privacy, rights and well-being of people written about. The final *pledge* deals with upholding the standards set forward.

The various other codes set forward by various professional and employee groups follow the two summarised here. However, specific mention of certain items should be noted, especially in radio and television broadcasting. In broadcasting, profanity, obscenity, smut and vulgarity are to be avoided, as is racial discrimination and stereotyping. Cigarette smoking to impress youth is cautioned against and the creation of a state of hypnosis is forbidden. Reference is also made to the educational role of television.

In the 1970s, an attempt to establish a National Media Council with private funds was pilloried, mostly by libertarians defending free speech. Indicative of the views expressed is the later defeat of an attempt to restrict the amount of advertising on television. This measure, which can be found in most, if not all, other developed countries, was defeated on the grounds that to do so would interfere with free speech.

Australia, Japan and the Netherlands

Australia, like the US, is both blessed and burdened by numerous codes of ethics, mainly drawn up by journalists. The foundation of most codes is that of the Australian Journalists' Association. The Australian Broadcast Commission amplified the eight main clauses of the Australian Journalists' Association code and added guidelines specific to electronic journalism, as well as explicit statements defining its relation to the government of the day. In 1975 the government proposed establishing a Press Council, including journalists, proprietors, editors and lay members, following the UK model.

The foundation of Japanese media ethics is in voluntary discipline and control. No newspaper laws exist nor are there any for the registration of journalists. *Nihon Shinbun Kyokai* is an industry-financed media council that works closely with the Motion Picture Moral Code Committee and deals with advertising as well as media content. This organisation, made up of veteran journalists who continuously monitor newspapers, has monthly meetings, warns offending papers, and refers recalcitrants to its Directors. It operates under six canons of journalism, which cover: news reporting and editorial writing; the principle of editorial comment; impartiality, tolerance and decency; guidance; responsibility, and pride. The role of the US in reconstructing post-war Japan has played a major influence in the operation of the Japanese media. At the same time, as noted previously, NHK, the national, publicly-owned educational broadcasting company is modelled on the BBC.

The flavour of the system can be gained from the manner in which political interviews and news gathering are organised. Japanese journalists must submit their questions in advance when interviewing any government minister. At government and large corporate briefings, journalists are provided with and accept 'administrative guidance'. Journalists from the main newspapers are granted an exclusive franchise to particular locations. All other journalists are forbidden. In exchange for this apparent exclusivity, the contents of any interview, including those with foreign journalists, are immediately circulated to Japanese and other foreign journalists through Kyodo, the Japanese wire service. When administrative guidance is not accepted, as it was not by Japan's largest commercial broadcasting station, TBS, in disregarding a foreign-ministry directive not to travel to the Soviet-held northern islands, the offender may be banned from briefings. TBS was banned, with nary a protest from other news outlets (*The Economist*, July 27 1991, p. 30). Similarly, although the relationship was known to Japanese journalists, it was the foreign-owned press that broke the news of the romance of Crown Prince Naruhito and Crown Princess Misako.

The Netherlands, like the Nordic countries and Japan, flourishes under a regime of voluntary control and self-discipline. Press laws, censorship and restrictions on journalists' activities are non-existent. The post-war Court of Honour was restructured in 1958 to become a Council of Journalism with jurisdiction only over its members and sanctions limited to publication of judgements. Present principles follow the codes of the International Federation of Journalists, and throughout the 80s and into the 90s journalists have been attempting to extend their influence on editorial content through involvement in editorial appointments. Since 1967, advertising revenue from television has been used to cross-subsidise the newspaper industry. The Netherlands have a highly developed regional press and a weaker national press.

Libel and other laws of constraint

While freedom of speech laws define the positive foundation of journalism, libel and other constraint laws such as contempt of court define the negative constraints within which journalists must operate. Rather than review the laws of each country in some detail, we will make some generalisations and distinctions.

In the main, differences between countries result not from different issues being covered by laws in place but from difference in emphasis. The common issues surrounding libel include identification of those responsible, burden of proof, appropriate compensatory action in libel actions, and considerations of personal privacy and the public interest.

In most developed countries, responsible parties in a libel case include many more than the author. Most often responsibility extends to the editor in his/her role as the person who reviews submissions and decides what to include and what not to include in putting together articles into a whole publication. It also commonly extends to the proprietor, whose responsibility is to have in place adequate review procedures to guard against libel. Responsibility can extend to the distributing companies such as wholesalers and news-stand or bookstore owners; however, usually these links in the chain are quick to withdraw publications and avoid being named in any suit. In France, such responsibilities are more formally coded and are more extensive than in most other countries. It is the custom that a newspaper or broadcasting company faces a stiffer penalty than the individual journalist. It is also not uncommon for the journalist's fine to be paid by his employer.

The balance of personal privacy and the public interest provides the basis for the most dramatic differences in the conduct and frequency of libel cases, and in court reporting. As we have seen in France, the personal privacy and the judgement of public officials is well protected. In Britain, the media must be quite circumspect in their discussion of individuals and of cases before the courts for fear of being charged with invasion of privacy or contempt. On the other hand, the Royal family seems to have no privacy at all as a result of the tireless seeking of information by the media (witness Diana pumping iron), the public's insatiable appetite, and certain amount of stories being fed to the media by various family members. That said, there is probably a great amount that the public never knows. In Canada, controls are generally less stringent than in Britain and more stringent than in the US. In the US, on the basis that public persons are virtually unprotected by privacy laws, it appears that the media can print or broadcast almost anything they please. For years there seems to have been open season on 'public persons' such as politicians and celebrities. On the basis that such people benefit from public exposure (in the case of celebrities) and that it is in the public interest to know (about the private lives of politicians) the private lives of these Americans have been opened to public view. This prying has been successful in driving more than one politician from a sought public office. Arguably, given the statements made by his murderer, the intensive coverage of John Lennon's private life led to his death. With regard to celebrities, certain American weekly tabloids have been shown to publish complete fabrications. Several successful lawsuits in the early 1990s have been won by movie stars against the *National Enquirer*, and this may decrease the printing of absolute fiction for a while. On the other side of the privacy issue, cameras have moved into the courtrooms of the nation and celebrated cases, such as the rape trial of William Kennedy Smith in 1991, are watched by sizeable numbers across the nation. He was found innocent.

As distinct from almost every other law in developed societies, it is often the case that in libel law the burden of proof rests with the accused. Often, mere correctness in fact is an insufficient defence, as is lack of intention to defame or otherwise reflect on a person's character. Increasingly, the economic interests of corporations are being protected with libel law, which is usually invoked by the persons responsible for taking actions in the name of the corporation. It would appear that the boundaries of free comment are most restricted in France; however, for the average journalist, more informal constraints can be extremely restrictive in other countries such as Germany or Norway. Laws applicable to corrections and reply also appear to weigh most heavily against the media in France and least heavily in Italy and the US.

Libel chill

Perhaps the most contentious area is what has been called libel chill. Basically, the term is used to reflect the power of the rich and powerful to protect their interests through mounting or threatening to mount a libel suit. A good example is Robert Maxwell's pursuit of Tom Bower's biography, entitled *Maxwell: The Outsider* (1988). When the book was first published by Aurum Press (owned by Andrew Lloyd Webber through his Really Useful company), Maxwell threatened lawsuits and managed to get the book pulled from most British bookstores. Maxwell also managed to persuade Bantam Books to trash a book they had already printed and were about to publish. The British bookstores retreated under threat and could only retaliate by refusing to stock an 'official' biography *Maxwell* by Joe Haines, written by a Maxwell employee and published in 1988 by a Maxwell company, with Robert Maxwell the copyright holder. Maxwell also bought the company that obtained the rights to the paperback edition of the Bower book. Interestingly, the original unofficial version was not substantially different in fact or in force from the official version. After Maxwell's death in 1991 the Bower book reappeared in a mass paperback edition, expanded and updated, and a third book was published, *Maxwell's Fall* by Roy Greenslade, a former *Mirror* editor.

Why can libel be so chilling? In a well-argued and -documented paper, Duxbury (1991) notes that under British law and derivative systems of law such as Canada's, the 'chilliness' of libel law for publishers and authors rests with the burden of justification or proof being placed on the accused: reverse onus in legal parlance. Once an action is mounted, the accused must defend him/herself. Libel insurance can run out even if it covers £1 million or more. Thus free comment about rich people can exact a considerable price. It is also the case that once a libel insurance company is involved, it calls the shots.

The plaintiff in a libel case risks little. The plaintiff must show that the words were published, that they were referring to the plaintiff and that they were capable of being defamatory. Defamatory meanings can derive from literal or ordinary meaning, popular innuendo (covering reasonable imputation) and legal innuendo (covering meaning that might be inferred by persons with special knowledge). This means that the accused may find it necessary to defend a meaning that was never intended or one of which s/he was unaware.

Defences available are justification, fair comment, privilege and consent. Justification means true in substance and in fact. Fair comment is described as 'fair and bone fide comment on a matter of public interest'. Consent means that the plaintiff assented to publication of the words in dispute. Privilege refers to the principle that 'there are occasions when it is in the public interest to promote freedom of expression or communication, even if individual reputation may be threatened' (all quoted in Duxbury, 1991).

The inside story

A knowledge and understanding of media law and policy are fundamental to understanding media operations. However, they do not provide a complete understanding of media operations. Elements of media practice that do not derive from law and policy also have major significance, for instance Lewis Lapham, the reputable columnist for *Harper's Magazine* notes 'I write a newspaper column twice a month for a syndicate and I am instructed by the syndicate never to write an article critical of the press. I can criticise the other institutions in American society, but if I criticise the media or the profession of journalism the piece isn't likely to make the paper' (Henry, 1988, p. 15). By 'instructed' Lapham may mean that at one point a representative of his employers specifically directed him in the manner he reports. That would actually be unusual. More commonly, an understanding develops in the industry between journalists, the government, editors, proprietors and press councils about what topics and treatments are permissible. On the basis of these understandings the norms of journalism, for instance the conservatism of the Norwegian media, are set. At the base of these agreed-upon operations are journalists who learn the rules and censor themselves. A valuable comparative perspective can be gained from a study of how foreign journalists saw the operation and control of their own media in comparison to the German media (Schultz and Hofmann, 1989).

In a discussion of journalistic self-censorship, Furhoff (1989) has noted:

> Another and more regrettable tendency is that the (Swedish) Press Council does not seem to be very effective. Year after year, it reprimands the same small group of extremely commercial newspapers for breaking the journalists' code. Yet just as regularly, these papers pay the relatively small fines imposed on them and continue to rely on sensationalism to build up circulation.
>
> (p. 46)

Furhoff also explores the positive and negative aspects of self-censorship, broadening the discussion to encompass the daily professional decisions journalists must make. He considers such questions as: Should teenage suicides as a form of political protest be given front page coverage? (They might encourage imitation.) If firm ideological commitments are likely to result in the commercial failure of a media outlet through the withdrawal of advertising, what priority should their expression have? Should issue-oriented campaigns push aside normal balanced coverage? Should journalists agree to embroider trivial subjects to fill space? Should journalists agree to fill an urgent deadline for a news hole when access cannot be gained to relevant newsmakers, or when insufficient time is available to obtain an accurate and full picture of a situation? What responsibilities does the reporter have to interview more than the powerful decision-makers on any issue? What responsibilities does the journalist have to gain further background to fill out wire copy, especially when insufficient resources exist for doing so? How should journalists deal with pressures from sources of information they rely on, or with the knowledge that written information provided by government or industry is unlikely to tell the full story, or with confidential sources who may want to time the release of certain information? If a journalist has political convictions, what responsibility does s/he have to write stories giving credit to parties with whom s/he disagrees, or to point out shortcomings in an institution (for example, child-care facilities) that s/he supports?

One point to remember in considering the behaviour of journalists, editors, owners and governments is that there is a great deal of subtlety to the interaction between these various players. It is rare to find journalists accusing their bosses of handing them orders to write on an issue from a particular perspective, contrary to the facts or to their conscience. If an editor wants a certain perspective taken, s/he will choose the reporter most likely to provide that perspective and may discuss the desired perspective with the reporter. In many other cases, the reporter is left with the 'responsibility' to do something that fits in with the perspective of the paper. The reporter knows that perspective simply by having worked for the paper for some time, by having read it prior to employment and by its general reputation in the profession. If a reporter turns up something that is not pleasing to the editor or publisher but cannot be faulted factually, the piece is either killed or, at most, it is suggested that the reporter produce something that balances the reporter's perspective with that of the editor or owner – although not in those terms.

Journalists and media outlets are not angels. The US State Department under the Reagan administration arranged news media interviews and concocted opinion articles opposing the Nicaraguan government that were placed in major media outlets. A vigilant media would have exposed such a ploy. The investigative arm of Congress concluded that the activities were misleading and constituted propaganda, violating a ban on the use of federal money for *propaganda not specifically authorized by Congress (Globe and Mail, 5 October 1987, p. A10) (emphasis added). Such a statement means, of course, that Congress authorises funds for propaganda and that the media advertently or inadvertently co-operate in its dissemination.

Relations between journalists and newsmakers

All journalists use a combination of officially available and informal information. Their ability to solicit information off the record is often a key to their success. Newsmakers and journalists have a mutual self-interest in co-operating with each other; when these interests become too self-serving, as they often do between journalists and politicians, the relationship becomes incestuous. Each extends favours to the other in exchange for future or past considerations.

The exploitation of information

Journalists are not hired as autonomous information-seekers and given the freedom to pursue and reveal what truth they personally deem worthy of their efforts. Their activities are constrained by their bosses, owners and/or editors, news directors, or anonymous bureaucrats who lay down policy and allocate the necessary resources to do the job. Their bosses, if they are not owners, are usually former journalists who have advanced to the editorial stage in the collection and organisation of information. The responsibility of these editors is to deploy human and material resources strategically on whichever fronts appear to be potentially active and then to sort through what information is gathered for the 'best stories'. From a business point of view, the media gather information and exploit its dissemination, either in the name of profit or public service.

In exploiting information either for profit or public service motives, the editor-managers must provide a credible and attractive information product that wins listeners, viewers or readers and advertisers to a sufficient extent to stave off the competition. In other words, their jobs are to maintain a market penetration rate and a balance of consumer (both audience and advertiser) satisfaction that does not leave room for a competitor to enter or gain market share. They must assemble a large enough audience in a receptive frame of mind to sell space to advertisers at a sufficient price to pay for production costs and to provide the requisite percentage of profit that the owner demands.

Hence the editor-manager (news director in television) becomes a gate-keeper, determining what will and will not get published. This involves not only a filtering function, but also a meaning- and identity-generating function. In other words, the gatekeeper (editor or news director, or for that matter any others involved) applies filters which select and transform raw information into stories which are then amalgamated into a produced package that reflects the identity and approach of the media outlet in the minds and consuming behaviour of its audience and advertisers (Lorimer and Rapley, 1991).

Academic research perspectives

Academic research conducted into the functions of journalists and editors has followed a number of paths. One portrays news as a constructed entity that reproduces the dominant ideology. The term 'dominant ideology' means the set of ideas that is commonly used to explain events in society – whether or not it is accurate. News is constructed by numerous journalistic means such as story format, use of beats, pursuit of accepted angles, use of authorities as primary definers of events and so forth. As Bennett, Gressett and Haltom (1985) put it, if news stories fail to reproduce the known and accepted power relations of society, then the news must be repaired to made it fit. Other research sees news in terms of the creative act of making the world comprehensible, consolidating or articulating culture.

Much of the academic work in this area tends to be slanted toward a basic gatekeeping model, for example, Epstein (1973), Gans (1979), Gitlin (1980) and Tuchman (1978). Simply stated, 'gatekeeping' presents media professionals as persons staffing a gateway through which all information must pass in order to reach the public. Gaye Tuchman's *Making News: A Study in the Construction of Reality* emphasises reality construction through the creation of frames of reference within which to present news. As Tuchman says, 'an occurrence is transformed into an event, and an event is transformed into a news story. The news frame organizes everyday reality and the news frame is part and parcel of everyday reality, for, as we have seen, the public character of news is an essential feature of news'. Some British work (see Gurevitch *et al.*, 1982 or the Glasgow Media Group's *Bad News*, 1976 and its sequels) has also been done on how the assigned work patterns of journalists, which are customarily defined by management, affect the information collected (Schlesinger, 1987). In an imaginative book called *Folk Devils and Moral Panics* (1972), Cohen traces the attribution of meaning and escalation in significance by those 'in authority' of some relatively contained concrete action. Cohen also points out the media's role in helping certain groups extend their definitions of the behaviour of others to name and control the lives of those named. In *Images of Welfare: Press and Public Attitudes to Poverty* (1982), Golding and Middleton extend their analysis into historical cultural attitudes, media ownership and long-term marketing dynamics of media outlets.

Two major studies by Ericson, Baranek and Chan (1987, 1989) also emphasise media construction and control of news. In *Visualizing Deviance*, the restricted use journalists made of information available was analysed. The authors noted that 'journalists tend to limit themselves to the 'performatives' of news releases and interview quotations from key spokespersons for particular bureaucratic organizations' (1987, p. 1).

There is also an extensive literature on balance and fairness. The work of Tuchman, the Glasgow Media Group and many other researchers demonstrates the limitations of the notion of balance as an analytical category (for example, Hackett, Gilsdorf and Savage, 1992). What is deemed to be the other side of the balance defines the issue in a particular way, as the semiologists point out.

Summary

This chapter examined the role of journalists in the media. It began with a professional profile to give a sense of the backgrounds, values and characteristics of journalists. It then reviewed the ideals of the profession in order to provide a sense of the principles that govern professional behaviour. That discussion also surveyed the range of approaches to those principles.

We then turned to international law and policy that has been developed as a guide to nations in their treatment of journalists. With this as a foundation we then reviewed EC documents dealing with the duties and rights of journalists. Following this pan-European perspective we then reviewed specific laws and policies of France, Germany, Italy, Scandinavia, the UK, the US, Australia, Japan and the Netherlands. In this review we attempted to give a flavour of the operation of the press and the media in each of those societies.

We then turned our attention to libel law as perhaps the most powerful constraint on the day-to-day practice of journalism. We noted how it affects journalism somewhat differently from country to country, and how its form, with the unusual onus on the accused in most countries, can profoundly affect social discourse in the media.

We concluded with a consideration of some of the internal workings of news organisations. First we examined the journalists' perspective, next the relationships between journalists and newsmakers, thirdly we reviewed the perspectives of news and information organisations and finally we examined what research has revealed of these dynamics.

References

Auby, Jean-Marie and Robert Ducos-Ader (1976), *Droit de l'information*, Dalloz, Paris.

Bennett, W. L., L. C. Gressett, and W. Haltom (1985), 'Repairing the news: a case study of news paradigm', *Journal of Communications*, 35 (2) (Spring), pp. 50–68.

Borovoy, A. (1990), 'From barricade to public forum', *Globe and Mail*, 9 October, p. A17.

Bower, Tom (1988), *Maxwell: The Outsider*, Aurum Press, London.

Broadcasting Complaints Commission (UK) (1993), *Twelfth Annual Report, 1992–93*, BCC, London.

Canada (1981), *Royal Commission on Newspapers*, Canadian Government Publishing Centre, Hull, Quebec.

Clement Jones, J. (1980), *Mass Media Codes of Ethics and Councils: A Comparative International Study on Professional Standards*, Reports and Papers on Mass Communication, Special Issue, Unesco, Paris.

Cohen, S. (1972), *Folk Devils and Moral Panics: The Creation of the Mods and Rockers*, MacGibbon and Kee, London.

Desbarats, Peter (1990), *Guide to Canadian News Media*, Harcourt Brace Jovanovich, Toronto.

Duxbury, Nancy (1991), 'Why is libel so chilling? An examination of Canadian libel law and the vulnerability of publishers', unpublished paper, Canadian Centre for Studies in Publishing, Simon Fraser University, Vancouver.

Eisendrath, C. R. (1982), 'Press freedom in France: private ownership and state controls' in Jane L. Curry and Joan R. Dassin (eds.), *Press Control Around the World*, Praeger, New York.

Epstein, E. J. (1973), *News from Nowhere: Television and the News*, Vintage, New York.

Ericson, R. V., P. M. Baranek, and J. B. L. Chan (1987), *Visualizing Deviance: A Study of News Organization*, University of Toronto Press, Toronto.

Ericson, R. V., P. M. Baranek, and J. B. L. Chan (1989), *Negotiating Control: A Study of News Sources*, University of Toronto Press, Toronto.

Furhoff, Lars (1989), 'Self censorship as seen by Swedish journalists' in Unesco Reports and Papers on Mass Communication, *The Vigilant Press: A Collection of Case-Studies*, no. 103, Unesco, Paris, pp. 45–52.

Gans, H. J. (1979), *Deciding What's News: A Study of CBS Evening News, NBC Nightly News, Newsweek, and Time*, Vintage, New York.

Gitlin, T. (1980), *The Whole World is Watching*, University of California Press, Berkeley.

Glasgow Media Group (1976), *Bad News*, Writers and Readers Publishing Cooperative, London.

Glasgow Media Group (1982), *Really Bad News*, Writers and Readers Publishing Cooperative, London.

Golding, Peter, and Sue Middleton (1982), *Images of Welfare: Press and Public Attitudes to Poverty*, Martin Robertson & Co., Oxford.

Greenslade, Roy (1992), *Maxwell's Fall*, Simon and Schuster, London.

Gurevitch, M. *et al.* (eds.) (1982), *Culture, Society and the Media*, Methuen, Toronto.

Hackett, Robert, Bill Gilsdorf and Philip Savage (eds.) (1992), 'Questioning balance: struggles over broadcasting policies and content', *Canadian Journal of Communication*, Special Issue, 17, pp. 1–142.

Haines, Joe (1988), *Maxwell*, Macdonald, London.

Henry, William A. (1988), *Media Freedom and Accountability*, Gannett Center for Media Studies, New York.

Humphreys, Peter J. (1990), *Media and Media Policy in West Germany: The Press and Broadcasting since 1945*, Berg, New York.

Lorimer, Rowland and Kellie Rapley (1991), 'CFUN: a commercial audience', in R. Lorimer and D. C. Wilson (eds.), *Creating Ideas and Information: Studies in Communications and New Technologies*, Detselig, Calgary.

Mowlana, Hamid, George Gerbner, and Herbert I. Schiller. (eds.) (1992), *Triumph of the Image: The Media's War in the Persian Gulf – A Global Perspective*, Westview, Boulder, Colorado.

Press Complaints Commission (1993), *The Press Complaints Commission*, PCC, London.

Schlesinger, Philip (1982), 'Princes' Gate, 1980: the media politics of siege management in Britain' in Jane L. Curry and Joan R. Dassin (eds.), *Press Control Around the World*, Praeger, New York, pp. 27–63.

Schlesinger, Philip (1987), *BBC News. Putting 'Reality' Together*, Methuen, London.

Schultz, W., and Hofmann, J. (1989), 'Control functions of the media in the Federal Republic of Germany' in Unesco, *The Vigilant Press: A Collection of Case Studies*, Reports and Papers on Mass Communication no. 103, Unesco, Paris.

Tuchman, Gaye (1978), *Making News: A Study in the Construction of Reality*, Free Press, New York.

Winter, James (1992), *Common Cents: Media Portrayal of the Gulf War and Other Events*, Black Rose Books, Montreal.

Chapter 6

Technology and communication

The literature on developments in the European Community in broadcasting, telecommunications and, to some extent, publishing is impressive in its accounts of technological and market possibilities. As this literature of development would have it, the time is at hand when any person may have any information product at any time in the comfort of his/her own home. As various directives and papers emerge from EC headquarters in Brussels and the Council of Europe headquarters in Strasbourg and debate ensues in the popular press, one question continually goes unaddressed: will the original driving force of development in broadcasting – and for that matter the driving force of any new mode of communication and representation – survive? The driving force we speak of is nothing more nor less than cultural and social enhancement.

The beginnings of broadcasting in the developed world were marked by a belief that this new form of communication could improve the lot of every person and every country. It could do so by means of the circulation of increased amounts of enlightenment and entertainment, bringing people increasingly in touch with one another and in touch with the achievements and activities of their society and civilisation. The exact organisation and emphasis of this ambitious social and cultural project differed from country to country as, very rightly, they should have. However, all countries, with the single exception of the US, deemed it desirable to create a public body, find a means of funding, and provide that public body with a general social, cultural and educational mandate to create a broadcasting system of benefit to society.

Since these beginnings, which, we should remember, are less than 100 years old, programming, audiences and consumption patterns have been established which demonstrate that in some circumstances broadcasting can pay for itself through one or both of subscriber revenues and advertising. In addition, technology is now almost fully capable of providing sufficient capacity and means of signal delivery that spectrum scarcity may be a restriction of the past. Technology, married with production economics and practices and predictable consumer behaviour, has the capability of ushering in a new era. That era would see current monopolies – whether held by national broadcasters, local cable companies, licensed private broadcasters, or international telephone, television and data signal carriers – replaced by a freer and more open market.

But what then happens to the great social and cultural project that broadcasting and electronic communications represented? This is where the drift of the EC literature is particularly instructive. In that literature there is much discussion of, on the one hand, the single market and the policies necessary to ensure the flows of goods and data across borders and, on the other hand, the vast potential inherent in technological variety – even as it converges. Much is made of the need for economic and technological co-ordination. Ad agencies are already gearing up to allow the transnationals to do their EC buying in one place. However, there is virtually no discussion of how the socially- and culturally-inspired organisation of broadcasting and the new electronic communication and information services are to be nurtured in this new era. To be concrete, there is virtually no discussion of content beyond a nod at national and pan-European quotas. In one sense, there ought not to be. The EC is a political and economic enterprise. Culture is to remain the job of national, regional and local governments, just as culture was 'off the table' in the Canada/US Free Trade Agreement and in the North American Free Trade Agreement (NAFTA), at least between Canada and the US.

But therein lies a rather stark contradiction: if broadcasting specifically and communications in general are activities of any social and cultural consequence, and arguably they will increasingly be turned over to free market forces, then to leave the social and culture to one side in designing a global or pan-European market is to mark the passage of an orientation to broadcasting that many would not want to relegate to history. The potential result is probably American television writ large which no one, including most Americans and recently the FCC itself (*The Economist*, 15 February, 1992, p. 25), touts as not being dominated by enlightened quality or broadly educational programming.

How large a role does technology play? Without new technology, specifically broadcast satellites, digital signals, signal compression, glass fibres, computers and the like, the whole enterprise would be impossible. So what will be the impact of this new technology and the production and market organisation and economics that it makes possible? It will create a new era. Worse or better than before? If we take a lead from theorists who have studied technology, the answer might best be phrased 'perhaps worse, perhaps better, certainly different'.

Technology defined

Western society is distinguished by its embrace of technology, an embrace which dates back to the days and writings of Sir Francis Bacon (1561–1626). Even though some theorists have misgivings about the technologisation of modern society, technology is absolutely central to its operation. The most we could do to combat a technological influence would be to slow it down or to insist on making informed choices, perhaps by requiring, as Julie James Bailey suggests, cultural impact statements for new technological or ownership proposals (J. J. Bailey, personal communication, 1990). But as biotechnology continues to be seen to 'hold such promise' and the rank of nations in the world economy is profoundly affected by who is first to develop new technology, such a slow-down is unlikely. A turn-around seems absolutely impossible.

Given that we are firmly in the clutches of the technological imperative, the task would seem to be to understand the most fundamental elements of an area of technology and what inherent tendencies there are in its application. Then we must invent laws and institutions to develop technology so that it is as universally beneficial as possible. In communications, patent and copyright laws and acts covering information, education, libraries, the arts, broadcasting and telecommunications are key. The institutions and practices that derive from those laws and acts are also crucial.

What makes these laws, practices and institutions critical derives from the nature of communication itself. Shannon and Weaver (1949, pp. 3–5) note that communication includes 'all of the procedures by which one mind may affect another'. Beniger (1986) maintains that information, which is the content of communication, derives from the organisation of the material world. Technology is the manner by which that organisation is brought about, thus technology is 'any intentional extension of a natural process'. (Beniger in Crowley and Heyer, 1991, p. 250).

For Beniger and others, the communications/information revolution, in both the evolutionary and turn-about sense of the word, is a revolution in control that began with bureaucracies and Max Weber's recognition of their function in modern times. It proceeded through such information inventions as interchangeable parts (after 1800), integration of production within factories (1820s and 1830s), the development of modern accounting techniques (1850s and 1860s), professional managers (1860s and 1870s), continuous-process production (around 1880), time-and-motion-management, or Taylorism (1911), assembly-line Fordism (1913) and statistical quality control (1920s). In communications industries, these control elements were complemented and enhanced by such specific reproductive and transmission technologies as photography and telegraphy (1830s), rotary power printing (1840s), the typewriter (1860s), transatlantic cable (1866), telephone (1876), motion pictures (1894), wireless telegraphy (1895), magnetic tape recording (1899), radio (1906) and television (1923).

Communication technology and the organisation of space

The march of the technology of communication and control has given rise to two fundamental changes: (1) the increased separation of information about a phenomenon from the phenomenon itself and (2) the reorganisation of space and power that results from that separation.

The separation of phenomenon and information can be explained as follows. A fisherman who has years of experience in a particular locale has access to a vast storehouse of knowledge expressed in the behaviour, feelings, superstitions and articulated understandings of fishing that are used to retrieve the past, explain the present and foretell the fishing future of that locale. Such is the wisdom of elders and locals. In contrast, fish researchers with access to computers, mathematical models, years of old records and several years of detailed data, gathered by communications satellites through infrared monitoring of weather and ocean currents, among other things, can likewise retrieve some of the past, explain the present and foretell the future. Such is the power of formal knowledge, communications and information-processing.

What does this do to the location of knowledge and power? The increased separation between a phenomenon and information descriptive of it allows a reorganisation of its spatial relations. Most significantly, it allows a shift in control from a multiplicity of scattered points, each proximate to a pheno-menon, to a central location that controls activities in a far-flung hinterland. As the information gathered increases – and it has increased enormously with digitalisation, computers, information-gathering satellites, transmission capability and information-processing capacity – the degree to which effective control can be exercised also increases.

Once the central processing centre has gained appropriate levels of infor-mation, it can begin to replace the on-location decision-maker. But the central processing centre can also introduce a further level of sophistication. It can bring in information about other locations, for example the state of world production, the state of markets, or even the state of government subsidies or restraints in other countries. It may even be able to predict more accurately events based on distant but related events.

This wider variety of information at the centre places greater power at the centre and tends to lessen the influence of the on-location expert. In fact, it may transform that person from a decision-maker into a person who responds to centralised analyses, a process sometimes called deskilling. The benefits of centralised information-gathering and analysis are often considerable. They also may disappear rather dramatically when the central information source is wrong, as it has often been in managing the North Atlantic cod fishery. Also, centralised information centres have a tendency to increase the exploitation of a resource. Thus, when mistakes are made, hundreds of hinterland producers may lose their livelihood.

The social and economic impact of separation of information and entity is extensive. First, information itself becomes a separate product that can be bought and sold. Second, as noted, increased power accrues to the centre. A third implication deriving from this separation and centralisation is an extension of the market into activities previously outside market forces. Thus, when rubber trees were discovered in Brazil and the properties of rubber were made known to Europeans, parts of the Amazon were transformed from untamed jungle into hinterland rubber farms and an integral part of the market system of Europe. When saplings were spirited out of the region and transplanted to a more human-hospitable climate, the jungle took over once again, as did the bats in the opera house in Manaus.

Some theoretical perspectives on technology

The French philosopher Jacques Ellul is generally regarded as an insightful if pessimistic theorist of technology. In his major work, *The Technological Society* (1964), Ellul's primary concern was to explore the past, present and future impacts of technological change. Of the many conclusions and observations he drew, four stand out in particular. The first is that all technical progress exacts a price; that is, while it adds something on the one hand, it subtracts something on the other. Secondly, all technical progress raises more problems than it solves, tempts us to see the consequent problems as technical in nature and prods us to seek technical solutions to them. Thirdly, the negative effects of technological innovation are inseparable from the positive. It is naive to say that technology is neutral, that it may be used for good or bad ends; the good and bad effects are, in fact, simultaneous and inseparable. Fourth, all technological innovations have unforeseen effects (Dizard, 1985, p. 11). A summary of this perspective might be that technology sets in motion powerful forces that rearrange the organising attributes of any society. Society must then invent social institutions to attempt to ensure that the technology in question is put to use for the greatest benefit for the greatest number. (We shape our tools . . . thereafter our tools shape us.)

A complementary viewpoint can be found in the writings of the Canadian philosopher, George Grant. In *Technology and Empire* (1969) Grant argues that the foundation of all modern liberal industrial and post-industrial societies is to be found in technique and technology: 'the belief that human excellence is promoted by the homogenizing and universalizing power of technology is the dominant doctrine of modern liberalism, and – that doctrine must undermine all particularisms' (p. 69). In Grant's view, then, the powerful forces which Ellul identifies are homogenising in their influence and hence are threatening the distinctive elements of societies that share the same technology. Raymond Williams (1975) has argued that television technology is an extension of the industrial revolution and feeds the mass society that industrialisation created.

Marxist American scholar Herbert Schiller (1984) has turned the above general perspective on technology around somewhat to expose a different angle. Schiller maintains that technological development and its application is an operating imperialist strategy on the part of the United States, designed to maintain economic and political dominance by technological prowess and induced technological gaps between the US and other countries. Moreover, he sees this imperialism as steered by multinational corporations, and stimulated by military research and development in communications hardware.

In contrast to these viewpoints, mainstream American scholars have been inclined to see technology as benevolent and technological change as progressive. American optimism stems from an economic history in which the development and use of machines to create wealth has been regarded as of widespread benefit to American society over the past two hundred years.

The physical foundations of communication technology

The physical foundations of electronic communications are to be found in sub-atomic particle/wave physics (otherwise called quantum mechanics) and the physics of light. Consider this passage:

> Some scientists are dissatisfied with electrons. This seems ungrateful. Electrons have served mankind [sic] well as carriers of energy; they have become adept as shufflers of information. Some of their attributes, however offend purists. They have mass, which makes them a bit sluggish. They have electric charges, which means they interfere with one another. Fortunately, there is something better around, something with no mass, no charge and no rival when it comes to speed: light. (*The Economist*, 'The optical enlightenment', 6 July, 1991, p. 87)

The result of this sub-atomic revolution has been the digitalisation of information encoding, transmission, switching, and decoding to produce a fully integrated electronic information industry where a photograph, a piece of music, and a written text, are all just so many zeros and ones.

Between physics and society

But is this enabling technology really that important? Researchers studying the social impact of new communication technologies are faced with an array of on-going basic technological changes. Often, enamoured of the technology, these researchers (e.g. Gilder, 1991) have construed social impact as a direct derivative of technological capacity. Such constructions fail to consider that it is the industrialised application of technology that has social consequence. For instance, whatever projections might be made about light-based communications, it is only that it is demonstrably cheaper, more flexible, and faster than particle technology that makes it significant. Of course, such capacities may depend on some basic characteristics of light such as the ability of beams to cross one another without interference. However, as attempts to market unwanted technologies demonstrate – facsimile in the 1940s and videotex beginning in the 1970s – impact and social significance depends on dissemination. And dissemination depends on how successfully a new technology can be introduced into existing patterns of life.

Technological difference, convergence and policy

The fact that technology becomes significant in its dissemination raises two other major points. The first is that traditionally, communication industries have been differentiated on the basis of their technology. Thus telephone companies were seen to be best at point-to-point communication requiring only limited fidelity but sophisticated switching. On the other hand, broadcast technology was seen to be good for single-to-multiple point communication, i.e. literally broadcast signals, and at a medium level of fidelity. Recording technology was seen to carry the highest demands in terms of fidelity and the lowest in terms of universality of distribution.

While the general public no doubt assumed that there was a technological base to this division of responsibilities, as Babe (1988, 1990) has pointed out, no such technological determinism existed. Telephones could easily have been turned into broadcast instruments, as they were in the very first example of voice telephony by Fessenden (see Fessenden, 1974), in early radio forms, and as they have been used in some Eastern European countries. If technological determinism did not exist then, it certainly does not exist now. The digitalisation of signals means that all forms of communication will be capable of being equal in fidelity. Cameras, computers, musical instruments, radio, television, cable, telephones, in fact all machines of information will essentially be doing the same job. They will merely be specialised computerised transceivers.

The second related point is that if technology was not the determining force, what was? The answer is: policy. Telephone and radio were separated in their functions in the early years by an agreement to share and split patents and for various companies to confine their activities to either telephone or radio. The modern policy/technology interface has been summarised nicely by several observers, including Robin Mansell (1992). Mansell notes that to choose a technology is to choose one industry for ascendance. Since all, by virtue of the technological convergence described above, are capable of doing the same thing, to choose an industry is to choose which players will be dominant and the nature of the regulatory regime that will provide the foundation for development.

The present state of technology is that since World War II, the size and capacity of computers has probably made more information-processing capacity available to the individual than both sides had in that war, at less energy per year than it would take for a fighter plane to fly one mission. Co-axial cable, which enhanced the number of signals one wire could transmit, has now been eclipsed in its capacity and efficiency by rare-earth doped, optical glass fibres. Signal compression has again enhanced transmission capacity by a sufficient level to make high-definition television feasible, whereas as late as the final months of 1991 it appeared not to be. Engineering studies have suggested to some commentators, such as Nicholas Negroponte, head of the Media Lab at MIT (Gilder, 1991), that radio communication may better be used for person to person communication (traditionally telephony) while wire might better serve the need to 'broadcast' similar signals to many people. The capacities of all these technologies are being maximised by adherence to a set of international standards to ensure system compatibility to produce Integrated Services Digital Networks (ISDNs), combining voice, data, facsimile and video in the same channels. The players in the game are newspapers and other information services, cable companies, the telephone companies, and satellite communication companies.

Rationales for and realities of technological development

While technology has a way of propelling itself by means of economic opportunity and our natural curiosity with objects and the way things work (which is encouraged by literacy), for technology to be seized upon and embraced by society requires more. The usual rationales that are used to encourage societal embrace of technology are based on some idea that this particular technology will improve the lot of humankind. The specific areas in which that improvement is purported to arise for communications are customarily in health, culture and education. In health, the spread of preventative, diagnostic, curative and emergency information is stressed. In culture, the dissemination of quality products inexpensively and more extensively is highlighted. In education, the spread of better information, designed more effectively for the learner, with the possibility of interactivity, supplemented by motivational devices and workplace relevancy is just a beginning.

Other positive impacts are claimed in the area of self-direction, social interaction, international and inter-ethnic tolerance, and even cognitive skills.

Satellites

The realities of technological development are somewhat different, as most theorists would predict. A well-known example of a known gap between rationales and realities involved the Satellite Instructional Television Experiment (SITE) undertaken by India, using an American satellite. Some 2,338 rural villages scattered across India received four hours of programming daily. The objectives of SITE were to contribute to family planning; to improve agricultural practice; to contribute to national integration; to contribute to school and adult education and to teacher training; and to improve occupational skills, health and hygiene. Some success was obtained in achieving the goals that involve the transmission of information. However, little restructuring of social relations or behaviour was observed. It has also been the general experience of TV-based education in the developing world that there is an insufficient infrastructure for the maintenance of a functioning system on a long-term basis. To obtain a constant source of electricity is a challenge in itself.

Communication satellites have not brought about a new egalitarian world but they have brought about extensive efforts at distance education both in the developed world and, for instance, in China, India, Indonesia and Thailand. While distance education does not necessarily require communication satellites, often the two are linked because satellites cope so easily with distance and distance education has been a feature of large, sparsely populated developed countries or large developing countries that lack a land-based communications infrastructure.

The marrying of satellite transmission technology or land-based technologies with computers has certainly enhanced the distance education experience. The Open University of the UK has more than 300 terminals installed in local study centres. Minitel, a electronic information service run by the French post office, has been used in France as a distance education technology. Computerised literacy programmes have been launched by the BBC and a number of projects have been introduced in Eastern Europe. The increased use of computers in these projects is indicative of the new area of emphasis that has taken over from communication satellites. That area is telematics, the marriage of computers and communication to produce modern systems of data communication. More generally, the term telematics seems to be used to describe anything that involves computers.

Telematics

To some extent the introduction of computers into the classroom has become the symbol of modernisation. The most radical of rationales for their introduction has been projected: positive effects on both cognitive process and personality development. The individualisation of the learning process has also been stressed.

There have been various developments in this area throughout the world. In Europe some countries have introduced computers at the level of technical and vocational training, while others have introduced them into the general education system. There are large-scale projects in place such as the Microelectronics Programme in Britain, the *Informatica Stimulerings* Plan in the Netherlands and in France, *Informatique pour tous*. In Hungary, since 1983 secondary schools have been equipped with one or more locally manufactured microcomputers. In 1985, after problems in dealing with Japanese characters had largely been solved, computers were to be found in senior secondary schools in Japan. By now they can be found throughout the school system. India has made limited inroads, having targeted 10,000 schools to receive microcomputers by 1990. In Latin America several countries, including Mexico, Brazil, Argentina and Cuba, have led the way through government action and the activities of private groups. Schools and libraries have been targeted in Mexico to receive microcomputers to assist in literacy training. Some effort has also been made in the Ivory Coast, with the assistance of Unesco (Jouët and Coudray, 1991, p. 43).

These investments represent an impressive allocation of resources and, to some extent, as microcomputers become an intrinsic part of any work environment, they are justified as part of a modern school curriculum. In terms of some of the more radical claims, computer-assisted teaching (CAT) appears to improve pupil performance, but no more than any other innovative method. Using CAT, there is an interaction between supervision and pupil age, with students requiring it at an early age and not benefiting from it later in life. Evaluations of the effects of Logo, a software program intended for use in the development of cognitive skills, on cognitive skills have proved contradictory (Jouët and Coudray, 1991, p. 44). Some factors which appear to affect the introduction of telematics into the classroom are the availability of high-quality educational software; the match between the software and the linguistic and cultural environment; teacher training; and the availability of significant additional budgets (Jouët and Coudray, 1991, pp. 44, 45).

Technology transfer

In being affected by cultural, linguistic and educational environments and the like, the potential benefits of communications technology are realised only to a limited extent. The communications literature that discusses such assimilation of new technologies is usually referred to as literature on 'technology transfer'.

Research on technology transfer reveals a number of insights. Generally speaking, direct causal correlations between introduction of technology and cultural patterns cannot be identified. Technically-oriented approaches to the introduction of technology are limited in their effectiveness. Assessment of the impact of domestic or endogenous manufacture of equipment has been embarked on by some countries such as Hungary, India and Brazil, but as yet the economic or social impact is not apparent. The importation of turn-key operations – in which the importing country has little to do except follow instructions and turn the machinery on – often proves of limited value for lack of prior study of needs, and because of an emphasis on the package rather than the content and the technology itself. Such transfers also create substantial long-term dependency relationships.

Negotiations of technology transfers would appear to have promise but often get bogged down in political and economic considerations while communication needs are bypassed. The effectiveness of transfers are also affected by limited exploration of the differing needs and dynamics of developed and developing countries. To give one obvious example, blowing desert sand, high temperatures and high humidity can play havoc with almost any electronic equipment. Massive importation of equipment may be of no value, as happened in China, until software and technologists are there to instruct users. Even attempts to create teleports, that is self-sufficient zones of advanced telecommunications and high-tech industries (known as little Silicon Valleys in North America), to serve as springboards for industrialisation have yet to prove themselves as immune to technology transfer limitations (Jouët and Coudray, 1991, pp. 37, 38).

A facilitative legal and policy framework

Currently, by international covenant, countries have the right to participate in communications development and to protect themselves from it. A country can object, for example, should an unwanted satellite signal spill over its boundaries. Japan has adjusted some of its satellite footprints in response to such objections. Countries also have the power to forbid the importation or exportation of any other form of information material or immaterial (i.e. books or electronic signals). On the other side of the issue, any country has the right to launch broadcast satellites, although it may first have to negotiate for a parking place, and any country can encourage internationally-oriented satellite operators to locate within its boundaries, as Britain and the US have done. These activities all take place within both international and national legal frameworks, as we explored in Chapter 3. Those frameworks make a considerable difference to the organisation of communication and information activity, as Lorimer and O'Donnell have pointed out (1992).

Technological development represents a continual challenge for legal systems and policy makers. Perhaps the greatest challenge is to ensure that the greatest number gain the maximum benefit. At times and in some countries this means assisting dissemination. At other times in other countries it may mean denying people access to certain technologies and content in order to promote a more universal distribution of other content via alternative technology. For example, in Europe cable TV has been a long time in coming; one reason is that it would have undermined state monopolies (Collins, 1992). In addition to these constraints the rights of individuals to 'seek, receive and impart information' must also be respected. The privacy of the individual must be respected: profiles of individual consumer behaviour by tracing their spending patterns potentially infringes on this right. To what extent this is now done by credit card companies is unclear; certainly, some monitoring is done in the name of the prevention of fraud. And many governments are positively rushing to market to sell their collected data. This brings forward the other side of the privacy equation – the security of the information system, be it a credit card operation or a databank.

Protection of intellectual property has also become an issue. First, are patterns of electronic signals eligible for protection, and if so over what period of time and under the regime of trademarks or copyright? Should vendors be allowed to sell products in which the vendor may confine the use and the time period of ownership? How should national laws be harmonised to allow international co-ordination if there are fundamentally different positions on these issues? What protection and compensation should creators of databases give to primary producers of information? Should both moral and economic rights be protected? Who has responsibility for libel in the chain of information producers, packagers, transmitters, and so on?

How should piracy be controlled? Given the historical record, and specifically the building of the American publishing industry on a foundation of piracy, what obligations should developing economies take on? This is a significant trade issue with the US and they have tied trade initiatives to reform in piracy. Studies have been undertaken (see Acheson and Maule, 1994 and International Intellectual Property Alliance, 1989), which show that computer, sound and video piracy are especially rampant. In India so many venues were showing pirated videos that the state introduced a licensing system to attempt to garner revenues. Although this was done, the videos shown continued to be illegal copies. The film industry of Egypt is severely crippled by the numerous bootleg copies made as soon as any film is finished. However, the motivation for many countries to take decisive action is not strong, as the effect of legislation would be primarily to protect the interests of the US.

The World Intellectual Property Organisation has been active in extending copyright protection to audio-visual authors and creators. While commendable, are such international organisations under any obligation to review the balance of benefit between various parties involved in copyright agreements? The position of music publishers and song-writers is especially troublesome. Traditionally, for a song to be protected it had to be written down and published. Music publishers agreed to publish songs, i.e. sometimes no more than print a few copies, and in return drove hard bargains with naive and usually young musicians, who not only gave control of the exploitation of the music to the publisher, but also granted the publisher up to 50 per cent of the future royalties. The Committee of Ministers of the Council of Europe has also been active in combating piracy in the field of copyright and neighbouring rights. In certain parts of the world piracy is rampant, notably in Asia and increasingly in Eastern Europe and Russia, and in other parts little is done to control the flow of pirated products. The use of artistic work for the promotion of commercial products without the permission of the original artist is also not uncommon.

Various sections of the media industry have an interest in seeing law and practice rationalised. In 1991 a breakthrough came with regard to Digital Audio Tape (DAT), at least in the US. Previously content producers had been reluctant to allow any of their products to be made available on DAT, essentially because virtually perfect copies could be made. Now producers have looked into their crystal ball and decided to accept the inevitability of home digital copying, whether on DAT or some future technology such as rewritable disk. In return for the producers ceasing to object, the hardware manufacturers have agreed to design in features which allow single copies but discourage copying from copies. Importers and US domestic manufacturers have agreed to pay 2 per cent royalties on the wholesale price of digital recording equipment with a maximum of US$8 or 3 per cent on each blank tape. This brings the US into line with such countries as Germany and with the intentions of the European Commission for 1992 (*The Economist*, 'In harmony', 20 July 1991, pp. 83, 84).

The changes which all communications technologies working together bring about has encouraged the European Commission to develop a policy to create an audio-visual area, a single market for European information products that will authorise the reception and retransmission in all member states of broadcasts which comply with a set of specific requirements. To undertake this task in areas such as television, quotas on the number of foreign programme imports are being proposed, along with the regulation of advertising and programming patterns that protect young people from pornography (EEC Green Paper 1989). In a complementary policy adopted in

October 1989, the countries of the European Community, the Council of Europe and four countries of Eastern Europe adopted an 'Audio-visual Eureka' plan for strengthening their television production capacity.

The philosophical approach one takes as to how information should be handled at the international level depends in part on one's definition of information. While information might be treated as a commodity, the European Court of Human Rights has ruled that information and televised exchanges come within the scope of services, as opposed to goods. Various international organisations are considering whether, for example, broadcasting should be a freely circulating service. Such a definition might help advance the debate on free trade versus balanced trade in information by recasting it as free trade or free circulation of information (Jouët and Coudray, 1991, pp. 27–32).

Perhaps the best way to organise a discussion of technology within a practical and concrete framework is to consider how it affects production, distribution and consumption of media materials.

Technology and production

The technological histories of the various media of production – printing in its various forms, radio, television, and film are not parallel. Printing began as a small two- or three-person operation and grew into a vast operation in which newspaper presses can cover areas almost as large as football fields. Radio began similarly as a small operation. The number of people customarily used to staff one station is still comparatively small – under a dozen – however, it is increasingly rare for radio stations to be single, stand-alone enterprises. The history of television is quite different, as is film production history. Indeed it is almost the opposite to that of the press and radio. The initial investment required to begin television production in its early days was substantial. Not only was the equipment bulky and expensive, but studios were required for shooting to take place. The financial investment required began with equipment and buildings; then crews of performers, writers, directors, technicians and make-up artists were also needed. The requirements of television were not unlike those of putting on a play. On top of these costs, there was no direct and immediate way to charge the consumer for reception and begin a quick cost recovery. Licence fees and advertising had already proven themselves in radio but until people began to buy sets, television production had to be financed at some risk to investors or at some cost to government. The situation in film was much the same, with high equipment, physical plant, and personnel costs.

In addition to expense, television and film were also hampered by immobility. As powerful as the visual image was, the equipment used did not allow real life to be readily captured. Means had to be devised for simulating life. Feature film drew upon the theatre and other performance art, such as vaudeville. Documentary film married the rhetoric of radio and the techniques of theatre with on-site footage collected with great organisation, effort and expense. As a later technology, and one that would carry both fiction and documentary programming, television drew on these roots but introduced techniques of its own – programme series, commentators with visual support and so forth.

Considerable technological development has ensued since those early days. We have ended up with an interesting technological, and hence communicational, environment. The press is dominated by large institutions that have the capacity to print vast amounts of information and advertising that is widely distributed to large communities in a short space of time. Over and above this elephantine character, the press has been allowed by governments to form itself into conglomerates. In so doing they have transformed themselves from elephants to dinosaurs, purely in terms of size of course. The newspaper press is quite similar to the general interest periodical press in terms of its size and method of production, although, as Driver and Gillespie (1993) point out, there are trends towards more decentralised operations. On the other hand, many book publishers are small. This is because it has become the custom to contract out their printing. No vast investments are required in plant and so one- to five-person operations are common.

The implications for content production of this small size and capitalisation are that books have become more heterogeneous than either the press or magazines in the range of content they produce. The continual emergence and disappearance of magazine titles is also a countertrend to what we are describing here. Undercapitalisation means that book publishing is more likely to be a medium with a fuller range of opinion than newspapers and magazines because there is much less in investment to lose. However, unlike journalists, who are salaried, book authors must fund or find support for their own research and take personal responsibility for their work: fact checking is extremely limited or non-existent; libel checking is more common. On the other hand, the wealth and employer/employee structure that is part of the newspaper and periodical industry allows for substantial research.

In the case of film, and even more so with television, production has moved in the same direction as books. The downsizing and downpricing of equipment, the expansion of the industry to encompass entertainment, education and industrial productions, the emergence of production rental shops as well as stand-alone post-production houses, have led both to mobility, hence relatively easy location shooting, and to the emergence of a plethora of small independent producers. This techno-industrial phenomenon, i.e. the existence of this community of independent producers, has put pressure on national broadcasters to increase purchases of productions from 'independents' and decrease in-house productions. Recognition of the contribution this industry could make was the moving force behind Channel 4 in the UK. In the US the networks are limited in the number of productions they may take on and 'out-source' many of their highly touted series. Of course, in many instances ownership ties exist between the outside producers and the networks. In France and Germany the participation of independent producers in providing programmes for broadcast companies has increased substantially over recent years. In Canada pressure has been exerted on the CBC and the National Film Board (NFB) to out-source, partly as a result of federal government budget cuts to thse organisations.

These changes from large to small players have paved the way for changes in content. In documentary work the changes have been most dramatic. On-location shooting is now commonplace, not only in the immediate environs of the broadcasting station but, by virtue of portable satellite transceiver dishes, anywhere in the world where one can point at the sky. The independents also tend, like book publishers, to produce a heterogeneity of content. The fact that we see very little of that heterogeneity on our television screens is a function of the organisation of distribution and the regulation of reception. But that too is changing. Distribution, the focus of discussion in the next section, is still controlled by large, highly capitalised operations. While they do not cite television broadcast figures, Curran and Seaton (1988) point out that the costs of establishing a cable television station are about £30 million. For a satellite television channel they are £300 to £400 million. These compare with about £10 million to set up and run a national daily newspaper, about £2 million to set up and run a local radio station and less than £10,000 to found a book publishing house.

To view politically and aesthetically diverse film and video a person has had to turn to sources outside the mainstream. Producer co-operatives formed to distribute such products have been common. Increasingly, non-broadcast cable channels are picking up such material. In the US, citizens can usually be successful in insisting on access to cable facilities; however, for this the producers gain little or no revenue. Community and interest groups also provide both publicity and distribution as do educational institutions, especially at the post-secondary level. While all these means of distribution are important, with production of an acceptable documentary running at not less than £12,000 it is extremely difficult to recover costs. Thus the vast majority of such material is underwritten by private- and public-sector bodies such as interest groups, governments, foundations, educational institutions and the like. While such funding tends to ensure solvency on a project-by-project basis, the audience reach of the means of distribution noted above is severely limited in comparison with broadcast or certain cable or satellite channel distribution. There also is a legitimacy attached to appearing on well-used channels.

Technology and distribution

The discussion of production has led us to distribution, but first let us backtrack and establish some fundamental elements of distribution. The central concern of Mark Hepworth's work in *Geography of the Information Economy* (1989) is with distribution. Now working in Britain, Hepworth did much of his initial research on the geographical manifestations of communications technology in Canada. He has described the evolution of the physical location of modern businesses in the context of developments in information technology. He used Canada's self-designated 'national newspaper', the *Globe and Mail*, as a case-study.

The *Globe* has always attempted to appeal to the elite of Toronto, Canada's largest city, which sees itself as the industrial centre of Canada. In appealing to this upscale market, it is continuously vulnerable to forays by other Toronto papers, especially the *Toronto Star*, a much higher circulation mid-market broadsheet. Much of the content carried by the *Globe* has always been of interest outside Toronto; however, the difficulty has been cheap and timely delivery of that information in such a large country. So, in 1978 the *Globe* set up a research and development collaboration with the *Los Angeles Times* and in October of 1980 began beaming up from Toronto an electronic facsimile to a communications satellite, which was beamed down again across Canada's five-and-a-half time zones to Vancouver, Calgary, Brandon, Ottawa and Moncton. The result in circulation figures is that sales outside Ontario have risen from 20,000 to about 150,000. The owners (Thomson) have managed to cut the costs and increase the size of the out-of-Toronto edition.

The *Globe and Mail* is not the only paper to be operating in this manner. The *Wall Street Journal* and *USA Today* not only distribute copies within North America by satellite, they do the same for Europe. Similarly, the London-based *Financial Times* and the *China Daily News* are imported to the US by satellite. When Robert Maxwell and Conrad Black were each trying to buy the *Jerusalem Post*, the purchase price appeared to indicate that both contemplated satellite delivery to centres around the world that might be interested in news from Israel.

A second, much changing area that Hepworth discusses is financial markets. Traditionally, firms have offered shares and other investment opportunities on a particular stock market in the country of their head office. Since the major stock exchanges of the world have become electronic and can be monitored from any location, not only does it become possible for traders to participate in markets far from where they are located, but also trading can take place during the working hours of many different stock exchanges. Putting together the trading hours of a variety of exchanges, for example London, New York and Tokyo, allows for a 24-hour trading day. Combined with more flexible rules about trading, this encourages wider participation and makes possible worldwide trading services for those who care to make the investment in communications technology. In short, parallel to our example of the fisherman, Knight (1984, p. 15) notes:

> In the days of domestic trading and before the technological era, [stock trading] information was best provided by people meeting in one place at particular times using facilities provided by a stock exchange floor ... It is clear the international capital markets lie not so much with those who provide a physical floor where trading can take place, but with those who control the information systems.

Which companies benefit? According to Stonham (1987), so far 24-hour trading goes on in a few large companies: 'The names involved [in Europe] are predictable so far: large companies like ICI, BAT and Glaxo from the UK; Honda, Hitachi and Matsushita from Japan, Royal Dutch Shell and Philips from the Netherlands' (p. 13). On the other hand, the market for on-line financial information is growing by 30 per cent per year (Hepworth, 1989, p. 174).

Other developments follow similar scenarios. For example, information services (teleports) have been seized by some municipal governments and countries as the basis for inner-city regeneration. Multinational firms are beginning to plan for flexibility between national locations in production to respond to labour costs, labour unrest, exchange rates and so forth. Hepworth argues that the delivery of components 'just in time' (for assembly) represents a trade of information for material capital.

Hepworth claims that information centres need not be located next to manufacturing centres. While true, it is also the case that information operations, just like businesses, require other services such as finance, labour and transportation, all of which are in place in traditional centres of manufacture. As noted, teleports have yet to prove themselves. However, if municipal governments in favoured climatic locations are aggressive in selling themselves, office rents continue to rise in old control centres, and if the banks are willing, the growth of head offices may take a different locational pattern than it has to date.

From a more general perspective and with regard to basic communication industries, distribution technologies have obviously had a major impact. National newspapers are now possible in large countries such as Russia, Canada, China, Australia and the US. The influence of smaller and lighter video recording and transmission equipment has suppressed the tyranny of distance. Courtesy of ISDN, any information gathered in whatever manner, as long as it is electronic or material form, can be made available anywhere in the world. Small but sophisticated television receive-only (TVRO) dishes, together with satellite systems and in-home, more powerful computers (the telephone can be seen as a small computer), are providing ever-easier information access to the average person. As if this were not enough, proposals now abound for ideas such as putting up larger and more powerful communication satellites, each capable of handling all channels now available in North America, if not the western hemisphere, some 65,000 km above the earth in geosynchronous orbit, double geostationary orbit. They have been dubbed 'death stars' by the cable industry, because of the threat they pose to cable signal delivery. Less lofty are the plans of Motorola to launch a flock of seventy-seven low-orbiting satellites that would form a system known as Iridium. The purpose of the system would be to allow customers to use pocket phones to phone from anywhere to anywhere on the earth's surface. Motorola has nine competitors. One is Globalstar, which proposes a system of forty-eight satellites to be launched by Loral, an aerospace company. Other consortia, such as one led by Hughes Aircraft, think three high-orbit satellites would do the trick.

Technology and consumption

Patterns of distribution pave the way for a discussion of the influence of technology on patterns of consumption. The most obvious consumer technology that has changed television viewing habits is the remote electronic channel changer. This device gives the viewer the power to change the channel quickly whenever s/he likes. When ads appear, zap, another channel appears. Slight boredom, zap, the viewer is gone. Two programmes the viewer wants to watch at the same time, zap, now one, now the other.

Video recorders (VCRs) have introduced 'time shifted' viewing. A programme can be recorded when broadcast and viewed at a later time or date. VCRs have also had an impact on the total amount of broadcast television watched. Together with rental shops they provide the viewer with a much greater ability to choose what to watch, provided, as always, that the material manages to gain entry to some channel of distribution. Rental shops themselves have an impact by allowing the consumer a broader choice of feature film and the ability to watch at a self-chosen time and without commercials. Through licensing, cable distributors can be prevailed upon to foreground national stations on a basic service and place foreign channels on a discretionary service in return for being granted a territorial monopoly. Regulation of the product mix in rental shops is more difficult and has yet to be attempted, except to exclude or classify pornography. Direct Broadcast Satellites (DBS) are also difficult to regulate, especially when their footprint legally crosses more than one border. The multiplication of channel capacity has also had a major impact on consumption. Basically the market has been fragmented and greater numbers of specialty channels are appearing – there is even a science-fiction channel in the US – fragmenting the market even further.

Not a great deal is happening in radio at present, although the increased fidelity of digital radio will certainly affect the recording industry. Some wire services are available over short wave, however, such services are unlikely to have any major impact on the general consumption of newspapers or television viewing.

In the press, the basic reorganising technological change is multiple printing sites for single national or international papers. Journalists are increasingly able to access electronic databases – sometimes up to 5,000 in the wealthier papers. They write their stories into computers. Printing presses are being computerised for a higher quality product. Some papers are providing electronic access to business news or other sections of the paper. No doubt this presages future changes in presenting stock market prices. With environmentalists biting at their heels, it will be hard for newspapers to justify the number of trees that are cut down to produce the paper on which the odd reader checks his/her stocks. Already papers are cutting down the size of their weekend editions.

Conclusion

'We shape our tools . . .' – with technological convergence and the current power of communications technology, the observation that policy is the key to technology, its industrialisation and impact is one to remember. '. . . thereafter our tools shape us' – the technological design of our future communication system will be played out largely in the arena of international politics and economics. While the international regimes, such as GATT, NAFTA, EC policies such as *Television without frontiers*, and the Berne Copyright Convention, that control international trade in communications products address consumer freedoms and target audiences with shared viewing habits, they are weak or do not address the needs of national and political communities and their cultures.

Summary

This chapter began with a review of technology in current policy development in the European Community. We noted the dominance of technological feasibility and its concomitant market-oriented thinking. We also noted the relative absence of cultural considerations from the discussion on the power and impact of technological progress and dissemination in communications.

We then put forward a definition of technology, outlined the nature of technology in general principle, discussed the manner in which the reorganisation of space, which communication technology makes possible, takes place and assessed its consequences. Following these sections we reviewed several complementary theoretical perspectives of technology.

From these heights we descended to a discussion of the physical attributes of communication technology albeit in the most basic and limited manner. As we noted, the significance of technology lies not in its capability but in the degree to which it is embraced by industry or society. We took note not only of current technological convergence but also of the role policy has played throughout history in the organisation of electronic communication.

We then turned to the rationales most often used for technological development and adoption, and contrasted them with the realities of technological impact. We discussed satellites and telematics as examples, and reviewed the literature on technological transfer. In addition, we pointed to the types of laws and policies that facilitate the adoption and application of technology.

In three final sections we reviewed the current state of technology in production, distribution and consumption across the media. In the final paragraph we returned to the theme of the interaction of technology, industry, policy and culture.

References

Acheson, Keith and Chris Maule (1994), 'International regimes for trade, copyright and investments in film and television' in Stuart McFadyen, Colin Hoskins and Adam Finn (eds.), *Cultural Development in an Open Economy*, unpublished report to Social Science and Humanities Research Council of Canada, Ottawa.

Babe, R. (1988), 'Emergence and development of Canadian communication: dispelling the myths' in R. Lorimer and D. C. Wilson, *Communication Canada*, Kagan and Woo, Toronto.

Babe, R. (1990), *Telecommunications in Canada*, University of Toronto Press, Toronto.

Beniger, James (1986), *The Control Revolution*, Harvard University Press, Cambridge, Mass.

Collins, Richard (1992), *Satellite Television in Western Europe*, rev. ed., John Libbey Acamedia Research Monograph 1, London.

Crowley, David and Paul Heyer (1991), *Communication in History: Technology, Culture Society*, Longman, London.

Curran, James and Jean Seaton (1988), *Power Without Responsibility: The Press and Broadcasting in Britain*, 3rd edn., Routledge, London.

Dizard, Wilson P. (1985), *The Coming Information Age: An Overview of Technology, Economics and Politics*, Longman, New York.

Driver, Stephen and Andrew Gillespie (1993), *Media Culture and Society*, 15(2), pp. 183–202.

Ellul, Jacques (1964), *The Technological Society*, Knopf (Vintage), New York.

Fessenden, Helen (1974), *Fessenden: Builder of Tomorrows*, Arno Press, New York.
Gilder, George F. (1991), 'Into the telecosm', *Harvard Business Review*, March–April, pp. 150–61.
Grant, George (1969), *Technology and Empire*, Anansi, Toronto, p. 69.
Hepworth, Mark (1989), *The Geography of the Information Economy*, Belhaven Press, London.
International Intellectual Property Alliance (1989), *Trade Losses Due to Piracy and Other Market Access Barriers Affecting the US Copyright Industries*, IIPA, Washington, DC.
Jouët, Josiane and Sylvie Coudray (1991), *New Communication Technologies: Research Trends*, Reports and Papers on Mass Communication, no. 105, Unesco, Paris.
Knight, J. (1984), 'The interconnection of European stock exchanges', *The Stock Exchange Quarterly*, December, pp. 14–16.
Lorimer, Rowland and Eleanor O'Donnell (1992), 'Globalization and internationalization: issues for publishing', *Canadian Journal of Communication*, 17, pp. 493–509.
Mansell, Robin (1992), 'Information and communication technology policy research in the UK: a perspective', *Canadian Journal of Communications*, 19(1), pp. 23–40.
Paltridge, Sam (1989), *Australian Satellites: Promises, Performance and the Next Generation*, Centre for International Research on Communication and Information Technologies, Policy Research Paper no. 1, Melbourne.
Schiller, H. I. (1984), *Information and the Crisis Economy*, Ablex Publishing, Norwood, NJ.
Shannon, Claude E. and Warren Weaver (1949), *The Mathematical Theory of Communication*, University of Illinois Press, Urbana.
Stonham, P. (1987), *Global Stock Market Reports*, Gower, Aldershot.
Williams, Raymond (1975), *Television: Technology and Cultural Form*, Schocken Books, New York.

Chapter 7

Media and audiences

In the previous four chapters we have outlined how law and policy, ownership and institutional organisation, professional goals and practice, and technology and its industrialisation influence the manner in which communications are organised and carried out. Audiences can be seen to play a parallel role to these four factors and it is the role of audiences that we explore in this chapter.

In the 1980s audiences began to come under close scrutiny by both the industry and researchers (e.g. Morley, 1980). Undoubtedly privatisation and the forces of competition for advertising revenue have contributed to the interest of media owners and their organisations in audiences. Prior to this increased scrutiny the image of audiences held by media owners and producers, at least in the private sector, was extremely limited. Their size, some basic demographic characteristics, consumption patterns and preferences, and responses to audience-building techniques were typically about the extent of that knowledge and understanding. With increased attention to audiences by researchers and industry, the area has become highly theorised and is becoming highly researched. The main contribution made by this increased attention has been to transform audiences from passive vessels into which media messages were poured to active, thinking human agents seeking information, entertainment and enlightenment by means of purposeful consumption and interpretation. Many scholars are increasingly reluctant to talk about media content outside the context of the receiving audience. Fiske (1989) calls for the binding together of the three-part entity of creator-content-audience as a reasonable 'unit of analysis'.

A theoretical synthesis: an interaction of meaning-generating systems

In this chapter we present eight approaches to the study of the audience; however, partly because they do not seem to account fully for what audiences make of the media, we will begin with a theoretical synthesis. There are two parts to this synthesis, which may be used both to understand media-audience relations and to understand and evaluate the different approaches to them. The first is that media-audience interaction is probably best conceived as an open discussion (on the part of analysts) of audiences (both as groups and as individual members) and media content and forms. In such a discussion we do not assume that the media pour meaning into audiences or audience members as if they were empty receptacles, nor that the media program audience members or audiences themselves in the same manner that a computer is programmed. Also we do not conceive of the audience as made up of fragile beings desperately seeking contact and meaning through the media. Most importantly, we take the position that media content cannot induce a member of the audience to act against or outside his or her own will.

What we do assume about both the media and the audience, and also about the cultures in which both exist, is as follows. Audience members, audiences as groups, the media, and the cultures in which they reside are meaning-generating entities which may affect one another. What does this mean? First, it means that media and audiences generate meaning in that they collect information (in a broad sense of the word), analyse it, synthesise it, and transform, reconstruct, or re-express it. Secondly, it means that while the media and the audience may affect one another, they do not account for one another because the interaction is always complex, multidimensional, and mediated by a choice process, which is complex in itself being affected by both situational and historical contexts. Finally, meaning generation is not confined to thinking and language. Meaning may consist of utterances, written words, silence, images, emotions, intuitions, imitation, or social action.

Because the relation between media and audiences is interactional but not predetermined, any consideration of the interaction between audience behaviour, media content, and cultural form must take place within a very broad framework, one that has the potential to encompass any and all elements of the interaction, including degrees of engagement.

Cultures, like audiences and like media programmes, are also meaning-generating systems. They generate their identity from their history, their laws, various institutions that mediate interaction, governing structures, opportunities afforded by their cultural and physical geography, and so forth. They generate meaning through interacting on the basis of this identity, in a particular style, and with the events of the day. How each as a totality responds domestically and internationally in time of plenty and in time of crisis is derived from the wealth, history, and present-day attitudes and responses of groups and individuals. The responses of cultures create meaning by exemplifying principles of action for both themselves and others to see; witness, for example, the 1992 Earth Summit in Brazil where the nations of the world were content to affirm platitudes but unwilling to adopt a framework of action that would turn around the degradation of the global ecosystem.

Stated succinctly, the synthesis we have proposed posits that lived reality at the level of the individual, the group, and the culture interact with media realities and with one another through a constant process of mutual selection, re-stylisation (or appropriation), transformation, and re-display.

An illustration

In an article in a popular Canadian magazine John Lekich (1982) provides an illustration of media-audience interaction. In an amusing and vivid manner, he illustrates the role television played in his 1960s childhood. He talks of his mother's attention to the set as a valued piece of furniture. He talks of his early wonder about how so many people came to be inside the TV set. He recreates the child's wonder and naive embrace of mother figures such as US television-actress June Allyson, his literal interpretation of Camay soap advertisements, and his persistent if not desperate attempt to touch the people behind the television screen.

Perhaps what makes his piece so interesting is the detail of his memories. These details evoke memories and the images come rolling back to anyone who grew up in the same era in North America, or who has seen re-runs. The memories include not only the content of the programmes but the entire family dynamic that the television programmes created: what restrictions there were on viewing, how late one was allowed to stay up, parental differences in viewing habits, involvement in programmes, and so forth. In short, he gives us access to his memory of the world created for him by his television set. Whether his model was any one of a number of famous television actors of the 1960s such as June Allyson, Van Johnson, Jimmy Stewart, Robert Young, or Donna Reed, they and the situations in which they were placed, including intervening commercials, provided the fabric of his dreams. As he says, based on the television world,

> My wife would be ideal. She would have no cavities, an embroidered hanky for each day of the week, and a hairdo with crash helmet durability. She would never do the upsetting things that mothers did, like making you eat creamed corn or sticking name tags on the inside of your underwear. At night we would walk up a long staircase to our separate beds, and read books across to each other. Just like Donna Reed.   (Lekich, 1982, p. 51).

The power of the article is that it makes the futility of calculating the relative influence of television as compared to social interaction, movies or books quite apparent. It forces us to recognise the extent to which the material presented on television can become fodder for a child's imagination.

Lekich and the various producers of the television shows he watched can be seen as independent but interacting with each other to create social and cultural meanings. Lekich was interacting with the programming through viewing. It was interacting with him through his willingness, along with millions of others, to tune in each week to these various shows and through the sponsors' interest in having access to him and his fellow audience members. In addition, the programmers made a conscious attempt to portray ideal-typical interactions to which their viewer could relate. The nature of this interaction is that neither is free from the influence of the other, yet neither is determined by the other.

Seven approaches to the study of audiences

Jensen and Rosengren (1990) and Lindlof (1991) have provided useful reviews of the development of recent audience research. Lindlof points out that the audience research with which he is concerned is qualitative and relies on inductive and interpretive methods. This approach can be distinguished from quantitative research, which deals with audience characteristics that can be counted, such as size, hours watched, etc. Lindlof also points out that, according to recent literature, the meanings audiences derive from texts or content are 'socially situated rather than resident in the text, author's intentions, or analytic categories of the audience that are imposed from without, [and] that qualitative audience research seeks to preserve the form, content, and context of social phenomena and analyze their qualities rather then separate them from historical and institutional surroundings' (p. 24). The perspective of this chapter is consistent with Lindlof's analysis. It is that audience behaviour and interpretations of media content derive from a combination of factors that include a) the personality and general outlook of the audience member b) his/her current state of mind (i.e. situational variables) c) the social situation in which the viewing is taking place, and d) the text or content.

Effects research

The idea of conceiving of the interaction between the audience and the media as effects derives from early survey research into the media conducted primarily by American social psychologists, such as Katz and Lazarsfeld (1965) and Klapper (1960). The primary question that interested these psychologists was the *influence of the media*. They were working to dispel the formulations of a group of European social theorists known as the Frankfurt School. The claim of the Frankfurt School was that the media were powerful instruments of social control that offered the masses false pleasures and in doing so destroyed human individuality and the possibility of critical thought (Adorno and Horkheimer, 1947, 1972). The ideological assumption of the American psychologists who set out to counteract these theories was that the media were democratic institutions that brought all people into the mainstream of the culture. They set out to document the 'effects' of exposure to the information and entertainment the media were able to bring into the homes and neighbourhoods of all Americans in the 1950s and 1960s.

At first these studies assumed the media would have strong, direct and specific effects on individual behaviour. It was thought, for instance, that TV influenced people's voting patterns at election time, or that the depiction of violence on TV might have harmful consequences, especially for young viewers. But to the surprise of the researchers, in general weak effects were identified. Having found weaker effects than anticipated, the task of reconceiving the nature of effects was addressed. Longer term, indirect and diffuse effects were sought. Thus recent research in this tradition has focused on such phenomena as the agenda-setting role of the media, that is to say, what issues are discussed and sometimes acted upon by, for instance, the government of the day. The message has also been more broadly conceived. Thus rather than looking for predictable voting behaviour, researchers tend now to look for positive or negative attitudes, for example towards a politician or political platform. Phrased a little differently, beginning with Gerbner (1969), researchers examined the effects of viewing behaviour on people's conception of social reality. This perspective has evolved into what is called 'cultivation analysis', wherein content is studied for its ability to encourage or cultivate a positive attitude in the viewer towards a particular person or perspective (see Morgan and Signorelli, 1990). In addition, the social context surrounding the audience has been increasingly differentiated, studied and named, where macro refers to the overall societal level, mezzo to the group or institutional, and micro to the personal or individual.

Effects analysis has received a great deal of criticism, essentially because researchers have not been able to identify clear, strong effects of media exposure. McLeod, Kosicki and Pan (1991) have attempted to revitalise the effects perspective through a reconsideration of the characteristics of the approach and the various critiques of it that have been mounted. Such developments have increased the usefulness of recent effects research. However, conceiving of the link between the media and people as 'effects' tends to narrow the scope of the questions one might ask about media-audience interaction, even when elaborations such as agenda setting and cultivation theory are introduced into the basic equation. Also, in any experiment or survey it is almost impossible to separate the influence of media content from the myriad other influences that exist in the environment. Because of the impossibility of controlling the prior exposure of audience members to the message in question, let alone what they have made of that exposure, it is very difficult to isolate the 'effects' of the media contribution to a wide selection of people's opinions or behaviour. Even in cases when one finds the 'smoking television set', a set – belonging to some individual who has committed a heinous crime – tuned to a channel that hours previously had shown a model of the crime committed, there is always more to the story. Specifically, there is human agency. For example, what in the person's background could make him (or her) vulnerable to internalising a message to act in an aberrant fashion? Consequently, discussion of the 'effects' of media on society becomes problematic.

Uses and gratification research

Uses and gratification research (U&G) began as a reaction against effects research (Blumler and Katz, 1974). Its central question is 'what do viewers do with the media'? From the beginning this approach was more attentive to audience variables, that is, the orientations and interpretations the audience brought to its selection of media content. Given its roots in social psychology, it has concentrated, not surprisingly, on the micro and mezzo level of social existence, in other words, the individual psychological and the social psychological. Little attention has been paid to the macro-social, the ideological, cultural, or political orientations of the audience. Recent work has spoken of never-ending spirals of uses and effects, where audience members look to the media for certain information (Rosengren and Windahl, 1989). Having gained it they behave in a particular way and then return to the media for further information, and so it continues. In fact, the two areas – effects and uses research – have been growing closer to each other and have become mutually complementary.

The major difficulty with uses and gratification research and theory is that it conceives of the subject as need-driven and thus plays down human agency. The nature of the research question tends to be as follows: given media exposure, what can be identified in the behaviour of the audience member that can be attributed to that exposure? In other words, although the focus is on what individuals do with the media, the emphasis is on the impact of the media on people's lives. In the end human agency is downplayed.

Cultural studies

Effects studies and 'uses and gratifications' developed in the US between the 1940s and 1960s. Both were heavily 'content' oriented, tended to rely on quantitative measurement, and assumed a simple psychological model of human 'needs'. Both were subsequently criticised by the 'cultural studies' approach to the analysis of the media, for lacking any critical perspective of either the character of modern (American) society or the role of modern media therein.

Cultural studies has two 'moments'. The first is the work of the members of the Frankfurt School in the 1930s and 1940s; the second is that of British cultural studies in the 1960s and 1970s. Both shared a commitment to a Marxist perspective on the analysis of modern societies. Karl Marx was a key thinker and analyst of modern societies, one of only a handful of intellectuals whose ideas have had a fundamental impact on modern life. The basis of Marx's ideas is that if you want to understand how a society really works you must look at how it meets the material needs (for food, shelter, clothing, and so forth) of its members. In other words, you begin a study of social life by looking at production: the manufacture of resources and goods that people need to maintain themselves and others. Modern, Western societies, Marx argued, were characterised by a new and revolutionary mode of production, industrial capitalism, where scientific techniques, applied to the mass production of an ever-increasing range of goods (or commodities, in Marx's terms), created wealth for the owners of capital (the factory owners). Modern capitalism, Marx argued, transformed all aspects of life: it changed politics, culture and social relations. It was a tremendous force with a double-edged potential. On the one hand, mass-production techniques seemed to offer the possibility of the end of scarcity. Material abundance might be available to all, if the techniques of modern manufacturing were somehow regulated in the interests of all. However, that is not the way things are in Western society. Indeed, it is a bitter paradox that while butter and beef mountains grow higher in the European Community, millions starve or live in hunger elsewhere in the world and even in Europe itself.

In Marx's analysis, the villain in the story is the capitalist, the property owner, who is motivated by a desire to accumulate an ever-increasing amount of capital and wealth. In other words, Marx argued, the system of production serves the interests of capitalists, who constitute only a tiny fraction of the population: the vast majority of people are workers and are exploited by the capitalist. They must sell their labour to him, and are thus dependent on him. They can be sacked, for whatever reasons. They have to fight to squeeze a living wage out of the owner of capital. At the heart of a Marxist analysis of modern society is the perception of a better life that could be shared by all. That better life is blocked by the private appropriation of wealth.

Marx's analysis of modernity is based on a view of a fundamental conflict of interest between the haves and the have-nots, between capitalists and workers. His ideas, of course, have had an enormous influence since the last century: their appeal to the poor and disinherited is obvious. They have shaped the political life of the twentieth century throughout the world; in most European democracies where mass parties developed they tended to split into those that represented the interests of the owners of property and those that represented the interests of workers. Experiments in socialism (the political application of Marx's ideas) lasted for over seventy years in the Soviet Union and Eastern bloc countries, and continue in China, Cuba, and elsewhere in the developing world today. Although state socialism (as the Soviet system was called) has clearly failed, and caused great misery and death for millions, Marx's ideas have not been entirely discredited. His emphasis on the fundamental importance of economic life for an understanding of how modern societies work, and his analysis of capitalist societies as based on deep social divisions and conflicts of interests remains a substantial and important contribution.

The Frankfurt School

Theorists of the Frankfurt School took up Marx's writings (which said little about political or cultural life) and tried to apply them to the analysis of twentieth century culture. Their ideas were formed in the inter-war period (1920–40). The leading members of this group of German intellectuals were Max Horkheimer, Theodor Adorno and Herbert Marcuse (see M. Jay, 1974, for a critical history of the work of the School up to the 1950s). At first they worked at the Institute for Social Research attached to the University of Frankfurt (hence the Frankfurt School), but when Hitler came to power they had to leave Germany because they were Jews, and they eventually settled in the United States. Adorno and Horkheimer were appointed to Columbia University in New York, where they remained until after World War II. In the late 40s they returned, with great honour, to Frankfurt, where they continued to work in the university until the 70s. Marcuse settled in San Francisco, where he made his major contributions (1954, 1964). He remained in the US and became a key intellectual 'hero' of the counter-culture in the 1960s.

These intellectuals argued that cultural life in modern times had been profoundly changed by the impact of capitalist methods of mass production. These methods were applied, in the last century, to the manufacture of the necessities of life in a manufacturing economy, i.e., material goods such as machinery, clothing, and so forth. But from the 1920s they were applied to the production of a new range of goods, products, or commodities – the terms are more or less synonymous. On one side were what we call 'consumer goods', such as the family car, gas and electric cookers, fridges, washing machines. Although these products, like the TV set, did not become mass-market items until the 1950s, when they did, they transformed the character of domestic daily life. On the other side were cultural goods or commodities. New forms of mass communication – cinema, radio, and photography (in newspapers and magazines) became subject in their development, manufacture, and distribution to capitalist methods of mass production.

Adorno and his colleagues argued that through such developments industrial capitalism penetrated ever deeper into cultural life, creating new forms of leisure and entertainment for masses of people on a scale hitherto unimaginable. They lumped these developments together under the umbrella term 'the culture industry' (Adorno and Horkheimer, 1977). Following Marx, they saw the application of capitalist methods to cultural production as exploitative of the mass of the population. They noted the concentration of ownership in Hollywood cinema, the American press and broadcasting. They noted the extent to which advertising supported these new mass media. They thought of the culture, or entertainment, industry as creating mass-produced forms of enjoyment that were standardised and uniform, that is, fundamentally all alike. Whether the products were popular songs or broadcast soap operas, they were all the same: they were mass produced according to standard formulae and were vehicles for the promotion of capitalism. Mass audiences could not resist the glossy appeal of the Hollywood movie, the star system, the easy exploitation of emotions in melodramas or gangster movies (Horkheimer, 1972).

Critical resistance to mass culture, impossible for the masses, was the object of 'critical theory', whose aim was to expose the exploitative character of contemporary, mass-manufactured capitalist (and largely American) culture. Most generally the Frankfurt school theorists saw these developments, along with the growth of monopoly capitalism (transnational corporations distributing their products all over the world) and of the strong, centralised modern state, as tending to increase the domination of social institutions over individual lives. The culture industry, in their view, destroyed individuality, created uniformity and conformity, and made resistance well-nigh impossible.

The Frankfurt School members have been accused of cultural elitism and pessimism, and very few people today would argue that the culture industries (a useful term) have the negative effects they claimed. Nevertheless the members of the Frankfurt School were right to point up the importance of analysing these industries as integral to global capitalism, and to question, in a critical spirit, their impact and effect on contemporary cultural life. The issues they addressed have a continuing relevance. In the forty years or so since they developed their analysis we have seen the continuing expansion of the culture industries to an extent that they now circulate throughout the world. *Jurassic Park* is not just a monster movie that has taken more money to make than any other in Hollywood history – it is a marketing extravaganza on an even more monstrous scale. Equally, Disneyworld (in the US and Europe) is part of that global process whereby tourism and entertainment converge, in a marriage of the leisure and culture industries, to reduce the world to a series of theme parks. Thanks to TV we've all been everywhere and seen everything, and it all looks the same – partly because you can stay in the same hotels, buy the same things in the same shops, in the same shopping malls, around the world. Consumer culture is inescapable. The trends that the Frankfurt School identified at an early stage, today dominate the globe.

British cultural studies

The impact of this growing mass culture in post-war Britain, and particularly on the working class, was a concern of a number of intellectuals in the 1950s, particularly Richard Hoggart (*The Uses of Literacy*, 1957) and Raymond Williams (*Culture and Society*, 1958–60) which complemented E. P. Thompson's conception of the formation of the English working class between 1780 and 1830 (*The Making of the English Working Class*, 1968). Hoggart established a small postgraduate Centre for Contemporary Cultural Studies at Birmingham University in 1964 and his colleague Stuart Hall took over as Director when Hoggart left in the late 60s. Hall's work with graduate students at the Centre in the 1970s has been increasingly influential (especially in the US) and largely defines what is today known as 'cultural studies'.

There are many accounts of the short history of British cultural studies from the 50s to the present (see Turner, 1990; McGuigan, 1992; Storey, 1993). For our purposes we can note two main lines of development: one focused on the analysis of working-class culture, particularly the culture of young working-class males, and then, in response to feminist critiques at the Centre, that of young working-class females (Women's Studies Group, 1978). A central concern was the use of mass culture, by both sexes, to create and define gendered identities for themselves. The choice of clothing, the kind of music you listened to, whether you had (for instance) a motorbike or a scooter – these things created your 'image' and defined your personality. Instead of individuals being manipulated by the products of mass culture – as the Frankfurt School had argued – it was the other way round. Individuals could take these products and manipulate them (subvert them) to create new self-definitions. The classic study of this process is Dick Hebdige's *Subculture: The Meaning of Style* (1979), which looks at how young white working-class males created identities for themselves through music: from mods and rockers in the 50s and 60s through to punk and beyond in the 70s. Particular attention was paid to the ambiguous relationship of musical styles and social identities, and particularly to the embrace of black music and the culture of young black males by young, white working-class males.

Another important strand in the study of contemporary culture, and central to this book, was the analysis of film and television. Two analytical approaches developed here (cf. Moores, 1990). The analysis of film worked out in the British Film Institute's journal *Screen* in the 1970s argued that the way in which the story was told (the techniques of editing, visual images, and so forth) controlled and defined the viewer of the film. The narrative techniques of cinema subtly but powerfully imposed their meanings on the spectator, who could not avoid being 'positioned' to see the film in a particular way (the notion of position refers particularly to the point of view that is constructed for the viewer through filmic techniques, the ways in which the viewer is, so to speak, 'put in the picture'). In a classic analysis of Hollywood movies, Laura Mulvey argued that the pleasures of this kind of cinema were organised for a male viewer, and that women (both in the storyline and as objects to be looked at) were merely instruments of male pleasure, objects of a male gaze (Mulvey, 1975).

Stuart Hall and his students, working on the analysis of television, wanted to develop a more open kind of analysis of how TV worked. They argued that TV tried to impose its meaning (its preferred reading) on viewers, but that it was quite possible for viewers to refuse the preferred meaning and develop their own interpretation of what they heard and saw. For example, TV news – it has been persuasively argued – tends to present industrial disputes in ways that favour the interests and point of view of management rather than the workers (see the Glasgow Media Group's *Bad News*, 1976). But it can be shown that viewers, and particularly blue collar/industrial workers, are likely to see through this ideological representation of news and question the way in which TV frames and interprets strikes in its news reports and presentations.

The key concept, in both film and TV analysis, was that of ideology, a term derived from Marx's writings, in particular *The German Ideology* (1974). The meaning of the concept has been much discussed (cf. Larrain, 1979, 1983; Thompson, 1980), but in essence it can be understood as follows. In a neutral sense ideology refers to a coherent set of social values, beliefs, and meanings (for example Catholicism, socialism, vegetarianism). In Marxist terms it is a critical concept that refers particularly to dominant or ruling-class values, beliefs and meanings, what came to be called the dominant ideology (for a critique of this concept see Abercrombie *et al.*, 1980, 1990). In classic Marxism, the analysis of dominant values was mainly in class terms. Cultural studies extended it to race (e.g. Centre for Contemporary Cultural Studies, 1982) and gender (van Zoonen, 1991). White, Western male values were central aspects of the dominant value system. The general idea was that through the ideological mis-representation of social reality, subordinate social groups (workers, women, blacks) were prevented from understanding how they were exploited or oppressed. The effect of ideology then was to maintain the status quo, to maintain the domination of the powerful over the powerless, by presenting versions of social reality that represented this process of domination as natural, obvious, right and just, in short, the 'natural order' or 'the way things are and ought to be'.

It was argued that British television reproduced the dominant value system, loosely understood as a class-based consensus that 'believed' in the monarchy, the Anglican church, Parliament, the rule of law, and so forth (Hall, 1978, 1980). Television worked to maintain belief in such things and to discredit ideas and attitudes that opposed them.

A major site in which 'dominant' values are reproduced is the news and current affairs programmes, in which powerful 'primary definers' (politicians, experts, the military) are routinely allowed to define the issues, to express their opinions and offer interpretations (Hall *et al.*, 1978), while alternative or oppositional interpretations of events are seldom if ever allowed expression. A poignant but somewhat extreme example derives from the continuing instability of Northern Ireland. There is, for instance, in TV news, only one definition of what is happening in Northern Ireland and it is one that is acceptable to the British government. Oppositional viewpoints are forbidden by the government. Members of Sinn Fein (the political wing of the Irish Republican Army (the IRA)) are banned from British TV (on the media and Northern Ireland see Curtis, 1984; Schlesinger, 1983). In the US this would be illegal as it would be a flagrant violation of the right of free speech as contained in the first amendment of the US Constitution.

According to Stuart Hall, although the media work to maintain the dominant value system it is by no means simply secured. It is not just imposed on people so that they cannot resist it (as the Frankfurt School and *Screen* theory tended to suppose). Dominant values are encoded in the media in complex ways, but they can be decoded by viewers in very different ways (Hall *et al.*, 1978). To encode something is to represent an idea within a particular system of meaning. To put an idea in words is to encode it in language; to put an idea in certain words is to encode it in a point of view or perspective, which is usually part of a larger perspective. To present a portrait of a person through interviews is to encode a representation of that person in a television-interview format. To decode is to take what has been encoded and interpret or make meaning of it.

In order to test this theory, David Morley (1980) looked at how viewers of a BBC television magazine programme in the 70s called *Nationwide* interpreted, made sense of, or decoded the programme. He found, as Hall had suggested, three different kinds of response: dominant, negotiated and oppositional. Some viewers 'bought' the values of the programme which, as its title implied, stressed national unity and strongly emphasised 'family values', suggesting that Britain was essentially a nation of white, middle-class families living in suburbia. Some viewers accepted the programme's preferred meaning, this consensual, harmonious representation of British society in which the conflicting interests of marginalised social groups (i.e. marginalised by this definition) were systematically filtered out. Other viewers took a rather more critical or 'negotiated' view of the programme, while a few groups of viewers (notably young blacks) rejected it altogether.

Morley's work was very influential and in the 1980s the cultural studies approach increasingly concentrated on how audiences made sense of the media. Ien Ang's (1985) study of how Dutch viewers responded to *Dallas* is a well-known example. This approach rejected the strongly deterministic view of the Frankfurt School and *Screen*, stressing that viewing was an active process. One recent commentator has suggested that all this amounted to re-inventing the wheel: this, after all, was what effects studies had discovered years before (Curran, 1992).

Feminist research

Feminist studies have much in common with cultural studies, but a very different history (see Franklin *et al.*, 1992). The approach first developed in the US in the late 1950s but has since spread all over the world. Like Marxism, feminism is deeply critical of the character of modern societies, which it sees as based on fundamental inequalities. But where Marxism locates the roots of inequality in capital ownership and class, feminism points to male domination (patriarchy) of women as the root of profound human inequalities and injustices. These inequalities are pervasive aspects of modern life. Men have economic, political and cultural power. Women do not. Men control public life, while women occupy the resigned marginal spaces of private life and domesticity. 'A woman's place is in the home' is a good example of ideological misrepresentation masquerading as common sense and proverbial wisdom.

How is it that such values (the ideology of patriarchy) continue to have such power? Why do women continue to be oppressed by men? To answer such questions feminist critics turned to look at how cultural products might contribute to 'naturalise' the oppression of women: advertisements were one obvious place to look (Williamson, 1978). Film, television and popular fiction were other obvious sites. The idea of gendered narratives was developed (Mulvey's work on film was influential here). There are types of stories (narrative genres) that appeal to, that 'speak' to male readers or viewers (adventure stories – the Western, or James Bond novels – are classic examples), while romances appeal to female readers (Radway's *Reading the Romance* (1984) is a key text). Similarly there was gendered television: feminist audience studies discovered the kind of radio and TV programmes that women preferred (see Hobson, 1980, 1982). Morley (1986) studied TV viewers in family settings and discovered a consistent profile of male and female preferences. One key programme category was TV soap opera with its largely female viewing audiences, and many studies have looked at what women enjoy in such programmes (Seiter *et al.*, 1989 is a recent study that reviews previous work).

Two recent articles, both in Curran and Gurevitch (1991), provide a context for this perspective. Liesbet van Zoonen (1991) argues that there is a great variety in feminist discourse. She notes that feminist research is drawn together by an 'unconditional focus on analyzing gender as a mechanism that structures material and symbolic worlds and our experience of them' (p. 33). Van Zoonen also distinguishes three traditions in feminist analysis, liberal, radical and socialist feminism. She notes that strategies for change derive directly from each of these perspectives, with the aim of either reforming existing media institutions or forming new feminist institutions.

Ien Ang and Joke Hermes (1991) take a much more radical approach. They criticise some of the underlying assumptions of a general feminist stance, noting that certain feminists have accepted a crude inoculation model of media effects on women. They call attention to work challenging such assumptions and call for a re-opening of the discussion of the female spectator. Noting that gender is socially constructed, essentialist and reductionist, they underline the necessity of investigating how women negotiate with the texts they encounter in the media.

Reception analysis

Cultural and feminist studies of the mass media in the 1980s increasingly turned to looking at how audiences made sense of cultural products, how they interpreted what they read, saw and heard. But it became apparent that to do this, it was necessary to attend not simply to the product itself (the novel, the film, TV play, and so forth), but, more generally, to the context in which the consumption of the cultural product took place. Reception studies thus broadens out to take into account the social setting in which audiences respond to the products of contemporary popular culture. This has been of particular interest to feminist scholars in a number of ways, because the household is a prime site for cultural consumption by women. When Janice Radway studied American women readers of romantic fiction she found that irrespective of what particular novel they might be reading, the women she interviewed emphasised the ways in which they transformed the activity of reading into a special moment for themselves: a moment when they took time out from domestic chores, responsibilities to husbands and children, and created a time and space for themselves and their pleasures. Thus the act of reading has a pleasure and a significance in itself. It is a way in which busy responsible women momentarily attend to their own needs instead of those of others. It is a moment of self-affirmation. This discovery points to the importance of attending to what lies outside the cultural products themselves. The *meaning* of romance fiction for Radway's readers was something more than the form and content of the stories themselves. The act of reading had ritual, affirmative meaning in itself.

Likewise work on how family members use radio, TV, newspapers, magazines, VCRs and satellite dishes (to take notable instances) shows how these things can be used for a range of purposes that have little to do with their content. A parent may watch a TV programme with a child to nourish their relationship, to maintain connections, rather than for what the programme is actually about. The dynamics of power relations between males and females, parents and children, older and younger siblings have been studied in relation to, for instance, who has access to the remote control of the TV set, or who can work the VCR (Morley, 1986). Ownership of a satellite dish in the UK has ambivalent social value, since it has a rather down-market image. Ownership may be justified as educative (valuable for the children) or as opening up new horizons (access to European TV culture) (Moores, 1993).

Attention to the domestic technologies of everyday life and their impact on the social lives of household members has been taken up historically in the reconstruction of the impact of such things as washing machines and other domestic aids (the electric vacuum cleaner was one of the first). More recently, of the uses of PCs and other state-of-the art gadgetry has been examined. In all cases the perception is that these things, beyond their use value or content, have other meanings and uses that link into the definition of life-styles and identities, the sociable relations as well as the small power struggles of everyday life. Reception studies thus further supports those views that reject the notion that cultural products control their users, by revealing the meanings that get grafted onto them by their users over and beyond their manifest content, meaning and use (see also Katz and Liebes, 1990).

In general, the attention of such researchers is directed towards what the audience brings to a viewing or decoding, the social context and the act of viewing. Bryce (1987), Collett and Lamb (1986), Hobson (1980) and Modleski (1984) have all described the manner in which various groups – women, men, families – watch television. Most notable are women, who juggle television watching with the simultaneous performance of domestic chores. Children often play and look up when their ears tell them that the plot is thickening. Men often watch programmes not of their own choosing. In some families and at some times, a switched-on television set may function as a conversation stopper or mediator rather than a source of watched pro-grammes. Scannell (1988) has analysed the manner in which broadcasting sustains the lives and routines of whole populations, while Silverstone (1981) and Hartley (1987) have discussed how television provides the basis for symbolic participation in a national community, or, in the cases of Belgium, Switzerland, and Canada, sometimes an international linguistic community.

Communication rules research (Lull, 1982, 1988) can be seen as a sub-section of reception analysis. It posits that patterns of media consumption can be explained by reference to a set of rules which can be developed by means of observation. The approach derives from an amalgamation of rules theory (Shimanoff, 1980) and ethnography of communication (Stewart and Philipsen, 1984). The rules that are derived from this form of analysis are not meant to be rigid, in that they may vary with the situation, the culture, and the politics of the actors and the situation (Lull, 1982, 1988), yet they may attain a moral or cultural force. Rule sets exist side by side with other rule sets, which may complement or contradict each other.

Structuration theory

It can be seen, in the above accounts, that there is a constant theoretical tension between approaches that stress the determining power of institutions to impose meanings on passive receivers 'in the grip of ideology' as Frazer (1992) puts it, and those approaches that emphasise that consumption is an active process of choice and meaning-making. This dichotomy has long been present in social science. There is a strong tendency in Marxist theory, for instance, to stress the power of institutional structures (or apparatuses) to determine the lives of individual subjects; Althusser's (1971) theory of ideological state apparatuses is a classic instance. Against that strong emphasis on institutions other sociological approaches stress human agency – that individuals can act on their own behalf, they are not simply controlled by social institutions that dominate and define their lives. The best-known attempt to reconcile these two opposing positions is the theory of structuration put forward by the British sociologist Anthony Giddens.

Giddens proposes that a theory of cultural production requires that we focus on human agency. We must understand practical consciousness, the indexicality or referential context, and the framework that speaking and talk provide for practical action. We must focus on the relation between discourse and cultural objects, material forms that convey cultural content from producer to consumer, creator to audience.

The key aspects of structuration theory are:

duality of structure – structuration is structure plus action where structure entails institutional constraints and linguistic codes and action carries those formal and informal constraints reproducing them in routinised social practices. Structuration theory thus closes the distance between micro and macro levels, between interpretive agency and a functional analysis of institutions.
knowledgeable human agency – human subjectivity entails an implicit and sometimes explicit knowledge of a rich array of implicit rules governing the understanding and carrying out of everyday actions, a practical consciousness. It is on this foundation that people understand and act.
double hermeneutics – social analytical knowledge entails the mapping and reinterpretation of knowledge which human agents already know.
time-space – structuration theory encompasses the blending of the temporal/historical with the spatial/geographical, for example, tracking the structuration path followed by an individual in his/her daily action with respect to various institutions   (Mitchell, 1989).

Given this orientation, Giddens (1987b) sees communications as central to our understanding of society. He is particularly interested in talk: 'Talk, carried on in the day-to-day contexts of activity, is the fundamental "carrier" of signification, because it operates in saturated behavioural and conceptual contexts. . . . Ordinary talk is precisely that "medium of living in the world" in which reference and meaning interlace' (p. 209). Although Giddens himself has not written much about mass communication, his ideas have considerable relevance for their study. With his own emphasis on the analysis of time and space and fundamental constraints on all fronts of social organisation and life, Giddens has also underlined the contribution made by McLuhan to opening up this topic. Scannell's (1991) recent compilation of studies, *Broadcast Talk*, owes much to Giddens.

Institutional audience research

So far we have discussed the interest of academics in studying the audiences of the mass media. But of course, from the beginning the media institutions themselves have been keenly interested in finding out what people read, listen to, and watch. Such information has practical value. It enables a TV or radio station, for instance, to discover who their audience is, its listening or viewing habits and preferences. Institutional audience research attends to basic questions such as when are people available – or not – to listen or watch (such research looks at audience habits) and then, when they are watching or listening, what it is that they like or dislike (such research studies audience tastes). Such information obviously has economic value, and commercial broadcasting is increasingly concerned to obtain ever more precise information about viewing audiences in order to sell advertising as the market becomes ever more competitive.

Traditionally such research concentrated on audience size: the bigger the audience for a TV programme, the more attractive it would be to advertisers. But from the 1970s, in the US, so-called 'quality demographics' tried to provide more accurate information about the kinds of viewer attracted to particular programmes. A programme might have a very large audience, but most of them might not have much disposable income. A programme with a smaller audience but with greater spending power could be more valuable and more attractive to advertisers. One example is the American police series, *Hill Street Blues*, which ran for several years in the late 1970s, and early 1980s. Although it was transmitted late in the evening and did not reach the mass prime-time audience, it had a strong following among younger, professional viewers, and hence could command premium charges on advertisements shown during the programme. It also earned prestige for the network, because it was regarded as up-market 'quality' television, winning prizes for the production team and actors.

But audience research has been essential for non-commercial broadcasting as well. The BBC set up its own Listener Research department in 1936 to answer questions about listener habits and preferences. Habits meant very simple things like when do people get up, go to work, return from work and go to bed. It meant questions like: 'do people watch more in the winter than in summer?' or 'do people in the south of England watch more or less than viewers in the north?'. As the answers to such questions were found programme planning (or scheduling) could be organised on a consistent, rational basis that tuned in with the daily habits and routines of the British people (Scannell, 1988). The other kind of BBC research was into audience taste preferences: the bulk of programme output on radio has always been music. But what kinds of music did people prefer to listen to: dance band music or orchestral music, opera, or chamber music? Listener research provided answers to such questions and helped broadcasters to make allocations about how much of each kind of music it ought to be playing over the air (on early BBC audience research see Pegg, 1983, and Scannell and Cardiff, 1991).

Since then broadcasting has become increasingly diverse and commercial. Competition for audiences, between commercial and public service broadcasting and within commercial broadcasting itself, has led to ever-increasing attention to the ratings. This would include basic demographic information as well as media-use habits, consumption patterns, psychological profiles, and so forth. Much of this information is collected under contract and is proprietary. It is therefore not all publicly available, although general patterns are known in the various industries and groups of researchers, such as the Group of European Audience Researchers (GEAR), exchange data and ideas. The second chapter of Ien Ang's book *Desperately Seeking the Audience* (1991), 'Audience-as-market and audience-as-public', contains a discussion of the relation of institutional research to the other types of research we have outlined above. Ang discusses how much institutional research tells producers how successful they have been in reaching their audience but leaves them profoundly ignorant about the precise ingredients of their success or failure.

In normal institutional research media consumption-oriented information is added to survey data that can be obtained through various sampling procedures within which particular groups may be identified. The relatively recent change in reporting procedures from diaries kept by audience members to people meters, in which people log in and out as they watch or cease to watch, has brought new information to the fore, first confirmed by Collett and Lamb (1986) by means of cameras built into television sets. As a result, we now know that many fewer have their eyes and minds glued to the tube than was claimed by those selling audiences.

Three important concepts which are basic to institutional audience research are:

1 *Reach*: the percentage of audience members that tune into a programme for some amount of time. Programme, daily, and weekly reach refer to the percentage of the audience that tunes to some part of the programme for some period of time during its showing, to the channel once in a day, or to

the channel once in a week respectively.

2 *Share*: the percentage of the average audience that tunes into a programme or channel at or over any specified time period.

3 *Viewing time*: the time spent viewing expressed over the period of a day, week, or longer period of time.

The difference between reach and share is particularly interesting. For example, in 1986 the audience share of BBC 2 in Europe was between 5 per cent and 10 per cent, however, the weekly reach of the channel was approximately 60 per cent. The range in daily viewing time was between 60 minutes (in Switzerland) and 209 minutes (in Spain), with an overall European average of 119 minutes. One would think that the spread of electronic television channel changers might make the actual if not the reported daily reach of many channels close to 100 per cent (BBC, 1987).

An extension from this type of research can be seen in niche marketing and the designing of services for niche audiences (i.e. MTV, sports channels, and so forth). The growth of subscription services is also attributable in part to the ability of programme distributors to provide specialised products.

For some time it was assumed, and many researchers have argued, that the size of the audience was all that was needed to determine the popularity of a programme. It turns out that audience satisfaction or appreciation is not consistently correlated with audience size. Thus, while large audiences may be delivered to advertisers by certain programmes, they may be delivered in a somewhat dissatisfied frame of mind. How they might differentially receive advertisers' messages has yet to emerge in the research literature, although it would be surprising if it were not available in the proprietary literature. Current research for all major media organisations relies on both appreciation and audience size, although in certain venues, for example, licence renewal hearings, one might never know it.

Yet another element of institutional audience research comes from qualitative data. Such data can come from in-depth interviews or such mechanisms as focus groups or group discussions. It is meant to provide some degree of insight into why audiences behave the way they do in their viewing and listening patterns. The evolution of academic research to the point it has reached with social phenomenological research may begin to bring institutional and academic research closer together. The marriage of normative data on how much and what type of media is consumed in what settings for what periods, with an understanding of the interpretation audience members give to their media consumption certainly has the chance of advancing our understanding of media consumption and perhaps to challenge such perspectives as cultivation analysis (Wober and Gunter, 1986). The kind of insight that may be provided is outlined in practical terms in the following section.

Building a picture of the audience

This chapter has so far provided a review of the theory and research applicable to understanding audiences. The remaining parts of the chapter will examine fairly direct questions about the audience, partly as an attempt to apply the reviewed theory and partly as an attempt to provide some direct answers to some rather obvious questions. What does it mean to be an avid or a casual media user? Indeed, what does it mean to have an imagination filled with the characters, events, and settings of the media that John Lekich wrote about in his article? Media producers would dearly love to have answers to these questions, as would advertisers, so let us see how far we can go.

The first answer to both questions is that it depends on the person and on the media elements. On the media production side, the same explicit or denotative message presented differently, that is with different connotations, will have a different impact. In different terms the message can be said to be polysemic, in short, it is open to a variety of interpretations. These differences notwithstanding, as Katz and Liebes (1990) have shown, audience members with widely divergent backgrounds will readily agree on the basic elements of the message or programme presented. What a particular message means to a particular person is probably unpredictable. This is the point on which effects research founders. Thirdly, the intensity of one's involvement can vary independently of the meaning one might extract from a message or programme. One film may lodge itself in one person's memory for life. S/he may use it as a foundation for social action, analysing social settings, understanding how individuals respond to stress, and so forth. Another audience member with approximately the same understanding of the film may see it as one of many examples of certain phenomena.

Given an essentially indeterminate range and intensity of interpretations, how and to what extent can we understand media/audience interactions? First, following the Katz and Liebes (1990) evidence, one must posit that there is some force behind the constructed reality that is presented. Thus the ideal-typical characters or families in their time and place are generally seen to be both ideal and typical by audience members, at least within their country of origin. (The export of such programmes to different cultures may mean that the interpretation of the portraits as ideal may change.) Next, we can assume that audience members may react negatively or positively to the presentation of the general ideal. They may generally accept or reject them.

From this point on the analysis gets considerably more complex. No doubt one could look up the multiplicity of verbs and potential modifying adverbs to be found in the dictionary to describe the potential range of reaction in individual audience members. The strength of the reaction, while different in different audience members, would most likely be related to the manner of presentation in the programme itself. Discussion, soothing music, laughter, and so forth, are designed to keep reactions low key. Other means can be used to heighten reactions, as horror movie producers know only too well. Such phenomena are not unknown or unrecognised in the research literature (see Jensen, 1990; Moores, 1990; Hall *et al.*, 1980; Bourdieu, 1984 and Eco, 1972). Moores (1990), citing Hall (1980, p. 134) in reference to this universe of readings, notes that polysemy should not be confused with unfettered pluralistic interpretation – the notion that any reading is possible.

Consider the police beating of Rodney King in April 1992 and the subsequent Los Angeles riots as an example of media/viewer interaction. When a home video camera caught four LA policemen beating up Rodney King one night after stopping him in his car, the video seemed to play into, with some poignancy, a well-established discourse on race relations. It is a discourse particularly entrenched in the US but current throughout the world: white official violent power meted out by both black and white policemen against the powerless underclass, that is, blacks. One might speculate that so accepted was this discourse as truly reflective of reality that 'while shock and concern were expressed', no race riots broke out when the video clip was aired across the US and around the world. One might even project some subtexts onto the events of the time. A first subtext would be the ordinariness of violence of this kind in the lives of Americans in the same position as Rodney King. Another might be an understanding of the ordinariness of this type of police behaviour in such a setting.

Whatever the reasons for the audience reactions, bearing in mind that the video was presented as news, thus having a certain truth value, a tense lull in the situation was introduced as America and the world awaited the charging and trial of the policemen. During this time, of course, there was ample opportunity for extensive discussion of the possible outcomes and what action would be appropriate. These discussions obviously would have been carried out in the context of the charges, which seemed to mock the act itself. The charges were 'using excessive force', charges that, judging from the video, seemed absurd since no force seemed necessary at all.

The first verdict of police innocence in October 1992 set off days of rioting and looting and hundreds of millions of dollars in damage. Quite an audience reaction! That the rioting should occur after the trial rather than after the beating, and that the media were well aware of its likelihood, would appear to indicate that at least the media and the rioters shared an understanding of the meaning of the event. To try to encapsulate that understanding: whereas police brutality is a fact of life, if the institutions of justice are going to condone such violence, then society and white people are going to pay dearly. It is interesting that the police did not predict the rioting and attempt to fend it off, both by an elaborated explanation of the basis of the verdict as well as a massive police presence.

As a media event, the home video of the beating was imbued with both the visual authority we are asked to give the news each night and the authority of an accepted discourse on race and power. If these were indeed the salient variables then an in-depth account of the reactions of black and white Americans would dwell on these themes. Were others prevalent that we have not thought of, they would emerge in interviews.

In general, building from spontaneous accounts or behaviour to a construction of events from interviews we can gain some sense of the manner in which audience members cognitively construe and interact with media content. Such analyses can be taken in a variety of directions.

A cultural analysis

If, as we claimed at the beginning of this chapter, cultures as well as the media and audience members are meaning-generating, how can this cultural phenomenon be observed? At a macro level it is to be found in the various structures we have outlined thus far. These are in the laws, policies, ownership patterns, professional ideals and technological developments characteristic of each culture. From a different perspective, they are also to be found in the viewing patterns of the audience.

A third view of the meaning-generating activity of a culture can be inferred from the predominance of sets of themes in media programmes, especially those that have high ratings. For instance, the steady diet in US television in the 50s and 60s of idealised families and fearless lawmen and particular types of comedy and variety probably reflects an unquestioning belief in progress and enlightenment in US society, and an attempt to appeal in a fairly monolithic but inclusive way to the polyglot US society. In Britain during the same period, the dominance of comedy together with the portrayals of endearing members of the servant and elite classes and dramatic productions with historical settings and some artistic depth no doubt affirmed crucial elements of the British social identity. The social reality approach of more current times in both the US and UK, as evidenced in *The Simpsons* and *EastEnders*, and the sneer factor inherent in such programmes as *America's Funniest Home-Videos* (the audience can feel superior both to those on film and those who would seek fame by submitting material) seems to suggest a different set of values.

Summary

A synthesis of various conceptions of the audience in media/audience theory and research suggests that such relations might usefully be conceived of as interaction between meaning-generating systems. Such a perspective provides a framework for explanation that represents media, audience members and cultures as ordered systems in interaction but in a non-deterministic fashion.

Seven approaches can be identified. They are effects research, uses and gratifications research, cultural studies, feminist research, reception analysis, structuration theory, and institutional research. All offer information and insight for an explanation but not a prediction of audience behaviour that is dependent on not only what the audience brings to the text or content but also the culturally specific references contained in the material. While cultural studies oriented to textual content have been dominant for some time, greater attention is now being paid to audience dynamics. Consideration of the social context of viewing adds yet further elaboration to the articulation of audience variables.

References

Abercrombie, Nicholas, Stephen Hill and Bryan S. Turner (1980), *The Dominant Ideology Thesis*, Allen and Unwin, Boston.

Abercrombie, Nicholas, Stephen Hill and Bryan S. Turner (eds.) (1990), *Dominant Ideologies*, Unwin and Hyman, Boston.

Adorno, T., and M. Horkheimer (1947, 1972), *Dialectic of Enlightenment*, Herder and Herder, New York.

Adorno, T. and M. Horkheimer (1977), 'The Culture Industry' in J. Curran, M. Gurevitch and J. Woollacott (eds.), *Mass Communication and Society*, Edward Arnold, London.

Althusser, Louis (1971), *Lenin and Philosophy, and Other Essays*, Verso, London.

Ang, Ien (1985), *Watching Dallas*, Methuen, London.

Ang, Ien (1991), *Desperately Seeking the Audience*, Routledge, London.

Ang, Ien and Joke Hermes (1991), 'Gender and/in media consumption' in James Curran and Michael Gurevitch (eds.), *Mass Media and Society*, Edward Arnold, London, pp. 307–28.

BBC (1987), *Handbook on Audience Research*, BBC, London.

Berger, Peter, and Thomas Luckmann (1966), *Social Construction of Reality: A Treatise on the Sociology of Knowledge*, Doubleday, New York.

Blumler, Jay and Elihu Katz (eds.) (1974), *The Uses of Mass Communications: Current Perspectives on Gratifications Research*, Sage, Beverly Hills.

Bourdieu, Pierre (1984), *Distinction: A Social Critique of the Judgement of Taste*, Routledge and Kegan Paul, London.

Bryce, J (1987), 'Family time and TV use' in T. Lindlof (ed.), *Natural Audiences*, Ablex, New Jersey, pp. 121–38.

Centre for Contemporary Cultural Studies (1982), *The Empire Fights Back: Racism in Britain in the 1970s*, Hutchinson, London.

Chomsky, Noam (1969), *Language and Mind*, Harcourt Brace and World, New York.

Collett, Peter and R. Lamb (1986), *Watching Families Watching TV*, report to the

Independent Broadcasting Authority, London.

Crook, Stephen (1989), 'Television and audience activity: the problem of the television/viewer nexus in audience research', *Australia and New Zealand Journal of Sociology*, 25 (3), pp. 356–80.

Curran, James (1992), 'The new revisionism in mass communications research: a reappraisal', *European Journal of Communication*, 5 (2–3), pp. 135–64.

Curran, James and Michael Gurevitch (eds.) (1991), *Mass Media and Society*, Edward Arnold, London.

Curtis, Liz (1984), *Ireland, the Propaganda War: The Media and the 'Battle for Hearts and Minds'*, Pluto Press, London.

Eco, Umberto (1972), 'Towards a semiotic inquiry into the television message', *Working Papers in Cultural Studies*, 3, CCCS, Birmingham.

Fiske, John (1987), *Television Culture*, Routledge, London.

Fiske, John (1989), 'Moments of television: neither the text nor the audience' in Ellen Seiter, Hans Borchers, Gabrielle Kreutzner, and Eva-Maria Warth, *Remote Control: Television, Audiences, and Cultural Power*, Routledge, London.

Franklin, Sarah, C. Lury and J. Stacey (1992), 'Feminism and cultural studies' in Paddy Scannell *et al.* (eds.), *Culture and Power*, Sage, London.

Frazer, E. (1992), 'Teenage Girls Reading *Jackie*' in Paddy Scannell *et al.* (eds.), *Culture and Power*, Sage, London.

Garfinkel, Harold (1984), *Studies in Ethnomethodology*, Polity Press, Cambridge.

Gerbner, George (1969), 'Towards "cultural indicators": the analysis of mass mediated public message systems', *AV Communication Review*, 17 (2), pp. 137–48.

Giddens, Anthony (1987a), *Social Theory and Modern Sociology*, Polity Press, Cambridge.

Giddens, Anthony (1987b), 'Structuralism, post-structuralism and the production of culture' in A. Giddens and R. Turner (eds.), *Social Theory Today*, Polity Press, Cambridge, pp. 195–223.

Glasgow Media Group (1976), *Bad News*, Routledge and Kegan Paul, Boston.

Goffman, Erving (1959), *The Presentation of Self in Everyday Life*, Doubleday, Garden City, NY.

Goffman, Erving (1967), *Interaction Ritual: Essays in Face to Face Behavior*, Aldine, Chicago.

Goffman, Erving (1979), *Gender Advertisements*, Harper and Row, New York.

Goffman, Erving (1981), *Forms of Talk*, University of Pennsylvania Press, Philadelphia.

Goffman, Erving (1986), *Stigma: Notes on the Management of a Spoiled Identity*, Simon and Schuster, New York.

Habermas, Jürgen (1979), *Communication and the Evolution of Society*, Beacon Press, Boston.

Hall, Stuart (1980), 'Encoding/Decoding' in Stuart Hall, Dorothy Hobson, Andrew Lowe and Paul Willis (eds.), *Culture, Media, Language*, Hutchinson, London, pp. 128–38.

Hall, Stuart, *et al.* (1978), *Policing the Crisis: Mugging, the State and Law and Order*, Macmillan, London.

Hall, Stuart, Dorothy Hobson, Andrew Love and Paul Willis (eds.) (1980), *Culture,*

Media, Language: Working Papers in Cultural Studies, Hutchinson, London.

Hartley, John (1987), 'Invisible fictions', *Textual Practice*, 1 (2), Summer, pp. 121–38.

Heath, Steven (1976), 'Narrative space', *Screen*, 18 (4).

Hebdige, Dick (1979), *Subculture: The Meaning of Style*, Metheun, London.

Hobson, D. (1980), 'Housewives and the mass media' in S. Hall *et al.* (eds.), *Culture, Media, Language*, Hutchinson, London.

Hobson, D. (1982), *Crossroads: The Drama of Soap Opera*, Methuen, London.

Hoggart, Richard (1992), *The Uses of Literacy* (originally published 1957), Transaction Publishers, New Brunswick, NJ.

Horkheimer, M. (1972), *Critical Theory*, Seabury Press, New York.

Jay, M. (1974), *The Dialectical Imagination*, Routledge, London.

Jensen, K. B. (1990), 'The politics of polysemy: television news, everyday consciousness and political action', *Media Culture and Society*, 12 (1), pp. 57–77.

Jensen, Klaus Bruhn, and Karl Erik Rosengren (1990), 'Five traditions in search of an audience', *European Journal of Communication*, 5, pp. 207–38.

Johnson, Richard (1986), 'The story so far: and further transformations?' in D. Pintor (ed.), *Introduction to Contemporary Cultural Studies*, Longman, London.

Katz, E., and P. Lazarsfeld (1965), *Personal Influence: The Part Played by People in the Flow of Mass Communications*, Free Press, New York.

Katz, Elihu, and Tamar Liebes (1990), 'The export of meaning: cross-cultural readings of American TV' in Peter Larsen (ed.), *Import/Export: International Flow of Television Fiction*, Unesco, Paris.

Klapper, Joseph (1960), *The Effects of Mass Communications*, Free Press, New York.

Larrain, Jorge (1979), *The Concept of Ideology*, Hutchinson, London.

Larrain, Jorge (1983), *Marxism and Ideology*, Macmillan, London.

Lekich, J. (1982), 'Horizontal hold', *Vancouver*, April, pp. 48–53.

Lindlof, Thomas R. (1991), 'The qualitative study of media audiences', *Journal of Broadcasting and Electronic Media*, 35 (1), pp. 23–42.

Lull, James (1982), 'A rules approach to the study of television and society', *Human Communication Research*, 9, pp. 3–16.

Lull, James (ed.) (1988), *World Families Watching Television*, Sage, London.

Marcuse, H. (1954, 1963), *Reason and Revolution: Hegel and the Rise of Social Theory*, Humanities Press, New York.

Marcuse, H. (1964), *One Dimensional Man: Studies in the Idealogy of Advanced Industrial Society*, Beacon Press, Boston.

Marx, Karl and Frederick Engels (1974), *The German Ideology*, Lawrence & Wishart, London.

McGuigan, J. (1992), *Cultural Populism*, Routledge, London.

McLeod, Jack M., Gerald Kosicki and Zhongdang Pan (1991), 'On understanding and misunderstanding media effects' in James Curran and Michael Gurevitch (eds.), *Mass Media and Society*, Edward Arnold, London, pp. 235–66.

Mitchell, David, B. (1989), 'Current issues in the foundations of social and communicational theory', presentation given at ICA meetings, Dublin.

Modleski, T. (1984), *Leaving with a Vengeance: Mass-Produced Fantasies for Women*, Methuen, London.

Moores, Shaun (1990), 'Texts, readers and contexts of reading: developments in the study of media audiences', *Media Culture and Society*, 12 (1), pp. 9–29.

Moores, Shaun (1993), 'Satellite TV as cultural sign', *Media Culture and Society*, 15 (4), pp. 621–40.

Morgan, M. and Signorelli, N. (1990), *Cultivation Analysis*, Sage, Beverly Hills.

Morley, D. (1980), *The 'Nationwide' Audience: Structure and Decoding*, British Film Institute Television Monographs, 11, BFI, London.

Morley, D. (1981), 'The *Nationwide* audience: a critical postscript', *Screen Education*, 39.

Morley, D. (1986), *Family Television: Cultural Power and Domestic Leisure*, Comedia, London.

Mulvey, Laura (1975), 'Visual pleasure and narrative cinema', *Screen*, 16 (3), pp. 6–18.

Pegg, Mark (1983), *Broadcasting and Society 1918–1939*, Croom Helm, London.

Radway, Janice (1984), *Reading the Romance: Women, Patriarchy and Popular Literature*, University of North Carolina Press, Chapel Hill, NC.

Rosengren, K. E. and S. Windahl (1989), *Media Matter: TV Use in Childhood and Adolescence*, Ablex, Norwood, NJ.

Scannell, Paddy (1988), 'Radio times: the temporal arrangements of broadcasting in the modern world' in P. Drummond and R. Paterson (eds.), *Television and its Audiences: International Research Perspectives*, BFI, London.

Scannell, Paddy (ed.) (1991), *Broadcast Talk*, Sage, London.

Scannell, Paddy, and D. Cardiff (1991), *A Social History of Broadcasting, vol. 1: Serving the Nation 1922–1939*, Basil Blackwell, Oxford.

Schlesinger, Philip (1983), *Televising 'Terrorism': Political Violence in Popular Culture*, Comedia, London.

Seiter, Ellen, Hans Borchers, Gabrielle Kreutzner and Eva-Maria Warth (eds.) (1989), *Remote Control: Television, Audiences, and Cultural Power*, Routledge, London.

Shimanoff, S. (1980), *Communication Rules*, Sage, Beverly Hills.

Silverstone, R. (1981), *The Message of Television: Myth and Narrative in Contemporary Culture*, Heinemann Educational Books, London.

Stewart, J., and G. Philipsen (1984), 'Communication as situated accomplishment: the case of hermeneutics and ethnography' in B. Dervin and M. J. Voigt (eds.), *Progress in Communication Sciences*, vol. 5, Ablex, Norwood, NJ, pp. 179–217.

Storey, J. (1993), *Cultural Theory and Popular Culture*, Harvester Wheatsheaf, London.

Thompson, Edward P. (1980), *The Making of the English Working Class* (originally published 1968), Penguin, Harmondsworth.

Turner, G. (1990), *British Cultural Studies: An Introduction*, Routledge, London.

van Zoonen, Liesbet (1991), 'Feminist perspectives on the media' in James Curran and Michael Gurevitch (eds.), *Mass Media and Society*, Edward Arnold, London, pp. 33–54.

Williams, Raymond (1958–60), *Culture and Society: 1780–1950*, Columbia University Press, New York.

Williamson, Judith (1978), *Decoding Advertisements: Ideology and Meaning in Advertising*, Boyars, London.

Wober, J. Mallory, and Barrie Gunter (1986), 'Television audience research at Britain's Independent Broadcasting Authority, 1974–1984', *Journal of Broadcast-*

ing and Electronic Media, 30 (1), pp. 15–31.

Women's Studies Group (1978), *Women Take Issue: Aspects of Women's Subordination*, Centre for Cultural Studies, Birmingham.

Woollacott, J. (1982), 'Messages and meanings' in M. Gurevitch *et al.* (eds.), *Culture, Society and the Media*, Methuen, Toronto.

Chapter 8

Media content

The previous chapter on audiences has completed the review of the five major factors that impinge on the production of media content. To review those elements: first are the laws and policies that set the formalities of media operations in place. Second is ownership or proprietorship; within proprietorship are the traditions and the demands of the form itself, the tendencies a particular medium encourages, and the preferences of the individual owner as s/he or it sets operational rules in place for the property that is owned. Third are the employees and other individuals that operate the particular media outlet. Not only do they play a role as individuals but also the ideals, traditions and practices of their profession or union play themselves out in a particular way in their particular work setting. Fourth, technology contributes not only by setting basic demands on the process and people involved in content creation, but also by the demands each particular medium places on the words, pictures, actions and context required. Finally, the audience, at least as it is perceived by media producers, affects the production or generation of content.

While forming an important context, by no means do these factors completely define the dynamics of media production. Within these constraints content producers work on the basis of their personal sensibilities and acquired skills to produce engaging content that will leave the audience entertained, enlightened, informed, and perhaps impressed. The purpose of this chapter is to focus on the detail of media production.

From one point of view content, as distinct from carriage, and encompassing both what is expressed and how it is expressed, is at the heart of the study of communication. A concern for content has, throughout history, been taken to be an important focus of study in material intended to have a lasting existence and a broad significance in society, that is to say, literature and the arts. The study of the ideas expressed in the literature of a particular epoch, by authors of a particular nation, even in one piece of writing by a particular author, provides insight into the society from which these works emanate as well as into the creative process of the individuals involved in their creation.

Content is also important in mass media material where, characteristically, there is a large audience and/or often repeated themes but where any individual instance is often not designed to have a lasting significance, for example one night's presentation of the news. In such content we find repeated ideas, information, constructions, interpretations and patterns of presentation and interaction. These repetitions and their variations provide insight into the society of which they are a part and into the institutions and individuals that manufacture media programmes.

Communication as representation

When we study content, we study the manner in which ideas and images are expressed or represented. This phenomenon is sometimes also called encoding, or symbolic production and symbolic systems. In general it is often referred to as representation. The study of representation is not meant to be an examination of the so-called 'truth' of statements. That is, it is not limited to commenting on whether a set of statements exactly corresponds to or describes what it purports to describe. Indeed, as researchers have focused attention on the process of representation, it has become apparent that attending to the accuracy of representation is misleading.

The study of representation is literally the study of re-presentation, pro-duction, or construction. Visual or musical ideas are constructed, just as events are constructed in narrative form. Different representations re-present ideas differently. Competing forms of representation are based on competing interpretations, for example, a different selection and emphasis of elements, or on the same interpretation in different media. The theories reviewed in the previous chapter are a good case in point. Each selects a certain set of elements of media-audience interaction for emphasis. At times, some repre-sentations are obviously better than others, perhaps because one or other is incomplete or inaccurate. But more usual in communication studies are analyses of competing representations of events and actions of everyday life in which the question of which is better is not particularly relevant. One representation brings a certain background set of ideas, interests, intentions or ideology to its task and draws out certain elements, while another brings other background and draws out other elements.

The study of representation, especially the representation of human affairs, is a study of *grounded, indeterminate systems*. There are an indeterminate number of ways of representing an object, action or event – another original drawing can always be made – but each of those ways is grounded in or focused on what is being represented, the person and/or medium doing the representing, and the audience for whom the representing is being done.

The concept of intertextuality deals with this phenomenon, as does the notion of polysemy. As we have seen, polysemy refers to the notion that any message is open to a variety – but not an infinite number – of interpretations. Intertextuality refers to the notion that both the style and content of authors is to be found in texts which preceded them (see Kristeva, 1969 or Barthes, 1968). Our knowledge of any one text depends on our knowledge and understanding of previous texts. It is often connected to genres, that is particular kinds of literary or artistic expression. The novel is a genre, and within it are many sub-genres (the thriller, romance, sci-fi, spy novel). There are many different kinds (or genres) of fictional narrative on TV: soaps, police series, westerns (very popular in the 60s) and sci-fi are obvious examples. Our understanding of these narrative genres is, in part, based on our understanding of the similarities and differences between them. *Star Trek*, one of the greatest 'cult' TV drama series, was derivative from an earlier (but very well known) Western series, *Bonanza*. These intertextual connections are part of the taken-for-granted knowledge, understandings and competences used by consumers of popular culture.

With regard to the polysemic character of the text, that is, its openness to a variety of interpretations, the utterance of a simple sentence provides a good example. 'Mary rolled her eyes' contains within it two elements basic to human understanding. One is the notion of intentionality, the second is the notion of causality. Both derive from the choice of the subject and verb. 'Mary's eyes rolled' has a much different meaning, an implied involuntariness. The statement also contains less fundamental meanings: our habit of placing the agent before the verb; the popularity of 'Mary' as an Anglo-Saxon first name; the tendency for common words to be mono- or disyllabic. As well as the expressed or denotative meaning of the statement, a meaning related to a female involved in a body movement, there exist a multitude of implied connotative meanings such as the ones suggested above. There is also a cultural dimension. In one culture first thoughts might go to humour, in another they might go to exasperation.

The implications of polysemy or the grounded indeterminacy of representation does not end here. Different systems of meaning derive from different media. In all that has been said so far we have been dealing within one system of representation – language. Many would argue that language is a most powerful and flexible system of representation. But that does not detract from the independent nature and value of other systems of representation, such as music and the visual arts. Nor can one system of representation encompass the full spectrum of the meaning of another. A painting cannot be translated into a prose essay, nor even poetry. Nor can a sculpture be transformed completely into a photograph or even a holograph. Inevitably, something is lost. In short, a multiplicity of meanings can be generated within one medium, and meaning can be generated within the multiplicity of media. Overall, because these representations can multiply indefinitely, we are dealing with a linked or correlated yet indeterminate system.

The implications of the indeterminacy of representation

The indeterminacy of representation tends to lead the study of communication content away from what has been taken to be the foundations of philosophy, science, and social science and more towards the foundations of interpretation we find in the humanities. In other words, it is primarily concerned with rhetoric – how things are said – and hermeneutics – how things are interpreted – rather than with truth value and reason, a perspective that we will outline more fully in our discussion of discourse analysis later in this chapter. That is to say, in the study of communication the importance of a statement is not limited to whether it predicts events, can be refuted by others, or generates other interesting hypotheses, all standards of science and social science. What is interesting in the study of representation is what it selects and how it re-presents or re-constructs, and what gives a particular representation its force, its ability to persuade, or its attractiveness. Whatever makes one author, painter or film more popular or revered than another, or even a novel more powerful than a film, cannot be satisfactorily discussed by reference to the relative 'truth' of each communication. Such media forms and individual works are more interestingly discussed in terms of their (rhetorical) force, in terms of the nature or style of their representation. In such discussions we can compare movies with books, paintings of battles with portraits, cars with clothes, or rock music with Greek society.

To compare media, movies may add a vibrancy that another medium such as print cannot provide. In addition, it may reach a wider audience. As examples of vibrant productions, the James Bond movies or those of Steven Spielberg are good cases in point. On the other hand, *The Magus*, by the English novelist John Fowles, appeared to lose much in the translation into movie form, perhaps because it was too literal and concrete. To take another example, the discussion of abstract ideas is changed when one moves from books to the popular press or to television. Television demands a necessary pluralism of sight, sound and personage that is absent in radio and print. More than a few minutes of the same person talking, no matter what the visuals, begins to undermine credibility. Just the opposite seems to hold for print.

In the history of the other social sciences, there has been a bias in favour of physical objects over verbal or other representational entities. Physical objects were seen as having a greater claim to an independent existence than representations of those objects. In fact, at times, representation has been subordinated to hypothetical entities, as in the case of language (representation) versus thought (a hypothetical entity). In the same way that the physical object was seen as somehow more fundamental than its representation, thought was postulated to be something that language only partially expressed. As a result, until recently in certain disciplines, representation was only studied as a secondary matter. As we will see later in this chapter, a first step in communication studies was to place representation at the forefront. The second step was to construct and examine the role of human agency in representation.

Signification

The postulation that the 'real world', or the empirical world of objects, and the world of representations exist on different planes, with the latter having secondary importance, led early media commentators to assume that there were true portrayals as opposed to biased portrayals (Bennett, 1982). The contemporary approach to the issue is to assume that physical objects and representations are two different but related aspects of the world. Such a statement places equal importance on representation and the object world, although this does not mean that objects can be represented as something they are not.

Even more recent to communication studies is the emphasis Giddens (1987a, 1987b) places on human agency behind the construction of those representations. All three – objects, representations and human agency – may be seen as 'real', with none subordinate to the others even though representation is derived from human agency acting on the object world. The reality of objects has been taken as given. The reality of representation has come from identifying systematic patterns of behaviour that are employed to collect and organise information. The reality of human agency has come from Giddens' analysis of missing elements in the equation. These patterns of human and media behaviour are a good example of signification, the creation and articulation of a structure for determining meaning.

In the everyday world of media operations, the beats that newspaper editors assign to reporters or journalists, for example, guarantee the presence of certain information and certain perspectives in the news rather than others. That pattern of presence and absence leads to the evolution of a point of view in the paper's overall operations. It also assigns certain meanings to – or signifies – certain relationships in a particular way. Similarly, what a television crew can obtain in the way of news is vastly different from what a single reporter writing news stories can present. Although the television equipment is invisible to the viewer and the television news seemingly puts forward a 'true picture', anyone who has been the subject of a news report is well aware of the obtrusiveness of the cameras and the degree to which they interfere with, influence, and distort an event, or more accurately, how they mould an event to what the technology and its users determine to be the demands of the medium. These media practices, the work habits of communicators, and, in general, the signification process that derives from these factors are as real as physical objects.

Theoretical perspectives on the study of content

The perspectives that are used to study media content are many. Some cast a wide net, taking into account the full context within which messages are formed and transmitted. In a sense each of the chapters in this book contributes to articulating that full context. Others cast a narrower net, focusing more intently on the content alone. There is also some overlap between content theory and audience theory. The purpose of this section is to introduce various approaches to the study of content. The seven – which might equally be said to be eleven – are literary criticism, structuralism and post-structuralism, semiotics, pragmatics, discourse and conversational analysis, modernism and postmodernism, content analysis, and media form analysis.

Literary criticism

The traditions of literary analysis and criticism reach back to Homer and continue through the ages with the Bible and other religious tracts as a central focus. Literary criticism in its modern form, as an academic discipline, is surprisingly recent. In the UK it was established in the 1920s when English was recognised as a degree subject at Cambridge. One of those involved in establishing the syllabus for English at Cambridge was F. R. Leavis; his ideas had an enormous influence on the study of literature, and were carried over later into the study of film and television. Leavis stressed the independence, or the autonomy of the text. He was not interested in such things as how the novel or poem under consideration was produced or its publishing history. Rather he was interested in the meaning of the text and to establish this was a delicate, discriminatory, critical act of interpretation.

Interpretation here meant interpreting what the author had in mind, as expressed in the text. The text was treated as the vehicle of an individual author-creator. Thus, in literary studies, texts were treated as the products of authors – the novels of Jane Austen, the plays of Shakespeare. Later, in film studies the same principle was applied. Students and scholars examined the films of Alfred Hitchcock or Howard Hawkes (both famous Hollywood directors of the 1940s and 1950s) or other famous directors. This approach, known as *auteur* theory (because it was developed in France in the 50s), treated the director rather than the script-writer as the creative originator of the film.

In the 60s this author-centred approach to the study of texts was strongly attacked. In a famous essay, 'Death of the Author', the French cultural critic Roland Barthes argued for an end to the author as the source of meaning in any text (film, novel, TV play). The source of meaning could only be the reader, since the text only becomes meaningful in the act of consumption. The effect of this startling reversal was the 'empowerment' of the reader. No longer chained to the dull task of trying to find out what Shakespeare 'had in mind' when he wrote *Hamlet* (an impossible task anyway, said Barthes), the reader was free to create his or her own meanings, to open up rather than close down the meaning of the text. Gone was the notion of the one true and authentic meaning of the text. Instead, any text, even the most humdrum realistic text, was thought to have a modest plurality of meanings. Texts were polysemic, they had a number of different possible meanings which the active viewer could uncover. Thus reading changes from the passive absorption of the text's imposed meaning, to an active exploration of the text's indeterminacy.

It can be seen how this shift in textual hermeneutics (i.e., interpretation) parallels a shift in audience studies away from the view of audiences as passive and powerless, at the mercy of the meanings imposed by the dominant values of the culture industry. It endorses that notion of the autonomy, or independence, of the act of viewing/reading. It supports a view of the power of readers/viewers actively to engage with and explore the meanings of cultural texts. This has been most vigorously argued by John Fiske (1987) in respect of television viewing.

The shift in emphasis towards the audience and audience interpretation did not obliterate textual analysis. Especially in literature and film departments textual analysis has continued to provide useful insights. An outgrowth of textual analysis has been analysis of the social production of literature and knowledge. This area has been opened up nicely, with particular attention being paid to publishing (see Darnton, 1976, 1979, 1982, 1989 and Chartier and Boureau, 1989). In addition, out of this tradition grew modern reception aesthetics, particularly in the work of West German scholars, reader-response theory, and psychological or sociologically-oriented textual analysis (Jensen and Rosengren, 1990, p. 212).

Structuralism and post-structuralism

An influential approach to the analysis of language and culture that became important in the 60s was structuralism – a general term for a particular way of analysing anything from an advertisement, to a fairy story, a movie, a TV-drama or language itself. The aim of structuralism is to discover the underlying pattern both of single texts and genres. The point is to try to see beneath the outer surface or 'skin' of narrative and get to the hidden, underlying skeletal structure that holds the body of the story together.

An early and seminal work that exemplified structuralist principles was the work of the Russian folklorist, Vladimir Propp, on the fairy (or folk) tale. Working in the 1920s, Propp collected over 400 traditional tales from Europe and was able to show that they all had a basically similar narrative structure. There were two parts to the analysis. The first was a set of basic lexical elements (all stories have some of the following 'items': a hero or heroine, a villain, a helper, and so forth). The second part was, rather as in a game of chess, the set of moves that propels the narrative from its beginning to its ending. Thus, something must happen to set the hero (usually male) in motion; at some point the hero's plans will be disrupted by the villain; and at some point he will receive aid from a helper (who may or may not be female) to overcome the obstacles in his way. Propp was able to reduce the apparent complexity of a great number of different stories to a simple set of underlying narrative elements that could be combined in a strictly limited number of ways. The structural analysis of narrative has subsequently been applied to James Bond novels and films (Eco, 1982; Bennett and Woollacott, 1987), to romantic novels (Radway, 1984) and to soap-opera (Geraghty, 1991).

A second influential scholar in the field of structuralism was the Swiss linguist Ferdinand de Saussure. Saussure (1974), also working during the 1920s, developed what was later seen as the structural analysis of language. Saussure felt it was impossible to analyse actual language, that is language in use, speech (or *parole* in Saussure's terminology). It was too vast, too elusive. No two utterances were alike. Speech was too fleeting, too trivial, too difficult to catch for observation and analysis. Saussure proposed that language could only be scientifically studied in the abstract, as an underlying set of linguistic structures (*langue*, in his terms) that could be combined together by any native speaker to produce an utterance (*parole*). Language is difference, he famously said. By which he meant that a small number of sounds can be combined in different ways to produce sound signs (what we would commonly call words). The study of the science of signs, later called semiotics, was founded by Saussure.

Other structuralists include the anthropologist, Claude Lévi-Strauss, the psychologist Jean Piaget, and the linguists Roman Jakobson and Noam Chomsky. Structuralism is not concerned with dialogue nor the negotiation of meaning in a particular setting. It divorces the 'text' from its moment of creation and reception. Lévi-Strauss extended structuralism beyond Saussure's theory of language into a social scientific world-view. He also extended the hypothetical power of the structuralist formula. He claimed to show in his work 'not how men think in myths, but how myths operate in men's minds without their being aware of the fact' (1969, p. 12). In this respect he differed from Noam Chomsky (1968), who saw the human subject in control through innately acquired linguistic competence.

The shortcomings of structuralism are several. Most important is the fact that it underplays the importance of the particular, the individual speaker and listener, or producer and consumer, of the communication. The moment and thus the context of creation and the audience, along with its situational dynamic, disappears. The speaker is posited as a silent centre of thought, action, aesthetic or moral judgement, the moment is universal and the audience is untheorised.

Post-structuralism brings the nature of the subject-creator forward as particular to a moment, often contradictory in his or her creative actions, certainly fragmented as a meaning-creating entity, and partly illusory in that while a person may create a message, he or she may not understand what he or she is talking about. In emphasising these elements, post-structuralism radically devalues authors and spins analysis out of control. While currently it has many detractors, the main contribution of post-structuralism is that it posits that 'narratives, images, or ideologies in general always imply or construct a position from which they are to be read' (Johnson, 1986, p. 299). Or, as Giddens (1987b, p. 213) suggests of Derrida's post-structuralist deconstruction, 'Derrida affirms the evanescence of processes of meaning: everything should be understood "as an active movement, a process of demotivating, rather than the structure given once and for all" ' (Derrida, 1981, p. 103).

Semiotics

Semiotics is the science of signs; as such it is an abstracted form of structuralism. There are three basic elements to semiotics: sign, signifier, signified. The sign is a concept meant to stand for a full and complete representation of an object or event or, as Roland Barthes (1968, p. 38) would have it, the amalgamation of signifier and signified. This is not to say that the sign is the combined totality of meaning of one instance of signifier and signified, for example, one time in which a word is used in reference to an object. Rather it is the emergent meaning inherent in numerous signifier/signified pairs, for example the many different times we use the word pipe to apply to various types of pipes. The sign is what emerges in our minds as a result of the many different times we come across a particular object of attention and its designation.

The object – or event or person – is the thing signified and the signifier is the device used to represent what is signified. The sign encompasses both. The signifier exists on the plane of expression (for example oral or visual representation), whereas the signified can be said to exist on the plane of content or reference (that to which the expression refers).

The semiotic analysis of popular culture has concentrated on the critical activity of decoding the hidden ideological meanings in anything, from all-in wrestling, striptease and the Louvre, to television, popular novels and advertisements (see Barthes, 1972). A semiotic analysis distinguishes between two levels of meaning – the denotative and the connotative. The denotative is the obvious, natural, self-evident meaning – what you literally see, for instance, in an advertisement. The connotative is what is implied but not actually said explicitly. To take a well-known example from Barthes, in an ad for Panzani spaghetti we see a picture of two packets of Panzani spaghetti, a tin of Panzani sauce and a packet of Panzani Parmesan cheese in a string basket resting on a table, with some tomatoes, onions, peppers and mushrooms spilling out of it (Barthes, 1977a). What you literally, obviously, see here is the denotative meaning of the image. Barthes goes on to discuss the second level, the hidden meanings in the image. First, there is a suggestion of healthiness and wholesomeness connoted by the fresh vegetables. Second there is a hint of what he calls 'Italianicity' in the image – the dominant colours are the same red, green and white of the Italian flag.

We have in the advertisement a modest plurality of meanings (a polysemy). On the surface is a denoted image which at first seems realistic, banal and obvious. But the image is saturated with implied or connoted meanings and values which, in combination with other saturated images to which they refer, form the basis of an ideology. Barthes thought the task of the semiologist to be that of unmasking the ideologies of a bourgeois, capitalist society, the connections between, say, the natural attractiveness of fresh food or a well-composed photograph and the interests of capitalist producers. In *Mythologies* (1972), he tried to unveil the naturalised mythical (ideological) meanings hidden in the everyday culture of France in the 1950s.

Although Barthes (1977a) later rejected this rather simplistic kind of analysis it was taken up in British cultural studies. Semiotic analysis, *à la* Barthes, became the preferred way of reading cultural texts (see, for example, Williamson's analysis of advertisements, 1978). Such analyses were mixed with the theory of ideology and a dash of structuralist narrative analysis. (For a review of this rather eclectic mix, see Woollacott, 1982.)

Pragmatics, discourse and conversational analysis

Although discourse analysis, pragmatics and conversational analysis have significant differences, they share a common ground by taking as their starting point that part of language rejected by Saussure, namely actual utterances (*parole*). These three research orientations are an important aspect of the so-called 'linguistic turn' in the contemporary social sciences, and are part of a wider development in a number of disciplines, including philosophy, linguistics, social psychology and sociology, in which ordinary language usage (conversation, talk) is taken as the object of study. From such studies a different view of language to that of structuralism (which, as we have seen, examines underlying, abstract linguistic structures) emerges.

The philosophy of ordinary language, first developed in the later philosophy of Ludwig Wittgenstein, and extended by the Oxford philosopher J. Austin, takes a pragmatic (practical) view of language. Language is almost always more than talk for talk's sake. To say something is to do something: to make a promise, or an offer, a refusal, an acceptance. Language as utterance is always a social act, and an interaction between two or more speaker/ hearers.

Philosophers, linguists and sociologists have been intrigued by what the concept of communication entails as a social interaction. In an attempt to deal with communication as social interaction a field of study has been reopened called pragmatics (Levinson, 1985). It has links to, but should not be confused with, American pragmatist philosophers such as John Dewey and C. S. Peirce. Nor should it be confused with the interpersonal psychology of Paul Watzlawick, Janet Beavin, and Don Jackson and their seminal book, *Pragmatics of Human Communication* (1967).

Central to pragmatics as articulated by Levinson and others is a recognition that all actual utterances are context-specific. That is to say, the meaning of what is said is related to the context in which it is said. To illustrate this notion consider a simple utterance such as 'give me that'. As an abstract written sentence we understand its general meaning, but we cannot know what 'that' is, or who 'me' refers to, or in what actual space the remark is made. In any actual conversational context all these things are quite clear and obvious. Of central interest to pragmatics is the study of implicatures (implied meanings).

Very often, too, in ordinary talk there is a difference between what is said and what is meant. Or, to put it differently, we very often express ourselves indirectly rather than directly. Instead of saying, for instance, 'pass the salt' we normally say 'could you pass the salt (please)?' Notice that this latter utterance is a request not a question, yet it is phrased as a question. If the person to whom it is said treated it as a question by answering yes or no (without actually passing the salt), we would be surprised or perhaps a little impatient. If we press our analysis further and ask why is 'could you pass the salt please' normally preferred to 'pass the salt', we might say because it is more polite. The notion of politeness here entails a notion of consideration for the other in the social interaction (Brown and Levinson, 1987).

A fundamental perception of pragmatics is that insofar as language is communicative (and not all utterances are), communication entails a co-operative principle, or attention to the needs, feelings and circumstances of others in the conversation. Thus, when we talk to others, we tailor the way in which we talk in order to take the other person into account: a parent talking to a little child, a teacher talking to a pupil, teenagers talking together, all design not only what they say, but how they say it to take the other person into account and thereby let them know that they are so doing.

This reopened pragmatics and the study of implicatures opens up a huge field of study, with considerable interest for the analysis of film, radio and television, though little work has been done on this as yet. Take one very obvious example. Voice is a crucial means of generating implicatures. If one says something in a slightly different voice from one's normal way of speaking, it will be heard by an associate as having possible implications. Maybe one is angry, sad, cross, affectionate or sexually aroused: all these things can be expressed by the tone of voice in which one simply says 'hello'. Since voice is the basic source of information on radio about the character, personality and state of mind of speakers, the study of voice implicatures can tell us a great deal about the communicative character of this particular medium of broadcasting (Brand and Scannell, 1991).

Van Dijk notes that discourse analysis is another perspective with a long history, dating back more than 2,000 years to the discipline of *rhetorica*. *Rhetorica* was oriented to persuasive effectiveness and dealt with the planning, organisation, specific operations and performance of speech in political and legal settings (van Dijk, 1985 [vol. 1] p. 1). A passage, speech or performance succeeded or failed according to the impact it made on its audience.

Discourse analysis points to media patterns and conventions and their success in being taken for granted, as evidenced in the satisfaction and understanding of audiences, and, more formally, in reviews. It also points to what is privileged in such apparently natural conventions, and provides a framework for understanding, for example, prime ministerial television appearances as discursive elements in political talk. A discourse analyst might note that beyond content itself, political debates represent a challenge mounted against the incumbent to dislodge that incumbent from a discourse of power. On the other side, it is the job of the incumbent to constrain the pretender in a discourse of questionable power-seeking. As van Dijk notes, ethnographers offer up a good general approach as follows: 'People of category x (men, women, elderly, leading persons, etc.), typically use form y (intonation, pitch, lexical item, narrative form, code, etc.) in context z (with a given purpose, speaking to a specific person, and in a given social event)' (vol. 3, p. 8).

Modern discourse analysis is a mix of sociology and linguistics applied to the study of discourse – units of expression longer than a single sentence (the standard work is Brown and Yule, *Discourse Analysis*, 1983). Thus discourse analysis looks at extended utterances, as in a conversation, or a monologue on radio (see Montgomery, 1991), dialogue on TV, and so forth. It has an intermediate position between pragmatics and conversational analysis, taking ideas from both but trying to develop a linguistic analysis of extended units of text. It is typically attentive to deixis (the contextual character of utterance), topic organisation and management (what is being talked about).

One variation of discourse analysis, sometimes called critical linguistics, has been strongly influenced by the mix of ideology, theory and semiotics found in cultural studies. For instance, Fowler (1991) has analysed discourse and ideology in the press, looking at newspaper representations of gender, race, power, authority and law and order.

Conversational analysis is a distinctive sociological approach to the analysis of naturally occurring talk. Pioneered by the American sociologist Harvey Sacks in the early 1970s, it depends on the audio or video recorder to capture a large corpus of talk on tape. Conversational analysis attends to the structure of talk-as-interaction by the careful analysis of its sequential character. Conversational analysis is interested to discover how participants in talk know, for instance, when it is their turn to speak, how they collaborate in topic maintenance and change, in ending talk, and in obeying other implicit rules of on-air conversational behaviour. Conversational analysis aims to show the ordered, orderly character of talk, how it works, and how participants work to make it work. A striking feature of talk that emerges from this type of analysis, is that there is nothing in the interaction that cannot be treated as relevant and meaningful. Conversational analysis has discovered the semantics of silence, showing that pauses or hesitations are always treated as meaningful and as generally implying disapproval, or as a prelude to a negative response. It has also shown the meaningful properties of seemingly meaningless speech particles (for example, uhuh, mmm, oh, oops) that ordinary semantics ignores (for useful reviews of conversational analysis see Levinson, 1985; Heritage, 1984, and Garfinkel, 1984).

Conversational analysis began with the study of ordinary, social chat in everyday contexts (especially telephone conversations). Since then it has moved out into the analysis of talk in institutional talk, including broadcasting. Some systematic work has been done on political talk (Atkinson, 1984), and especially the political news interviews on radio and TV in the UK and USA. A key to conversational analysis's work on broadcast talk is the demonstration of the institutional character of radio and TV talk, and the various ways in which it is designed with absent listeners or viewers in mind. For instance, in the broadcast political interview, the broadcaster – the host – always begins the talk, closes it down and asks the questions (thereby controlling the definition of the topic to be talked about). John Heritage (1984) has shown that unlike in ordinary talk, there are no response tokens in broadcast interviews such as mm, uhuh, or oh. Such responses are systematically absent to avoid seeming to exclude the viewer/listener or giving him/her the feeling of eavesdropping on a private conversation. At the same time the withholding of response tokens maintains the neutrality of the broadcasting institution in respect of what is being said. The inclusion of 'noddy shots' – the reporter nodding at what the politician is saying – is to prove that the politician is in fact talking to someone and not thin air.

Modernism and postmodernism

Modernism and postmodernism are terms that are closely connected to the notion of the modern: the perception that we live in a historically unique kind of society that is radically different from all previous historic (and prehistoric) societies. How did this happen, and what are the characteristics of a modern society?

The process of modernisation is closely connected with economic and political transformations, the creation of urban, industrial societies (Marx was the first great analyst of this development) and their political institutions (the modern nation-state). This process has had a profound impact on how members of such societies experience their lives. This is what is termed the experience of modernity. Modernity refers to the character or quality of modern life; the definition of modernity is another matter and while there are many different manifestations and differences in definition, you will get a sense of what we mean by modernity in the following discussion.

Modernism, as opposed to modernity, refers to literary and artistic expressions of the experience of modernity. Modernism in the arts and literatures of Europe developed in the late nineteenth century, and reached a climax in the inter-war period (1920–1940). Modernism tried to give expression to what the French poet Charles Baudelaire called 'the shock of the new'. In a famous phrase he defined modernity as 'the transient, the fleeting, the contingent: it is the one half of art, the other being the eternal and immovable'. The paradox for 'modern' art was how to catch and fix in permanent form what essentially seemed to escape capture and expression – the transient, fleeting experience of the new. In art, the schools of impressionism, post-impressionism and expressionism were all early attempts by modernist painters to express the impermanence of modern life. To catch the new meant rejecting old forms, above all realism. The exploration of form rather than content was a characteristic feature of modern art, think of Picasso or the sculptor Henry Moore.

The theorists of the Frankfurt School were modernists, particularly Theodor Adorno. Adorno believed that the only way that culture could critically resist the all-embracing domination of the culture industries was through an artistic modernism that resisted commodification. To resist commodification was to resist the process whereby the culture industry transformed cultural forms into commodities (economic goods) designed for easy consumption. Thus, Adorno argued, works of art were loaded with meaning and required, for their full appreciation, a great deal of knowledge. He affirmed the ensuing difficulties in understanding and appreciation because they were indications that art was successfully resisting easy consumption and hence the grip of capitalism, the profit-motive and the market-place. A writer like James Joyce (*Ulysses*), a painter like Picasso (*Guernica*) or a composer like Schöenberg – all notable modernists – resisted easy consumption and thereby resisted the mass market, preserving the integrity (the independence) of artistic creativity. It is not hard to imagine how such a perspective leads to elitism.

Since the late 70s there has been a growing debate about whether modern society is moving into a new postmodern phase. It is argued that economically, politically and culturally the world has moved beyond its formative 'modern' character of the nineteenth and early twentieth century. Economically, Fordism (the production-led – rather than consumer-led – assembly-line production methods of a limited number of products, pioneered by Henry Ford) has been replaced by post-Fordism. Post-Fordism goes for careful product research before production is launched, flexible production methods yielding a greater variety of products, and a shorter shelf-life for each. Politically, the nation-state, as a society that shares allegiance to a common set of values, ambitions, religious symbols, and so forth, is under increasing strain. Culturally, the distinction between high culture (modernism) and mass or popular culture has collapsed.

There was some truth in the Frankfurt School's perception that mass production imposed its standardised uniform products on consumers. They said of early Ford automobiles that you could have one in any colour you wanted – as long as that colour was black, the only one produced by the company. Now, it is argued, in the postmodern world a limited number of standardised uniform products is almost a thing of the past. Now, when a movie is made in Hollywood it will be tested, with alternative endings, on trial audiences before general release. The ending preferred by the trial audiences will be the version of the film that is released. The most obvious site of such developments is the high-street retailing sector. The shopping malls of Western Europe and North America offer a staggering variety of products, in food and clothing, with a faster and faster turnover of new lines. Even the continual emergence and disappearance of stores themselves is an indication of courageous attempts to find consumer niches not satisfied by others. Production, and especially retailing, is becoming more and more diversified, fragmented, and specialised.

These developments have a considerable impact on the culture industries today. Consumer choice is sovereign. Reflecting a higher value attached to consumer choice than the 'public interest', European governments have withdrawn support for public-service radio and TV since the early 80s. A greater proliferation of mostly commercial channels targeted at specialised audiences defines the broadcasting industries today. General interest magazines are increasingly being pushed aside by speciality titles. Pop groups and radio stations are continuously inventing 'new' music and labels in search of unserved niche markets. And all this proliferation of consumer culture is linked, albeit loosely, to the growing diversification and fragmentation of contemporary societies, politically and culturally.

Looking back in comparison, until the 60s in the UK it was easy to invoke through the BBC's services a sense of national unity, a common loyalty to Queen and country. Since then Britain, like all other European countries, North America and Australia, has become increasingly multicultural. The global migration of peoples has increased enormously since the 50s, and continues to increase. In a multicultural society there are many different cultural identities and lifestyles. The analysis of lifestyles and the creation of products for such lifestyles (discussed in Chapter 7 under Cultural Studies) recognises and celebrates the diversity of ethnic and sexual identities. Postmodernism acknowledges, celebrates and rationalises this increasing diversity.

Postmodern culture has no rational core of meaning at its centre. There are no deep meanings or truths. Everything is on the surface, and the surface shimmers with a myriad of glittering differences. Collins (1989) notes that postmodernism is a manifold of many decentred discourses, none of which are privileged (cf. Bakhtin, 1981), is historically self-conscious of its own project, and searches for ways of integrating historical and contemporary stylistic concerns with those of local cultures. Postmodernism affirms the development of sub-genres and attends to different taste cultures, for example opera lovers, rock music fans and so forth.

The character of knowledge in postmodern society has changed. It is no longer possible to believe in 'grand narratives' that claim to explain the underlying or true meaning of modern society. Marx, who constructed a narrative of historical emancipation from feudalism to capitalism to socialism, along with all those thinkers who believed in democracy-as-progress, were deluded. They tried to impose, as it were, a single storyline on history (as in previous epochs Christianity had done), which they thought of as a linear progression from superstition and barbarism to civilisation and rational enlightenment. Postmodernism simply refuses to believe such stories (Lyotard, 1984). It sees history as infinitely more complex and uneven in its development.

The collapse of Soviet socialism in the late 80s is taken as a proof of this general diagnosis of the times. State socialism was the most grandiose effort to impose the narrative of progress, technical efficiency and the rational society upon a huge and diverse mix of subject-peoples. When this monstrous delusion finally collapsed, that diversity, kept down by the permafrost of Stalinism, has proved to be a tragically explosive mix of clashing ethnic, religious and national identities.

Having taken note of the strengths of the postmodern framework, we should hasten to add that postmodernism underplays the importance of the dominant discourse, the dominant set of values and attitudes that underpin much of the institutions and operations of societies.

An analytical technique: content analysis

In contrast to the above approaches to content is a technique called content analysis. We have termed it a technique because, although it has been used extensively, especially in the US, and even boasts a feature-length film shot in homage of its analytical power (*Midway Island*), it lacks theoretical but not methodological underpinnings.

Above all, content analysis is quantitative. After a first overview, the content analyst sets up units of analysis – phrases, sentences, nouns, verbs, adjectives, paragraphs, column inches, placement, accompanying illustrations, categories of spokespersons quoted or cited, and so forth. Secondly, the analyst determines meaning categories or themes that appear to be salient to a particular piece of communication. They may be salient on the basis of the focus of the author or on the basis of the interests of the analyst. With units and categories in place, the analyst then counts various types of occurrences and perhaps their partnership with other types of occurrences, that is, words with pictures, long pieces with prominent placement. On the basis of these frequencies of occurrence and their relations with others, the analyst can provide a reading of an article, a newspaper, a treatment of an issue over time and by numbers of media outlets, and so on. Not just occurrences are noticed. Non-occurrences may be just as important. Content analysis is also useful in comparisons. Thus during the military rivalry of the USSR and the US, the media treatment of comparable actions by both sides could be analysed.

For example, a content analytic study of the coverage of Latin America in the US press revealed that the dominant definition of news, that is what was most often reported about Latin America was disasters, for example earthquakes and volcanos. During the 70s there was a gradual shift towards a definition focused around dictators and banana republics. And more recently, as we will see in Chapter 9, there has been a further shift. Such an analysis is revealing not only in terms of the triviality of the actual news definition of an entire continent, but also in terms of its significant absences – the failure to offer any serious account of the economic, political or social developments of that region. Content studies are also able to show over-time continuities and changes in the representation of issues, social roles, attitudes to authority, and so forth. Likewise, content studies of social representation have pointed to the distribution of those who come to define the social order and who are seen to be important social actors. In the main they are white males and professionals. Black males are portrayed as crooks, athletes or musicians.

In the US, content analyses are often performed not on the individual stories themselves but on news coverage (Berelson, 1972). The conclusions of such studies mostly have to do with the manner in which news is organised and what picture of the world is thereby presented to the reader, listener, or viewer. The discussion can then proceed to considering the implications of such a news structure.

Other content analyses of news can examine anything from a set of news programmes to an individual news item, story, photograph, or visual. Generally, researchers attempt to define the logic of the presentation, for instance the positioning of the various elements in the piece or the totality of pieces being considered. The point is to work towards an articulation of the internal relations among those elements. For example, attention may be drawn attention to the fact that labour is usually associated with on-the-street events such as recurring disorder, while management is often used to provide analysis in the context of the controlled, peaceful, quiet environment of a plush executive office (see the Glasgow Media Group's studies on news discussed and cited in Chapter 7). The implications of this way of using sources is that, even in a lock-out, labour is shown as the instigator of the stoppage and management as the patient victim. From the point of view of semiotics, such studies thus tend to show the signification process of newsmaking: what is deemed to be important and how it is placed within a meaning system. What is the nature of the news story? How does it reproduce the dominant ideology?

Other studies of news deal with what gets included in the news and what does not. These studies then tend to turn away from content and toward the process of news-gathering and the influence of professional ideals and the goals of owners (see Gans, 1979; Tuchman, 1978, Schlesinger, 1978).

Some of the serious difficulties with content analysis are based on the lack of theorisation of the media. Content analysts tend to provide relatively unsophisticated readings of their findings. Thus in very few instances are normal patterns of media treatment given. Similarly, the role of the media as sources for repeated confirmations of themes of community consolidation is rarely considered. The standard media treatment of transgressors is unknown. The contextualisation of repeated mentions of particular events, actions, attitudes, and so forth, is rarely fully discussed and sometimes goes unmentioned. Insufficient analysis of the constructed scenario is given to allow a person to determine whether further treatment of the issue outside the time period mentioned would lead to much different conclusions.

Media forms and meaning structures

The foregoing analytical frameworks provide understandings of the structures and implicit meanings of content that span all media. Another framework of analysis that can be used as a complement to any of the above frameworks is derived from McLuhan's notion of the medium as the message. In short, the presentation of meaning is constrained by the medium itself and how it forms and carries content.

In the day-to-day world of journalism, journalists, newsmakers, and news consumers alike have realised that the various media consistently select certain elements for emphasis. That selection leads to a bias about events that varies across each medium. The best example is the television news team as compared with the single newspaper reporter. Not only is the news team more intrusive on the event itself but also a television news story is uncompromising in demanding good visuals as part of the story. On the other hand, a newspaper story depends for its strength on various elements, including analysis. Each medium organises and encourages particular elements of content and particular relations between those elements. These elements and relations are both distinct to each medium and forever shifting with the creativity of the practitioners in each: they provide the background to the effectiveness of any individual piece. The following sections will examine a number of important media forms and their biases.

The advertisement

The advertisement is an invention of profound significance to capitalist society. It lies at the very foundation of the commercial mass media, for it allows production and distribution of information and entertainment across a wide segment of the population at very little cost to the consumer. For a surcharge paid on every other consumer product, an advertising industry of immense size and power has been developed in the United States, and in other capitalist nations to a lesser extent.

In commerce, advertising has increasingly become the means whereby producers launch products and maintain sales. In the past the performance of a product and hence consumer satisfaction were supplemented by advertising to increase or maintain sales, but now markets are created by advertisers launching new products. Consumer satisfaction is anticipated, sometimes by means of market tests. As numerous commentators have pointed out, we are either threatened or tempted by advertisers into buying advertised products. The advertiser creates the need and then persuades us that this product fills that need. Advertising also bypasses product performance by boasting enough so that the boast, rather than the performance, becomes reality.

Advertisements customarily are created by advertising agencies. During the twentieth century, these agencies have played a central role in the development of advertising as a persuasive communication process. The agencies taught producers about consumers, telling them how to pitch their product with the audience in mind, how to layer their goods with symbols structured to persuade the consumer to purchase, and to feel satisfied with his or her purchase. On this basis, advertising campaigns are created. They are then followed up with audience research to measure how the audience is interpreting the pitch and responding to the product.

Because so much is at stake and the constraints of space or time are so great, there is an astonishingly high investment involved in the making of advertisements. It is not at all uncommon for a 30-second advertisement to cost more to produce than a 30-minute programme. Millions of pounds of production investment in the advertised product hang in the balance. Moreover, no surface is safe from advertising, be it a shoe bottom, a space craft, the sky, toilet doors and paper, or mountain sides. Advertisements are the graffiti of the business world.

To summarise a general example of the advertising and market development process briefly, the producer first selects a target market. Some prized attribute of high-status members of this market, such as attractiveness to the opposite sex, is inextricably linked to consumption of this product. Using this process, the producer generates sales in the target audience. Sales are also made to people who envy, and aspire to be like, those who are part of the target market. Members of the target market essentially are presented with an idealised, supercharged image of themselves that they can consume through the purchase of a never-ending stream of products purported to be crucial to the lifestyle and values they represent. Consuming these articles not only feeds narcissism but also provides a means of gaining status.

An interesting aspect of advertising is the relation of the product to the advertisement particularly when brands are essentially identical in their basic defining characteristics, for example taste and alcohol content for beer, cleaning capacity for detergent. In North America, as a result of market research, beer companies have identified what image consumers have of themselves and their product and what is appealing about that image. They have then designed ad campaigns based on an idealised version of that image. Attributes are given to the product, such as the purity of the ingredients or the esoteric technology of the brewing process that are meant to appeal to the consumer in that they fit into his or her self-image. At the same time, attributes are given to the depicted consumers that are also designed to flatter. In this environment, the obvious distinctive attribute of the product that one might think would be the basis of choice – for instance the taste of beer – is noticeably underplayed. But even more interesting, the actual tastes of the competing brands are so similar that they are virtually indistinguishable and certainly indescribable.

This convergence of product attributes amongst competing brands gives companies a great deal of power to manipulate the image of the product and the consumer in order to capture a particular market segment (Grady, 1983). It also places market share and brand control in the hands of the spin doctors – the advertising agencies that design the ad campaigns and the marketing managers who capture market share based on the size of promotional funds.

The end result is that while the market is dominated by large companies who invest heavily in marketing, two significant vulnerabilities emerge. The first is the emergence of generic products with virtually no advertising expenses. The second is the emergence of small players with a genuinely different product. These vulnerabilities are very real and are constantly in play whether the product is beer, soap, music, books and authors, films, and so forth.

Once the marketing game is in play, it has a life of its own. Consumer boredom, which may also be conceived of as the market's 'neophilia', or love of the new, keeps the advertising world turning. Such boredom also influences the development of products and the application of technology to consumables. It is nothing more than the added 'play value' the product gains that makes manufacturers consider putting holograms on cereals and chocolate bars.

Three other types of advertising are significant. The first includes advertisements for a company rather than its products. This type is usually called a corporate image ad. It promotes an image of the corporation rather than a particular product or product line. In some cases, such as the advertisements of the energy industry, the responsible nature of the individual company or the industry as a whole is put forward explicitly with a content of concern that has either been demonstrated by the public or that the corporations have discerned through market research.

A version of the corporate image ad is the advocacy ad. It can be found in the advertisements of United Technologies, a company that obtains a good number of contracts from the American military. Over the years it has placed advertisements in an American magazine, *The Atlantic Monthly*, in which United Technologies takes a position on a variety of public and social issues ranging from the so-called governmental to the educational. Advocacy advertisements are not as common outside the US. Perhaps the more central role of American business in American society encourages companies like United Technologies to place such advertisements.

There is also the ad that masquerades as a piece of reporting. It has been called a variety of names, one of which is advertorial. This is descriptive material on, for example, the contribution of a company to the larger economy, which is prepared for print publications, apparently written by a journalist, but in fact written by an employee or agent of the company or agency that is the subject of the article. Television info-mercials, half-hour programmes foregrounding a particular product, are similar to advertorials. They now account for over US$1,000 million in sales in the US.

This leads to a last form of advertising, called product placement or plugging. Until the last decade or so, Hollywood producers portrayed themselves as putting out 'pure entertainment'. By this they meant that they did not systematically attempt to promote products, take political stances, or teach public morality. This was not quite the case, of course. Billy Wilder's movie,

One, Two, Three (1961) blatantly plugged Coca-Cola, and the blacklisting from the industry during the late 1940s and 1950s of persons who were purported to be Communists demonstrates how ideologically sensitive Hollywood was and is.

Miller (1990) notes that the Hollywood product has become more sullied. He reports that plugging products in movies is so rampant that some movies are being turned almost completely into advertising vehicles: 'Friendly producers send scripts to [Associated Film Promotions] weeks and even months before filming starts, and the company analyses them scene by scene to see if it can place a product – or advertising material, a billboard perhaps – on, under or behind the stars' (p. 48). Miller adds that the plugsters choose projects that offer them maximum control, even telling the producers precisely where they want to see clients' brands. 'The plug, in other words, must not just "foreground" the crucial name or image but also flatter it – that is, brightly reaffirm the product's advertising' (p. 48). This is clearly exemplified by the plugs for Pepsi in the three *Back to the Future* movies starring Michael J. Fox, who also appeared in Pepsi commercials on TV. In the movie *Texasville*, 145 product placements were made. Wasko, Phillips and Purdie (1993) have provided a useful analysis of plugging.

The expansion of plugging in movies illustrates a more basic relationship between content and advertisement. In every medium, the content of the programme or publication is closely allied with the perspective of the advertiser. No advertiser is going to support a publication or programme with content adverse to their kind of values. The delivery of large audiences who are alienated from advertised products is hardly going to gain the support of the advertiser. As a result the news media must wend their way between the discourses generated by all parties. They must balance what the various vested interests say with what other groups say, such as the public, the government, and the experts. Above all, they cannot forget advertiser sensibilities while, of course, not ignoring 'undeniable facts'.

The news story

The news story is a distinctive informational form that differs in its structure according to the medium within which it appears. However, all news stories share certain fundamental characteristics. Richard Ericson, Patricia Baranek and Janet Chan (1989) developed a set of criteria to describe the characteristics of events that made them newsworthy. The criteria of newsworthiness they discuss have been usefully summarised by Desbarats:

- Simplification – an event must be recognised as significant and relatively unambiguous in its meaning.
- Dramatization – a dramatized version of the event must be able to be presented.
- Personalization – events must have personal significance to someone.

- Themes and continuity – events that fit into preconceived themes gain in newsworthiness.
- Consonance – events make the news more readily when they fit the reporters' preconceived notions of what should be happening.
- The Unexpected – unexpected events that can be expected within frames of reference used by reporters are newsworthy.   (1990, p. 110)

These criteria of newsworthiness are important to bear in mind as background to a consideration of the characteristics of news stories in individual media.

A more traditional description of the characteristics of the news story posits that such stories are organised according to an inverted pyramid. This means simply that a summary of the 'important information' is put at the beginning followed by the development of the story and the context in which it happened. By 'important information' journalists mean the five 'w's', one 'h', and one 's-w'. That is to say, the story leads off with *who, what, when, where, why, how*', and then '*so what*'. Journalism textbooks also emphasise clarity and conciseness. Language must be simple and straightforward. Clarity is achieved by avoiding clichés, jargon, and excessively complex phraseology. Conciseness is partially achieved through the use of the active voice. Neither unnecessary words nor redundancies should appear. Pace and tone are crucial. Ideas must be introduced at a pace the reader can understand. The tone of the story must reflect both subject matter and treatment of the material. Obviously, what is concise in *The Times* or the *New York Times* is wordy for *The Mirror* or the *New York Daily News*. Also, what is wordy in the US may not be in the UK.

Finally, leads are important to stories. Most often they are direct, sometimes giving the five 'w's' in the first sentence. They must also serve to capture the readers' attention and orient them to the story. Delayed leads come in the second paragraph or sentence and exploit the curiosity of the reader established by an introductory delay.

The inverted pyramid has allowed the development of newspaper tabloids. They gain their name from the half-sized format of the pages, which makes them easy to read en route to work by public transit. The tabloids are meant to be a quick and easy read, often complemented by soft porn and low-level boosterism of actual and potential advertisers. They play into the predispositions of their readership, which are determined by market research, more than the broadsheets; events are often overdramatised and are interpreted as signals that things are often out of control. Headlines regularly emphasise the bizarre. In the week of 1 October 1992 some examples from a variety of weekly tabs were:

Singing duck sounds just like Elvis
Teacher swallows live baby mice
People near death hear the same heavenly music

Psychic killed in car wreck brings herself back to life
Di was never shy – she took her first lover at 16
Wife disguises self as chair to catch cheating husband
Family flees talking doll
Boy castrates himself because his parents didn't take him to the zoo.

Whether one sees them as vigorous and entertaining, or as intrusive, insensitive, and malicious, the tabloids' superficial treatment of stories periodically rouses disquiet in the UK about standards regarding privacy, libel, contempt, confidentiality, and slander. However, as an editorial in (Conrad Black's) *Sunday Telegraph* pointed out, if the Thatcher government had really been outraged by the excesses of 'the gutter press', then she would not have bestowed knighthoods on its editors and elevated its proprietors to the House of Lords (*Guardian Weekly*, 1 July 1990, p. 9).

The inverted pyramid and the medium of print mean that the journalists must tell the story, even if they use liberal doses of quotations. This places the journalist and indeed the paper in a particular position in the mind of the reader. The angle taken on stories, what is brought forward and emphasised and so forth, is taken to be the perspective of the individual reporter and the paper. The discussion of context and the provision of analysis develops the implicit position taken in the opening of the story. To assume that the angle taken on a story necessarily represents the view of the reporter, the editor, or the owner of the paper is, to a degree, the old problem of blaming the messenger, a problem around which neither journalist nor reader can steer. The reporter and editor are seen to be intervenors in the construction of the news even if they might not want to be. It is they who must tell the story. And while the tone of the press today is much less blatantly partisan than it has been in the past, the medium itself prevents the press from removing itself from this role as intervenor, interpreter, or mediator.

Events versus issues

One further point, already mentioned in passing, must be emphasised. With the five 'w's' up front, and with the constant emphasis on human interest and so on, what the news brings us is events rather than issues. As any public interest group knows (especially Greenpeace), any amount of informed analysis about a particular issue will never bring it onto the front pages. But an event, whether chaining oneself to a fence or barricading major traffic routes, may produce saturation coverage. Prior provision of information and analysis to a columnist is a good method of getting some of the issues discussed. But the event itself moves the issues to front and centre in the public agenda.

From the point of view of the public, and that of conscientious journalists, the irony of produced media events is that the produced event may obscure the importance of the real event. For example, the security provisions and counter-demonstrations to such major events as first ministers' meetings and UN special conferences such as the Earth Summit may obscure the significance of the event.

Television versus print

The most obvious difference between newspaper news stories and television news stories is the dominance of visuals. These visuals are not merely moving pictures that complement a text written up much like a newspaper text and then spoken by an announcer. The visuals structure the story and a text is built around those visuals.

The nature of the video camera is that while it is extremely intrusive for the actors of an event, it is quite invisible to the viewer. It claims by its ability to record sound and picture a veracity that no other medium can match. It apparently cannot lie. In its ability to record an event, barring intentional distortion, it brings the news to us from the mouths of the participants. What we see are snippets of the actual happenings, together with interpretations by on-the-spot observers and participants.

The trick for television news producers is to edit the material in such a way that the edits also appear unobtrusive. The visual coverage of the event must be simple enough to orient the viewer, but it must not appear incomplete. The sentences and phrases that are recorded and subsequently used in the final piece must be succinct and directly relevant. The speakers' identities must be obvious and they must have an obvious validity as observers or participants. Politicians who can speak in 'clips' and who can move comfortably on camera are often the people sought out for background to stories.

What is primary in the television news story is not the interpretation of the story by the reporter out of all the information he or she can glean. Rather, it is the directing of the news crew interviewer and interviewees to create the elements of a story that can then be pieced together as a snippet of life.

The camera versus the reporter

The major difference between the newspaper news story and the television news story derives from the camera, the position in which the reporter or interviewer is placed as a result of the camera's ability to present facsimiles of real events. Instead of being in a position of messenger, the interviewer and his or her crew acts as a solicitor of information from others. Presenting that information and synthesising it, television news producers are apparently removed from a primary role of interpretation. They merely provide the means whereby the story and the participants can tell what they have to tell. In synthesising the news, producers are apparently uninvolved. They merely manage the news by placing it in an understandable format. All this is a result of the dominance of the visual element. The camera never lies, or so we are led to believe.

However, it frames and its operators edit. It puts some things in the picture and keeps others out. It can emotionalise with the extreme close-up or provide a 'more objective' panorama. It can present the authoritative distance of the medium close-up against a neutral cardboard backdrop or include an entire visual environment and attendant mood. If the camera does not actually always lie it certainly tells its own version of the story.

Investigative television reporting

One common observation about television investigative reporting is that it has become a non-fiction adventure story. This construction has been applied to the US programme *60 Minutes*, where each of the permanent star investigative reporters is presented as an inveterate single-combat-warrior seeking after truth in a corrupt world, exposing the liars and cheats of the world to the public eye.

Given the flexibilities and power of the television medium, television investigative reporting demands an extremely high level of trust from the audience. The credibility of the programme and host is absolutely essential. As an illustration of the necessity of that trust, we reviewed the scripts of an award-winning programme in which Canada's pre-eminent investigative reporter, Eric Malling, inquired into the safety of the highly computerised Airbus A320 (Canadian Association of Journalists, 1991). Some of the techniques we noted follow.

The first technique used by Malling was to set up a test pilot, Michel Asseline, the man who piloted the A320 that crashed at the Paris air show in June 1988, as a credible witness. As the transcript reads, Malling establishes Asseline's credentials, his consistency, his reasonable tone in responding to questions. Into this environment the programme introduces an Airbus Industrie spokesman, Robert Alizart, whose first comment and therefore first impression, chosen by the programmers and edited in from any point in any interview done with Alizart, is that Asseline owes his life to the plane. It is difficult to avoid the implication that Asseline was an ungrateful man. Were the editors justified in placing the comment there, that is, did the wider context of the interviews give them the confidence that Alizart had that attitude? We don't know. We can only trust that it is not a severe distortion.

Malling then introduces further evidence that appears quite damaging to Airbus Industrie. It is intercut with elaborations and other evidence from Asseline. The programme producers mount the seemingly damning evidence building a case and then confront a second Airbus Industrie spokesman, Yves Benoist, who seems to obfuscate, to escape, to want to change the subject. (Bear in mind that Benoist was not played this crafted story-building and then asked to respond but interviewed in a context unknown to the viewer.) As if cornered, the programme then presents the Airbus spokesmen building countercharges into their obfuscation.

Note that the Airbus Industrie spokesmen have not been introduced sympathetically as credible witnesses. Rather they have been intercut into a story line with established, sympathetic characters and a mounting accusatory dynamic. They are presented and confirmed in the viewer's mind as defensive mouthpieces for a company probably all too willing to risk the lives of the general public for reasons of hubris and profit.

The question can be asked: did these spokesmen actually build these countercharges into their obfuscation? Or, perhaps, did the obfuscations come much later in the interview when the officials were tired of trying to explain the company's perspective to Malling? Whatever the answer, and returning to the story, in response to their countercharges Malling inserts the name of their apparently intended victim, Asseline. Then, immediately after naming Asseline, in a surprising move, Malling articulates the charges Airbus seems to want to make directly against Asseline but dare not for reasons of libel, calling him obsessed and giving the reasons. By apparently reversing himself, having previously presented Asseline as credible, and himself as sympathetic to Asseline, Malling further discounts the credibility of the Airbus spokesmen by seeming to put words into their mouths, extending their counter-attack against this Dreyfus.

Malling then provides an editorial synopsis and moves to new evidence from other credible pilots in other situations that essentially support Asseline. Other information and words are used to gain sympathy, if not credibility, for the allegations. Indian Airlines buys fifteen planes, must ground them, 'bleeding the airline of $60 million', 'feeding allegations in parliament', and so on. More stonewalling from Airbus spokesmen is edited in. This stonewalling is punctuated by an edited-in statement from Asseline in which he portrays himself as a loyal and talented employee who, as he says 'then suddenly, for four seconds, . . . becomes a mad dog'.

The programme then expands first to a comparison with some particularly accident-free aircraft, Boeing's 757 and 767, then to the general unreliability of computers and how they can crash, associating this line of discussion with 'temporary loss of control' and 'unplanned excursions', and so the story goes.

The point, and it is easy to overlook when carefully chosen words and compelling images are passing by on the television screen, and one does not have the advantage of reading slowly, checking back, and reading again, is that 'the story' is a constructed one. It is constructed from hours of tapes, where interviewees know only what they are told about what their adversaries say (which is often very little), and where the editors not only choose what they will allow their interviewees to say but also when and in what context. This is not to say that this programme gave a false impression. However, after reading the transcript or, especially, after seeing the programme, flying in an Airbus A320 can be an unnerving experience. On the other hand, there have not been any major disasters attributable to the computer control over the aircraft, the target of the story by Malling.

And so we return to trust. Obviously there are limits to the distortion programme producers can introduce. But television provides substantial flexibility. From numbers of disparate interviews one can weave a single coherent story with villains and victims, where the villains condemn themselves with their own words. The audience can only rely on professional journalistic ethics and the need to maintain credibility over the long term. In certain situations, for example war, social unrest, the McCarthy era, that may break down.

Soaps

Radio soap operas were originally developed in 1930 in the US by a school teacher named Irna Phillips and first broadcast by radio station WGN, the station owned by the Chicago Tribune (Williams, 1992). The program was *Painted Dreams*. In 1933 an advertising agency, Bleckett-Sample-Hummert, developed three shows for its soap company clients and went on to become a soap opera factory (LaGuardia, 1977). The soaps were both a popular cultural form and designed to socialise a home-confined female audience with disposable income into the art of consuming. In a sense, soaps represented the life of the fictitious satisfied consumer whose worldly needs were entirely taken care of by the various products that she had purchased for her family. Once these needs were satisfied, she could turn her mind to dreaming of a richer, more fulfilling life found in the Gothic and romance novels of the thirties. However, pure fantasy was not the only powerful opiate. Not long after the soaps had established themselves in the US, a kind of realistic fantasy programme was developed featuring characters who were professional people, whose lives were made of the stuff of fiction – they were important politically, became wealthy and famous, had wonderful romances, and so forth. In this manner an illusion of reality was developed that has carried through to the present day. Our discussion of the soaps will take us through this illusion into the dominant themes of present-day soaps and then into the grammar of the medium, the devices used to achieve the realistic illusion.

Along with news, soaps are the most analysed kind of narrative genre on TV. They have been of particular interest to feminist studies because they are a preferred form of entertainment in many countries for female viewers. Analysis has concentrated on the form and content of soaps and on the pleasures they offer viewers.

A basic distinction is drawn between the narrative structure of soaps and classic narrative. In classic narrative the story has a beginning, middle and end: the movement of the narrative is strongly organised towards the resolution of the story's riddle, or enigma, that is, to the final moment when the hero kills the villain (as in any James Bond story or Clint Eastwood western); the cop finally catches the criminal, the murderer is exposed (Agatha Christie), or the heroine marries her man (or nowadays gets into bed with him). The story, then, focuses on one primary character (male or female) and moves to a final moment in which all is explained and everything is resolved. THE END comes up and the credits roll.

But soaps have no sense of an ending. They are 'open', never-ending narratives, in sharp contrast to the 'closed' stories of classic narratives. In the US, the daytime soap *All My Children* has been running since the late 1930s – first on radio and then from the 1950s on TV. In the UK, the BBC radio serial *The Archers*, has been going since 1951, while on TV *Coronation Street* has been on continuously since 1961. Furthermore, soaps have no obvious single hero/heroine. What is created in the narrative is a social world of the entwined lives of maybe a dozen or more characters who are intermittently but continuously present in the story. Thirdly, where the classic narrative has usually only a single story line, with perhaps a sub-plot, in soaps there are several different stories running at the same time that often overlap with each other (see Geraghty, 1991 for an excellent early account of the structure of soaps).

These are the most basic features of the narrative structure of soaps. In terms of their content and style – what they are about, how characters and plot are presented – some distinctions need to be made. In the US a distinction is drawn between daytime and prime-time soaps. The former are shown in the afternoon and achieve relatively small but loyal audiences of female viewers and college students. The latter are shown at peak viewing times in the evenings and often have strong family audiences. Prime time soaps have higher production values (are much more expensive to produce) with glossy sets and costumes and a tendency to focus on the lives of the rich (*Dallas, Dynasty*).

A further distinction needs to be made between the style of British and American soaps. British soaps are shown in the early evenings (between 6 and 8 p.m.) and achieve family audiences. They are increasingly popular with young viewers, and have become part of the culture of school children (especially *Neighbours* and *EastEnders* – see Buckingham, 1987). British soaps are often described as being realistic in contrast with the melodramatic style of American soaps (or Brazilian *telenovelas*). They tend to deal with working-class life and experience, whereas American daytime soaps are more middle class and prime-time soaps are about the super-rich.

British soaps are realistic in the way that the life-world of the story is organised to correspond with (to be essentially similar to) the ordinary life-world of viewers. The actors look and sound like 'ordinary people', the script sounds like ordinary talk, the location is life-like (the East End of London in *EastEnders* looks plausibly like the real place though in fact it is filmed on a special location in West London near the BBC's television centre). The things that happen in the story are not implausible, the characters have some psychological realism and depth of personality. Melodrama reverses all these: it is sensational, artificial and exaggerated in terms of characters, action and setting. It is much more like a fairy story than a realistic story: it creates a fantasy world, remote from everyday reality, into which readers and viewers escape for the duration of the tale.

Dallas is a classic melodramatic narrative. The appearance of the actors is stylised. Victoria Principal, who played Pam Ewing (married to Bobby) for several years, was an icon of Hollywood notions of feminine beauty. The script is not like ordinary talk. A high level of emotion is always in play. The characters are continuously hating, loving, taking revenge, having identity crises, and seeming to play real-life monopoly with real dollars. The story often defies the logic and plausibility of realistic narrative. In a famous episode, Bobby Ewing was killed off at the end of one season of *Dallas* (unlike daytime soaps, prime-time soaps do not run continuously throughout the TV year). In the following season the ratings dropped, and so in the next season Bobby was resurrected from the dead to revive flagging audience interest (it was suggested that in fact he hadn't died, but had simply had a bad dream).

The pleasures of these kinds of narratives have been much discussed. Far from being, as in the common perception, mindless rubbish for passive couch-potatoes, they create a high degree of audience involvement and enjoyment. The infamous case in Brazil of an actor murdering an actress off-screen who was spurning his advances on screen, is *à propos*. In Brazil, more attention was paid to this than to the December 1992 impeachment of ex-President, Ferdinand de Collor (Guillermoprieto, 1993), which was going on at the same time – and not just because the actress's mother was writing the scripts.

All soaps focus on interpersonal relationships in an everyday context (usually the family, but often an institution – hospitals, schools, police stations and prisons are favourite locations). The more you watch, the more you get out of it, because the more you know about the lives of the characters (their past biographies) the more you are able to assess how they will react in their present dilemmas. Soaps create expert viewers. Regular fans remember a great deal about the past of the narrative and use that knowledge to interpret what is presently going on the stories.

A prime pleasure of watching soaps is gossip – talking about the story with others (there is always, of course, a great deal of gossip going on in the soaps themselves). Watching soaps is not a solitary individual activity but a social and sociable act. There is plenty of evidence that regular viewers watch in groups – with friends, family or schoolmates. And the story is discussed before, during and after each episode (Hobson, 1980; Morley, 1986; Buckingham, 1987). In the UK, soaps are part of the general public discourses of daily life. The lives of soap-opera stars, both in the stories and outside, are staple news items in the British tabloid press. In the early 80s a love affair between Mike Baldwin and Deirdre Barlow in *Coronation Street* was the talk of the whole country, and was minutely discussed and monitored in the popular press. Should Deirdre leave her husband ('boring' Ken Barlow) for the more glamorous Mike? The nation was divided. More recently William Roache, who plays the part of Ken Barlow, sued *The Sun* for an article saying that he (the actor) was as boring as the character he played (he won, just).

In the course of studying soaps, academic perceptions of them changed. At first it was supposed that they were the essence of that common criticism of television – they were trivial, mindless entertainment. Gradually it was understood that the pleasures soaps offered were real, that they had an important sociable role in daily life, and that their narrative structure (unlike any other kind of narrative in any other medium) was linked to the character of the medium of broadcasting itself. Such a shift in attitude implied a revaluation of everyday life itself, and led to renewed interest in understanding its character and effect on social relations in contemporary societies.

The illusion of reality and the ability to exploit these themes would not be possible without a cinematic code appropriate to the genre. That cinematic code is characterised by a number of techniques. Primary is the long, peering, extreme close-up, a framing technique that allows the viewer to search the face of the actor for its expression of emotion. This technique also encourages feelings of intimacy. The long, extreme close-up is enhanced by being taken from eye level. The viewer becomes the eye of the camera, intimately involved and yet quite separated from and unaffected by events. Similarly, the slow pace of the drama allows the viewer time to read in a depth of emotion, and thus encourages the prediction of events and interpretation of reactions.

Music videos

In a fashion similar to the soap, music videos, particularly rock videos, have emerged from the demands of producers to socialise an audience into an increased purchasing of their product. The difference between the soaps and music videos is that the product to be purchased is part of the promotional vehicle used to bring it to the attention of the audience. Music videos are visually enhanced versions of the records that the audience is intended to purchase.

The sudden explosion of rock videos and rock video television shows is not accounted for by the fact that these manage to express something that no other medium has done quite as well. Rather, rock videos make cheap television, just as playing records makes cheap radio. Suddenly, costs of a half-hour original television show dropped from £1,000 to £1,500 a minute to approximately the same amount for a half-hour. The beauty of the beasts was that they assembled quite sizeable, high-consuming audiences whose attention could then be sold to advertisers.

As with each of the media forms discussed in this chapter, rock videos have evolved from other forms in the media. Movies featuring rock stars such as Elvis Presley, Richard Lester's iconoclastic movies with the Beatles, and filmed recording sessions or concerts were the precursors of the rock video. Rock videos themselves were around in the industry for several years before they exploded into television, first in the UK and then in North America.

In contrast to the soaps, rock videos are as fast-paced as any movie or television ad. They feature jump cuts, crazy juxtapositions, and an intense bombardment of images somewhat inspired by the song's rhythm and lyrics but certainly not constrained by its literal meaning. They appear to take their inspiration from the 'visual effects' of movies, providing, again in contrast to the soaps, surrealism rather than realism. Their sets are often reminiscent of non-representational sculpture, and appear to reduce modern living to an anticipated future without a clear reflection of human values and detail. They serve also to partition the rock market through easy visual identification of rock, heavy metal, rap, dance music, and so forth. Insofar as they take their lead from visual effects (which require more money than imagination), they allow the purchase of market dominance; such a situation places performers such as Madonna, whose record companies will afford lavish extravaganzas to promote their songs, at a considerable advantage over less established artists. Carefully choreographed and staged videos, like those produced by Quincy Jones for Janet and Michael Jackson, guarantee heavy rotation on video playlists.

Many videos are a means for the fan to engage in a rather straightforward voyeurism. The focus of the video is the individual artist or, in the case of a group, primarily the lead singer acting as chief protagonist. The nature of the dominant vision in rock videos can best be contrasted with the literary, filmic, and choreograph-based imagination apparent in Leonard Cohen's award-winning production, *I am a Hotel* (see Lorimer, 1988). There, while ample use is made of visual effects, the effects almost continually contribute to the ongoing narrative and draw on established symbols of Western literature.

As with other communication forms, patterns of content can be seen in current rock videos. Bondage, especially of women, and restriction of all kinds are used, particularly in the more extreme forms of heavy metal. Violence, disembodiment, chaos, explosions, and destruction are also present. Chase scenes, or their visual metaphorical equivalent, are often used. The fragmentation and fetishisation of the female body is matched by aggressive phallic display. And while those are elements of the dominant form, other artists such as Michelle Shocked, Melissa Etheridge, and Alannah Myles feature women in positions of authority.

Rock videos are also similar in their structure to such movies as *Graffiti Bridge*, *Purple Rain*, and *Flashdance*. The notion behind these movies, according to the creator of *Flashdance*, Tom Hedley, is visual rather than narrative. Hedley sees 17- and 18-year-olds as involved in the creation of an interior musical that they act out, thereby creating the style they use to live their lives. He claims that such people take their inspiration from fashion photographs and magazine illustrations. They invest in such idealisations an individual interpretation and a dynamism built on popular music, thus ridding the pictures of their frozenness in time. Their personal style of living results from this process.

Hedley's conceptions are similar to Goffman's (1974) dramaturgical perspective. They are also consistent with more recent research, such as that by Fornas, Lindberg, and Sernhede (1988). As Curran remarks:

> The underlying assumption of this and similar research is that popular culture provides the raw material for experimenting with and exploring social identities in the context of a postmodernist society where the walls of tradition that support and confine them are crumbling. In this case, rock music is viewed as a laboratory for the intensive production of identity by adolescents seeking to define an independent self.   (1990, p. 154)

Mechanisms of media/culture binding

The task of the advertiser is to sell the audience an image of itself with the advertiser's product ingratiated into that image. The task of the media in general is to insinuate itself into social life in general and, as Eco points out with his alligator-shirt example (see Chapter 2), they have been quite successful in that regard.

The media interact with everyday life in various ways. Catchy tunes played countless times or repeatable phrases that float through one's head at the oddest times are not infrequent, nor are they intended to be. And they are not confined to advertisements. The media teach us how to kiss, how to smoke cigarettes (Humphrey Bogart had a style that was immortalised in his movies and even reappeared in a popular song in the phrase 'Don't Bogart that joint, my friend'), how to rob banks, how to play with toys, how to dance. The list is endless. But the interaction is not a one-way process. The media take their content out of the lives of real individuals and groups. Everything, from surfing movies to portrayals of the life and times of a now dead but famous writer, emerges not from a vacuum but from real life.

In the movie *Fast Times at Ridgemont High*, released in 1982, California valley talk, introduced to mainstream radio by Frank Zappa's daughter, Moonunit, was crystallised in the lead character, a thick, dope-smoking surfer played by bad boy Sean Penn. Associated with this California-based teenage slang were beach fashions. The fashions were reminiscent of those of the drop-out, oppositional, surfing crowd of the early 1960s. However, they had been mainstreamed to attract urban dwellers and middle America by two phenomena. The first was recreational surfing typical of Californian coastal youth and of their cousins, the sons and daughters of middle America who found it easy enough to take holidays near surfing/holiday haunts in California, Florida, Texas, Hawaii, and Surfers' Paradise in Australia. The second was skateboarding, which created a demand for the clothing in inner-cities throughout North America and Europe.

The language and fashion gradually spread, as much through the activities of surfing and skateboarding and the beach-oriented, West Coast-based fashion industry as by media presentations. In the late 1980s the language received a giant prod from the creators of Teenage Mutant Ninja Turtles. Through the TMNTs in movie, cassette, comic, toy, and TV programme form, highlighted in the character Michaelangelo (he of the whirling nunchakus), the language was picked up in caricatured form with his overuse of yo, narly, rad, cowabunga, dudes, surf's up, and so forth.

In addition, the beachwear and the lifestyle it represented were marketed in and out of the advertisements by beach volleyball, at first an opportunity for watching young men and women in bathing suits, but later a convenient vehicle for all sorts of sponsors – and now a demonstration sport in the Olympics. By the late 1980s and early 1990s, beachwear was thoroughly integrated into and even dominant in North American mainstream fashion. Even the mini-characters sold by McDonald's in the 1990s to families of hamburger-buyers presented the surfing motif.

Nor were the seasons to interfere. Snowboarding has also gained prominence with complementary fashions, separate from downhill skiing and with echoes to their surfing roots. All of these elements are, of course, rooted in postmodernism, with its penchant for recombining eye-pleasing elements from any tradition.

Mainstreaming

All forms of media presentation carry elements of someone's lived reality to broader audiences, in many cases from a segment of society into the mainstream. For example, Elvis Presley took southern black music and transformed it into something white teenagers would consume, largely by being white and being able to combine the energy of both black and white youth. Mainstream white North American radio stations did not play recordings by blacks in this genre. This is not the sum total of what Presley did, but it was the basis of his fame. Lesser-known examples of popular singers taking musical material from its folk origins, stylising it, and offering it up for mass consumption, include Carl Perkins, Jerry Lee Lewis, the early Beatles and Stones, and Sinead O'Connor. The phenomenon is known equally in popular music and in classical music. Béla Bartók was a pioneer user of sound recordings to collect folk music, which he then used as the basis for his classical compositions. Anton Dvořák's *New World Symphony* transformed southern black music, as did George Gershwin, into contemporary orchestral form.

In the 1980s one of the most notable mass-market entertainers to draw on music from non-mainstream cultures is Paul Simon. His album *Graceland* brought black South African missionary township music to the Western world in a manner that was enormously successful and compelling. Simon has a history of such success dating back to his use of traditional English balladry ('Scarborough Fair/Canticle') and to his hit based on a South American folk tune, 'El Condor Pasa'. Besides being enormously successful and giving the world a feel for some of the music of black South Africa and a sympathy for black South Africans, *Graceland* provided a platform for black South African groups, notably Ladysmith Black Mambazo.

One point should be emphasised about this process of media/culture binding and interpenetration. In picking up material from other sources the mass media transform it, whether it is clothes, music, or, as we will see in the next section, information. At a first level they stylise it for mass audiences, smoothing its edges and in general making it distinctive – although not so much so that it does not have mass-market appeal. They also transform it to suit the particular characteristics of the medium. The movies, for example, require visual overstatement of a fashion style for that style to be noticed. In being picked back up in the world of mass fashions, that overstatement does not disappear. This process thus tends to encourage extremes. Consequently, when movie costumes emphasise aggressiveness (through military-inspired styles) or sexual characteristics (through the portrayal of high-class prostitutes), styles also follow that overstatement.

Media presentations and social and political agendas

The interpenetration and binding of culture and the media is not confined to the domain of entertainment. As the Rodney King/LA riots example showed, real political, economic, and social events interact with the media, which in turn shapes events and media treatments in the future.

A number of recent events of global significance have provided opportunities to watch the interaction of the media. First was the Falklands War waged by Britain against Argentina in 1982. In that altercation Britain put strict controls on the media, yet Margaret Thatcher still lashed out against the BBC for its unpatriotic coverage that was critical of British actions (see newspaper accounts of the time). Then in 1983 the Americans invaded Grenada and sealed the island off from all travel, thereby freezing the press out entirely. The majority of the press corps sat on neighbouring islands and received reports on events. Following Grenada, realising that the United States was not beyond invading a country on the excuse of protecting even one American life, Nicaragua waged what might be termed an information war against the United States. In a public manner it asked Soviet advisers to leave, did not import advanced Soviet weaponry, and generally attempted to avoid any actions that could be construed as a provocation for invasion. These very public acts were moves in a media-based information war in which the Sandinista government attempted to make it a greater embarrassment for the US to invade than it would be a victory to oust the Sandinistas. The Sandinistas won the information war and, indeed, the military war. They could not, however, win the economic war mounted against them by the United States. In February 1990 a rival party, with $40 million in assistance from the US, was elected to office.

The actions of the Chinese in Tiananmen Square in June 1989 show yet again the role of the media in social and political agendas. In China the expulsion of Western journalists and the clampdown on information sources indicate a perception on the government's part of the potential influence of the media. One can account for much of the way the Gulf War was handled by proposing that it was a performance on the part of the US for world audiences, choreographed by means of media control to present the US as the most powerful nation of earth and as global policeman. Even the involvement of other nations such as France and the UK could be seen as an attempt on their parts to share centre stage.

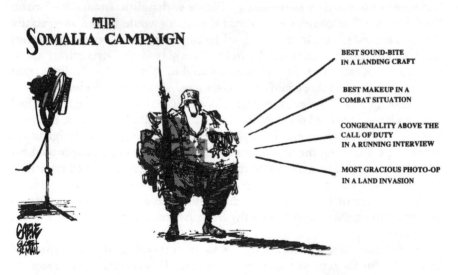

THE SOMALIA CAMPAIGN

BEST SOUND-BITE
IN A LANDING CRAFT

BEST MAKEUP IN A
COMBAT SITUATION

CONGENIALITY ABOVE THE
CALL OF DUTY
IN A RUNNING INTERVIEW

MOST GRACIOUS PHOTO-OP
IN A LAND INVASION

Source: The Globe and Mail, 11 December 1992. Reproduced by permission.

Obviously, as the Somalia cartoon illustrates, the media play a role in shaping world events. An interesting aspect of this process is that whereas sometimes we ask whether the media should intervene and do not come to a conclusive answer, in other instances that question is not even asked. Nuns, monks, teenagers and ordinary citizens have burned themselves for the television cameras. Soldiers have murdered in front of the camera. US state treasurers have committed suicide with cameras rolling. Some of these events were obviously performances for the media. Such events pose the question of whether the media should intervene in such events, for instance to stop someone burning him or herself, and if so, under what circumstances? The same question is not asked with regard to the actions of politicians or nations. Should and could the media intervene to prevent wars, perhaps by attempting to mediate or by revealing secret information?

The freedom of the media to create meaning

The examples given in the previous section concern the role or interference of the media as they go about their task of collecting, constructing and disseminating images and information. However, these examples do not address the limitations on the media in terms of defining issues, or *creating a discourse* within which issues are defined (see Mitchell, 1988).

In Birmingham, England in 1968, a Conservative politician, Enoch Powell, made a speech designed to sweep away an artificial consensus on race that had been constructed by the media in alliance with politicians and the British Civil Service. That consensus was that the media would ignore any racially oriented protestations. In the words of Jeremy Isaacs, a television producer: 'Television current affairs deliberately underplayed the strength of racist feelings for years, out of the misguided but honourable feelings that inflammatory utterances could only do damage. But the way feelings erupted after Enoch Powell's speech this year was evidence to me that the feeling had been under-represented on television, and other media' (quoted in Braham, 1982, p. 280). Powell received 110,000 letters containing 180,000 signatures in the days following the speech. Only 2,000 did not express approval for what he had said. The majority of the letters of support contained reports of real and imagined sufferings that white Britons had experienced as a result of the immigration of 'black' people (British citizens as a result of their country's membership of the Commonwealth) from Africa, India, Pakistan, and the Caribbean.

Enoch Powell opened the floodgates to an outpouring of feeling that had had no means for representation in the media. This situation illustrates the potential peril the media court in defining issues in terms that may be laudable but which insufficiently reflect the construction their audience puts on events and issues.

Media and reality: media devices and real life

While few people in this era would identify so strongly with the characters and interaction of a novel that they would confuse the world of the novel with their day-to-day world, the intermingling of media realities and lived realities is more likely to happen in television and film. Soap-opera characters, for example, regularly receive letters from viewers advising them of the intent of other characters or giving them gifts for their forthcoming television marriages. Some observers have suggested that this means the viewers do not distinguish between real life and the soaps. It may be more the case that they want to test the system. If they send gifts, will their gifts be included in what the couple receives? Or if they warn the character of the intent of another, will a warning be built into the plot somehow?

When we move out of literature and into other media, whether radio, television, or movies, the distance between reality and signification shrinks. To take another example, in 1939 Orson Welles produced a radio play called *The War of the Worlds* in which he presented, in pseudo-documentary style, an invasion of Earth by Martians. Great numbers of listeners phoned in, some as the programme was being aired, reporting sightings of the landings of other Martians. Some listeners seemed genuinely in fear of their lives.

Other producers have attempted to use this intermingling of reality and media play to their commercial advantage. The makers of everything from laser guns to controversial documentaries are delighted by serious academics decrying the denigration of human values illustrated by some aspect of their commodity. It is publicity that translates into a larger audience. Canada's National Film Board and the makers of a small, rather insignificant documentary on nuclear war entitled *If You Love This Planet* were delighted to have the work labelled foreign propaganda by US authorities. It helped win them an Oscar.

Media violence

George Gerbner has concentrated his research over the years on the portrayal of violence on television (see, for example, Gerbner, 1977). He has argued that the frequent use of violence results from it being a cheap way to portray power. But his central concern has been the effects that this constant use of violence has on television viewers. In his studies Gerbner has pointed out how people who watch a great deal of television overestimate the amount of violence in society. They tend also to have a 'bunker mentality,' to protect themselves from what they perceive to be a violent world. In spite of the broad acceptance of Gerbner's work and analysis, certain British studies (for example, Wober and Gunter, 1986) have not been able to replicate Gerbner's results.

In a variety of studies of children's play, Bandura (1976) has shown that those children who watch a great deal of television tend to engage in more aggressive play than those who watch less or see none at all. Also, following a television session in which aggression has been shown, there is an increase in the amount of aggressiveness in the interactions between children. Tannis Macbeth Williams (1986) has done similar studies in Canadian communities newly exposed to television. She has found an undeniable change in children's play after the introduction of television. One of the noticeable changes is an increase in aggressive play.

In all of these studies, obviously, only a certain amount of control over the exposure of the subjects to the media can be achieved, and only a certain level of confidence in the results is appropriate because of other such uncontrolled variables as socio-economic status. There is also the experimental and cultural environment which may be particular to one lab in one country. Then there is interpretation. Is an increase in aggressive play a bad thing? Does it translate into increased aggressive or violent adult behaviour or to the acceptance of violence or, in general, to a violent society? Obviously, the violence of previous centuries was not brought about by the media. So do media role models of today have a unique burden of guilt to carry? Whatever each case, there is little doubt that Bandura's work points to effects that make sense if one takes a more analytic perspective, as we have done in this chapter by postulating persons, cultures, and the media to be meaning-generating systems in interaction with one another.

Howitt and Cumberbatch (1975) and Messner (1986) make a case for television violence having no effect on viewers. In their discussion of pornography, Howitt and Cumberbatch also claim that while sexual depictions are sexually arousing there is no evidence to suggest that sexual crimes are caused by sexual arousal. As the call by various members of the US Congress in the summer of 1993 for less television and movie violence demonstrated, the public, and now the politicians, disagree.

Pornography and erotica

In discussions of pornography a distinction is often drawn between pornography and erotica. The former is considered unacceptable, the latter permissible. This argument usually asserts there is nothing wrong with sexually stimulating literature for adults, whereas there is something wrong with portraying the sexual exploitation of females or children.

While such a distinction can be made, another viewpoint questions the acceptability of erotica. Erotic magazines for men do two things. First, they idealise the female body. Only attractive women are photographed and, in addition, the photographs are touched up to remove what are regarded as imperfections. Second, they give men easy access to (pictures of) naked women in poses intended to encourage fantasies and masturbation. By providing erotica for the young male market, its producers have the potential to encourage unrealistic expectations on the part of young men. When this idealised form is combined with an unimpeded visual access, a rather dramatic rift emerges between community norms and the norms of the medium. The presence of such erotica is a continual challenge to the norms of the community. If one were to assume a direct effect, that is, an internalisation, of these materials, one would assume that rather large numbers of young men walk around in a state of wonder as to why they can have easy visual access to beautiful women in magazines whereas they have no such thing in real life. To carry the matter one step further, it might be similarly argued that rather large numbers of young women compare themselves to the idealised form presented in these magazines and must deal with the environment created by the circulation of nude pictures among their male peers.

In the same manner in which sexual portrayals challenge community standards, so do other portrayals, whether they are violent, idealisations of family, or dramatic or even humorous portrayals of the life of anyone the media care to portray. The positive side of such portrayals is that they provide the viewer with another view of life besides the one he or she lives. Such a view may encourage a striving for excellence, or a movement from the farm to the city, or vice versa, in order to take advantage of what is offered in a milieu other than the one in which one has grown up. On the negative side, they may discourage an allegiance to community values in favour of the values of a world of signification.

Even knowing this, it is a separate question of whether and how much such portrayals should be controlled and by whom. Different countries address this question differently, with the most distinctive being the US. In the early 1990s the Supreme Court of the US allowed that laws against the burning of crosses were restrictions of free speech. The Ku Klux Klan were, no doubt, delighted with the verdict.

Summary

The nature of representation, or as the semioticians would have it, signification, is a construction of meaning that refers to aspects of the real world and expresses that meaning within symbol systems such as language. This realm of meaning-making is not subordinate to that of physical objects. Its study involves understanding the nature of polysemy, of grounded indeterminate systems, that is to say, the possibility and dynamics of a finite but unpredictable number of interpretations focused on or grounded in the object, event, or phenomenon being represented. The study of communication is closely aligned with interpretation, an activity more characteristic of the humanities than science or social science.

A variety of approaches are used to analyse content. They include literary criticism, structuralism and post-structuralism, semiotics, modernism and postmodernism, pragmatics, discourse and conversational analysis, content analysis, and media form analysis. Each has particular strengths and draws out various aspects of meaning-making. Some that are used to study media/ audience interactions, such as cultural studies and feminist analysis (see Chapter 7), are also used. And each approach contains a beginning sketch of – if not an entire perspective on – society.

The various media forms and the genres within them structure meaning in a manner that largely escapes the study of representation as outlined by most social scientific approaches. For example, newspaper news stories build on the standard inverted pyramid. Television news stories are organised primarily by the intrusion of the camera as opposed to the reporter. Soap operas have developed their own set of portrayed social relations and visual techniques to present an intimate, universal world. Rock videos bombard the viewer with technological gimmicks, and lavish production.

The media bind themselves to society through a process of interpenetration of media content and lived reality. Often they massage and present material from the margins of society, making it acceptable and available to the mainstream. The media are not free to create social values which do not exist, even though they may affect the manner in which social values are played out. By searching after monopolies in market segments the media are free to pander to special interests and, ultimately, prejudice. The interpenetration of reality and media representation is problematic, especially with regard to violence and pornography.

References

Atkinson, J. Maxwell (1984), *Our Masters' Voices: The Language and Body Language of Politics*, Methuen, London.

Bakhtin, Mikhail (1981), 'Discourse in the novel' in Michael Holquist (ed.) (1981), *The Dialogical Imagination*, University of Texas Press, Austin.

Bandura, Albert (1976), *Analysis of Delinquency and Aggression*, L. Erlbaum Associates, Hillside, NJ.

Barthes, Roland (1968), *Elements of Semiology*, trans. A. Lavers and C. Smith, Hill and Wang, New York.

Barthes, Roland (1972), *Mythologies*, Johnathan Cape, London.

Barthes, Roland (1977a), *Image-Music-Text*, Fontana, London (see in particular 'The rhetoric of the image', and 'Change the image itself').

Barthes, Roland (1977a), 'The death of the author', in *Image-Music-Text*, Fontana, London.

Bennett, Tony (1982), 'Media, "reality" and signification', in M. Gurevitch *et al.* (eds.), *Culture, Society and the Media*, Methuen, Toronto.

Bennett, Tony, and Janet Woollacott (1987), *Bond and Beyond: The Political Career of a Popular Hero*, Methuen, New York.

Berelson, Bernard (1972), *Content Analysis in Communication Research*, Hafner, New York.

Braham, Peter (1982), 'How the media report race' in M. Gurevitch *et al.* (eds.), *Culture, Society and the Media*, Methuen, Toronto.

Brand, Graham and Paddy Scannell (1991), 'Talk, identity and performance: *The Tony Blackburn Show*' in Paddy Scannell (ed.), *Broadcast Talk*, Sage, London.

Brown, G., and G. Yule (1983), *Discourse Analysis*, Cambridge University Press, Cambridge.

Brown, P., and S. C. Levinson (1987), *Politeness: Some Universals in Language Usage*, Cambridge University Press, Cambridge.

Buckingham, D. (1987), *Public Secrets: EastEnders and Its Audience*, British Film Institute, London.

Canadian Association of Journalists (1991), 'Should pilots trust Airbus?', *The Eye Opener*, Canadian Association of Journalists, Ottawa, pp. 2–15.

Chartier, Roger and Alain Boureau (1989), *The Culture of Print: Power and the Uses of Print in Early Modern Europe*, Polity Press, Cambridge.

Chomsky, Noam (1968), *Language and Mind*, Harcourt Brace, New York.

Collins, Jim (1989), *Uncommon Cultures: Popular Culture and Post-Modernism*, Routledge, New York.

Curran, James (1990), 'The new revisionism in mass communication research: a reappraisal', *European Journal of Communication*, 5 (2–3) June, pp. 135–64.

Darnton, Robert (1976), *The Widening Circle: Essays on the Circulation of Literature in Eighteenth Century Europe*, University of Pennsylvania Press, Philadelphia.

Darnton, Robert (1979), *The Business of Enlightenment: A Publishing History of the Encyclopédie, 1775–1800*, Belknap Press, Cambridge.

Darnton, Robert (1982), *The Literary Underground of the Old Regime*, Harvard University Press, Cambridge, Mass.

Darnton, Robert (1989), *Revolution in Print: The Press in France, 1775–1800*, University of California Press with New York Public Library, Berkeley.

Derrida, Jacques (1981), *Positions*, Althone, London.

Desbarats, Peter (1990), *Guide to Canadian News Media*, Harcourt Brace Jovanovich, Toronto.

Eco, Umberto (1982), 'Narrative structure in Fleming' in B. Waites *et al.* (eds.), *Popular Culture Past and Present*, Open University, Milton Keynes.

Eco, Umberto (1984), *The Name of the Rose*, Warner Books, New York.

Eco, Umberto (1986), *Travels in Hyperreality*, Harcourt Brace Jovanovich, Orlando, Florida.

Ericson, R. V., P. M. Baranek, and J. B. L. Chan (1989), *Negotiating Control: A Study of News Sources*, University of Toronto Press, Toronto.

Fiske, J. (1987), *Television Culture*, Routledge, London.

Fornas, J., U. Lindberg, and O. Sernhede (1988), *Under Rocken*, Symposium, Stockholm.

Fowler, R. (1991), *Language in the News*, Routledge, London.

Gans, Herbert (1979), *Deciding What's News: A Study of CBS Evening News, NBC Nightly News, Newsweek, and Time*, Pantheon Books, New York.

Garfinkel, Harold (1984), *Studies in Ethnomethodology*, Polity Press, Cambridge.
Geraghty, Christine (1991), *Women and Soap Opera: A Study of Prime Time Soaps*, Polity, Cambridge.
Gerbner, George (1977), *Trends in Network Drama and Viewer Conceptions of Social Reality, 1967–76*, Annenberg School of Communications, University of Pennsylvania, Philadelphia.
Giddens, Anthony (1987a), *Social Theory and Modern Sociology*, Polity Press, Cambridge.
Giddens, Anthony (1987b), 'Structuralism, post-structuralism and the production of culture' in A. Giddens and R. Turner (eds.), *Social Theory Today*, Polity Press, Cambridge, pp. 195–223.
Goffman, E. (1974), *The Presentation of Self in Everyday Life*, Penguin, Harmondsworth.
Goldenberg, Susan (1984), *The Thomson Empire: The First Fifty Years*, Methuen, Toronto.
Grady, Wayne (1983), 'The Budweiser gamble', *Saturday Night*, February, pp. 28–30.
Guillermoprieto, Alma (1993), 'Letter from Brazil: Obsessed in Rio', *The New Yorker*, August 16, pp. 44–56.
Heritage, John (1984), *Garfinkel and Ethnomethodology*, Cambridge University Press, Cambridge.
Hobson, D. (1980), 'Housewives and the mass media' in S. Hall *et al.* (eds.), *Culture, Media, Language*, Hutchinson, London.
Howitt, Dennis and Guy Cumberbatch (1975), *Mass Media Violence and Society*, Elek, London.
Jensen, Klaus Bruhn and Karl Erik Rosengren (1990), 'Five traditions in search of an audience', *European Journal of Communication*, vol. 5, pp. 207–38.
Johnson, Richard (1986), 'The story so far: and further transformations?' in D. Pintor (ed.), *Introduction to Contemporary Cultural Studies*, Longman, London.
Kristeva, Julia (1969), 'Le mot, le dialogue et le roman' in *Sémeiotiké, Recherches our une sémanalyse*, Editions du Seuil, Paris.
LaGuardia, Robert (1977), *From Ma Perkins to Mary Hartman: The Illustrated History of Soap Opera*, Ballantine Books, New York.
Lévi-Strauss, Claude (1969), *The Raw and the Cooked*, Cape, London.
Levinson, S. (1985), *Pragmatics*, Cambridge University Press, Cambridge.
Lorimer, R. (1988), 'A reflection on technology and culture: the case of music videos' in R. Lorimer and D. C. Wilson (eds.), *Communication Canada*, Kagan and Woo, Toronto.
Lyotard, Jean-François (1984), *The Postmodern Condition: A Report of Knowledge*, University of Minnesota Press, Minneapolis.
Messner, S. F. (1986), 'Television violence and violent crime: an aggregate analysis', *Social Problems*, 25, pp. 397–415.
Miller, Mark Crispin (1990), 'Hollywood: the ad', *The Atlantic Monthly*, 265 (4), April, pp. 41–68.
Mitchell, D. (1988), 'Culture as political discourse in Canada' in Rowland Lorimer and C. D. Wilson (eds.), *Communication Canada*, Kagan and Woo, Toronto.
Montgomery, Martin (1991), 'Our Tune: a study of a discourse genre' in P. Scannell

(ed.), *Broadcast Talk*, Sage, London.

Morley, D. (1986), *Family Television: Cultural Power and Domestic Leisure*, Comedia, London.

Pollack, D. (1984), 'Mister Flashdance', *Saturday Night*, October.

Propp, Vladimir (1970), *Morphology of the Folktale*, University of Texas, Austin.

Radway, Janice (1984), *Reading the Romance*, University of North Carolina Press, Chapel Hill, NC.

Saussure, Ferdinand de (1974), *Course in General Linguistics*, Fontana, London.

Schlesinger, Philip (1978), *Putting 'Reality' Together: BBC News*, Constable, London.

Tuchman, Gaye (1978), *Making News: A Study in the Construction of Reality*, Free Press, New York.

van Dijk, Teun A. (1985), *Handbook of Discourse Analysis*, vols. 1, 2, 3, and 4, Academic Press, London.

Wasko, Janet, Mark Phillips and Chris Purdie (1993), 'Hollywood meets Madison Avenue: the commercialization of US films', *Media Culture and Society*, 15 (2), pp. 271–94.

Watzlawick, Paul, Janet Beavin and Don Jackson (1967), *Pragmatics of Human Communication: A Study of Interactional Patterns, Pathologies, and Paradoxes*, Norton, New York.

Williams, Carol T. (1992), *It's Time for My Story: Soap Opera Sources, Structure and Response*, Praeger, London.

Williams, Tannis Macbeth (1986), *The Impact of Television: A Natural Experiment in Three Communities*, Academic Press, Orlando.

Williamson, Judith (1978), *Decoding Advertisements: Ideology and Meaning in Advertising*, Boyars, London.

Wober, J. Mallory, and Barrie Gunter (1986), 'Television audience research at Britain's Independent Broadcasting Authority, 1974–1984', *Journal of Broadcasting and Electronic Media*, 30 (1), pp. 15–31.

Woollacott, J. (1982), 'Messages and meanings' in M. Gurevitch *et al.* (eds.), *Culture, Society and the Media*, Methuen, Toronto.

Chapter 9

Information flow: the geopolitics of entertainment and information

An overall examination of media content is revealing because the form and dynamics of content are the result of a process which begins with the evolution of communicative enterprises out of their societies, and continues through the creation of laws, policies, professions, practices, and technology in pursuit of entertainment, information and perhaps education. The content of the media, as well as its predominant genres, patterns of concerns, and programme mixes, reflects the societies in which they reside.

In a heterogeneous world where both individuals and nations have differential access to producing and distributing media content, it is similarly revealing to examine the creation and distribution of media products amongst nations. One might undertake this task with the following question as background: In what manner do nations through their mass media manage to inform, educate and entertain their audiences about their own and other societies, especially their governance? This question is the focus of this current chapter.

The doctrines of free speech, a free press, free flow of information, and a free and open information system, especially about the affairs of government, are entrenched as ideals and to some extent as practices in Western societies. These doctrines contribute to the continued existence of developed Western societies as democratic, free and open. Most of us understand about free speech and a free press. We value highly the right to hold our own opinions, to speak freely about those opinions and not to fear the consequences of doing so. We also understand the need for a free press. Hardly a week goes by without the media bringing some major issue to our attention. The media are our eyes and ears on the world and the conscience of the powerful. Arguably, one major contributing factor to the social, economic and political collapse of the former USSR was the inability of people to speak out at the same time as they were increasingly informed about societies beyond their borders.

These principles of free speech and a free press are complemented by the notion of free and open information, especially that collected by governments in the name of the democratic governance of people. If the freedom to speak exists without a right to know what is going on, then such a freedom is an empty one. A free press requires open access to information about governments and the dynamics of society that governments collect and create. This principle can be extended to other institutions in society, although the determination of exactly how much and what type of information should be public requires careful consideration. Only with such access can the media make informed comment on government policies. Freedom of access to information has been late in developing and it is a fragile freedom in every country in the world, with the possible exception of some parts of the operations of the US government. Whatever other shortcomings there are in the manner in which the US media and information system operates, there is no question that the US is the world leader in entrenching the principle of and procedures for open access to information. This freedom to know is applied both to government and corporations whose stocks are publicly listed on stock exchanges. The major difficulty in its application is that it does not extend to military, security and intelligence matters, all of which can be broadly defined.

A logical extension of free speech, a free press and a free and open information system is the freedom to make information and ideas known as widely as possible, most commonly encompassed by the term free flow of information. The principle behind this extension of free speech is unassailable. Not to allow the free circulation of ideas and information in a democratic society would be to render ineffectual the preceding freedoms – free speech, a free press, and free and open information.

However, the actuality of facilitating free flow of information introduces a paradox. Western societies have allowed the private sector to own most media of communication, and have allowed those media properties to become larger and more powerful than the average citizen. In allowing such corporations to serve as the major facilitators of the free flow of information by gathering, organising, producing and distributing it for profit, we have subjected these activities to the regimen of the market. In not placing controls on programme allocations in relation to advertising or to any great extent on the size of communications enterprises (e.g. single enterprises versus conglomerates), we have increased the strength of competitive struggles to achieve market dominance by making it possible to achieve substantial wealth and power through ownership of media outlets. In not using national boundaries as control mechanisms for the outflow and inflow of news, information and commentary, the nature of the information mix and therefore the cultural context within smaller, poorer, less developed and less dominant countries is strongly affected by cheap information imports from large, rich, developed and dominant countries.

In short, by making information an exploitable resource we have transformed the democratic and journalistic ideal of free speech and freely circulating information into an ideal of producers who wish to be free to exploit any market anywhere in the world. In doing so we have also laid the foundation of the entertainment and information industries. The result, in a nutshell, is that while these industries make copious quantities of certain types of entertainment and information widely available, such as world politics, international commercial trends, or environmental issues, as well as adventures, dramas and comedies, competition in the market to produce 'the best product for the least cost' means that market forces also suppress the circulation of another type of valuable information. This latter type of information is local information and entertainment, for which there is not a wide market. This material costs a substantial amount to produce, requires well-trained and, at times, courageous journalists and creative programme producers, and does not generate much, if any, profit. Yet such entertainment and information is the foundation for the coherence and development of a society – at least in the normal way we might tend to think about the natural formation and evolution of a community.

There is one other difficulty with the application of the principles of free speech, a free press, the right to know and free flow of information. Information and entertainment, and specifically the news, are neither disinterested nor without cultural bias. Knowledge is organised to serve the interests of those who collect it – advertently or inadvertently. Reporters conceive of what information is to be sought, what elements of it are important, and how it should be discussed. For those who are written about and who have no access to telling their own story, the consequences can be rather drastic. As Smith (1980) says: 'To be imprisoned inside the misinterpretation and mis-understanding of others can be a withering form of incarceration. It is a fate which can afflict whole nations and cultures as painfully as individuals' (p. 27). Similarly, entertainment programmes are created out of a shared culture and are best and most fully appreciated by members of that culture. To be assailed daily by the diversions of a society that is not one's own, chattering to itself using images and allusions that at best one knows vaguely, tends to bind one to that culture in admiration or rejection or some mix of both. As such it is an intrusion that separates individual members of a society from each other and from their society.

Consider the organisation of the following remarks and the interests served by its point of view. The quotation comes from J. M. Stanley, the man who found Livingstone in 'deepest Africa'. He had this to say to the Manchester Chamber of Commerce: 'There are 50 millions of people beyond the gateway to the Congo, and the cotton spinners of Manchester are waiting to clothe them. Birmingham foundries are glowing with the red metal that will presently be made into ironwork for them and the trinkets that shall adorn those dusky bosoms, and the ministers of Christ are zealous to bring them, the poor benighted heathen, into the Christian fold' (Smith, 1980, p. 25). Stanley might have spoken of distinct societies, subtle kinship relations, knowledge of medicinal herbs, and musical forms unheard by the European ear. But he did not. His information was collected under the inspiration of a socially accepted doctrine of colonialism, in which the pursuit of loot, markets and the Christian faith were subsumed into a single quest, which was undoubtedly emotionally uplifting for his audience in imperial England.

Consider a second example:

> The American networks have a clear mind-set. What does it mean for Washington? How will the president handle this? How will it affect our relations abroad? It is a kind of imperial outlook, easy to develop if you're a superpower. In a sense it's easier to write for the Amnets [the American television networks, CBS, NBC and ABC] because the focus is always so sharp. In international relations, if it doesn't affect the US it scarcely exists.
>
> (Brian Stewart as quoted by Frum, 1990)

Third World nations have claimed for some time that the manner in which the developed world collects information continually puts the developing nations at risk by portraying them according to Western, developed-world news values instead of evaluating them in their own context.

A theoretical framework: metropolis and hinterland

The geopolitical view that an inevitable difference of interest exists between communities and that this difference derives from the structural relation of communities to each other is well-accepted. One theory that describes these relations, most often used by geographers but also by economists, sociologists and communication analysts, is variously called metropolis-hinterland, centre-periphery, centre-margin, empire-colony and several other combinations of the above. Its major proponent was the economic historian and communications theorist, Harold Innis. Metropolis-hinterland theory can be applied equally to global, national, regional or local affairs. Some of the same dynamics were identified by various Marxists such as Marx himself, Engels, Gramsci and Althusser. Out of the writings of these latter theorists grew the 'media imperialism' thesis. As Roach claims, common sense tends also to suggest media imperialism in the following way: '(1) culture and communication influence society; (2) culture and communications produced in a capitalist system convey a capitalist ideology; and (3) this ideology helps to reproduce capitalism' (Roach, 1990, p. 293).

The metropolis-hinterland version of events may be summarised in the following manner. A metropolis or centre or empire is a seat of power. As such it engages in social, economic, cultural, political and military practices that prioritise and organise not only itself but the activities of hinterland communities that may, or may not, be under its political control. (See Beale, 1988 for a discussion of transportation and communications in this context.) Accordingly, North America and Stanley's Africa were 'explored' by various European powers for what they could contribute to European economies. The European economies were the metropoli and colonisers, reaching out into homelands that they transformed first into frontiers and later into hinterlands to gather materials to enhance their power and wealth. Much of the history of the period is a description of how well those colonies functioned as hinterlands, for example, how well the fisheries, timber, fur, rubber, mineral, cotton and other trades served the Europeans.

The activities of the emissaries to and inhabitants of the hinterland – the explorers, missionaries, traders and settlers – were governed by the centre. If the centre needed fish, fish were caught, not to eat in the colonies but as a cash crop. If the centre needed fur for fashionable beaver hats, then fur was gathered. If the taste for furs radically declined with changes in fashion, as indeed it did, then the whole of the economic, and therefore social and political, activity of the periphery was altered. Not only did various traders become bankrupt, but the primary producer, the aboriginal, often starved. Like all single-commodity producers, the native people who came to rely on trade with Europeans were completely vulnerable to market fluctuations, whether they were caused by the fickleness of fashion then, or now, the concerns of environmentalists and animal-rights activists.

The ideology of empire was also promoted by the centre. The Canadian Prairies were touted as the 'breadbasket of the empire'. More than one British immigrant farmer, inspired or not by Kipling, saw himself as manning the 'outpost of empire' on the Canadian frontier. If he faltered in his vision, he could rely on his children, who were encouraged in their school books to see themselves accordingly.

In the general case, the relations of the hinterland, not just to the centre but also to other points on the periphery, are centre-dominated. Two neighbouring hinterland producers are more liable to be producing goods in competition for the market of the centre than to be producing goods that complement each other. Also, transportation routes radiate out from the centre like spokes on a wheel. There are few connectors between the spokes.

To reiterate, the metropolis or centre or empire organises the activities and life of its hinterlands, periphery or colonies as well as its own. The relationship between hinterland and metropolis is never static. Despite attempts to prevent it, and depending on such factors as richness of natural resources, education, the nature of the indigenous culture and effective political control, in due course colonies may establish themselves as centres in their own right. Blessed with wealth and a population that understands the nature and mechanisms of the metropolis, that evolution can be quick. In other circumstances it can be slower.

Communications can be seen as the control system that allows the metropolis-hinterland relation to function. In the European colonial period, beginning before Marco Polo and ending with Marconi, information was carried physically. Now the transmission of information is instantaneous. From the hinterland come messages of the extent of found resources and their exploitability, not just in physical terms but in terms of the culture of the hinterland. From the centre come the orders to proceed, to pace exploitation, as is done with diamonds, or to abandon. Communications extends the society, the political and economic system, the culture, religion and technology of the metropolis. It reinforces the way society is organised by extending it. This relationship gives to communications its geopolitics (see Innis, 1950, 1951 and Smith, 1980).

Information flow

Two types of communications activity illustrate the extensive influence of centre-hinterland relations on world communication. The first is the activities of international news agencies. The second is in the sales and exchange of media products around the world. We will examine these two areas, and the more recent literature that questions the 'media imperialism' hypothesis. We will then consider policy initiatives in the European Community to see whether they appear to be framed with any sensitivity to the debate on media imperialism.

The international news agencies

On any single day there is a high degree of similarity in the media coverage and treatment of stories; this is especially true with international stories. The reason is that most media outlets subscribe to common sources for their foreign material, one of four global news agencies. While as many as 1,200 news agencies operate in the world, the four large Western agencies are Reuters, Agence France Presse (AFP), Associated Press (AP) and United Press International (UPI). According to Unesco, as of 1988 their output was as follows: AP, 17 million words per day; UPI, 14 million; Reuters, 1.5 million; and AFP, 1 million (Unesco, 1988; 1.54 as cited in Roach, 1990). In 1980 Anthony Smith (p. 72) claimed that the output of these four agencies was 34 million words per day, a figure close to those of Unesco in 1988. Smith also noted that those 34 million words represented nine-tenths of the entire foreign news output of the world's newspapers and radio and television stations. Roach reports that, in contrast, TASS (now replaced by a very diminished Interfax and ITAR) produced 4 million words while many smaller agencies were dwarfed by such output, for example the Inter-Press Service in

Latin America (IPS), 150,000 words per day, the Non-Aligned News Pool (serving the Non-Aligned movement, Third World nations not aligned with either superpower), 100,000 words per day, the Pan-African News Agency (PANA), 20,000 words, the Caribbean News Agency (CANA), 25,000 words, and the Gulf News Agency, 18,000 words per day. Other international agencies worth noting are the German agency DPA (Deutsche Presse Agentur), EFE of Spain and Kyodo of Japan.

Dominance by the large

The Western agencies maintain dominance over the market by means of a variety of factors. Sheer size is the most important but state assistance is another (e.g., AFP and formerly TASS), as is low or no profit (UPI, AP, and formerly Reuters). AFP operates with indirect subsidies through the purchase of the service by offices within the French government. Reuters, AP and UPI depend on a vast subscribership to support their operations. AP and UPI make little profit. The profit is to be found in their newspaper members. UPI, off and on, verges on bankruptcy. This combination of factors blocks effective competition and ensures the dominance of these voices. Consequently, until recently, much of the Western world has come to rely on these agencies. The last decade has brought new players into the picture, particularly CNN. Complementing the agencies and CNN are the US television networks, the BBC, and the foreign correspondents of individual media outlets. These latter agencies, and probably CNN, rely on the news agencies to monitor 'hot spots' and to make decisions on the deployment of personnel. They then make deployment decisions and follow a breaking news story in greater depth. In short, the global agencies are the dominant players and set the context for other information-gathering.

The colonial roots of the globals

A review of the dynamics and history of the news agencies and their relations to national governments points out why the identity of the agencies is so important. Smith (1980) maintains it is impossible to examine the global news agencies without considering their relation to capitalism. He maintains that capitalism is as much an information system as a system of finance and production.

The organisation of finance, exploration, resource exploitation, trade, manufacture, and information with respect to each element of this process was the foundation of contact between Europe and other world civilisations. Moreover, they were structured in such a way to benefit Europe. Europe defined itself as the coloniser, the spreader of the one true civilisation and religion to a heathen world. For a time, the communication of information depended on its physical carriage along with goods and people from Europe to the colonies and back. Eventually, submarine cables laid along sea routes and across land outpaced the speed of physical carriage. The British especially were eager to put the latest and best communications technology in place to span their empire. The dominant position of the British company, Cable and Wireless, reflects the history of Britain in this period.

The news agencies built their commercial empires on the backs of the colonial information system and transformed the whole scope of news dissemination. Founded by a Frenchman, Charles Havas, in 1835, the first news agency grew out of a translation agency that then sold its translations to newspapers. With the coming of the telegraph, the number of newspapers the agency could sell to increased enormously. With the primacy of national interests in the nineteenth century and the division of the world into various European 'empires', other nationally-based agencies soon emerged. The first two were begun by two of Havas's employees, Bernard Wolff (Germany) and Paul Julius Reuter (England).

Havas, Reuter and Wolff were all expansionist entrepreneurs working at the edges and propelled by the energy of three European empires. The world was split three ways among them, with Havas gaining monopoly control of Latin America, which he held from 1870 to 1920, when his monopoly was broken by the US-based United Press Association. From his base in Britain, Reuter took over the Low Countries and moved into Austria, Greece and the area surrounding the Black Sea. Thwarted by the refusal of *The Times* to use his service, he provided information for other, mostly provincial, British newspapers. His service was so credible that he was allowed to use British government telegrams as a source of news from India. Reuters was seen as an independent news service operating at arm's length from the British government; however, during World War I, the managing director of Reuters doubled as director of propaganda for the British government.

The entry of the Americans

World War I brought the United States and the American news agencies onto the world stage. The obvious connections between the European agencies and their national governments and the virtual news blockade of Latin America provided the Americans with the opportunity to move out of their domestic confines. So successful have the Americans been in their operations that Smith (1980) claims that the whole of Latin America operates on the same news values as the US.

The territorial monopolies have disappeared and been replaced with a scale of operations that ensures market dominance. As we noted earlier, the big four claim 90 per cent of the world's foreign news. However, since the entry of the American agencies during and following World War I, a variety of other agencies have attempted to gain a foothold in the international market. Some, such as the Chinese agency, Xinhua, have been national efforts, while others, representing numbers of developing countries, have been aided by Unesco, such as IPS, the Inter-Press Service of Latin America, or the news service of Caribbean nations. Many of these latter agencies have exchange or service relations with parallel organisations in other regions and also with the larger agencies to give them access to world news in exchange for what they provide on the local scene.

Inevitable problems arise in the use that other countries and regions make of the material the big four create. Smith cites the coverage of Surinam independence: not a single Latin American paper carried the story on its front page on Surinam's first day of independence, 26 November 1975, despite Surinam being in South America (1980, p. 71). Apparently the absence of coverage was simply the result of the US agencies not feeding the story.

At times there are also problems of access to news sources for all but the most powerful and global of news outlets. Third World agencies and news outlets typically have problems gathering news. This is even the case for less-than-first powers. When Canada's first astronaut was being interviewed shortly before he was launched into space, individual interviews were scheduled for Voice of America, AP and UPI. Twenty minutes were set aside for all Canadian journalists (*Saturday Night*, March 1985 p. 27).

The performance of the news agencies: the bias of news values

During the 70s and 80s the most publicised shortcoming associated with the global agencies was the type of coverage given to Third World countries. The general view was that there was an overemphasis on tragedy and disaster. Table 4 summarises the actual pattern of coverage in the early 70s. It shows 'crime and criminal violence' as the third most frequent category sent out by the Latin American bureaus – after 'foreign relations' and 'domestic government and politics'. But at the level of the Associated Press trunk wire in the US (the stories selected at the central US office to be sent to all US subscribers) 'crime and criminal violence' jumps to 48 per cent, almost four times higher than any other category. Smith reports a study by Harris which indicated that the weakest aspect of the agency-created news story was the presentation of the Third World in a rather sketchy and ethnocentric form (1980, p. 91).

Global news flows

Hester (1974) identifies another major contributing factor to the distortion of the news from the Third World. While the definition of news causes journalists to select a certain minority of events out of the possible universe of

TABLE 4 *Subjects of AP Latin American news*

Subject categories	From Latin American bureaus %	On US AP trunk wire %
Accidents	5·01	2·34
Agriculture	0·86	1·36
Art, culture and entertainment	1·16	0·00
Crime and criminal violence	13·81	47·66
Disasters	3·61	11·72
Domestic grovernment & politics	15·65	14·06
Economics and business	7·58	2·34[a]
Education	1·04	0·00
Foreign relations	19·19	6·25
Human interest features	2·81	5·47
Labour	2·20	0·00
Military and defence	1·16	0·00
Miscellaneous	1·04	0·78
Prominent people	1·47	3·91
Religion	0·79	1·56
Science and medicine	1·34	2·34
Sports	23·23	0·00[a]
Totals (%)[b]	101·93	99·79
Number of items	1,636	128

Notes
[a] A few sports items were retransmitted on AP sports wires in the United States. A few business items were used on the AP-Dow Economic Wire.
[b] Totals do not equal 100 per cent because of rounding.
Source: Al Hester (1974), 'International news flows' in Alan Wells (ed.), *Mass Communications: A World View*, Mayfield Publishing, Palo Alto.

events, several filtering or gatekeeping processes further select the material that ends up in the newspaper. The content of the media reflects the application of news values several times over. They are applied by the global agencies, by the reporters for the national bureaus, by the national bureaus themselves who decide what to feed, by the media who subscribe to the agency services and by the individual users of the media. As they are successively applied by people who have a very limited knowledge of the country being discussed, it is easy to understand why certain subjects of AP Latin America News – such events as coups, floods, buses crashing into ravines and debt defaults – are over-represented.

An ensuing debate

The debate that ensued in response to this pattern of information flows was protracted. Few newspeople denied the existence of a systematic distortion of what the developed world receives as news about the developing world. Most were also prepared to accept that the distortion arose through the definition of news. But they also noted that it is precisely that definition of news that sells papers and captures audiences for television. Soft news on development, for example, is not read. It is not even picked up by neighbouring countries and regions in the Third World when it is provided. The relative lack of success of the Soviets with their short-wave radio services compared to the BBC points to the crux of the problem in assessing how far one can go in using the media for the direct presentation of ideologically-based issues (see Smith, 1980 and Robinson, 1981).

The central issue with regard to the agencies can be illustrated by examples. If the US government relies on ABC television news for information on foreign events, as a spokesperson for ABC claims in the television documentary, *Inside TV News*, might we not assume that an American viewpoint pervades the operation? And if the BBC can be berated in the British House of Commons for failing to provide a sufficiently British perspective on the Falklands War, can we not assume there is a certain pressure on all journalists to maintain a national perspective? The answer seems to lie in Brian Stewart's comments quoted at the beginning of this chapter about his work for NBC. Those comments are absolutely unambiguous in supporting the notion that any news organisation reflects a set of values, often those of the primary audience for which it is providing news.

Smith uses the example of the overthrow of the Shah of Iran to clinch the argument that the news agencies provide an ethnocentric perspective on foreign news. Smith points out that prior to the collapse of the Pahlavi dynasty, there was no inkling in the Western press that the reforms brought in by the Shah were becoming less and less acceptable to the people of the country. The Ayatollah Khomeini was portrayed, if at all, as a religious zealot and not given any credibility as a spokesperson for a firmly entrenched set of values. The British press reported on the jobs lost to British and American firms, ignoring the plight of the Iranians themselves. The land reforms that consolidated the Shah's power did nothing to put land in the hands of a greater number of people, and these reforms obliged the country to import 50 per cent of its food, where previously it had been self-supporting. In the American press, the land reforms were presented as positive modernisations. After thousands had been killed in riots during the Shah's regime, the regime was still presented as having a broad base of popular support. In general, a viewpoint emphasising modernisation versus reactionary religious zealotry was put forward. The power of the Iranian revolution to sustain itself suggests that it was much more than the actions of hundreds of religious zealots.

Four more recent examples of similar distortions of reality can be identified in the Western press: the reporting on Saddam Hussein and Iraq prior to and following the Gulf War, which transformed Hussein from a friend to an enemy; the coverage of political activities in Burma (also known as Myanmar); the long silence of the press about events in East Timor; and the portrayal of Romania and the Ceausescus. With regard to Romania, how a Stalinist dictator with a human rights record far worse than the majority of the Communist bloc leaders could be so warmly embraced by the West prior to the collapse of communism in Eastern Europe points to the follies and tragedies that ideological rivalry can create. The story of how the West propped up the Ceausescu regime and suppressed information about conditions within the country will be a sorry one, once it is told. So will be the stories of East Timor and Burma.

International trade in television programmes

In the same way that world news is dominated by a few very large players, so are the information and entertainment industries, especially television and movie production. The major difference between the entertainment and news industry is that the Americans currently play an even larger role in entertainment than they do in the news agency business.

To provide some historical perspective, as Figure 4 shows, in 1985 many nations and virtually all of the Third World were substantial importers of television programmes, especially fiction and variety. The patterns that appear in Figure 4 also reflect political alignments (Eastern Europe and the USSR), geographic and cultural similarity (Eastern and Western Europe), relative wealth in regional terms (Nigeria in Africa), colonial history and language. Most importantly, however, the data reflect free flow of information in action. Highly dramatic is the 98 per cent consumption of domestic programmes in the US, and secondly the 92 per cent consumption of domestic programmes in the former USSR. At the time these data were collected the US and USSR were the two superpowers, fully capable of making extensive use of information and entertainment generated by other nations.

The diagrams reflect the ability of the superpowers to serve virtually all of their own needs and hence their domestic markets that are effectively closed to importation. The figure also illustrates the difficulties for small and developing nations as net importers. Not only must they pay for programmes in hard currency, the markets of larger, more powerful nations are effectively closed to them. This centre to hinterland flow echoes and re-echoes from the global through the hemispheric and continental, to the national, regional and local levels. That is to say, just as on a global scale the US and USSR severely

TOTAL PROGRAM OUTPUT (U.S.)
(100% = 17,344,100 minutes)

TOTAL PROGRAM OUTPUT (Canada; Montreal area excluding cable TV)
(100% = 65,376 minutes)

TOTAL PROGRAM OUTPUT (Latin American)
(100% = 670,088 minutes)

TOTAL PROGRAM OUTPUT Western Europe
(100% = 247,739 minutes)

TOTAL PROGRAM OUTPUT (U.S.S.R.)
(100% = 22,080 minutes)

TOTAL PROGRAM OUTPUT (Eastern Europe)
(100% = 62,449 minutes)

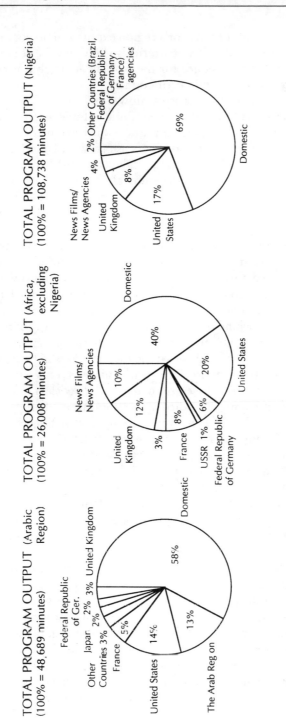

Figure 4　Domestic and imported television programmes

Source: UNESCO, *Reports and Papers on Mass Communication* by Tapio Varis, No. 100 International Flow of Television Programs. UNESCO, Paris, 1985. Reprocuced by permission.

limit imports, so certain countries of a region export and do not import from the region (Nigeria in Africa). This pattern also holds for the dominant media centres of nations which produce for the whole country but rarely acquire programmes from regions within their country.

A more recent study of international flow of television fiction provides a more detailed understanding of the geopolitics of television entertainment (Larsen, 1990). The study surveys a number of developed and developing countries and includes three interpretive case studies. Data from 1980 are compared with 1984 in Denmark, Italy, the Netherlands, the UK, Yugoslavia, Canada and the US. The study also includes information about selected countries in Latin America, Asia and Africa. Unfortunately, although an informed discussion is presented on Italy and Holland, detailed data were not available.

The major finding of the study is substantiation of the US as the dominant source of imports for television fiction programmes in all countries. That dominance appeared to be slowly but steadily increasing over the years 1980–84 in developed countries. The second finding is that the UK is a weak second as a source of imports. However, weak as it is, we then move into also-rans trailing far behind these two leaders. Thirdly, many of the countries surveyed look first to the US, and then to the UK for programmes. If they look beyond these two sources it is a cursory glance at others in their linguistic or regional group. Of the Western European countries, only Denmark looks further than these three sources of materials. Yugoslavia was the most cosmopolitan of the countries studied in its importation of programmes from many different countries. Fourth, every country except Yugoslavia, even the US, found itself importing more programmes in 1984 than in 1980. Fifth, although this does not appear in our tabular reporting of the data, the subcategories of fiction that account for US dominance are series, movies, TV movies, cartoons and to a lesser extent serials and mini-series. TV plays are not a US strong suit. Table 5 provides the exact figures.

For purposes of comparison, Table 6 presents data from a selection of developing countries. There are several notable similarities and differences. First, the US dominates here, as well as in developed countries, as the major source of imported programmes. Secondly, in contrast to developed countries, in all the countries presented except Thailand there is a lessening of US dominance over the years 1980–84. The UK is either very weak or has no presence. If there is any candidate for the weak and growing second spot it would be Japan. Thirdly, regional interchange is strong in Chile and Malaysia. Fourth, European ties are visible in the Congo. Fifth, whereas Chile, Malaysia and the Congo draw programmes from a variety of countries, Thailand and Bangladesh do not. In summary, language, region, colonial history and superpower politics account for most of the variation in the patterns of data.

TABLE 5 Fiction programming by genre and country of origin for an average sample week in five developed countries, 1980 and 1984 (%)

Country	Denmark 1980	Denmark 1984	Yugoslavia 1980	Yugoslavia 1984	UK 1980	UK 1984	Canada 1980	Canada 1984	US 1980	US 1984
Domestic	13	9	30	29	57	47	22	22	92	87
Imported										
US	35		35	36	40	44	55	62		—
UK	26		7	6	—	—	9	8	6	10
France			7	2			10	5	1	1
Italy			3	2						
USSR			4	7						
Australia					3	6				
Canada							—	—		2
Others	26	91	15	17	0	4	4	4		
Total imports	87	91	71	70	43	54	78	79	7	13

Source: Peter Larsen (ed.) (1990), *Import/Export: International Flow of Television Fiction*, no. 104, Unesco, Paris.

TABLE 6   *Fiction programming by genre and country of origin for an average sample week in five developing countries, 1980 and 1984 (%)*

Country	Chile		Malaysia		Thailand		Bangladesh		Congo	
	1980	1984	1980	1984	1980	1984	1980	1984	1980	1984
Domestic	3	8	10	17	27	20	15	25	13	14
Imported										
US	56	46	72	70	47	55	85	75	35	32
UK	2	2	5							
Argentina	4	1								
Mexico	6	3								
Puerto Rico		3								
Brazil	3	3								
Venezuela	1	2								
Japan	3			2	4	10				
France									29	31
Germany									7	7
Italy									3	3
USSR									10	12
Australia										
Canada										
Indonesia			1	3						
India			6	5						
Hong Kong			5		21	16				
Others	22	32		2					2	1
Total imports	97	92	89	82	72	81	85	75	86	86

Source: Peter Larsen (ed.), (1990), *Import/Export: International Flow of Television Fiction*, no. 104, Unesco, Paris.

What general conclusions can be drawn? First, information flow patterns support the established position of dominant producers and also the general geopolitical thesis of centre to hinterland flow. Second, in all countries except the US and the UK less than 50 per cent of television fiction is domestic product. The reason is simple: as Table 7 indicates, the costs of production are substantial in comparison with the costs of importing programmes. To be blunt, patterns of import exist for economic reasons not for reasons of reaching the greatest number of viewers with a programme with which they will be satisfied. Substantiation for this view comes in a variety of situations where it has been shown that indigenous productions are usually more popular in a domestic market than the globally successful distributed products. The only caveat that should be made to this generalisation is that comparison is often made between 'one off' domestic programmes or special national series. These programmes are produced only occasionally. When compared, as they are, with long-running series such as *Dallas*, it is not surprising that they make a good showing.

TABLE 7   *The direct costs of BBC produced and purchased programmes by category*

Programme category	Cost per hour (£) 1991–92
Parliamentary broadcasting	23,000
Purchased programmes	38,000
Sport	40,000
News- and daily news-related programmes	65,000
Religion	81,000
Music	89,000
Features documentaries and current affairs	94,000
Children's programmes	106,000
Continuing education	123,000
Schools broadcasting	145,000
Light entertainment	159,000
Drama	481,000
Overall	**90,000**

Source: *BBC Annual Reports* (1992).

The third conclusion that may be drawn is that importation of programmes, cheap as they are, still means that there is a considerable drain on national resources in the form of foreign currency, especially in developing countries. Importing and displaying foreign programmes generates few jobs and earns little hard currency revenue.

A fourth conclusion is that the dominance of US programming can be explained in three ways. First is that it already has a dominant market presence. Once established in the market, it is difficult for a product to be pushed out by competitors. Secondly, according to one of the case studies by Hoskins and Mirus (1990) included in the Unesco publication that presented the data reviewed here, US dominance can also be explained by means of an economic analysis. They point out that the large, rich, polyglot, competitive, private-sector market of the US is an ideal breeding ground for world products that can amortise approximately 80 per cent of production costs. The risk for countries with smaller, poorer, more homogeneous, non-competitive, or public-sector oriented producers is much higher. Thirdly, and not unrelated to the second point, is that through devices including a range of characters, kinship relations amongst them, plot, setting, sex, violence, attractive actors, camera work, general production values and (series) form, US producers have developed an entertainment genre that supports a host of possible identifications and projections made by a multitude of audiences (see Katz and Liebes, 1990).

A Unesco study provides even more recent data on television consumption in general. The time period of the study was 10 days in March 1991. Five European countries were surveyed, Bulgaria, Hungary, Italy, the Netherlands, and Sweden. Unesco has provided extensive analyses of the television distribution and consumption. We have selected four tables as a summary of that data and present them with Unesco's permission. They are presented as Tables 8 to 12.

Table 8 provides a summary of the domestic and foreign content that was broadcast over the national channels of each country listing the amount of programming and the country of origin. Note that overall, 65 per cent of programme supply was domestic, that 20 per cent was from the US, and that less than 9 per cent was from the rest of Europe. Table 9 summarises the consumption patterns of the content made available and from which country they originated. In approximate terms, the consumption patterns follow the supply statistics. Overall, 83 per cent of consumption was of domestic programs, 13 per cent was of US programmes and 3 per cent was of programmes from the rest of Europe. Tables 10 and 11 step back from national broadcasters to show all sources of supply and consumption. Thus in both tables lines one and two must be added together to indicate the percentage of supply and consumption that is accounted for by national broadcasters. That percentage, considering all countries together, is 39 per cent of supply and 86 per cent of consumption. This large difference between supply and viewership (i.e. consumption) is an indication of how much television viewing is accounted for by satellites. Nineteen per cent of programming available comes from satellite overspill and 42 per cent comes from satellites purposefully aimed at the country in question, whereas 1 per cent of programme consumption from satellite overspill and 13 per cent from satellites purposefully aimed at the country. Finally, Table 12 indicates what types of

TABLE 8 Country of origin of total programme supply on national channels during the study period (minutes and %)

	Bulgaria Min.	%	Hungary Min.	%	Italy Min.	%	Netherlands Min.	%	Sweden Min.	%	All Min.	%
DOMESTIC	8380	61	12622	70	55246	58	14161	78	14345	81	107754	65
Austria	0	0	0	0	377	0	0	0	90	1	467	0
Belgium	0	0	74	0	0	0	0	0	0	0	74	0
Czechoslovakia	196	1	586	3	0	0	0	0	10	0	792	0
Denmark	315	2	0	0	0	0	188	0	60	0	563	0
Finland	0	0	18	0	0	0	0	0	370	2	388	0
France	769	6	354	2	962	1	80	0	0	0	2165	1
Germany	132	1	1064	6	1033	1	236	1	30	0	2495	1
Hungary	177	1	0	0	0	0	0	0	0	0	177	0
Ireland	0	0	60	0	0	0	0	0	0	0	60	0
Italy	989	7	296	2	–	–	200	1	5	0	1490	1
Netherlands	10	0	0	0	0	0	–	–	95	1	105	0
Poland	0	0	21	0	0	0	0	0	0	0	21	0
Spain	436	3	0	0	0	0	0	0	0	0	436	0
Sweden	0	0	97	1	0	0	60	0	–	–	188	0
Switzerland	0	0	31	0	59	0	0	0	0	0	59	0
UK	403	3	756	4	1185	1	597	3	620	4	3561	2
Yugoslavia	0	0	27	0	85	0	90	0	0	0	202	0
USSR	263	2	184	1	0	0	0	0	140	1	587	0
Other Europe	302	2	0	0	0	0	0	0	140	1	442	0
All Europe (not domestic)	3992	29	3568	20	3701	4	1451	6	1560	9	14272	9
USA	826	6	1252	7	27788	29	2395	11	1685	10	33946	20
Canada	0	0	25	0	0	0	148	1	0	0	173	0
Australia	20	0	0	0	0	0	249	1	0	0	269	0
Japan	0	0	0	0	1589	2	0	0	0	0	1589	1
Brazil	0	0	112	1	0	0	0	0	0	0	112	0
Other Asia	0	0	0	0	0	0	30	0	0	0	30	0
Other Latin America	0	0	0	0	3711	4	0	0	0	0	3711	2
Other (not Europe)	0	0	45	0	0	0	98	0	0	0	143	0
Coproduction d/f	344	3	80	0	580	1	55	0	145	1	1204	1
Coproduction f/f	0	0	375	2	2079	2	287	1	0	0	2741	2
Unknown origin	98	1	0	0	130	0	196	1	0	0	424	0
All imports = T_s-S	5280	39	5457	30	39578	42	4909	22	3390	19	58614	35
Total	13660	100	18079	100	94824	100	22070	100	17735	100	166368	100

Source: Pebren Sepstrup (1992), *Transnetionalization of Television in Five European Countries*, Unesco, Paris.

TABLE 9 *Country of origin of total programme consumption on national channels during the study period (minutes and %)*

	Bulgaria (E) Min.	%	Hungary Min.	%	Italy (E) Min.	%	Netherlands Min.	%	Sweden Min.	%
DOMESTIC	1049	58	805	53	1590	68	770	78	1098	83
Austria	0	0	0	0	6	0	0	0	1	0
Belgium	0	0	4	0	0	0	0	0	0	0
Czechoslovakia	4	2	61	4	0	0	0	0	0	0
Denmark	28	0	0	0	0	0	3	0	0	0
Finland	0	0	1	0	0	0	0	0	0	0
France	102	6	35	2	9	0	0	0	0	0
Germany	18	1	156	10	16	1	21	2	6	0
Hungary	8	0			0	0	0	0	0	0
Ireland	0	0	4	0	0	0	0	0	0	0
Italy	286	16	30	2			7	1	0	0
Netherlands	0	0	0	0	0	0			1	0
Poland	0	0	1	0	0	0	0	0	0	0
Spain	61	3	0	0	0	0	1	0	0	0
Sweden	0	0	0	0	0	0	0	0		
Switzerland	0	0	1	0	0	0	0	0	0	0
UK	52	3	65	4	27	1	16	2	28	2
Yugoslavia	0	0	1	0	0	0	0	0	0	0
USSR	10	1	41	3	0	0	0	0	2	0
Other Europe	48	3	0	0	0	0	0	0	0	0
All Europe (not domestic)	617	34	400	26	58	2	48	5	38	3
USA	88	5	265	17	533	20	112	11	176	13
Others	2	0	10	1	116	6	32	3	0	0
Coproduction d/f	60	3	31	2	29	1	2	0	4	0
Coproduction f/f	0	0	0	0	20	1	13	1	0	0
Unknown origin/missing	0	0	16	1	0	0	4	0	0	0
All imports = T_S-S	767	42	722	47	762	32	211	22	218	17
TOTAL	1816	100	1527	100	2351	100	981	100	1316	100

Note: Figures for country of origin concerning Bulgaria and Italy estimated.
Source: Pebren Sepstrup (1992), *Transnationalization of Television in Five European Countries*, Unesco, Paris.

TABLE 10 Total programme consumption during the study period, in minutes over the study period by main programme categories

Origin of supply	Bulgaria Min.	%	Hungary Min.	%	Italy Min.	%	Netherlands Min.	%	Sweden Min.	%
National origin	1049	57	805	49	1590	68	770	44	1098	72
Foreign origin nationally distr.	767	42	722	44	762	32	211	12	218	14
Spill-over (nat.av.)	6	0	–	–	–	–	411	23	10	1
Satellite (nat.av.)	8	0	105	6	–	–	731	42	196	13
Total foreign	781	43	827	51	762	32	983	56	424	28
TOTAL	1830	100	1632	100	2351	100	1753	100	1522	100

Source: Pebren Sepstrup (1992), *Transnationalization of Television in Five European Countries*, Unesco, Paris.

TABLE 11 Total programme supply during the study period, in minutes by main programme categories

Origin of supply	Bulgaria (W) Min.	%	Hungary Min.	%	Italy Min.	%	Netherlands Min.	%	Sweden Min.	%	Total Min.	%
National origin	7086	55	12622	24	55246	58	17161	8	14345	25	106460	25
Foreign origin nationally distr.	4628	36	5457	10	39578	42	4909	2	3390	6	57962	14
Spill-over (nat.av.)	0	0	9388	17	0	0	69401	34	2314	4	81103	19
Satellite (nat.av.)	1139	9	26217	49	0	0	111457	55	36060	64	174873	42
Total foreign	5767	45	41062	76	39578	42	185767	92	41764	75	313938	75
TOTAL	12853	100	53684	100	94824	100	202928	100	56109	100	420398	100

Source: Pebren Sepstrup (1992), *Transnationalization of Television in Five European Countries*, Unesco, Paris.

TABLE 12 Consumption of imported programmes on national channels by main programme categories (average viewing time in minutes per week)

	Bulgaria		Hungary		Italy		Netherlands		Sweden	
	Min.	%	Min.	%	Min.	%	Min.	%	Min.	%
1. Drama/movies	347	90	286	79	342	90	92	88	102	94
2. Light entertainment	7	2	41	11	34	9	9	9	2	2
3. Music	18	5	5	1	4	1	0	0	0·5	0
4. Sports	0	0	23	6	0	0	0	0	0·5	0
5. News	0·5	0	2	1	0	0	0	0	0	0
6. Information	2	1	0·5	0	0	0	2	1	4	4
7. Arts/humanities/ science	3	1	2	1	3	1	2	1	1	1
8. Education	6	2	1	0	0	0	0	0	0	0
9. Religious	0	0	0	0	0	0	0	0	0	0
10. Other/not attr.	0	0	0	0	0	0	0	0	0	0
TOTAL	384	100	361	100	381	100	106	100	109	100

Source: Pebren Sepstrup (1992), *Transnationalization of Television in Five European Countries*, Unesco, Paris.

foreign programmes are watched in each country. Notable here is the domination of drama and movies at 94 per cent followed by light information at 4 per cent and entertainment at 2 per cent, and arts and humanities programmes at 1 per cent.

In overview, and speaking in global terms, both information and entertainment markets are dominated by the US and, to a much lesser extent, the UK. What is the nature of some of the media products that account for this dominant market share?

Consuming exported cultural products: heartburn or health?

One of the better-known studies of the ideological content of entertainment products is Dorfman and Mattelart's *How to Read Donald Duck: Imperialist Ideology in the Disney Comic* (1975). The authors document a case for a high level of ideological intrusion into material assumed by most to be free of 'political' content.

On the basis of an extensive review of some 200 Disney comics available in Latin America, Dorfman and Mattelart claim that the Disney world denies the political realm, yet simultaneously has a clear politics, centring on personality characteristics and family interactions. Donald Duck leads the life of the idle rich, yet he has the consciousness of the dominated. He blames his constant unemployment on his personality, just as he sees the rich as 'lucky' in that they seem to 'attract wealth'. Moreover, the rich are made morally legitimate by being unhappy victims of their wealth. These politics are profoundly personal in being most strongly affected by the personalities of those involved. The stories are highly adventuristic and lack any exploration of the crucial nurturing elements of childhood, especially the guidance of child-parent relations. For Huey, Louie and Dewey, who have only their Uncle Donald and no parents, it is not unlike a prettified Dickensian orphanage. This message is not all that different from what Thomas and Callahan (1982) have characterised as typical of *Dallas* and other American TV family drama. That message is: Come join us, if you can; it's very lush where we are. But if you can't make it, be consoled in the knowledge that we are very unhappy.

Other countries are presented in the Disney world as caricatures based on the very symbols those countries use to attract tourists. Such names as 'Unsteadystan' (Vietnam), 'Aztecland' (Mexico), 'Inca Blinka' (Peru) and 'Sphinxia' (Egypt) mock Third World countries. More significantly, they provide a basis for a distorted self-knowledge, a device that divides Third World people among themselves in negative stereotypical understandings of one another. People who object to oppression are dismissed as eccentrics and charismatic egomaniacs, and are trivialised (for example, Soy Bhien and Char

Ming). Protest movements are portrayed as completely lacking in serious-ness. The people can be diverted from their causes by a lemonade stand.

The exploitation of the Third World is legitimised by comparisons. The ducks, working with the unknowing collaboration of the natives, are con-trasted with the up-front criminality of the Beagle Boys. The ducks, implicit citizens of the US, are put forward as representatives of 'civilization, wealth and industrialization'. As such, they lay claim to the treasures and resources of Third World backwaters that would merely be corrupted if they knew the value of their own wealth. The politics of exploitation and, at times, of outright robbery and injustice are cleansed in the waters of innocence we normally attribute to the imaginative world of the child. It is justified impli-citly as a process of civilising and modernising.

Dorfman (1983) has extended this type of analysis in a more recent publication, in which he discusses how figures such as Babar and the Lone Ranger reflect class-based power dynamics while at the same time appearing to be innocent of such politics.

Domestic trade in information and cultural products

While communications may be studied as a separate entity with its own dynamics, it is also part of a social system. It both complements and reinforces the manner in which society is organised, especially in the produc-tion and distribution (i.e., the domestic trade) in goods.

In overview, the production of 'national products' by one or more major urban centres of a country creates jobs at the centre and fewer in the hinterland. The production of media products, dealing as they do in informa-tion, entertainment, images and symbols, extends the interpretations and priorities of the centre into the hinterland. In so doing it suppresses hinterland expression and priorities. This suppression is most noticeable in countries with distinct hinterland populations, for instance, the Scots and Welsh in Britain, the Basques in Spain and indigenous peoples in Australia, New Zealand, Latin America, North America and, most recently, the people of the various republics of the former Soviet Union. The dynamics of this suppres-sion have been explored vividly in two Canadian National Film Board productions entitled *Magic in the Sky* (1981) and *Distressed Signals* (1991). The stories encapsulate a great deal about the impact of modern communica-tions, one at the national level, the other at the international level.

Magic in the sky

Canada began experimenting with communications in the North because of the irregularity in radio signals. The problem was that the same electrical disturbances that produced the northern lights also interfered with radio signals. At times radio was perfectly adequate; at other times it was impossible. The quality of the signals was improved, but various experiments showed that the interaction of radio signals and this electrical activity in the atmosphere was inevitable and that there were firm limitations on the use of radio signals as a means of communication in the North. Reliable communications in the North could not depend on the airwaves. Since land lines were impossible, the answer was satellites.

Canada launched its first communications satellite in 1972, with immediate experimental use in the North. By the late 1970s satellite reception was commonplace. Early satellites were designed to enable individuals and communities to communicate with each other. Because the satellites were relatively low-powered, powerful ground stations were required to send and receive signals. Once this was discovered to be a satisfactory means of communicating, development followed quickly. Satellite power was increased, as was the capability to transmit numbers of signals until, with a four-foot stationary receiving dish, it was possible to receive good-quality signals of any kind, including television.

Suddenly, communication between individuals and communities was 'enhanced' with the possibility of receiving as many or more channels as any southern Canadian could. By means of satellites and receiving dishes, people in isolated northern communities who had communicated with the outside world only by short-wave radio, had suddenly been catapulted into the modern world.

The significance of these developments for Inuit and other northern native communities was considerable. In place of traditional values of sharing, television programmes, especially game shows, introduced young people to individualism and greed. Social status was linked not to an ability to provide for more than one's own family, but to the ability to collect and hold material goods for oneself. The personal politics we have discussed as endemic to popular culture items, where status is conferred on those of particular body types, with particular ethnic backgrounds and with particular personality traits, suddenly became the way the outside world worked. Most of all, consumerism, the necessity of having all manner of consumer products, as well as the necessity of a culture producing all manner of consumer products, became a guiding force. All these things were made doubly attractive by the sumptuousness of the settings in which both advertised products and entertainment programmes were presented.

Imagine having lived in an environment where a crackling radio brought sporadic items of world news on an erratic basis. The qualities of the technology itself suggest distance. Contrast that with sitting down one day and seeing the crowded, bustling streets of London, Paris, Beijing, Moscow, Delhi, Tokyo or New York, in real time. Contrast a whining and crackling radio bringing in news important for survival to the daily fare of murders, assassinations, coups, wars, plane crashes and social and political unrest that make up the evening television news. Suddenly, the detritus of the modern world was injected into the daily life of northern native people in just as pervasive a manner as DDT found its way into the remote northern habitats of the gyrfalcon, the polar bear and even the musk ox.

The world information and communications order

In this examination of information generation and international information flow, several points have been made. The first is that information is gathered, organised and distributed according to a doctrine that applauds free access to information, freedom of expression and the free flow of information. These notions are rooted in the liberal democracies of the industrialised world. The major characteristic of these democracies is a sufficient political consensus to allow for the coexistence of a number of sets of overlapping interests. This coexistence is enshrined in information policy by the respect paid to press freedoms, a respect that allows for private ownership of the press and free inquiry, expression and distribution. It is a stable society indeed that can hand over to the market-place the generation and responsibility for distribution of ideas!

These freedoms have contributed to the political, social and economic health of the developed world. However, their entrenchment and extension to other areas of the world has led to less-than-ideal outcomes. For example, the global news agencies were built to serve the expansionary interests of first Europe and then the US. Considered as equal players, nations of the Third World are not served well by these agencies. Citizens of neighbouring Third World countries often know of each other through exception-oriented news and information-gathering and editing processes of the developed world. Stories about them are written and edited by people who have sketchy and simplified notions of their countries and peoples. Myths are held to be true, despite obviously contradictory social phenomena.

A similar problem exists with regard to education and entertainment. A massive, highly capitalised industrial production of books, movies and television programmes, based in the US, either blots out or distorts our knowledge of other cultures and national expression. In short, the press traditions and media practices that have protected and are protecting the liberal democracies of the developed world are ill-suited to serve the developing world. While developed nations gain the information they need to remain rich and free, the developing world receives little it can use to begin to take control over its own affairs, let alone redress the gross inequalities between North and South. In more political terms, having gained political independence and having expected to gain overall sovereignty, the nations of the Third World are discovering the degree to which they are dependent – even for the very low standard of living they have achieved – on the information institutions and markets of the developed world. Trade and information routes still run to the old imperial centres rather than between points of the periphery. Participation in international markets demands the acceptance of certain business practices and ultimately the evolution of a certain class of people, whose manner of thinking and overall ideology must be consonant with those of the business world in which they live.

This pattern of global information creation and flow, who owns and controls it, along with its characteristic content, is termed the world information and communications order. The systematic jeopardy it introduces to some nations, especially those of the Third World, and the systematic advantage it creates for others, especially the US, as well as other developed countries, are the reasons why there emerged a call for a new world information and communications order.

The new world information and communications order

Conceptually, the call for a new world information and communications order arose out of an attempt to redress the imbalance in how the various nations of the world were served by the evolved international system of communication. Politically, it arose from a shift in the balance of power in the United Nations, and specifically within Unesco in the early 1970s. With the achievement of formal political independence, Third World nations, the vast majority of which were former colonies of Europe, obtained an independent voice in the United Nations and considerable influence over such agencies as Unesco.

Three points of debate

The international debate focused – and to some extent still focuses – on three points. Historically, communication services together with evolved information technologies have allowed dominant states to exploit their dominance. Through historical patterns and enabling technology, such as communication satellites, they have assumed a presence in the cultures and ideologies of less dominant states, that is, other nations throughout the world. Whether that presence comes through being the only source of foreign news or from beaming satellite signals into another country, such a presence is strongly felt by nations of the Third World.

The second central point of the international debate is that economies of scale in information production and distribution threaten to give increased dominance to those already dominant. However, any attempt to counteract a

worsening situation must avoid feeding into the hands of repressive governments that would curtail freedom of expression and information circulation.

Thirdly, the mobilisation of technology has been accomplished by a few
transnationals as a vehicle for the exploitation of markets rather than to
serve the cultural, social and political needs of nations. In other words, the
large corporations have seized the opportunity to develop and use communication technologies, but they have employed these technologies primarily to exploit the value of these audiences to advertisers, as opposed to
providing information, education and entertainment to these audiences for
their benefit or for the benefit of the larger cultural whole.

Moves by the developing world

International debate over the design of a world information order coalesced
in 1978 around the MacBride Report, a 312-page report by a Unesco
commission that studied communication problems on a global scale. The
underpinnings of this report are found in two principles that were accepted
by two intergovernmental conferences, the first held in San José de Costa
Rica in 1976 and the second in Kuala Lumpur in 1979. They are: 1.
'Communication policies should be conceived in the context of national
realities, free expression of thought, and respect for individual and social
rights' (Unesco, 1980, p. 40); 2. 'Communication, considered both as a
means of affirming a nation's collective identity and as an instrument of
social integration, has a decisive role to play in the democratization of social
relations in so far as it permits a multidirectional flow of . . . messages, both
from the media to their public and from this public to the media' (Unesco,
1980, p. 41).

A few words of interpretation are in order. To conceive of communication
policies as national realities rather than as the right of any individual to
communicate with any other individual in any place in the world is a
fundamental delimitation of free flow of information. The casting of communications in terms of 'national realities' puts in place a respect for a
collectivity, the nation. It also recognises the contribution that information
can make to that collectivity. However, respect for collectivities can be
abused and become unnecessarily restrictive of individual freedoms. Hence,
communications policies must also be conceived 'in the context of free
expression of thought', which curtails the ability of the state to infringe on
individual freedom and insists on an acceptance of plurality. In other words,
individual ideas should be freely considered in order that the collectivity can
enrich itself.

A third element of this first San José principle further limits the freedom of
the national collectivity: communication policies should be conceived in the
context of 'individual and social rights'. Such a phrase has direct reference to

the Universal Declaration of Human Rights to which all nations are signatories.

The second principle, accepted by the intergovernmental meeting in Kuala Lumpur, restates the San José principle in terms more satisfactory to those concerned with bringing about a new world information and communications order. It puts forward the integrity of a culture or nation, 'its collective identity and social integration', while maintaining that communication has a key role to play in enhancing that identity through its power to democratise information flow. While it is difficult to object to such a principle, it is a potential threat to the vast economic interests of the producers of information and cultural products in the developed world. Not only is it threatening to the standard content of entertainment programmes, but also it challenges technologies that only serve to increase the flow of information from the centre to the periphery.

The apparent reasonableness of the San José and Kuala Lumpur principles has been pitted against the interests of dominant nations and information producers. The objections of the Western press have been particularly strong, and not without reason. From the point of view of the owners, the possibility of collapse of foreign markets is alarming. From the point of view of journalists, while the MacBride Report and the debate on the new world information and communications order came up short of recommending the licensing of journalists (indeed, it stated that 'we share the anxiety aroused by the prospect of licensing and consider that it contains dangers to freedom of information' [1980, p. 236]), many journalists saw the report as chipping away at the freedom they need to do their job properly.

There are those (for example, McPhail, 1981) who adopted the Third World position and argued that developing nations should be allowed to develop print and electronic communication systems that foster their national development and integrity as separate and distinct cultures, just as many developed nations now do with electronic media. Anthony Smith took a quite different perspective in *The Geopolitics of Information*, maintaining that there was little doubt that the developing nations had a legitimate complaint. However, Smith was troubled by the statements of the strongest proponents of fundamental change. In his view they did not seem to capture how humankind might be improved through a different use of information, communications, knowledge and entertainment; rather, Smith saw in these writings the heavy hand of bureaucratic control.

The publication of the MacBride Report, with its challenge to Western information ideology, provided a focus for the extreme disenchantment of the US. A fairly sustained attack against attempts to introduce state control and to curtail the free flow of information was mounted by the US government and the journalistic community, led by the *New York Times*. In the mid-1980s Ronald Reagan took the US out of Unesco, persuading the UK and

Singapore to come along. This reduced Unesco's budget by one-third and the departure of Amadou Mahtar M'Bow, its director general, signalled a change of direction.

Roach (1990) has detailed the effective reversal of Unesco, in spite of continuing Third World support for the redressing of imbalances in information flows. She has also noted the continuing refusal of the US to rejoin the organisation, in spite of that change of direction. All that the US has granted is the recognition that imbalances in information flows do exist. Its proposed solution is to encourage others to produce and to compete in the market-place for information and entertainment products.

Countercurrents of geopolitical thought

It is certainly interesting to consider the body of evidence that has been presented detailing the systematic disadvantage of smaller, poorer nations as a result of Western information policy, in light of the current nature of international debate and of academic reflection on the information order. For instance, much has been made, as we noted in Chapter 7, of audiences and their tendencies to interpret content according to their own shifting and unpredictable priorities. This 'discovery' of what every child knows perfectly well and informs his/her parent in every argument about watching certain programmes, has been heralded not only for the welcome attention it pays to the audience but also because it challenges the thesis that the media can be imperial and impose their values on an unwilling public. Similarly, attention has been drawn to the difference in interests between the state and large corporations and the lack of control the state actually has over its resident corporations. It is asked 'How can the state use institutions which it cannot control, as agents of imperialism?' This question assumes a fairly narrow definition of 'the state' and the necessity of a fairly direct relation between state and media corporations. But whatever the adequacy of the questions, in combination with other points, the media imperialism thesis has been called into question, primarily in the countries that have the most to gain – the US and the UK (see Tomlinson, 1991).

The challenges to the media imperialism thesis that have arisen are significant because they derive from a more general trend in world affairs. The 1990s have seen cultural and ideological politics replaced with the politics of economies as a primary focus of concern. This shift of concern has occurred not only as a result of the collapse of the USSR but also because of a number of other factors, including the haemorrhaging of developed economies and the growth of production enclaves in the Third World. With this shift to economics over culture, society and ideology, many developing countries are seeing their future in economic integration within large trading blocs. The simple reason for this change is widespread poverty and privation in a world of plenty. Their reasoning is that participation in global trade will bring the wealth necessary to assist in economic – and, if it is wanted, cultural – development.

What impact is this general trend having on the global information order? The case of Reuters tells a great deal. Musa (1990) notes that since the 1960s Reuters has been transformed. It is now the world's largest electronic publisher, specialising in providing financial data from markets around the world. While for many years it had never made a profit, profits have grown fifty-fold and by 1985 the company was valued at £1.5 billion. By the late 80s Reuters' revenue looked like this: 56 per cent from the sale of money market and foreign exchange information; 13 per cent from client systems; 12 per cent from securities information; 10 per cent from commodities information, and 9 per cent from media services (i.e., the provision of news). This decrease in the importance of providing news – it used to account for the lion's share of revenue in Reuters – is not a result of contraction of those services but rather massive growth in the financial information sector. Reuters has even found room to accommodate some of the desires of Third World governments in making news from government initiatives. Why? Because such information is important for investors. Obviously, government programmes indicate where governments are spending and the likely impact of such programmes on the labour market, political stability, in general the environment for doing business, is valuable information. In short, as portrayed by the Western press, the Third World has been transformed from a place of amusing and tragic incompetence to a place where corporations and individuals may make their fortunes. To put it somewhat differently, Boyd-Barrett (1992) has observed that the slowly increasing wealth and industrialisation of the Third World is combining with a recognition of the issue of distorted news coverage to produce a steadily expanding production and circulation of alternative information.

With the increased domination of economics, the nature and value of information changes. If governments can be said to be upset when they miscalculate the political drift of a country – based partly on media coverage – there is no doubt that investors will be livid over such miscalculations. To be sure, they will put every conceivable pressure both on their home country and the countries in which they invest to maintain an healthy investment climate. And they will pay handsomely for reliable information that allows them to move their money as needs be to make healthy profits.

Within Third World countries themselves things are also apparently changing. The change is apparent as well as real because, while one can point to significant examples of, say, television and film production, and in Asia hardware production, the statistics on international information flows presented earlier tell a much more accurate story. In general, trade balances are as bad as ever. What we see emerging here and there in the Third World are production enclaves. These enclaves oftentimes have their roots in attempts by the state to increase production for the domestic market. But in their final form they are often a fiefdom of an aggressive media mogul, a hard-fought-for prize that constitutes a stranglehold on a domestic market and (as a result) a foundation for global export.

The Brazilian (TV Globo) alternative

A good case in point is Brazil's TV Globo. In 1985, Brazil earned US$20 million in exports to Portugal, other Latin American and Spanish-speaking countries, Italy, France, the Netherlands, Switzerland, the UK and Germany. These exports were dominated by the production of Roberto Marinho's TV Globo. A New Yorker article provides a revealing discussion of the *telenovelas* and the politics of Brazil (Guillermoprieto, 1993). It also provides some information on the career of Marinho and his rise to become a global producer.

The foundation of Brazil's export activities are TV Globo's *telenovelas*, effectively soap operas with outdoor settings. Inside the country the *telenovelas* are complemented by a down-market form called *teletemas* or *casos verdade* (true cases), where members of the audience are encouraged to write in and suggest stories based on their own experiences. There also exists an up-market form called *seriados*, mini-series related to Brazilian realities. The formula for TV Globo's success appears to be copying the production-line techniques of US soap operas, the development of technical and creative talent and average production costs of US$105,000 per hour (Marques de Melo, 1990).

On the basis of this content, the production techniques outlined above, and a massive export push, TV Globo has been gaining a significant presence in international markets. This presence has caused US government spokespeople and a goodly number of academics to question the media imperialism hypothesis. They note that if someone from as poor a nation as Brazil can rise to become a significant global producer, how can it be said that the Americans dominate the market to the exclusion of everyone else? The answer, of course, is that rich and powerful capitalists can be found in every corner of the world.

Televisa Mexico

The case of Televisa Mexico is even more apropos. Televisa is a private media conglomerate that dominates its home base, Mexico, and for some time it dominated the US Spanish-language television market. Sinclair (1990) notes that Televisa was set up in Mexico as a closing of ranks by the private sector in face of challenges from the Echeverria government in 1976, following the San

José, Costa Rica meetings of Unesco. Televisa emerged as a powerful player, controlling 70 per cent of advertising in the country in 1987. It has numerous subsidiaries operating within and outside the country and has consistently supported the national oligarchy and ruling party of the country, the Partido Revolucionario Institucional (PRI). As well as owning television stations it engages in in-house production. In 1989 it transmitted 24,500 hours of television, 60 per cent of which were produced in-house, and it exported to 35 different countries. It was also involved in setting up a communications satellite, PanAmSat. So powerful was it, and so in tune with the US government's approach to communications, that Ronald Reagan signed a declaration that PanAmSat was in the national interests of the US, a move which may have contributed to Reagan's ambassador to Mexico being appointed head of Televisa's international satellite division.

Like TV Globo, Televisa produces a large number of soap operas but also translates many US productions into Spanish for re-export to the Spanish-speaking world, second in numbers only to English speakers. Televisa also managed to gain control over Spanish-speaking broadcasting in the US until 1986, when the Federal Communications Commission decided that it could turn a blind eye no longer. Not long after, US interests began to buy into the company and its subsidiaries and it has lost some of its holdings to US interests. It then turned to Latin America and the Spanish-speaking world and has established itself as a formidable regional power.

Behemothic variety

Beyond taking note of such companies as TV Globo and Televisa and their ability to become world players, the question can be asked: what is the significance of such players in the debate over the balance of information flows and content reflective of domestic culture? A number of points can be made. First, the participation of large corporations domiciled in countries other than the US in world entertainment markets does not represent an exchange of cultural products amongst cultures and nations. Secondly, the nature of the material produced by such corporations should be examined. Soap operas, with their mixture of sex, hubris, jealousy, intrigue, family quarrels – in short, the intricacies of personal life – are like game shows. They attract large audiences but have very little to offer us in terms of enlightenment. Thirdly, an examination of the economic structure of all nations, including those of the Third World, indicates that rich and powerful corporations can be found everywhere. Often they arise as national saviours, large enough to compete on a world stage and rich enough to offer a genuine cultural alternative to the imported product. Once they have achieved a domestic market dominance and a notable level of profitability they play out their role as international capitalists driven by the bottom line.

In *The Age of the Behemoths*, Anthony Smith has revisited international flows of information and entertainment. Smith notes that through its control mechanisms, and within a framework of domestic policy, the state may create a regime which encourages or discourages the evolution of both national and internationally-oriented, domestically-owned firms. Smith argues that internationally aggressive media conglomerates are emerging out of a variety of not necessarily predictable places, for instance, out of the print industries in Germany, television in Italy, hardware manufacture in Japan and out of cable and telecommunications in the US. TV Globo in Brazil and Televisa in Mexico would be two additional examples. Further, he argues that regulatory measures are discouraging international growth in certain areas where one might expect it, for instance, the US television networks. Curtailed from growth for so long, the networks have developed corporate cultures in which aggressive growth scenarios are not considered, and nor are there qualified persons within the firm to plot such manoeuvres.

The same point can be made in a wider and positive context. While on the international level the smaller nations are vying for a voice, competition also exists within nations for a hearing. To say that the design and content of the modern media re-express the power relations of the state is to provide an initial overview. However, such a statement tends to encourage a perception of the state as a monolithic entity. In fact, power blocs within the state often vie for appropriate representation. The most obvious example of such competition is between regional and national services. The call that the regions, as opposed to the nation, have on resources for media production differs significantly from country to country. As we have seen, in Germany and the Netherlands regionality is strong; in Germany it is a result of the ideological preference of the Allies following World War II. In Britain, Italy and France significant regional claims are allowed, although even in these countries the national outweighs the regional significantly. In the US, regionality is often absent at the level of the South, the Midwest, or the East Coast, but exists most prominently in the local, i.e. the individual town.

It is interesting to compare the call regions have between countries and project onto that comparison patterns of economic development. The economic strength of the various regions of Germany, for example, complemented by the vesting of constitutional control over broadcasting in the *Länder*, arguably has contributed to the dispersed economic growth and stability of the Federal Republic as a whole. In contrast, the concentration of production, power and media in the south-east of England to the detriment of other areas – the decline of Edinburgh as a Scottish publishing centre is especially notable – arguably has led to substantial regional dislocation and unemployment. Media production and content realities reflect the evolution of this dominant single metropolis, regional licences notwithstanding.

European trade in information and cultural products

Perhaps the most exciting development in communications is the stated goal of a unitary market in the European Community. The EC represents a community of more-or-less equal states, each with distinctive cultures, many with healthy production, particularly media production facilities and capabilities. On the one hand, the driving goal is to rationalise and integrate production so that economies of scale can be realised throughout the community. This would allow Europe to become a third industrial force to rival North America (the US with its free trade partners) and Asia (led by Japan but backed up by Taiwan, Hong Kong, South Korea, China and so on). On the other hand, because the partners in the EC are distinctive and equal, there is reason to believe that it is the intent of most member states that this integration will not come about through the subordination of certain states to the dominance of others. In short, it is reasonable to conclude, and the promulgation of certain EC policy papers such as *Television Without Frontiers* (1984) supports this notion, that the ideal state of union would include a federation of production epicentres that allow for cultural sensibilities to co-exist with competition for entertainment markets. Time will tell.

The possible collapse of the EC into a set of purely dominant-subordinate relations, in which Germany leads, perhaps followed by the UK and France, would not bode well for either economic or communication and cultural industry relations between the developed and developing world. If balanced trade in cultural products can be achieved, perhaps with a freer market in entertainment products, then perhaps the EC will provide the model and the morale to work around the momentum of centre-hinterland relations.

What does theory have to offer?

Perhaps the most important point to remember in the debate over balance in information and entertainment flows is that ideas and images do not subjugate people irrevocably. No one ever totally lost their freedom from being exposed to the wrong balance of foreign versus domestic content. Nor do empires live forever. Colonies grow, become independent, and sometimes become empires themselves. As Larry Pratt and John Richards argue in *Prairie Capitalism* (1979), hinterlands are not forever bound in a dependency relationship to a centre. Given that domestic audiences have a preference for domestic programmes, national policies that provide the means to produce cultural material may lead to linked development in the production of cultural and entertainment products. Secondly, there is little reason why public entrepreneurship in the form of regulatory and/or policy action with respect to imports cannot be used to make room for domestic products and domestic players. Once in place, these players and products can then move beyond their domestic markets. Once export activity is in place the way is paved for expansion and finally independence.

Summary

In this chapter we have outlined perhaps the most fundamental issue facing communications today: how can the world community design a communications system for equal benefit to all?

The prevailing ideology of the role of the media within developed Western countries is that they must be free of government control and have freedom of access to information, and that, as an extension of free speech, they should be free to distribute information into all markets (the free flow of information doctrine). This doctrine plays squarely into metropolis-hinterland dynamics, which are well understood as favouring metropoli over hinterlands. However apt the free flow doctrine might be within a country, and its aptness depends very much on development philosophy, between countries it pits the market-seeking forces of media conglomerates against the responsibilities of national politicians to assist their country and its culture to develop.

The global news agencies and trade in television programmes are vivid historical and contemporary illustrations of a free press (also media) in action. The news agencies provide inexpensive information around the world; however, certain biases are introduced into that information in the way it is collected, by whom and for what dominant set of users. The domestic geopolitics of information are not unlike global geopolitics. Generally speaking, the greatest benefit accrues to the economies of the producers and organisers. Patterns of production, import and export in news are parallel to those in the entertainment industry, the difference being that the US dominates more singly in entertainment.

The patterns of information flow have been called a world information and communications order. The inequitable treatment of all nations has produced a call for a new world information and communications order. In the late 70s and early 80s it appeared that this call would have some impact on international information flows. However, the determined resistance of the US has borne fruit and both Unesco and many communications analysts are turning away from the thesis of Western media imperialism.

The trend towards a general concern with economies rather than societies and cultures has led not only to a vast expansion of information circulation around the world but also to a reassessment of the notion that Western developed nations dominate the world information order. Much has been made of examples of Third World production and the active decoding capacities of audience members. Less has been made of more general statistics on information flows. Independent of empirical evidence, it would appear that all nations will be required to make their own way in designing their own media environment and that they will not be able to use international agencies to aid in that regard.

The evolution of a single market in the EC that recognises the cultural role of communications and therefore the separate and distinctive needs of member states may provide a model for ameliorating the shortcomings of a bald acceptance of free flow of information forces in the context of existing patterns of industrialisation.

References

Althusser, Louis (1971), *Lenin and His Philosophy*, New Left Books, London.

BBC (1992), *Annual Report*.

Beale, Alison (1988), 'The question of space' in R. Lorimer and D. C. Wilson (eds.), *Communication Canada*, Kagan and Woo, Toronto.

Boyd-Barrett, J. O. (1982), 'Cultural dependency and the mass media' in M. Gurevitch *et al.* (eds.), *Culture, Society and the Media*, Methuen, Toronto.

Boyd-Barrett, J. O., and D. K. Thussu (1992), *Contra-flow in Global News*, John Libbey, London.

Dorfman, A., and A. Mattelart (1975), *How to Read Donald Duck: Imperialist Ideology in the Disney Comic*, International General Editions, New York.

Dorfman, Ariel (1983), *The Empire's Old Clothes: What the Lone Ranger, Babar, and Other Innocent Heroes Do to Our Minds*, Pantheon, New York.

European Communities Commission (1984), *Television Without Frontiers*, Green Paper on the establishment of the common market for broadcasting, especially by satellite and cable, COM(84) 300 final, Office for Official Publications of the European Communities, Luxembourg.

Frum, Linda (1990), *The Newsmakers*, Key Porter, Toronto.

Guillermoprieto, Alma (1993), 'Letter from Brazil: Obsessed in Rio', *The New Yorker*, August 16, pp. 44–56.

Hester, Al (1974), 'International news agencies' in Alan Wells (ed.), *Mass Communications: A World View*, Mayfield Publishing, Palo Alto.

Hoskins, Colin and Rolf Mirus (1990), 'Television fiction made in USA' in Peter Larsen (ed.), *Import/Export: International Flow of Television Fiction*, no. 104, Unesco, Paris, pp. 83–90.

Innis, Harold (1950), *Empire and Communication*, University of Toronto Press, Toronto.

Innis, Harold (1951), *The Bias of Communication*, University of Toronto Press, Toronto.

Katz, Elihu and Tamar Liebes (1990), 'The export of meaning: cross-cultural readings of American TV' in Peter Larsen (ed.), *Import/Export: International Flow of Television Fiction*, no. 104, Unesco, Paris, pp. 69–82.

Larsen, Peter (ed.) (1990), *Import/Export: International Flow of Television Fiction*, no. 104, Unesco, Paris.

Marques del Melo, José (1990), 'Brazilian television fiction' in Peter Larsen (ed.),
    Import/Export: International Flow of Television Fiction, no. 104, Unesco, Paris,
    pp. 91–4.
McNulty, Jean (1987), 'The political economy of Canadian satellite broadcasting',
    paper presented at Canadian Communication Association meeting, May, Mon-
    treal.
McPhail, Thomas (1981), *Electronic Colonialism: The Future of International
    Broadcasting and Communication*, Sage Publications, Beverly Hills.
Musa, Mohammed (1990), 'News agencies, transnationalization and the new order',
    Media Culture and Society, 12(3), pp. 325–42.
National Film Board (1981), *Magic in the Sky*, directed by Peter Raymont, produced
    by Peter Raymont, Arthur Hammond, NFB, Ottawa.
National Film Board (1991), *Distressed Signals*, produced by Tom Perlmutter, John
    Walker, Kent Martin and John Taylor, NFB, Ottawa.
Pratt, Larry, and John Richards (1979), *Prairie Capitalism: Power and Influence in
    the New West*, McClelland and Stewart, Toronto.
Roach, Coleen (1990), 'The movement for a New World Information and Com-
    munication Order: a second wave?', *Media Culture and Society*, 12(3), pp.
    283–308.
Robinson, G. J. (1981), *News Agencies and World News: in Canada, the United
    States and Yugoslavia*, University of Fribourg Press, Fribourg, Switzerland.
Sepstrup, Pebren (1992), *Transnationalization of Television in Five European
    Countries*, Unesco, Paris.
Siegel, Arthur (1973), *Politics and the Media in Canada*, McGraw-Hill Ryerson,
    Toronto.
Sinclair, John (1990), 'Neither West nor Third World: the Mexican television
    industry within the NWICO debate', *Media Culture and Society*, 12(3), pp.
    343–60.
Smith, Anthony (1980), *The Geopolitics of Information: How Western Culture
    Dominates the World*, Faber and Faber, London.
Smith, Anthony (1991), *The Age of Behemoths: The Globalization of Mass Media
    Firms*, Priority Press, New York.
Thomas, Sari, and Brian P. Callahan (1982), 'Allocating happiness: TV families and
    social class', *Journal of Communication*, 32, pp. 184–90.
Tomlinson, John (1991), *Cultural Imperialism*, Johns Hopkins University Press,
    Baltimore.
Unesco (1978), *The World of News Agencies*, Commission for the Study of Com-
    munication Problems (MacBride Commission), Working Paper no. 11, Unesco,
    Paris.
Unesco (1980), *Many Voices, One World: Communication and Society, Today and
    Tomorrow* (MacBride Report), Unipub, Paris.
Unesco (1988), *Draft World Communication Report*, Unesco, Paris.
Varis, Tapio (1985), *International Flow of Television Programs*, Reports and Papers
    on Mass Communication, no. 1010, Unesco, Paris.

Chapter 10

Mass communication and culture

Media and society

In Chapter 1 we drew attention to how the dominant media of communication, which derive from their host society, organise that host society. In his examination of Western civilization Harold Innis proposed that the communication systems of the Greeks and then the Romans were not just a means for relaying messages but were systems that encouraged certain social relations, economic organisation, selective self-preservation, and ways of conceiving of the world that altered Western civilisation fundamentally. In other words, these communication systems were modes of representation that emerged out of, implied, and even demanded a particular social organisation.

Societies in which oral communication was dominant, Innis noted, were time-biased, that is to say, they were biased in favour of the preservation of themselves over time, towards the building of tradition. On the other hand, societies in which written communication was dominant were space-biased, that is to say, they were biased in favour of extending themselves over space, towards the building of empire. This simple dichotomy was both evocative and appealing, even though, as later work has shown, the situation is not nearly so straightforward.

Innis's basic equation caught the attention of Marshall McLuhan, the scholar of English literature who was most intrigued by the modern condition and James Joyce. After examining 'the making of typographic man' in *The Gutenberg Galaxy* (1962), McLuhan turned most of his attention to transforming Innis's dichotomy into a trichotomy, adding 'electronic society' to the equation. McLuhan's enterprise was to articulate the fundamentals of electronic society as something quite different from oral and literate society. Some of his notions – probes, as he called them – were compelling. Some were obviously wrong, others merely evocative or provocative, partly because McLuhan saw himself as a latter-day James Joyce, giving voice to concerns about the media that emerged out of British modernism in the 20s and 30s

(Tiessen, 1993). But such notions as 'the global village' and 'the medium as the message', or his idea that the electronic media were our 'outered intelligence or nervous system' were clearly powerful insights into and predictors of the dynamics of our evolving, electronic, globally organised information society.

While many have taken Innis and McLuhan as proposing that literate and electronic processes replaced oral and literate communication respectively as they achieved dominance, it is probably more accurate and useful to think of these processes as incremental. In being incremental, the development of literate and electronic forms have extended the multiplicity of means of communication available in society. For example, as outlined in Chapter 1, electronic communication has extended oral, audio-visual and textual processes. Consequently, the position of contemporary society is one in which we have a multiplicity of enormously flexible communicative capacities which can project a voice, an image, or a text from any point where funding and equipment are in place to innumerable similarly endowed points anywhere in the world.

The notions of Innis and McLuhan laid the foundation for thinking about the manner in which communicational forms play a structuring role in society. At one very general level encompassing historical and cultural comparisons, the balance of media use in a particular society, that is to say oral, literate and electronic media use, may be seen playing itself out in the organisation of society as a whole. However, given the multiplicity of mass media forms – books, magazines, newspapers, television, movies, radio, computer communications – and the differing patterns of both dissemination and use, a more detailed description of the mass media is needed to understand how communicational forces differentially affect societies and groups within societies. Literacy rates, newspaper, magazine and book publishing consumption figures, together with data on the numbers of television and radio sets and computers per capita, tell the beginning of that story. International information and communication flow, and values and attitudes tell more about the nature of societies as, in fact, do the nature and use of the mass media.

The mass media

The dominant media of communication in modern society are a combination of mass print and electronic media, that is, newspapers, magazines, books, radio, television, data communications, video and film, together with increasingly available point-to-point communications capacity – the telephone, and various other forms of computer communication. These media forms exist against a backdrop of prevailing social assumptions, face-to-face communication, various social institutions and practices, and other forms of communication such as architecture and religion. The media encompass numerous genres and/or formats – novels, compilations of daily events, newspaper columns, dramatic presentation, visual synopses of world events, investigations, comedy, still pictures, documentaries, game shows, talk shows, and so on. These many different genres and formats run the gamut of print and electronic possibilities. They fall short in an inability to facilitate unmediated person-to-person or face-to-face communication. They also fall short by virtue of budgetary and editorial constraints placed on them by the organisation of media production. Serious enlightening drama is a fading genre in the increasingly commercial world of television.

These content forms are produced within institutional structures that have only recently evolved. That is to say, while mass communications itself is not new, its current forms are. Those current forms are a set of print- and electronically-based secular institutions existing as an extension of either the business community or the state (in the name of the public), and which profess to represent the interests of the people.

These media, through public spending, advertising, and/or engaging text and images, have integrated and ingratiated themselves into our lives so that, at times, we and they appear to be one and the same. At times, we as members of the public are vehicles for representing their symbols in the same way that they are vehicles for representing our behaviour. However, even though society and individuals are inextricably interwoven with media processes, the mass media are also separate institutions of production, as we saw in Chapter 2, dedicated to the creation of content, using particular technologies, within formal institutions; acting according to certain laws, professional codes and practices, carried out by persons occupying certain roles; conveying explicit and implicit information, entertainment, images and symbols to mass media audiences.

Conceiving of the mass media as encompassing this seven-point framework gives us a tool to fill out the McLuhan/Innis framework. It also provides a preliminary sense of mass communication as a particular cultural phenomenon in the context of developed Western societies.

Policy and ownership

The cultural orientations of the modern mass media are readily apparent in the examination of law, policy, ownership, professionalism and technology. With regard to law and policy, a number of dimensions are significant. They include the level and nature of direct involvement by the state as defined by statute; the existence and extent of policy in telecommunications, broadcasting, satellite and cable and cultural industries; policy on programming;

import and export policy on services and specifically cultural products; media investment opportunities; ownership restrictions; laws, policies and practices applicable to the media professions; the adoption of technology and technology policy, national and regional divisions of responsibility, opportunity and funding; public- and private-sector opportunities and challenges; policy goals, and so on.

These dimensions of law and policy were explored in Chapters 3 and 4. To review the case of France as an illustration, the myriad ways in which the French state inflects the operations of seemingly every element of its media is most telling. The French state achieves this inflection through a wide range of mechanisms, beginning with culture as a first priority. This includes an emphasis on culture at all levels of government; specific encouragement for business and public support of culture; licensing according to cultural indicators; direct financial aid to cultural industries and creative cultural workers; distribution assistance for media that meet certain cultural criteria; ownership regulation across the cultural industries; laws that enhance the prestige and the operation of the journalistic profession; low interest and forgivable loans (they do not have to be repaid) to cultural enterprises; a technology policy that considers cultural impact; the founding and maintenance of cultural institutes; liaison with and entrenchment of culture within education; the subsidisation of foreign distribution of French media products; domestic consumer subsidies and other forms of demand stimulation, and so forth.

On the other hand, Germany's approach to culture can be seen most readily through the combination of policy and patterns of ownership and ownership behaviour, especially the broadcasting industry. The vesting of responsibility for broadcasting in the *Länder* after World War II tells the story of Germany's past aggression and its subsequent control by the Allies. The various attempts by Konrad Adenauer to found a national television network, with his doctor and a neighbour on the board of directors, speaks to the desire of Adenauer, but certainly not of all Germans, to speak for Germany with a single voice. The growth and ideological stance of the Axel Springer group, in spite of ownership concentration laws, also indicates tolerance of press dominance by a single individual and, given the content of the papers, a *bürgermeister* mentality – an overacting concern with the local and with the comforts of home. The vehement opposition to Axel Springer by other sections of German society reveals the resistance of many Germans to any resurgence of extreme right propaganda and politics. Similarly, the ability of the Springer Verlag group to maintain its prestige and market position as a scientific publisher, because of and in spite of Robert Maxwell, who, in the 50s and early 60s held world distribution rights to Springer Verlag's publications, is telling, as are the many small operations that keep Germany amongst the artistic *avant garde*.

The seeming greater national presence and organisation of press and film production, importation and distribution in Germany, in contrast to the *Länder*-based broadcasters, has provided a foundation not only for greater press influence over television in Germany but also for comparatively greater industrial growth in the print media over television companies. At the same time the contrasting organisation of the press and broadcasting has seemed to encourage a higher value to be placed on literary values and art in Germany than might otherwise have been the case had television been more dominant on the national scene.

Continuing with a cultural perspective on these national media matters, the evolving industrial form and position of the UK is particularly interesting. Whether one focuses on the privatisation of British Telecom, the expansion of private broadcasting, the attempt to set up southern England as a film, satellite broadcasting and technological development centre, or the auction of broadcasting licences, the passage of the period of benign state dominance in communications – the BBC was popularly known as 'Aunty' or 'Aunty Beeb' – is marked. In the context of the policies of other European countries, it is odd to see so much of Britain's economic momentum complementing US free-market policies. In communications, this complementarity begins with the absence of both the US and the UK from Unesco and continues through a variety of different policies with regard to television production, copyright, film production, cable, satellite usage, and so forth. If the US is the free marketeer to the world, both in ideology and in its position on the laws and practices of other nations – it can be remarkably blind to its own transgressions – then Britain appears to be the free marketeer in its relations with the EC, with a similarly distorted self-image. In this context, and in the context of culture, one begins to have an understanding of why the French and sometimes other Europeans speak of a monolithic Anglo-Saxon viewpoint, with English as a world language.

The above general cultural read-out of institutional forms in national contexts is one approach to the subject. Another is Anthony Smith's (1991) more particular hypothesis that it is domestic policy which has most strongly influenced the history of organisational form and practice. Noting, as we did in Chapter 9, that the great American television networks have not become global predators, Smith argues that this can be accounted for by the internal structures and viewpoints that have evolved as a result of FCC anti-trust restrictions that have been applied at the domestic level. The other side of the coin, he explains, can be seen in some of the globalising initiatives of the variously-domiciled media moguls, for example the Italian, Silvio Berlusconi. Smith believes that their aggressive globalising behaviour can also be accounted for by the nature of the regimes within which they have become accustomed to operate. Of course, such a hypothesis is just an innovative version of the thesis that ownership form is of significance to the understanding of firm and industry behaviour. But Smith's innovation is nevertheless stimulating within a cultural perspective because it broadens the purview. Ownership may be seen as a fundamental mechanism for the organisation of resources. The organisation of resources is a foundation of power. Economic power translates into political power, and political power provides a foundation for ideological dominance. Ownership also expresses, at one and the same time, domestic social values and an international stance – two quite different consequences of a single reality. Thus while Japan may use both state and industry to rebuild a domestic economy, it may also choose to set that achieved market savvy and productive power to work to capture global markets. It may thereby achieve a world power status that would otherwise be unattainable. Similarly, France may use the state to protect all forms of domestic communications industries. In doing so it may adopt a state-led authoritarian and arrogant attitude to international trading rules and relations that would be unacceptable in and from other, more powerful, countries.

In short, the cultural consequences of communications law, policy and ownership patterns are salient cultural indicators of the approach and priorities of the cultures in which they reside.

Professionalism

With the consideration of the influence of professionals and journalists the plot of the cultural story thickens. The existence of the *Universal Declaration of Human Rights*, to which all developed countries are signatories, along with pan-European agreements on the ethics and practice of journalism, is certainly culturally significant. The founding of journalistic practice in the Western world on notions of both freedom of speech and conscience as well as protection against infringement of privacy provides for a common cultural foundation at the level of principles. However, because of the generality of such principles, it also provides for cultural variation in both the application of these principles and the balance of one against the other.

The specific clauses of the 1971 Munich *Declaration of Rights and Obligations of Journalists* elaborate on free speech and privacy and give insight into the character of UK and European society and the perceived role of the journalist. For instance, the obligations not to use unfair methods in collecting information, to respect the privacy of others, to rectify any published information, to observe professional secrecy, to act in accordance with one's conscience, and not to act contrarily to the policies of an information organ in which one is employed, if carried out in practice, would distinguish a European journalist from many of his/her colleagues in North America. Such clauses provide both an outline of some of the boundaries of the profession and a bulwark for journalists to fall back on if challenged. Their acceptance by society is an indication of the positive value society places on journalists and the recognition of the need for rules of conduct, if not laws, to allow them to perform that function.

However, such clauses, even if they are only accepted by journalists and not their employers, do not mean that there are not substantial cultural differences between the various countries. In the many different Scandinavian documents dealing with the press and media there can be found a disinterested, dispassionate fairness that is inspiring from one perspective, and speaks to an intrusive bureaucracy from another. The fact that owners' groups have made statements against disguising advertising content as journalism adds to the picture of Scandinavian media operations. So does the acceptance by journalists of the principle of not naming government bureaucrats and others unnecessarily for minor infractions. The situation is almost the exact opposite in Italy where personally intrusive, sensationalist reporting is, if not the norm, then certainly easily found.

In the context of a hierarchy of influences, the foundations of journalism in France are, quite predictably, not to be found in arrangements worked out on a firm by firm basis, as they are in Germany, but are derived from a code dating back to 1881. The considerable protection of journalists in France grants both protection and privilege that is difficult to find elsewhere and speaks to the value the state places on professionalism as well as state involvement. It is not surprising then that French journalists are positively oriented to the state and fiercely loyal to their profession. Nor is it surprising that there is a low level reporting of government corruption and a low level of public concern that the French government might be involved, for example, in sabotage of environmental groups.

In the UK, privileged access to government information, for example the parliamentary press gallery, in a political system in which the first assumption is secrecy, is combined with a stubborn insistence on the part of press owners to minimise any involvement with written codes of practice to produce a unique, class-bound, competitive 'market-place' reality. This reality, primarily characteristic of the press, is, or at least has been, balanced by the public-service orientation of radio and TV. However, with commitment to the public good, as opposed to the private interest, on the wane in Britain one might expect a stronger 'market-place of ideas' to gain influence in broadcasting.

In contrast to all of the above is the single principle, free speech orientation of the US press and media system. Freedom of speech is paramount in US society and it is defended strenuously, especially by the US Supreme Court. Other complementary laws, notably libel laws, allow for a particularly strong reading of freedom of speech. Such arrangements give rise to almost the opposite kind of public debate than exists in France. Whereas in France protective mechanisms abound to keep public debate 'civilised', in the US few holds are barred, creating a free speech free-for-all that would crush other societies.

Another side of the media profession involves other media creators such as novelists, poets, film-makers, cartoonists, television producers, script-writers, photographers, programme planners, censors and classification boards, and so on. The traditions of journalism are well understood and indeed well founded in the principles of freedom of speech, the obligation to seek information in the name of the public, the duty to respect the truth, and the respect for privacy. In contrast, similar guidelines that derive from a sophisticated analysis of its role in society do not exist for those involved in the creation and distribution of fiction. True, in the US and Australia and probably in other countries, codes have been drawn up by various groups that reflect some of the notions of journalists' codes, such as fairness, balance and respect for privacy. However, in practice it is difficult to observe their impact. Certainly they are unknown to society at large.

The issues are certainly real enough. What obligations do individuals and organisations involved in the production of fiction and entertainment have to the society within which they work and from which audience members will come? What potential is there for a constructive contribution by enter-tainment forms that does not detract from freedom of expression? The possibility of making a constructive contribution to society is an accepted concern, for example in the marketing of television fiction for children. In industry magazines, children's programmes are advertised as having 'positive social values'. This means that although there may be lots of explosions and mayhem, and the 'good guys' square off against the 'bad guys', irreparable maiming and killing of human beings is fairly absent and an attempt is made to convey values of which society (specifically parents) would approve. The existence of censors in some countries and classifiers in others, as well as the literature on violence and pornography, address the same central concern – the positive contribution that the media may make to the community of which they are a part.

The liberal viewpoint on the role of entertainment is that the audience has the right to prior knowledge of potentially offensive content in such media as feature films. In the case of television, those of liberal persuasion in North America feel that a person should have the right not to have their living-room invaded by portrayals of offensive values (Martinez, nd). However, these tolerant attitudes appear to have been eclipsed in early 1993, at least in North America. Calls by various groups, including the US Congress, for a diminution of violence seem to be obtaining a hearing.

The absence of a sustained and engaging discourse in the communications literature and in society on the ideals and realities of fiction and entertainment producers, parallel to the literature dealing with the positive contribution that journalists make to society, perhaps derives from the relatively recent emergence of the electronic media and their extensive carrying capacity for fiction and entertainment. Perhaps the lack of a parallel concern with the potential contribution to society that entertainment could make derives also from the coupling of artistic freedom to freedom of speech in modern historical times. Occurring when it did, the emergence of the independent artist resulted in the affirmation of a discourse of resistance. The role of the artist was to reveal the warts and follies of society and to resist its confines, be they physical restraints, conceptual categories or material wealth. Yet, if we think broadly, the role of the story-teller has always been and continues to be important to society. We are brought together through understandings and viewpoints that are shared and that allow us to make sense of ourselves, our neighbours, our society and others.

Whatever the reason for this issue not having a place of significance on the social and political agenda, at least until recently, the emergence of both theory and professionalism of fiction and entertainment production within the context of their possible contribution to society also has been late in coming. Indeed, in attempting to write about it here, because writing in the area is so limited, the spectre of a potentially serious infringement on artistic freedom looms large. However, the possibility of infringement notwithstanding, three concepts would appear to be useful for thinking about fiction and entertainment production that go beyond, but do not replace, artistic freedom and freedom of speech. They are entertainment, enlightenment and cultural development. Here we mean entertainment in the sense of amusement and enjoyment. Enlightenment here means causing an audience member to see something in a different light or from a different perspective, in such a way that he or she gains further insight or understanding. Cultural development we mean as something which has the potential to help build on cultural patterns that reflect the particular ideals of a culture and that may or may not be shared with other cultures.

It would seem that were these three concepts considered by media producers as professional ideals, a potential for an increased positive contribution by entertainment products to society might be realised. It would also appear that such an orientation allows both for contributions that are directly supportive of the status quo, and for others that are resistant to or critical of it. To enlighten and to work towards cultural ideals does not have to be trudging work. Similarly, to amuse is not all smiles and laughter. This orientation represents an attempt to situate fiction and entertainment production and host cultures within the context of a) individual, creative, artistic and freedom of speech values, b) the role of the historical and modern role of the story-teller and the clown, and c) the political, economic, technological, and administrative forces of modern life. It is meant only as a possible beginning.

Technology

Just as media policy, ownership and professionalism reflect fundamentals of the host culture, so does the development, adoption and application of technology. Europe and the UK have fallen behind in the development and adoption of communications technology. Whereas television was invented in Britain and the education systems of the UK and Europe are fully capable of sustaining these countries at the leading edge in research, development, and application of technology, they have not held such a position for a consider-able time. Their relatively weak position as technological players in relation to the US, Japan, and even Canada and Australia, can be attributed partly to the strength of the public sector and cultural commitments across Europe. Having created perfectly adequate print and electronic media forms to reflect their culture and to serve the public's need and desire for information and entertainment, the UK and Europe, dominated by public broadcasters and a limited number of channels, did not see the need for the development and adoption of new major technologies such as cable, which is not to include technological refinement. Therefore technological development did not take place in these locales and it was left to the Japanese and North Americans.

Against this cultural orientation to technological development in the UK and Europe, countries with different needs acted differently. From a founda-tion in the military sector, the US proceeded with the development of com-munications technologies of all kinds. Japan's desire to be the world supplier of communications hardware caused it to look for innovations that would be adopted by consumers. Canada's need to distribute signals inexpensively to distant points over a sparsely populated landscape through electromagnetic interference also caused it to participate in inventing and adopting new technologies. In each case, markets existed or were created to sustain such development. In short, while European technology policy was appropriate from a cultural perspective, as a result of technological development over the years the technology policies of other countries have now created forms that have provided content delivery opportunities of which Europe can also make good use. Not being in the communications technology development game throughout this period has placed Europe in a catch-up position.

The response of Europe as a whole and of the various European countries to the necessity of catching up can be interpreted in cultural terms. France has been attempting to keep Japanese hardware at bay through protective poli-cies. It is attempting to become a European supplier by matching production in certain instances and developing distinctive devices in others. Meanwhile, the Dutch-based Philips has been forming consortia in direct competition with the Japanese. In the UK, the privatisation of British Telecom in the atmosphere of global competition has transformed that company almost magically. British Telecom is emerging as a major player in global markets, outplaying many who have been participants in that market for some time. The British are also attempting to bring about a free market in hardware and software in Europe to provide a 'domestic' market of sufficient size for global competition in all areas. The British position on copyright is slightly different in that the favoured option is the maintenance of some elements of national territoriality at least in a transition phase, that is, UK copyright as distinct from English-language copyright within the EC. British media planners are as aware as the French of the importance of policy in the evolution of dominant technological forms. However, where the French are prepared to use policy quite openly as a trade barrier, British industrialists and government bureaucrats are oriented to an apparently more open policy which protects achieved domestic market position and power and opens export markets at the same time. On the pan-European front, the potential adoption of a European high-definition television standard will be carried through as an attempt to maintain Europe as a distinctive market. Whether this is possible in a region of as many languages as Europe and with strong linguistic allegiances is yet to be seen.

Media and audiences

Understanding the cultural implications of law and policy, ownership, professionalism, and technology is relatively straightforward; that is to say, certain policies, practices, and/or technologies favour certain cultural organisations and outlooks. And differences in communication systems between countries both derive from the distinctiveness of their host cultures and provide a foundation for their continuation. However, understanding the cultural implications of audiences as they influence the communicational enterprise is another matter entirely. First, as the multiplicity of approaches to studying audiences suggests, a straightforward and comprehensive method for understanding audiences does not exist, let alone their interaction with the media. Some approaches conceive of audiences as passive and akin to vessels into which media messages can be poured, albeit carefully. Such an approach, while limited in its view of audiences, is not entirely lacking in validity. Its validity arises from the tendencies of audience members at times to use the media as vehicles for escape from the worries of the world and as reliable conduits of important information and analysis. Other approaches conceive of audience members as active meaning negotiators critically engaged in assessing media portrayals and the significance of such portrayals. Still other approaches conceptualise audience/media engagement to emphasise other elements such as gender and cultural identification. In short, understanding the nature of audiences is a complex and multifaceted challenge.

The second constraint that exists in understanding the cultural influence of audiences is that the various models that content producers use to guide them in the creation of media products are a profound influence on the formation and organisation of audiences. To be concrete, programmes are designed for certain groups based on variables such as age, language, taste, nationality, gender and personal orientation. Much less frequently are they designed for groups based on such variables as occupation, ethnicity, cultural background, or political orientation. The hinterland nature of the programme *Northern Exposure*, for example, is expressed primarily through personal and situational idiosyncrasy rather than economic or social marginality. This means that audiences – as opposed to cultural groups – tend to form around the organisational variables of media producers. Thus what might be considered a cultural influence of audiences could be argued to be derived from the choices made by the media in creating content. Real social groups do not organise around the programmes they watch, except in the extreme case of fan clubs.

Thirdly, notwithstanding the constraint that audiences are created by the organisation of the media and media products, comparative audience studies have not been undertaken as attempts to understand the nature of various cultures. The closest that we have come is to such studies is commentary on success rates for global products such as *Dallas, Anne of Green Gables*, or *Robinson Crusoe*. It appears that to carry such commentary further into systematic study is to risk entering a formulation that is currently taboo – the serious discussion of national culture and character.

However, we do understand that audience members are human agents who make specific media choices for particular reasons. Those reasons are as diverse as the reasons for people engaging in any other social activity. In addition to having access to entertainment, enlightenment, or information, media consumption may contribute to social bonding, to individual expression, or a host of other things. As any election campaign demonstrates, members of the public are sophisticated analysts of media presentations. They have a developed ability, after several exposures, to separate presentation from reality. Members of the public also seem to have a growing awareness of themselves as media consumers, especially of television and film. And as that awareness develops, there seems to be a turning away to media that offer a greater variety of information, perspectives and thoughtfulness.

Media content

The specifics or particularities of culture are directly visible in media content. The productions of a culture are the expression of its values and orientation, its legacy to civilisation. Patriarchy, hubris, nurturing, the boundaries of tolerance, the relation of the personal to the social, points of tension that allow for humour – all are cultural indicators.

Cultural production exists in dynamic tension with the society of which it is a part. Light entertainment may re-express the values or realities of society. News and current affairs patrol the boundaries of the acceptable or usual, mostly in the world of business and politics. Works of artistic value provide insight into often unrealised aspects of society. The genius of the artist and of all creative cultural workers is to select what matters, express it in a form that is engaging, and entice the audience to reconsider – to inspire a creation by a creation – to cause a double hermeneutics.

Given that media content so vividly reflects culture it is somewhat peculiar that culture has come forward only recently as a salient element in the interpretation of media production. Is this really so? Consider the status of culture in the approaches to media content that were presented in Chapter 8. In structuralism, post-structuralism and semiotics, culture is at some remove. It may be inferred from the detail of the clusters of signifiers and signifieds but with some difficulty, for often the task of identifying underlying generalities blurs the particular. The central task for all three of these approaches is the identification of underlying generalities to which the particular makes reference or from which the particular draws. The focus is on the creation of meaning and mind, not the warp and woof of social interaction. Lévi-Strauss, for example, makes no attempt to connect the transpositions he observed in myths to any cultural reality: he implies that they are arbitrary. Post-structuralism draws out the vulnerability of this generality-oriented enterprise by pointing to the ephemeral and transitory nature of the subjects and events being examined. But post-structuralism does not carry its inquiry further to an examination of cultural roots of subject viewpoints and embedded events.

Pragmatics, discourse and conversational analysis do better, as do modernism and postmodernism. The difficulty with the first three approaches is that they are tied to situations, to communicative interaction. However, their micro situational concentration tends to produce a framework too particular to take on culture in a satisfactory manner. In the identification of general discourses and patterns, elements of culture can be and certainly are identified and, thereby, these three approaches may make a valuable contribution to an understanding of cultures. However, the articulation of the key elements of a particular culture is certainly not a first concern.

Modernism, while falling into an analysis of the discourses of the elite, opens those discourses from which much can be learned about the ideas that underpin the culture from which they emanate. Postmodernism is referential to both ways of living and styles of expression. It is a commentary on the contemporary human condition. At the level of the larger play of social forces postmodernism has offered insight. Yet at the level of cultural particularity the postmodernist agenda often seems, for its opaqueness, to be modernist in design.

Content analysis concentrates far too greatly and reductively on what is actually said within the confines of a particular article, news organ, dramatic presentation. In being so closely focused on a definable entity it extracts and isolates the ideas from their social context and from the production processes from which they are born. Media form analysis similarly tells us much about media forms but little about the producing culture. Only when we back away from media forms far enough to see their transformative character on their host society *à la* McLuhan can such an approach tell us very much about a host culture. And even then it is at a high level of generality.

So what then do we learn of culture from cultural production? Probably more from the poem than either the poet or the analyst. If we can gain from the analysts we might best turn to the pioneers. The original insights of Propp, the opening salvos of the semiologists, the probes of McLuhan are both crude and delicately insightful. In making fresh cuts into the soil they were forced to deal with fundamentals. Their work can be continuously revisited for insights into the cultural dynamics of Western civilisation.

Geopolitics

The geopolitics of communication and information is a read-out of the interactions of national cultures in a global context. The sites of those interactions are in international agencies and meetings such as Unesco, the International Telecommunications Union, spectrum management conferences, and copyright deliberations. But they are also in the policy and practical decisions that are made within individual countries to produce the patterns of global information and entertainment flows that were presented in Chapter 9. Cultural orientations can also be seen in policy statements and stances. The US insistence on the maximisation of free speech as the sole governing principle in broadcasting and the media is reflective of the individualism of US culture. It also flies in the face of a more measured European position. The US position is reminiscent of the post-World War II attempt by the US government and its media to export their First 'free speech' Amendment to Europe. As Blanchard (1986) notes, the attempt failed because it lacked recognition of the full set of cultural, contextual realities of journalism law and practice.

Patterns of information flows provide a view of historic patterns of international relations. The maintenance of book and other print markets by the UK, for instance, which have now grown to other media markets, are based on old colonial ties. Their survival is both interesting and surprising given, for example, the indolent exploitativeness of British firms in Africa (Gedin, 1991). Essentially the oft-repeated story of educational publishing 'in the colonies' involves a single British company outwardly embracing the goals of indigenous development while privately doing much to maintain a stranglehold on the market. There are those that dispute such a story (see Hill, 1992), and in counterpoint to this exploitation is the 'reasonably objective' public-service orientation of the BBC's World Service. But the surprise is that British Empire geopolitical values continue to be expressed in buying patterns and direct genuflective statements in Commonwealth countries. And similarly, the direct exploitation of markets by France also remains and is tolerated by both former and present French colonies. When these echoes from history are combined with on-going initiatives in spectrum management, information flow policy, geostationary orbit deliberations, actions and interpretations of satellite footprint overspill, it is surprising that the affairs of the global regulatory bodies are not more fractious than they are.

Amidst the politics of the domination of world information and entertainment markets is the new dynamic of computerised point-to-point communication. Think of the power of the telephone, a cheap, commonly available instrument of communication designed for input from anyone, anywhere and possible transmission to anyone else, anywhere else. Add to it the power of the computer – the ability to transmit an encyclopedia in seconds, to store, retrieve, select, organise. The result is a changed communicational dynamic that is individualised, empowering, and text-based. The cultural implications of this changed media environment are profound. Already television and movie production enclaves in Third World countries are emerging for First World markets. No doubt people working in daily contact with potentially the whole world are changing their views of themselves, their country, and their place in the world. And while the new technologies, as the Internet and information highway concept appear to indicate, play into the interests of the mega-corporations, they also may empower smaller people and smaller players. What the future will bring is difficult to say.

A closing note: communication and cultural identity

Many of the major factors that we have been discussing in this book – technological advance, the postmodern condition, national broadcasting systems, cultural industries, established patterns of proprietorship, professionalism, and geopolitics – come together with more general elements of politics, economics and culture to produce what has been called the politics of cultural identity. Cultural identity is based on patterns of information exchange.

We noted in the third paragraph of this book one pattern of information exchange: 'where speech is the only means of communication the group is small, and face to face interactions define and organise the scope of social life'. In modern life, however, a much different pattern of information exchange exists. Most notable is its multiplicity in terms of information sets and communicational processes. Communication in modern life not only pervades the many dimensions of social life (cf. Chapter 2), but also it combines speech with books, newspapers, magazines, television, sound recordings, films, cable, radio, telephones, computers, data processing and transmission, satellites, e-mail, electronic bulletin boards, videotex, insurance and health records, electronic shopping services, credit card information, government databanks, and so forth. Thus not only are communications more complex but also the foundations of social groups are many and varied. Neighbours, work colleagues, community groups, political groups, school-parent groups, professional associations and unions, e-mail discussion groups, subscriber groups, fan-clubs, are all based on different sets of information and a variety of communication processes. Neighbours are defined by geographical space and communicate primarily by face to face communication. E-mail discussion groups are defined by access to electronic networks, are somewhat immune to space variables, and use only computer terminals and text (on screen and on paper) for communication (video is coming, voice is controlled by the telephone companies). In contrast, other groups might be defined by, say, educational experience and use a broad set of means of communication. Professional groups may involve communicational patterns based on face to face interactions, contact with colleagues from school, telephone and group interaction with local colleagues, information exchange based on subscriber groups to professional magazines and journals, national associations, international associations, specialist groups, and so on. And besides all the groups we are aware we belong to are those that may be identified by others. Companies that purchase information packages based on consumption patterns through credit-card usage or health information, subscriber lists, and government databases, may group us into a category of which we are entirely unaware. They may base a sales pitch to us on that basis.

This multiplicity of information sets and communicational processes leads, in social life, to nations made up of a variety of individuals from a host of different backgrounds each of whom, in terms of everyday life, has a multi-faceted cultural identity. Thus as a person gets up in the morning she may juggle the role of mother with a workplace identity, thinking about both as she and her family start the day. She joins a commuter group on the way to the office, served by both a transportation system and of interest to certain advertisers. During the day in the performance of her job she may act as a member of an office peer group, as a professional, a boss, a citizen, a group of

Doc Marten's wearers, an electronic bulletin board subscriber, and so forth. In short, we each live a life of sometimes minute-by-minute shifting identities. Were the question to be asked 'what are the dominant elements of your cultural identity?', who knows what any individual might answer? And two people living parallel lives could easily answer differently.

For every social process there is a politics, a power dynamic, a vying for influence. And so there is a politics of cultural identity, a contestation for influence. For some time, certainly the whole of the twentieth century, those politics of cultural identity beyond the family and the local have been strongly national in character. A primary collectivity to which Europeans and North Americans have made reference is the nation. (Contrast tribal or ethnic loyalties, which make it difficult for African and other European nations such as Yugoslavia to survive.) Exceptions notwithstanding, beyond face to face experience, many people have thought of themselves as belonging to a nation. They have had a fairly deep identification with their country. Such allegiances are no accident – from the time our birth is registered with officialdom we are citizens of a country and its institutions.

But the information environment is changing the balance of allegiances and hence the dynamics of cultural identity. Most notably, allegiances to nation-states appear to be weakening. In some cases, a new consumerism is emerging where buying cheaply is more important than buying the products of one's own country. In other cases what is emerging is an ethnicity that has been suppressed, for example, in Eastern Europe. In the EC, labour mobility laws are combining with encouraged workplace loyalties to emphasise allegiance to the firm and to greater Europe. The connections between expatriot and home communities, in fan-dom, especially of musical forms and sports teams, in formation of audiences that are responses to market specialisation of magazines and specialty television channels, all disregard national boundaries.

What role does communication play? Generally speaking, as the magazine-television channel example above indicates, communication contributes to a new politics of cultural identity through the re-formation of audiences. The passing or weakening of national television monopolies, national film industries, national newspapers, national magazines and book publishing, and their replacement with pan-national or global entities, some of which are general but even more of which are specialised, at least in the developed world, is substantial in its influence. In the information environment the individual consumer, professional, tradesperson, and so on is served more thoroughly as a consumer, professional, or tradesperson, than he is in terms of his location or citizenship. While certain institutions – the state, the courts, the schools, and the remnants of public broadcasters – serve citizenship, cultural industries, especially when they are entertainment industries, do so less and less. TV-carrying satellites, films, and the recording industry, to name three clear examples, serve consumer-taste clusters that have been developed and defined by the production forms of the entertainment sector. There are parallel spaced-based phenomena. Los Angeles is the third largest American city. European financial transactions are centred in London. European political-economic bargaining is focused on Brussels. The third largest English-language publishing industry is in India. Enclaves again (cf. Chapter 9) but this time not production enclaves.

The admonition of the environmentalists to 'think globally and act locally', which encourages a transnational cultural identity, takes on a different meaning in this context. As national institutions weaken through economic integration and through migration, individuals may do well to orient themselves to their village and to the wider world, paying less attention to national governments who have very limited abilities to act decisively. Citizens of the developed world can afford what Brazilian peasants cannot – to be concerned with the Brazilian rain forest. Feminists of the developed world are politically and culturally enfranchised to a sufficient extent that they can be concerned about the position of women around the world.

This swirl of changing elements in cultural identities and its attendant politics have been discussed in a particular context by Richard Collins (1990). He has argued that the dependence of nations for their continued existence on a congruence in political institutions, the structure of the economy, and cultural production has not been proven. He argues his point using Canada as a case-study, pointing out that Canadians have, since the advent of broadcasting, first listened to and then watched at least as much American programming as Canadian, certainly more if we focus on light entertainment and drama. Yet Canada survives. I have challenged this reading of Canada and its media environment elsewhere (Lorimer, 1991). But more important than whether Collins is correct in his analysis is that the shift in the communications industries from nationally-mandated, publicly-oriented and -owned institutions to commercial pan-national entities (which itself is encouraged by national laws and policies [cf. Lorimer and O'Donnell, 1992]) is changing local, national, and international cultural landscapes and thus cultural identities.

In societies with built-in allegiances to the dominant group and dominant ideology – the Anglican, white, middle class – many are marginalised, sometimes abhorrently through ethnic cleansing. Within a commerce that is oriented to segmented markets, and within a society that affirms pluralism, marginality may become more akin to a node on a neural network – a point where certain information and realities are processed, dealt with and fed back into the neural net, which is not dominated by a central overarching control. However, non-consuming marginal groups may not be served at all and may atrophy. (Not all can be left to commerce.) The important point is that the attractiveness of the emerging politics of cultural identity is not predetermined by its structure (i.e., decentralisation and plurality over centralisation and a dominant identity) but rather the elements that make up that structure (tolerance, resentments, social policy, and so forth). What appears most sure is that plurality is part of the contemporary condition. Perhaps the reason why the backlash to this contemporary condition as seen in religious fundamentalism and ethnic upheavals is so virulent is that its presence is so real and so apparently threatening – just as the theory of evolution was seen as threatening to Christianity.

As we enter the twenty-first century there is sure to be both a lively argument and an aggressive staking of claims. The media moguls have already prepared themselves – for battles with each other and for a struggle with states who might pare them back through national laws. There is a real need for policy and planning for, at least for the moment, most of the power to affect the social and cultural environment beyond the local, through the provision of information, enlightenment and entertainment, is vested in nations. Should nations, or organisations of nations, step aside, the field would be left to commerce. And whatever one might want to say about commerce, as Jane Jacobs (1992) argues, it is probably not the sector to be entrusted with balancing all the interests of society. Should states retain a position of influence and should they use that position to foster the articulation of a multiplicity of realities as they are known, believed to be, and experienced, and within a positive pluralism, we might very easily have a delightful future.

Summary

In this concluding chapter we have revisited the main issues of this book from a cultural perspective. We have noted throughout that every aspect of communication is intimately connected to its parent culture, at the same time noting the formative influence of communication on that culture. The influence or interpenetration begins at the most fundamental level, involving the invention and use of oral, print and text, audio, and audio-visual communication forms. It continues through the institutionalisation, professionalisation, legal, policy, ownership and technological foundations of communication as they are played out in each country. These factors in concert form an infrastructure for the creation and consumption of information and entertainment, the quintessential cultural manifestation of modern mass communications. This information and entertainment is then exported and imported around the world, both augmenting and dissipating the cultures in which it takes up residence. The contemporary world is abuzz with change. Both the content and form of communication are contributing to changing cultural identities. There is a continuing need for them to do so within a framework which both recognises and affirms changing social realities.

References

Blanchard, Margaret A. (1986), *Exporting the First Amendment: The Press Government Crusade of 1945–1952*, Longman, New York.

Collins, Richard (1990), *Culture, Communication and National Identity: The Case of Canadian Television*, University of Toronto Press, Toronto.

Gedin, Per, I. (1991), 'Private enterprise publishing in Africa', *Logos*, 2 (3), pp. 133–9.

Hill, Alan (1992), 'British publishers' contribution to African literature', *Logos*, 3, pp. 45–53.

Jacobs, Jane (1992), *Systems of Survival: A Dialogue on the Moral Foundations of Commerce and Politics*, Random House, New York.

Lorimer, Rowland (1991), 'Review of *Culture, Communication and National Identity*', *Media Culture and Society*, 13, pp. 581–3.

Lorimer, Rowland and Eleanor O'Donnell (1992), 'Globalization and internationalization in publishing', *Canadian Journal of Communication*, 17, pp. 493–509.

Martinez, Andrea, *Scientific Knowledge about Television Violence*, CRTC, Ottawa: nd.

Miller, James (1990), 'France confronts the new media', in S. Thomas (ed.), *Communication and Culture: Studies in Communication*, vol. 4, Norwood, NJ, pp. 325–41.

Smith, Anthony (1991), *The Age of Behemoths: The Globalization of Mass Media Firms*, Priority Press, New York.

Tiessen, Paul (1993), 'From literary modernism to the Tantramar Marshes: anticipating McLuhan in British and Canadian media theory and practice', *Canadian Journal of Communication*, 18 (4), pp. 451–68.

Glossary

ABC American Broadcasting Corporation, a major US radio and television network

access, free the provision of unimpeded availability of, e.g., information

addressability the ability to send electronic signals to a particular location, as in the telephone system

advertorial an advertisement written in editorial form and presented as normal journalism

advocacy advertisement a position statement on a social issue paid for by a corporation

affiliates privately-owned television or radio stations associated with either publicly- or privately-owned networks

AFP Agence France Presse, a French wire service operated with the assistance of the French government

agenda setting determining priorities, usually of governments by the media

airwaves the atmosphere, space though which radio waves pass

aligned (non-aligned) countries that are, or are not, politically aligned with a superpower

AM amplitude modulation

Amnets American (television) networks

amortise reduce to zero the original research, development and initial or set-up production costs of the production of a commodity

analytic/descriptive journalism the relative balance between analysis and description in any piece of reportage

AP Associated Press, an American news agency

ATT American Telephone and Telegraph, a US telephone and communications hardware conglomerate

audience people who read books or other materials, watch television, listen to radio, go to performances, etc.; people who consume media, cultural or informational products

audience share, reach and viewing time (see **share**, **reach** and **viewing time**)

Audio-visual Eureka plan a Council of Europe policy for strengthening the television production capacity of countries of the European Community

auteur **theory** a theory of textual interpretation that relates a work to the author and to the body of work produced by that author; in film the author is taken to be the director, not the script-writer

BBC British Broadcasting Corporation

BBC model an approach to broadcasting based on a national public monopoly with an accompanying mandate to serve the public interest

behemoth extremely large beast or corporation

Berne Convention the basis of international copyright law requiring,

amongst other things, that foreign
authors be treated in the same way as
domestic authors and that there be a
minimum number of years of
protection of a copyrighted work

bias, media the emphasis which a
particular medium places on a certain
selection of content elements, e.g.,
pictures by television

Birmingham School the media
commentators of the Centre for
Contemporary Cultural Studies at the
University of Birmingham, who
developed the Marxist-derived school
of thought which evolved into cultural
studies

blasphemy contemptuous speaking or
writing against religious deities

borrowing power the ability to obtain
loans

bourgeoisie the business class

broadcast to send out a radio signal via
the airwaves intended for the reception
of any within a certain radius of the
transmitter

broadcast licence permission given by an
authorised government body to
persons or organisations to carry out
broadcast activities

burden of proof in Western law the
accused is presumed innocent until
proven guilty and therefore the burden
of proof rests with the accusers,
usually the state; in libel law – after it
has been shown that certain words
were written without authorisation
and that they could be potentially
damaging – the burden of proof rests
with the person accused of libel to
show that words written are not
libellous

buy-outs the purchase of operational
companies

cable 1. usually coaxial cable used to
bring television and radio signals to
home from a central transmitter (and

receiver) of signals; 2. the industry
which provides cable services.

calumny a false or malicious statement
designed to injure someone's
reputation

CANA Caribbean News Association

Canadianisation the creation of a
balance of TV programming and
media products in which imported
content far outweighs domestic
content

capitalism a system of commerce based
on the freedom of individuals to own
and control property and to hire others
for wages; a form of society deriving
from this system of economic
organisation

carriage the carrying of communication,
e.g. as done by telephone companies,
as opposed to content; in regulation a
distinction is drawn in order to discuss,
for instance, the carriage and the
content activities of a television
network

CAT computer-assisted teaching

causality the state of being a result or
effect of something else

CBC Canadian Broadcasting
Corporation, the publicly-owned
national television and radio network

CBS Columbia Broadcasting System, a
major US radio and television network

CD compact disc (containing digital
signals)

cellular composed of different cells or
electronic sending and receiving units
that can function unhindered by the
different functioning of other cells
adjacent to them

censorship preventing the expression of
ideas and/or information

chain a group of horizontally integrated
companies, as in a group of
newspapers owned by the same
company

CIS Confederation of Independent
States, states that have elected to

confederate with Russia to form a new grouping following the collapse of the USSR

classic narrative a story that has a beginning, middle and end and in which the movement of the narrative is strongly organised towards the resolution of the story's riddle, or enigma

CNC Centre National du Cinéma, French organisation providing assistance to film-makers

CNN Cable News Network based in Atlanta, Georgia, owned by Ted Turner

cognitive pertaining to thought

Colbertism the involvement of the state in a contributory manner in the affairs of people and business enterprises giving rise to subtle state control

collectivities groups

colonial ties trade and other relations between empires (centres) and colonies (hinterlands)

colonisation the transforming of a region or nation into a colony administered and serving the interests of the nation or group that brings about the transformation

columnist person, usually an established reporter or known expert, who provides either information or analysis, or both. The columnist brings a personal interpretation to events and attracts an audience because of that personal orientation or interpretation

commercial media outlets outlets that are owned by private groups or individuals and exist as profit-seeking enterprises

commodification the transformation of things, events, people into products that can be consumed, e.g. movie stars

commodities things one can purchase

communication, communications 1. sending, giving or exchanging information, the spreading of

intelligence; 2. the media organisations involved in 1.

communications hardware equipment such as radios, television, satellites, wire, cable, etc.

competition policy government-enacted rules and laws designed to ensure that the interests of the consumer are served by the promotion of competition in the market-place

Complaints Commission a body set up to receive complaints about the press or broadcasting that may be either voluntary or gain its authority from a government act

concentration of ownership the growing restrictiveness of proprietorship to a few large corporations

conductor a substance capable of transmitting an electric current

conglomerate a company that combines a variety of linkages, usually inclusive of horizontally- and vertically-integrated companies and sometimes cross-ownership; a media conglomerate does the majority of its business in the media, a general or non-media conglomerate has its foundation in non-media firms; a company which contains within it many companies carrying on a variety of businesses not necessarily related to one another

connotative implying, as opposed to naming directly

consent (within libel law) the plaintiff assented to publication of the words in dispute

consortium a group, usually of institutions, gathered together for a common purpose

constitutional derivative from a country's constitution

consumer-led products that come to market as a result of an analysis of the real or potential wants and needs of consumers

consumerism an orientation which emphasises the role of the individual as a consumer or purchaser of goods and services

content what is expressed in any medium and how it is expressed

content analysis a quantitative technique that sets up units of analysis – phrases, sentences, nouns, verbs, adjectives, paragraphs, column inches, placement, accompanying illustrations, categories of spokespersons quoted or cited – sometimes within a thematic context, counts them, and discusses them as indicative of the true meaning and perspective of a communication

contestation a vying or competition as in a contest

contextual taking account of the surrounding concepts and ideas in which, for example, a word is used

contextualisation placing something in its appropriate surround or environment

conversational analysis interpretation of social interaction and communication based on a conversation model, e.g. taking turns in speaking, maintaining and changing topics, and obeying other implicit rules

copyright the exclusive right to reproduce a work; this right belongs to the author and is composed of a property right, which may be assigned to others, and a moral right, which may not be assigned but may be waived

corporate image advertisement an advertisement designed to promote a company, perhaps as a responsible corporate citizen, rather than its products

Council of Europe body based in Strasbourg, France, founded in 1949. Aims to achieve greater unity between its 31 members and 7 'special guests' of the CIS, to safeguard their European heritage, facilitate economic and social progress through discussion and common action in economic, social, cultural, educational, scientific, legal and administrative matters, and maintain and further pluralist democracy, human rights and fundamental freedoms. Organs are Comittee of Ministers, consisting of the foreign ministers of member countries, and Parliamentary Assembly 212 members elected or chosen by the national parliaments of member countries in proportion to the relative strength of political parties. The Council has a broad mandate, compared with the EC's limited economic mandate. Among its achievements are the European Convention of Human Rights (1950)

critical linguistics a mix of ideology theory (dealing with class, gender, race and equality) and semiotics (objects, referents and larger meaning systems) as found, for instance, in cultural studies

cross-ownership ownership of more than one media enterprise in the same market in more than one medium, e.g. newspapers and radio

cross subsidisation the subsidising, usually by a single company, of one service, e.g., local telephone calls, from profits made on another service, e.g., long-distance calls

crowd see **small group**

CRTC Canadian Radio-television and Telecommunications Commission, Canada's regulatory body for broadcasting and telecommunications

cultivation analysis an examination of content for the way in which it may encourage or cultivate a positive attitude in the audience member towards a particular person or perspective

cultural allegiances the loyalty a person feels towards particular social or cultural groups

cultural colonisation the subordination of one culture to another

cultural development social change which builds on established cultural patterns reflecting the particular ideals of a culture

cultural diversity the many different characteristics of the people of a country or culture; a term usually used to describe a government policy designed to encourage citizens of a country to affirm their distinctive backgrounds

cultural identity the defining characteristics of a culture

cultural imperialism the tendency of one culture to export its ideas and values to other countries with the effect of undermining the cultural values of the recipient country

cultural industries companies engaged in the production of commodities that reflect and develop societal values, e.g. publishing, film making, sound recording

cultural production the writing and publishing of books, performance of plays and music, the mounting of exhibitions, as well as the holding of public gatherings in which people may entertain, enlighten or inform one another

cultural studies a field of study derived from a Marxist perspective that extended the analysis of class to race and gender and that, in general, examined the nature of the cultural relations of the society being studied

cynicism a negative or sneering approach focused on finding fault

DAT Digital Audio Tape, a consumer technology that allows the recording of sound by digital means in the home

databank see database

database a compilation of retrievable information, usually in electronic form and accessible by computer

DBS Direct Broadcast Satellite, a geostationary communications satellite that receives signals from earth and sends them back with sufficient strength to be received by homeowners

decency not pandering to vicious instincts

decoding to receive an expressed idea and to interpret it; the act of an audience member putting an encoded idea into their own terms

defamation injuring a person's good reputation by means of insults, or interference with the course of justice

deixis the contextual character of utterance (in discourse analysis)

democratic ideal the emancipation of the individual through the granting of such rights as free speech

demographic 1. related to the statistical study of populations; 2. (n) a group that may be identified through statistical analysis of populations

denotative simply naming, not implying

deskilling simplifying jobs, usually with technology, so that the level of skills required are downgraded and thus skills are lost

diachronic change over a period of time

dialectical examining truth or validity by question and answer

digital expression in digits, i.e. 0s and 1s

digitisation the coding of information in digits

discourse analysis a form of analysis oriented to media patterns and conventions, or what category of person uses what conventions in which context to mean what

discursive pertaining to discourse

disinformation untrue, trivial or irrelevant information

disinterested uninvolved but not uninterested

distribution a key element in communications and cultural industries that may make or break companies, domestic or international products

doctrinaire following a doctrine without full consideration of the practical implications

doctrine the principles or tenets of a point of view or school of thought

dogma the often rigid application of principles sometimes to situations beyond their applicability

dominant ideology the set of ideas that is commonly used to explain events in society

dramaturgical an approach to understanding social activity that derives from the theatre, from directing a play

droit d'auteur French copyright law founded on those human, personal or moral rights most strongly expressed as perpetual, inalienable and imprescriptible. Perpetual rights forbids anyone at any time claiming ownership, or 'paternity' of a work, or destroying its 'integrity' by unfaithful reproduction, distortion or multilation. Inalienability of personal rights means they cannot be sold or otherwise transferred to another person, although they may be waived. Imprescriptibility forbids the taking away of such rights by any state or other authority

duopoly exclusive control over the supply of a market by two companies

economic system the sum total of rules, laws and regulations which govern the affairs of commerce; the system that deals with the allocation of scarcity

economies of scale efficiencies in costs that can be achieved via repetition of

some aspects of the production process and deletion of others, e.g., printing 10,000 copies of a book once the presses have been set up instead of 1,000

ecu the unit of currency for the European Community

editor person who creates a package of information based on the efforts of others such as reporters. Editors may have limited responsibilities, e.g. the city editor, whereas the Editor (in chief) takes overall responsibility for the editorial content of the newspaper, magazine or news programme. (Copy editors are the exception to this definition. Their responsibilities are to ensure that the material is presented in the best way possible.) The designation 'editor' is applied differently in book publishing, but the basic principle of creating a coherent package of information is the same

editorial independence the freedom of editors to act independently and not to be influenced by advertisers or media owners

editorialisation editorial comment

educational infrastructure 1. the basic framework of education, e.g., institutions, learning materials, teachers; 2. the provision of usually free education by societies resulting in its members acquiring the understandings, skills, and attitudes they require to be productive members of society

EFE the Spanish news service

effects research observing impact of the media on human behaviour

egalitarian oriented to equality

electrification the transformation of society or information processing into electrical form, in contrast to, say, print on paper

electromagnetic wave a wave propagated through space by simultaneous periodic variation in the electric and magnetic field intensity at right angles to each other and to the direction of propagation; a radio signal, television signal, or light wave

elite the few who are considered superior or more powerful in a group

embedded taking account of the surround (of context)

encoding to formulate an idea, to put an idea into a symbolic system, for example, language, or a television programme

Enlightenment an intellectual movement of 18th-century Europe that questioned tradition and emphasised the primacy of reason

enlightenment causing an audience member to see something in a different light or from a different perspective so that he or she gains further insight or understanding

entrepreneurs persons who engage in new activities or undertakings usually, but not necessarily, of a commercial nature

epic a long narrative story or poem done in a grand style with a focus on heros and heroines

erotica literature, photographs, paintings, etc. intended to be sexually stimulating

essentialist reduced to the bare bones or 'supposed' essential elements

étatisme political theory that sees social and economic matters as primary responsibility of the state. Usually refers to France, where the state participates both as a public sector entity and in the private sector through partial ownership of commercial ventures

ethics, journalistic the set of ideals, rules of conduct, duties and responsibilities of journalists; the literature that deals with the contribution of journalists to the media enterprise

ethnocentric a point of view derived from one's own culture and experience

ethnography the detailed description of social behaviour, usually of a group or setting

ethnomethodology an investigative method designed to uncover the implicit rules of behaviour in a particular social setting

European Community customs union first established among six countries and later extended to another six European nations (as of 1992). Intended to remove all obstacles to the free movement of capital, goods, people and services between member states; to allow for the creation of a common external trade policy and common policies for agriculture and fisheries. The institutional infrastructure, centred in Brussels, is composed of the Commission, the Council of Ministers, the Economic and Social Committee, the European Investment Bank, the Parliament, and the Court of Justice. Its revenue is partially derived from duties collected at the external frontier of the EC and a proportion of national receipts from the VATs of members

Expressionism a modernist school of art concerned with the impermanence of modern life and the exploration of form; intended to convey direct expression of feeling or emotion, e.g. van Gogh, Strindberg

facsimile transmission electronic transmission, usually via telephone lines, of printed matter by means of a technology dating back to an 1843 patent

fair access provision to individuals (households or businesses) of telephone and telecommunications services at a price that takes into account what others must pay, as distinct from what it might cost a utility to provide a service to a particular location

fair comment (within libel law) fair and bona fide comment on a matter of public interest

fair play media operations in which unofficial charges are not published, private rights are not invaded 'without sure warrant of public right as distinguished from public curiosity', and the duty to correct promptly and completely is acknowledged.

Falklands Islands islands off the coast of Argentina, also known as the Malvinas, that belong to Britain

federal the national government of federated states, i.e. those having states within a larger national state

Federal Communications Commission (FCC) the US broadcasting regulatory body

fetishisation excessive preoccupation with an object or thing

Fininvest the main holding company of Italian investor, Silvio Berlusconi

First Amendment the 'free speech amendment' in the US constitution, stating that Congress shall pass no law limiting freedom of speech

fixed satellite services closed systems, not intended to be accessed by the general public, used to transport signals from one point to another on earth, e.g. from an uplink programme provider to a cable company that then distributes the signal to its customers

flagship an operation providing a quality or upmarket service that serves to demonstrate the ability of the company to provide quality service

flow, information a summary concept describing the imports and exports of goods, specifically information and entertainment products

footprint the area of the earth within which a satellite signal can be received

at a certain strength

Fordism the production of a limited selection of commodities via assembly line techniques. Henry Ford (1863–1947), after whom Fordism is named, was also known for paying his workers relatively high wages

foreground literally, the front (opp. background); may be used as a verb to indicate the emphasis placed on something

fourth estate the media, as distinct from the church, landowners and bourgeoisie. The OED defines an estate as an 'order or class forming part of the body politic and sharing in government'

fragmenting segmenting, dividing into parts

frame both a noun and a verb drawing attention to the boundaries that a picture, story, or other means of communication places on that to which it refers

franchise an independently-owned business operation licensed to operate under a generic name, e.g. McDonald's

Frankfurt School a school of thought led by three German intellectuals, Max Horkheimer, Theodor Adorno and Herbert Marcuse, who argued that cultural life in modern times has been profoundly changed by the impact of capitalist methods of mass production

Freedom of or Access to Information Acts statutes providing for the accessibility of government information; in the UK and derivative systems government information, to which citizens can request access, belongs to the Crown; in the US government information belongs to the people and they may demand access to it

freedom of speech the right of any individual to speak freely on matters of concern without fear of retribution

freedom of the press 1. the freedom of the press and other media to exercise the right to free speech, usually in the name of the public good; 2. the freedom of press and other media owners to pursue market interests unhindered by the state

freenets electronic, computer based, message and information systems accessible by anyone with access to a computer for no charge

gatekeeper a person who controls access to media publication or broadcast, and shapes what gains access according to the identity or character of the media outlet for whom he or she works

GATT General Agreement on Tariffs and Trade, an international agreement aimed at bringing about freer trade around the world

generic products products that do not claim to be a special brand of something, e.g., plain, unbranded or unnamed soap

geopolitics politics as they are affected by geography

geostationary orbit an orbit situated directly over the equator in which objects rotating around the earth are always in a fixed location relative to the earth

geosynchronous orbit an orbit twice the distance of geostationary orbit which similarly allows for objects to remain in a fixed position relative to the earth

GHz gigahertz, a radio frequency unit equal to 1,000 million cycles per second

glass fibres see **optical fibres**

global village the organisation of society brought about by the possibility of instant communication between any two or more points in the world

globalisation the transformation of an activity to take into account a world-wide orientation

GNP gross national product, the total value of all goods produced by a nation

Gramsci, Antonio an Italian Marxist social theorist best known for the concept of hegemony

grand narratives all-inclusive stories that claim to explain the underlying or true meaning of a society

Gulf War the war of 1990 between certain Western military forces led by the US and legitimised by a UN resolution against Iraq after its invasion of Kuwait

Gutenberg, Johannes the first person in the Western world to use movable type, i.e. individual letters that can be used to typeset one page and then used again to typeset the next page

Havas a news agency based in Germany

HBO Home Box Office, a US movie channel

hemispheric related to a half of the world, i.e. western, eastern, northern, southern

hermeneutics the science of interpreting meaning

heterogeneous composed of difference (opp. homogeneous, meaning the same)

high culture the representation through art, literature, behaviour, custom of the values of elites or of the ideals of those who control society, often including conscious experimentation with the form of expression

high-definition television has more than twice the number of lines in its picture than conventional television (525 lines in North America; 625 in Europe). It is also wider and a greater amount of definition in the picture is achieved due to greater density of lines in the same space. The picture is clearer and can be made larger before it begins to appear grainy.

hinterland a geographical area, activities

of which are organised in relation to a metropolitan centre

homogeneous made up of similar parts

horizontal integration a group of companies all carrying on the same business, allowing for economies of scale by efficiencies through the streamlining of in-common needs

house agreement a set of rules that apply to a particular media outlet

hubris pride, particularly pride that is overweening, overambitious, scornful, or transgressive of moral law

human agency the notion that human beings control their behaviour through purposive action

human rights the freedoms that are or should be granted to all individuals in every society according to the Declaration of Human Rights

hyperreality acutely presented or perceived reality

hypothetical entities, things or processes that are believed to exist but that are difficult to prove the existence of

icon 1. a revered or sacred object of the Eastern church; 2. a visual, highly meaningful image by virtue of it referring to much other than itself

iconic pertaining to visual images

ideological vehicle the use of a media outlet for purposes of stressing a particular set of ideas

ideology a coherent set of social values, beliefs, meanings; in Marxist terms it is a critical concept that refers particularly to dominant or ruling class values, beliefs and meanings, which came to be called the dominant ideology

impartial unbiased

imperialism actions taken towards the end of building and maintaining an empire

implicatures implied meanings

Impressionism a modernist school of art

oriented to expressing the impermanence of modern life and involving the exploration of form; intended to convey subtle moods and impressions as they appear to the artist at the moment of creation, e.g. Monet, Manet, Renoir

indeterminacy of representation the inability to fully and completely account for or describe something

indexicality the connection of an element to a larger whole, i.e. as signifier to sign

indigenous original to a region, in contrast to people, animals, objects, etc. introduced later

individualisation tending towards serving the needs of individuals

industrial capitalism the form of society which developed in countries in which the main activity was industrial production and the control of that activity was in the hands of capitalists, i.e. the business or commercial sector as opposed to the state or the landed gentry

Industrial Revolution the transformation of the major activity of human society from agriculture to manufacturing of goods

industrialisation move towards manufacturing and commodity production, e.g. from agricultural production

inferential the drawing of inferences or conclusions

informatics the combination of computers and electronic transmission of information

information environment the sum total of what information is available, in what form, through what means, accessible via what procedures, and for what cost

information sets groupings of information dealing with a particular subject from a certain number of sources

information sovereignty the ability of a nation or community to control the dissemination of information across and within its own boundaries to preserve its cultural integrity and distinctiveness while maintaining basic human rights freedoms to seek, receive and impart information

infrastructure the necessary capacities underlying a particular activity, e.g. roads for the distribution of goods

innuendo a statement injurious to a person's reputation on the basis of reasonable imputation that might be made; when confined to a group with special knowledge this is referred to as legal innuendo

institutional audience research research that provides useful information about audiences usually for media institutions, e.g. on reach, share, demographic character, etc.

institutional feudalism the domination of an activity by an institution in such a way that the institution can control the activities of individuals

Integrated Services Digital Network see **ISDN**

integrity in copyright law, the characteristic(s) of the work that makes it a whole and what it is; an author has the moral right to protect the integrity of his or her work and to prevent others from using it in ways of which she or he disapproves because it changes the nature or denigrates the work

intellectual property the set of rights that accrue to an author by virtue of the work expended in the creation of a literary, dramatic, artistic, or musical work

intellectual sovereignty the development of ideas in a manner not directly derivative from the ideas of other societies

INTELSAT the consortium of companies, many national telecom companies, that own and operate a set of satellites used to beam signals between countries

intentionality done by choice and with purpose

Interfax a non-state news agency founded in September 1989 as a faxed bulletin of Radio Moscow and a Soviet–French–Italian joint venture known for political news, exclusive interviews, business and macroeconomic information; it publishes 21 periodical bulletins in Russian and English, with a staff of 420 in the former Communist bloc, 220 of whom are in Moscow; it has 60 foreign subscribers

International Telecommunications Union (ITU) UN-sanctioned international organisation of nation-members of the International Telecommunications Convention, founded in 1865. Function is to develop telecommunications, allocate the radio frequency spectrum and regulate telecommunications at the international level

internationalisation tending towards the international, when used in contrast to globalisation the term refers to a balance of trade between countries as opposed to a centralised control of production usually overseen by multinationals

interpenetration elements of one thing becoming part of another and vice versa

intertextuality pertaining to the referential character of texts; the meaning of phrases, ideas, and points of view derives from the manner in which related ideas, phrases or points of view have been explored in other intellectual works

inverted pyramid the presentation of a story in a form in which 'who, what,

when, where, why, how and so what'
are addressed at the beginning,
followed by the development of the
story and the context in which it
happened

invisible hand the notion proposed by
Adam Smith that the market-place
works in the best interests of society in
general by encouraging individuals to
pursue their own self-interest and
economic opportunity

Iridium a hypothetical system proposed
by Motorola to launch a flock of 77
low-orbiting satellites that would
allow customers to use pocket phones
to phone from anywhere to anywhere
on the earth's surface

ISDN Integrated Services Digital
Network, a set of international
standards for digital signals of all
types, carrying voice, data, facsimile,
video, etc. to ensure compatibility and
encouraging technological
convergence

ITAR (or **ITAR-TASS**) the much cut-
back and renamed (from TASS)
Russian news agency (Information
Telegraph Agency of Russia),
apparently now operating without
KGB personnel under its cover; most
bureaus in Africa and Asia have been
closed as well as some in Russian
towns; it has about 3,500 employees,
900 of whom are journalists, with 75
based in foreign countries; it has 120
subscriber-customers in foreign
countries. A separate organisation,
Novosti, provides news and features.

ITC Independent Television
Commission (of the UK)

ITU see International
Telecommunications Union

jump cuts a sudden change of shot from
one camera position to another

justification (within libel law) true in
substance and in fact

Khomeini the Ayatollah that replaced the
Pahlavi Shah of Iran

kHz kilohertz, a radio frequency unit
equal to 1,000 cycles per second

Kipling, Rudyard a British writer known
for his enthusiastic eloquence on the
British Empire

knowledge infrastructure the sum total
of information, skills and
understandings that have been
acquired to allow the operation of, say,
a television station

Ku Klux Klan a US-based secret society
of men who profess Protestantism and
white supremacy

Kyodo the Japanese news agency

langue the shared language system which
we use to generate individual
utterances

lead the opening of a story

lexical elements the words of a story, the
elements of a story

libel 1. a published written statement that
does damage to the good reputation of
a person; in France and the US libel can
express true facts, in the UK and
derivative systems truth is an absolute
defence against an accusation of libel;
2. any false or insulting statement

libel chill the threat, real or imagined,
under which authors and publishers
live that they will be accused of libel
and need to expend considerable sums
of money to defend themselves

liberal not subject to common prejudices
or conventions nor strongly tied to
traditions, especially the rule of
elites

liberal pluralism an approach to society
which affirms a variety of perspectives
within a range consonant with the way
in which a society, usually a capitalist
society, is organised

libertarian a doctrine stressing the liberty
or freedom of the individual, not to be
confused with liberal

lifestyle advertising advertising that depicts an idealised way of living, which usually includes an emphasised depiction of a consumer product

linear comes from line, progress along a single line

linkages (forward and backward) supply or demand connections between producers

literacy the ability to read and write

literary criticism the analysis of literature, at times dealing with the effectiveness of the author in creating his or her intended response and at other times descriptive of the referential framework from which the author drew in creating the text

lived reality life as it is experienced; ordinary behaviour

loss-leader attractive item likely to be sold in quantity that is sold at below normal mark-up, and sometimes below actual cost, in order to attract customers, who also spend money on other goods priced with normal retailer's mark-ups

Luxembourgian refers to the relatively undemanding character of the regulation of media operations allowing for companies based in that country to pursue commercial imperatives with little hindrance by the government of Luxembourg

macro societal at the level of society as a whole

Madison Avenue the street in New York where many advertising agencies are located, often used to mean the advertising industry

magnates persons who have considerable financial and business holdings

mandate a responsibility given legally or via another outside authority to pursue a certain purpose, as in cultural mandate, to pursue cultural ends as opposed, for example, to economic ends

Marconi, Guglielmo (1874–1937) inventor of radio telegraphy, which was the first electronic means for the transmission of intelligence

market theory the general approach to commerce that takes the position that a free market is the most efficient way of serving the best interests of the largest number (see also **invisible hand**)

marketplace of ideas the notion that trade in commodities, in this case intellectual property, is an appropriate arbiter of the value of ideas to society

Marxism an approach to studying society that derives from the writings of Karl Marx, who emphasised the control of the means of production as a fundamental dividing element in society separating and placing in conflict the interests of workers and capitalists

mass audience a convenient shorthand term for the great numbers of people who constitute the 'mass entertainment' audience; rather than being conceived as homogeneous, vulnerable, and passive, the mass audience is better conceived as a great number of individuals of heterogeneous backgrounds who use the media for a great variety of purposes

mass communication 1. the practice and product of providing leisure entertainment and information to an unknown audience by means of corporately financed, industrially produced, state regulated, high technology, privately consumed commodities in the modern print, screen, audio and broadcast media; 2. communication to large audiences

mass culture the representation through a variety of means of the characteristics of the mainstream of society, often seen as an aggregate

meaning-generating entity something existing that is complete in itself which seeks information, processes it, and may act on or in relation to it

media form, media content a differentiation that draws attention to the influence of both the medium in which something is expressed and what is expressed

media vehicles, second-order mass media items of media content that become capable of carrying other items into the mass market

media/cultural binding the adhering of media to the culture in which they reside or in which they display products through presentation of elements of that culture

melodrama a story that is sensational, artificial and exaggerated in terms of characters, action and setting; remote from everyday reality

mezzo institutional, e.g., the media, the mass audience

MHz megahertz, a radio frequency unit equal to 1 million cycles per second

micro individual, e.g., an audience member

minder person charged with ensuring appropriate behaviour in another; in the context of the media and the military, a member of the military who supervises journalists to ensure that they obey the set restrictions under which they are allowed to work

modernism literary and artistic expressions of the experience of modernity which attempted to resist its influence by avoiding easy appreciation and consumption

modernity modern life which, some say, is characterised by continual change

modernisation the creation of urban, industrial societies through economic, political and social transformations

mogul someone with conspicuous

power or influence in a defined area of activity

monopoly exclusive control over the supply of a particular product for a market

monopoly, natural regulated exclusive control of supply which has been granted by society because competition seems wasteful. In compensation society usually assumes a watchdog or regulatory role to oversee the monopoly's activities in the name of the consumer interest

moral rights the set of rights associated with intellectual property that are vested in the creator by virtue of a work being originated by the creator; moral rights may be held, waived but not assigned to any other person; moral rights are distinct from property rights and are not taken to be material, most often they are associated with the integrity of the work

multiculturalism a policy designed to promote the development of a variety of cultures within a larger context, usually a nation; policies to encourage citizens to affirm their cultural roots

multifaceted many sided

multilinguality policies directed at providing services in more than one language

multinational corporations corporations that operate in more than one country, also known as transnationals

Myanmar Burma

mythologies a set of stories relating to a people, their gods, heroes and origins

NAFTA the North American Free Trade Agreement (between Canada, the US and Mexico) in which 'culture' was said to be off the table between Canada and the US, allowing Canada to assist the development of cultural industries

nation-state a sovereign political unit composed of a body of people who

share linguistic, historical and ethnic
heritage

national public monopoly a monopoly
given to a publicly-owned corporation
to serve the needs of a nation in a
certain area of activity, e.g. telephone
service

National Socialists the German Nazi
party

NBC National Broadcasting
Corporation, a major US television
and radio network

networks a group of television or radio
stations, not necessarily owned by the
same person, that group together for
mutual benefit

newsmaker person who tends to be the
subject of news reports and/or
commentary

newsworthiness the characteristics of
occurrences, events, and people that
make them likely to appear in the news

NFB National Film Board (of Canada), a
government-owned corporation that
produces films, mainly shorter than
feature films

NHK the Japanese public broadcast
company

non-representational art art that does not
depict objects as they may be seen in
reality

North and South a manner of
differentiating poor (developing) and
rich (developed) countries derived
from the fact that the former are
mostly in the Southern hemisphere
while the latter are mostly in the
Northern hemisphere

numeric pertaining to numbers

objectivity having a real, substantial
existence outside the point of view,
emotions, or imagination of the
observer; unbiased

oligarchy a form of government or, more
generally, a system of control in which
power is in the hands of a few

oligopoly a small group of companies,
usually large, which control market
supply

ombudsman a person responsible for
assuring that persons are treated fairly
by institutions and governments

optical or glass fibres thin filaments of
glass made pure enough and shielded
on the circumference so that many
light patterns can be transmitted
simultaneously for long distances

orality characteristics, usually of society,
which derive from oral, face-to-face,
conversation

Organization of American States (OAS)
regional organisation within the UN,
headquartered in Washington, DC.
Originally founded in 1890 for
commercial purposes, now aims to
strengthen peace, security, democracy
and economic, social and cultural
development among its members

overspill signals from communications
satellites that may be received in
countries that surround the area at
which the satellite is aimed

PANA Pan-African News Agency

pantheon all the gods of a people

parking place the point of placement of a
geostationary satellite in orbit around
the earth

parole the actual words of an utterance

particularity uniqueness or
distinctiveness

partisan a person supportive of a
particular political party or country

paternity the term used to describe the
personal rights which accrue to those
who create intellectual property

patriarchy a social system ruled by
fathers or males

PBS the Public Broadcasting System of
the US

phenomenological dealing in experiences
as perceived by human beings as
opposed to what 'they really are';

oriented to human creations such as
culture

phonetic alphabet alphabet in which
each letter stands for a sound (as
distinct from, e.g. Chinese, in which
characters represent objects, ideas,
etc.)

piracy theft of intellectual property, often
by persons based in a country that does
not recognise the laws of another

plagiarism using the words of another
without attribution

plugging or product placement the
placement of commercial products
in entertainment or information
vehicles for the purpose of advertising
them

plurality more than one

policing, self the monitoring and
disciplining of industry members by an
industry association to which industry
members belong

policy the set of rules, laws, and practices
that govern the manner of operation
of, say, the broadcasting industry

policy process the manner in which
policy comes to be established

political economics the consideration of
economic phenomena inclusive of the
political arrangements which allow
them to exist and function

polyglot made up of many different
languages

polysemic open to a variety of
interpretations

popular culture the representation
through a variety of means of the
values of people in general, at times
inclusive of their many and different
tastes and values

pornography literature, photographs,
painting, etc. dealing with sexual
matters that has no redeeming value
and usually denigrates people or
sexual activity

post-Fordism production led by prior
market or product research, flexible

production methods yielding a greater
variety of products, and a shorter
shelf-life for each product

post-Impressionism a modernist school
of painting responding to the
impermanence of modern life and
involving the exploration of form, e.g.
Seurat

post-industrial societies societies that
increasingly rely on non-industrial
production, e.g. service industries, for
increases to the productivity and
wealth of society

postmodernism the view that there is no
rational core of meaning at the centre
of modern society; a search for the
integration of the historical, the
contemporary and the local; a view
that no longer affirms the existence of
central stories and myths which bring
people of contemporary society
together

pragmatics an approach to
communication that deals with what
people actually say and emphasises the
context-specificity of utterances; more
generally the term is taken as dealing
with the relations between symbols,
interpretations, and users

press the newspaper business (also,
literally, a printing press)

privacy the right not to have one's
personal life discussed in the media;
such rights do not formally exist in
Britain and are weak in the US

private interest the values of private
citizens, commercialism, the pursuit of
profit

privatisation the transfer of publicly-
owned enterprises into the ownership
of private individuals or corporations

privilege (within libel law) the principle
that there are occasions when it is in
the public interest to promote freedom
of expression or communication, even
if individual reputation may be
threatened

probes as used by McLuhan, probes were new, original, seemingly bright ideas that might or might not turn out to make sense. By using this term, McLuhan was indicating that he was testing ideas in putting them forward

produced event a staged happening for the benefit of an audience

product placement see **plugging**

production values the amount spent per measure of content, e.g. minute of film in the final product

production-led products that come to market as a result of the capacities and/or inclinations of producers, and for which the producer expects that there will be a market

promulgation to make publicly known a statute

propaganda material meant to persuade rather than to explain or enlighten

property rights the rights pertaining to the ownership of property; intellectual property rights pertain to the ownership and material benefit one may gain from intellectual work

proporz a system for hiring journalists in Germany in which a balance is maintained in a particular media outlet by hiring individuals representative of a number of different political parties

provincial pertaining to a province (of Canada)

psychological realism the characters seem plausible, perhaps to the point of an audience member being reminded of someone she or he knows who is 'just like' the character

public good see **public interest** and **democratic ideal**

public interest the investment that a national group or other polity has in preserving or developing the best of its values and ideals

public see **small group**

public service publicly-owned, volunteer, or co-operative institutions and associations which place the interests of society first

quotas a system specifying the quantity and source of content that can enter a country or be broadcast by a particular station

rare-earth doping use of a group of chemical elements called rare earths in optical fibres. They share the following characteristc: their electrons rise to a higher than normal energy level when stimulated by a laser; after stimulation they emit light, which can serve as an amplifier to telecommunication signals passing along the fibre

rate balancing the setting of tariffs for certain types of services, usually telephone, as in local versus long-distance

RCI Radio televisione Italia, the publicly-owned Italian television network

reach the percentage of audience members who tune into a programme for some amount of time

realism fidelity to life as seen and experienced

reception analysis research directed at what the audience brings to a viewing or decoding the social context and the act of viewing

redress compensate usually for previous behaviour that was not warranted

regime implicit or explicit principles, norms, rules and decision-making procedures in international trade, often defined in an identifiable agreement such as GATT

regionalism policies directed at providing services to reflect the variance in culture between regions of a country

regulation the control of communication activities in accordance with principles laid down by statute

regulatory that which controls or

regulates
reporter person who reports on the events and issues of the day by collecting information and turning that information into a story (for whatever medium). Reporters are usually assigned stories or beats (e.g. the courts) by their bosses, who are referred to as editors. The term 'journalist' is often used to refer to reporters, editors and columnists
representation the production or construction of ideas or images in a communicative form
reprographic rights the rights to reproduce, usually by means of photocopying, a copyrightable work
Reuters a British news and information agency
revisionism reinterpretation
rhetoric the manner in which an argument or interpretation is presented
right of reply the right of a person to reply to statements made in the media
Royal Commission a high-level commission of inquiry set up by the government of the day to inquire into a situation (most often used in Britain and Commonwealth countries)
royalties a percentage of receipts received by copyright owners from those who trade in intellectual property
run-on prices prices set for commodities that reflect a large production run and where development and other set-up costs have been already recovered

samizdat underground writing circulated by clandestine means in Eastern Europe
saturation coverage appearance in all forms of news and all outlets
scrambled signals satellite signals that have been mixed up or encrypted by means of computer program, and must be descrambled, unencrypted or

straightened out to be received as a clear sound or picture signal on a normal receiver
SCS Satellite-to-Cable Systems (opp. is DBS)
segmented divided into parts
self-censorship the tendencies of journalists and editors to restrict the point of view taken or subject-matter addressed, usually by considering the likely impact on proprietors or advertisers
semiotics the theory of the social production of meaning from sign systems; the science of signs; an abstracted form of structuralism
seriados serials or series
share the percentage of the average audience who tune into a programme or channel at or over any specified time period
sign a physical form (e.g. a word, gesture or even an object, such as a rose) that is used by someone to refer to something else (e.g. an object, a feeling) and is recognised as such; the totality of associations, thoughts, understandings, or meaning brought about by the use of symbols in reference to an object, thing, person, etc.
signal compression the encoding of an electrical signal in such a way that it requires less capacity for its transmission, e.g. television picture transmission only sends changing elements rather than the whole picture
signification the articulation of the connections of, say, an object to its referents
signified the mental concept of what is referred to (e.g. an object as we think of it when we hear a word)
signifier the physical form of the sign, i.e. symbols such as words
sitcoms situation comedies
slander an oral utterance injurious to a

person's reputation

small group, crowd, public in a **small group** all members know each other and are aware of their common membership; the **crowd** is limited to a single physical space, is temporary in its existence and composition and if it acts, it does so non-rationally; the **public** is customarily large and widely dispersed

Smith, Adam a Scottish philosopher known for his writings on the free market and less well-known for his writings on the limitations of the market

soap opera a form of radio or television series invented in 1930s based on the notion of a continuing story and emphasising the personal trials and tribulations of the characters

social responsibility the notion that the media have a responsibility to contribute positively to society and that they should be aware of their privileged position

social time and space the organisation of space by society, e.g. working-class and middle-class neighbourhoods may be divided by railway tracks or a river; social time is also structured e.g. happy hour, tea time

solicitor a lawyer qualified to advise on all legal matters

sovereignty to have sole control

space allocation allotment of a place in geostationary or geosynchronous orbit for a communications satellite

space biased societies which were able to preserve their central organisation over extended territory, e.g. the Roman Empire

space law law that governs the use of space, beyond the air space immediately above a nation in which, for instance, planes might fly

spectrum the electromagnetic spectrum, including radio and television signals and also light

spin doctors persons, usually former journalists, responsible for presenting information in a light most favourable to their clients

Stalinism communism under Joseph Stalin, a particularly repressive form of communism in which many were killed to eliminate counter-revolutionary elements

state communism the control of commerce and society by states adhering to communist principles

state control the control of non-government activities by the state, either directly through ownership and control or through indirect means such as budgetary control

statute a written law passed by a country's government

Stoic philosophy a metaphysical system stressing the correspondence between humankind and nature as a whole, and advocating suppression of passions

stonewalling resisting, standing up against

structuralism a method and theory which emphasises the formal relation of elements in a meaning system to each other; a particular way of analysing that attempts to identify the underlying skeletal structure holding the body of the story together

structuration theory a perspective oriented to understanding the role of human agency in the context of the meaning making and to considering fully the persuasive attributes of the media

subliminal not rising to the threshold of consciousness

surrealism transcending the real as it is conceived by day-to-day intelligence; more than real

symbolic production the manner in which ideas and images are expressed or represented, encoding, representation

synchronic the structure of language or an idea examined at one point in time (opp. diachronic)

syndicated comes from an organisation selling material for simultaneous publication in a variety of places, e.g. a newspaper column

tabloids or tabs half-size newspapers convenient for reading in limited space that often provide bare-bones stories; tabs often engage in yellow journalism, i.e. prying into the private and personal lives of the rich and famous in order to discover scandal

take-over assuming control from others, as in the take-over of one company by another, when the one taking over purchases controlling interest of the company being taken over

TASS the news agency of the former USSR (Telegraph Agency of the Soviet Union), founded in 1925, that worked under the Council of Ministers of the Soviet Union and later reported directly to the President of the USSR; it had, at its peak, 5000 workers, 1000 of whom were journalists; it had bureaus and correspondents in 110 countries and a daily output of 750 newspaper pages in eight languages

Taylorism named after Frederick Winslow Taylor (1856–1915), whose time-and-motion studies observed industrial workers and work processes with a view to minimising extraneous elements to the work and thus increasing industrial efficiency

technological convergence the ability of numbers of technologies to accomplish the same goals

technological determinism the notion that technology is an autonomous and powerful driving force in structuring society or elements of society

technology an instrumental manner of thinking, usually enhanced by pieces of apparatus requiring operational procedures, often used in a social and institutional context

technology transfer the assimilation of new technologies by societies other than those involved in their development

telcos telephone companies

telecommunications any transmission, emission or reception of signs, signals, writing, images or sounds, or intelligence of any nature, by wire, radio, visual or other electromagnetic system; communication over a considerable distance, which may exclude broadcasting; when used in the plural it refers to the activities and/or the industry associated with this form of communication

telegraphy telegraph technique (electronic transmission of letters of the alphabet)

telematics the marriage of computers and communication to produce modern systems of data communication

telenovelas Brazilian soap-opera

telephony pertaining to telephones

teleports self-sufficient zones of advanced telecommunications and high-tech industries to serve as springboards for industrialisation

Televisa Mexico a Mexican television company, operating in Spanish, that grew up under state protection and then was sold to US interests

temporal pertaining to time

textual-numeric composed of letters and numbers

theorised having being subjected to the application of theory

Thoth the Egyptian god of words, speech and writing usually depicted as having the head of an ibis and the body of a man

time biased societies able to preserve their central organisation for certain periods of time in history

Toronto School the Toronto School is said to be composed of scholars who based their research on Marshall McLuhan and Harold Innis, who lived and worked in Toronto

transfrontier crossing national boundaries

transmission movement from one place to another without disturbance

transnational spanning more than one nation, as in a transnational company

transponder a radio relay, a receive-transmit channel on a communications satellite

Trud newspaper, originally Soviet, now Russian, run by the labour unions; circulation of 22 million prior to perestroika, by summer 1993 circulation of 1.2 million

turn-over change, replacement, sales

TV Globo a Brazilian television production and broadcasting company owned by Roberto Marhino

TVRO dishes (TeleVision Receive-Only) antennae, originally saucer shaped

typographic, typographic man pertaining to printed material, social processes derived from printing

undercapitalisation a lack of financial resources

underground press the publication of material in which the identities of the publishers and sometimes the authors are unknown, often against the law of the country

Unesco United Nations Education, Science and Culture Organization based in Paris

UPI United Press International, a US news agency

uses and gratification a theory of media focusing on how audience members use the media, i.e. for information, for entertainment, for conversation, etc.,

and what satisfaction they get out of it

USSR Union of Soviet Socialist Republics, now replaced by the CIS

value-added services usually companies offering extras such as voice mail to basic services such as telephone services

vernacular speech of ordinary people

vertical integration a group of companies linked by common ownership which exist in a supply-demand relation to one another, as in a sound recording company and a radio network

VHF very high frequency (radio waves)

videotex a technology for accessing texts and graphics from a central computer using a relatively simple home terminal

viewing time the time spent viewing expressed over the period of a day, week, or longer period of time.

voice mail telephone message systems that serve the same purpose as answering machines – they take messages that can later be retrieved by the person called

voluntary control (or self-discipline) the media in the Netherlands, Scandinavian countries and Japan flourish under a regime of voluntary, as opposed to legislated, control

voyeurism the pleasure some gain from viewing the privacy of others, especially sex acts

WARCs World Administration Radio Conferences, for allocating use of the radio spectrum

Xinhua the Chinese news agency

Zeitgeist the feeling of the times, the moral character of a period in history

Index